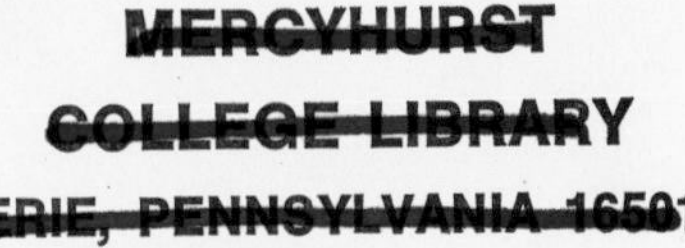
MERCYHURST
COLLEGE LIBRARY
ERIE, PENNSYLVANIA 16501

THE DREAM SELLERS

Perspectives on Drug Dealers

Richard H. Blum and Associates

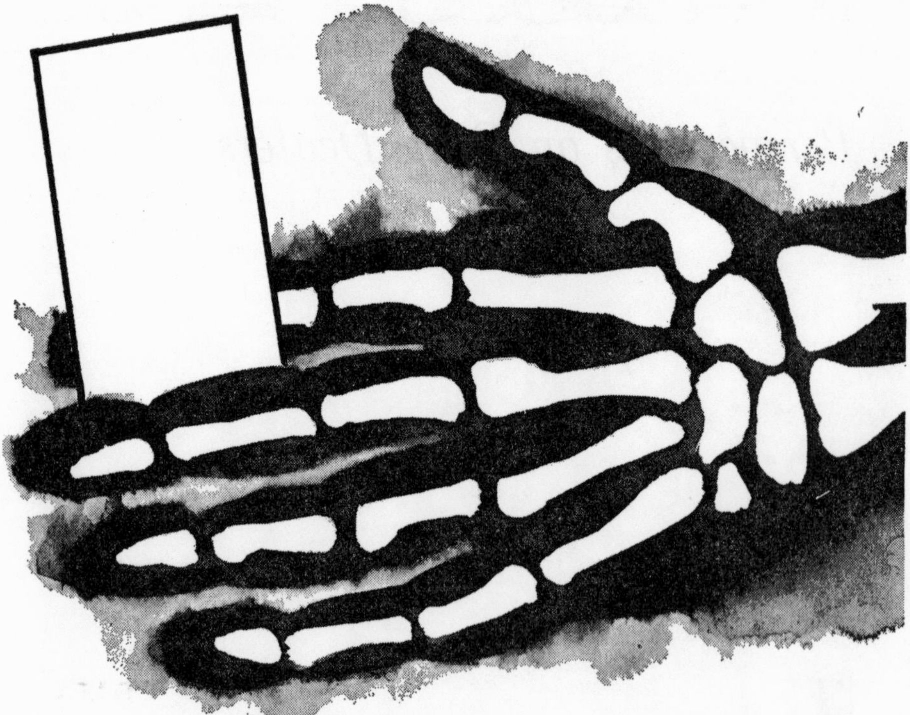

THE DREAM SELLERS

Jossey-Bass Inc., Publishers
San Francisco • Washington • London • 1972

THE DREAM SELLERS
Perspectives on Drug Dealers
by Richard H. Blum and Associates

Published in Great Britain by
Jossey-Bass, Inc., Publishers
St. George's House
44 Hatton Garden, London E.C.1

Library of Congress Catalogue Card Number LC 79–184960

International Standard Book Number ISBN 0–87589–119–5

Manufactured in the United States of America

JACKET DESIGN BY WILLI BAUM

FIRST EDITION

Code 7209

THE JOSSEY-BASS
BEHAVIORAL SCIENCE SERIES

General Editors

PREFACE

These are times of much public concern with drug "abuse," particularly the illicit use of heroin, LSD, amphetamines, barbiturates, and marijuana. These are also times when most citizens are deeply worried about rising crime rates in the United States. In both, young people are particularly implicated in the statistics. The two issues merge in one phenomenon, that of drug dealing. The drug dealer, because he is involved both in drug abuse and in nondrug crime—where he is likely to be linked to violence and other delinquency as well as to "vice" per se—is therefore of considerable interest.

This public interest, fed at the least by worry if not by anger and possibly inspired by misinformation and fantasy as well, has generated a number of images. One hears of sinister figures lurking in school yards to seduce the innocent by inviting them to take candy laced with drugs, of vice kings living fabulously rich lives as heads of vast criminal empires, of young girls hooked on heroin earning their next fix either by selling their bodies or by selling drugs, or of foreign intelligence agents conspiring to bring drugs to our shores. Dramatic stuff, but is it so?

Also, in this period when drug laws are undergoing change, some basic assumptions are stated by policy makers about drug dealers and about drug users. Sharp is the contrast made between dealers—those "responsible for enslaving the minds and bodies of the young"—and the users/abusers, who, misguided or ill, are more to be pitied than scorned. This contrast is made at least in the context of the criminal law, which is asked to go light on users and heavy on dealers. The question is: Are dealers different from users or are they the same? Other policy questions arise too; for example, is there evidence that maintaining or increasing the penalties on dealing will be effective?

Young people sympathetic to drug use and to dealing are not without their own public voice and access to the press, where they express a very different point of view. Quite unlike those who hold the peddler to be the devil incarnate, these advocates contend he is a noble missionary carrying good things to deserving people, a new kind of priest ministering chemically to cure the ills of spirit and flesh. Can it be? Are dealers in fact unmoved by greed and motivated by higher purposes?

Whether they subscribe to the picture of the dealer as satanical, as distinct from the user, or as pure in heart, many citizens would likely opine that drug dealers as people are at least different enough from ordinary citizens to merit attention. Most would further agree that illicit drug use these days is extensive enough to justify examination of the dealer as "cause" of abuse, because without him drugs would not be available.

Depending upon their special interests, citizens are also likely to find merit in examining the dealer as a person, his career and situation, and the operation and consequences of some of our current policies which bear on him, all of which the studies of my colleagues and myself attempted. For example, the educator may be interested in estimating the prevalence of drug dealing in schools in relationship to the number of users. He may also want to know how dealers differ from users and how both groups in turn differ from straight students. On the basis of such information perhaps it will be easier than it now is to assess the magnitude of the drug dealing problem in schools and to see it in relationship to the personal, academic, and family differences which set the dealer apart. We offer such information in this volume.

Those in mental health, medicine, and other helping professions also have an interest in drug dealers. They may want to know what happens to young dealers who seek treatment in a modern psychiatric facility and how those who treat them deem it best to approach that task. They may also wish an understanding of family patterns and childhood and adolescent drug histories of those young people who come to them for care. What events, for example, constitute the sequence from being drug naive to being an armed trafficker making thousands of dollars a month? How do dealers characterize their own lives and what gains and losses do they count? What about the reformed dealer? Can he teach us about developments beyond dealing? These too are questions to which my colleagues and I address ourselves.

If dealing is important, so too is not dealing, for understanding of the one implies comprehending the other. Also, the image of dealing may be unduly restricted if one thinks only of young people or adults identified as criminals. These two premises led us to examine the absence and presence of illicit practices among "respectable" older folk who had opportunities to distribute illicitly—namely, pharmacists, detail men, college faculty, narcotics law enforcement officers, and physicians. In several of these samples we sought to identify factors associated with illicit or questionable practices and, conversely, with conformity to the law-abiding norm. In the case of physicians we went beyond distribution to others and examined self-prescription to see how in this professional group, as in young people, personal factors linked to drug use were also linked to distribution. As is usually the case our curiosity was more whetted than satisfied by our findings, but we believe that other professionals—for example, pharmacists, physicians, pharmaceutical industry personnel, vice officers, and professors—will likewise be interested in what emerges from the inquiry.

The official serving in the administration of justice—whether as policeman, probation officer, judge, or prison administrator—may be interested in estimates of the impact of arrest on dealers or in the differentiation of dealers so that arrested versus nonarrested dealers can be characterized. Perhaps, too, they are concerned with what happens when youthful dealers go to juvenile correctional centers or their adult counterparts go to prison; do they straighten up or is there drug traffic in the "joint"? Curiosity about how police departments set their priorities for drug law enforcement and how they work in practice—including what it costs to arrest a dealer and what the risk of arrest per dealer per year is—may be expressed by citizens and legislators as well as by enforcement personnel. We have, in our studies, sought to gather data bearing on these interests and in Blum and associates (in press) present those data along with policy comments and recommendations.

The foregoing are samples of the questions the authors had in mind as we undertook work on drug dealers. We wanted at least to learn enough about dealers in California to get some idea of their development, their views, and their lives, and to be able to compare different groups with one another. We wanted too to be able to look at dealers in various settings: junior high schools, high schools, colleges and universities, the streets of Oakland, the Haight-Ashbury, communes, Europe, and elsewhere. We wanted to gain a perspective on dealing by looking at drug practices in a variety of young dealer groups, in adult offender groups, among older respectable people, and before as well as after arrest. Because we wanted to go beyond an accounting of personal lives to an initial wrestling with policy, we had a particular interest in how current policies work out in practice. Thus, we examined police departments, juvenile halls, and prisons. We also took a brief look at international traffic and at what drug dealers sell (the matter of drug purity).

All this work on drug dealers and dealing cannot be presented in one volume. The present book focuses on the dealer. Blum and associates (in press) focuses on dealing, issues and policies. Blum and associates (1972) is of a different order and focuses intensively on the youthful etiology of drug "abuse" within the family. The origins of the present studies may best be understood as a development arising from our earlier work. Interests arising in the course of that work indicated that further inquiries should attend to (1) the phenomenon of drug distribution with particular attention to the dealer himself; (2) the workings of present policies of intervention, which are, for the most part, matters of criminal law; and (3) the origins of the personal interest and involvement in illicit drugs necessary to using or dealing (in some cases leading to problem outcomes—being ill or in trouble)—that is, a study of family values and dynamics and subsequent child-rearing practices. This volume contains the results of inquiries addressed to (1) above. It is hoped that it will provide knowledge helpful in understanding drug dealers and how one might best respond to them. The other works cover (2) and (3) above.

Acknowledgements

I wish first and foremost to thank the 2,579 citizens, most of them young people and many of them drug dealers, who gave us their time and spoke to us of their experiences so that we might learn about the complex and troublesome phenomenon which drug dealing is. Second, I wish to thank the many volunteers who worked on the thirty-seven subprojects which constituted our effort to put drug dealing and the people who do it into some perspective. Without those volunteers most of these projects would have died aborning. Third, I wish to acknowledge the support of the sponsors, originally the Bureau of Drug Abuse Control in the Food and Drug Administration, Department of Health, Education, and Welfare, and later the Bureau of Narcotics and Dangerous Drugs, Department of Justice. This work was performed under their contract number J-69-13. The presentation contained herein represents the findings and viewpoints of the authors and does not necessarily reflect the position of the Bureau of Narcotics and Dangerous Drugs.

I wish also to acknowledge the considerable help rendered by the following affiliates and assistants: James Alums, Diane Bausek,

Gerald Bausek, Ralph Benson, Bernard Christopher, Frances Riley, Raymond Faber, David Green, Rosemary Gutt, Lewis Harris, Thirza Hibner, Vivian Hausen, Margaret Huntsberger, Therese Jordan, Ann Kilborn, Dinah Kramer, Mary Klein, Thomas McDonell, Janet Pagen, Doris Schwartz, Gerald Wright, David Southern, Sanford Feinglass.

The support of those individuals who provided exceptional aid ranging from institutional access to personal advice is gratefully noted. I thank Caroline Coon, RELEASE, London; John Ingersoll, director, Bureau of Narcotics and Dangerous Drugs; Stephen Pittel, Department of Psychiatry, Mt. Zion Hospital, San Francisco; Haskell Brazell, Student Health Service, San Francisco State College; Lawrence Wolfe, Peninsula Medical Group, San Carlos, California; Loren Beckley, Probation Services Department, San Mateo County (California) Health Department; Robert Day, School of Pharmacy, University of California, Berkeley; Anadi Roy, Department of Statistics, Stanford University, and Department of Statistics, University of Lucknow (India); Earl Whitmore, Sheriff, San Mateo County (California); Gene Stewart, assistant sheriff, San Mateo County (California); Donald Coslett, Sergeant, San Mateo County (California) Sheriff's Department; David E. Smith, Department of Pharmacology, University of California Medical Center (San Francisco), Haight-Ashbury Free Clinic, San Francisco; Norman Sears, Napa (California) State Hospital; H. B. Spears, Home Office Drugs Branch, London; Charles Gain, chief, Oakland (California) Police Department; R. K. Procunier, director, California Department of Corrections; John Kramer, Department of Psychiatry and Department of Pharmacology, University of California, Irvine, formerly with California Rehabilitation Facility, Corona; Charles Richardson, Richardson Data Processing Services, Palo Alto, California; Dan Casey, Bureau of Narcotics and Dangerous Drugs; Nora Shaykin, University of Sussex (England); Raymond Le Gouze, Department of Social Studies, Brunel University (England); John Pearson, Department of Social Studies, Brunel University (England); John Kaplan, Stanford Law School; Michael Schofield, Health Education Council, London.

The assistance of the following institutions and agencies is also acknowledged: RELEASE (London); Institute for the Study of Drug Dependence (London); National Addiction and Research Centre (London); Great Georges Community Arts Project (Liverpool); St. Clement's Hospital (London); St. Giles Centre (London); The Salvation Army (Chelsea); Home Office Drugs Branch (London); Bureau of Narcotics and Dangerous Drugs; Folsom, San Quentin, and Soledad prisons; Duell Training Center (Tracy, California); San Mateo County

(California) Sheriff's Department; Palo Alto (California) Police Department; San Francisco Police Department; and the Oakland (California) Police Department.

Associates

The associate authors for this volume are Desmond Banks (coauthor of Chapter Fifteen), Noel W. Barker (coauthor of Chapter Seventeen), Eva Maria Blum, Gail A. Crawford (coauthor of Chapter Seventeen), Emily Garfield (coauthor of Chapter Twenty-Four), Mark Garfield (coauthor of Chapter Twenty), David Garvin (coauthor of Chapters Nineteen and Twenty), Patrick H. Hughes (coauthor of Chapter Seventeen), Jerome H. Jaffe (coauthor of Chapter Seventeen), Peggy Joseph (coauthor of Chapter Twenty-Four), Edward Lewis, Jr. (coauthor of Chapter Twenty-Five), Thomas Martinez (coauthor of Chapter Twenty-Two), Nicholas Munson (coauthor of Chapters Twelve and Twenty-Eight), Lee Ross (coauthor of Chapter Twenty-Two), Suzanne Schumann (coauthor of Chapter Seventeen), Jean Paul Smith (author of Chapter Five and coauthor of Chapter Twenty-Six), Robert Spaan (coauthor of Chapter Twenty-Two), Alan Sutter (author of Chapter Sixteen), Jonathan Wolfe (coauthor of Chapters Twenty, Twenty-One, and Twenty-Five, and author of Chapter Twenty-Seven). All other chapters are by me; some are also coauthored by me.

Stanford, California RICHARD H. BLUM
January 1972

CONTENTS

For information on which chapters were authored or coauthored by the associates, see pages xiv, xix, and xx.

TWO: COMPARING DEALERS

THREE: COMPARING SETTINGS

FOUR: COLLEGE DEALERS

ASSOCIATES

DESMOND BANKS, *Release, London (coauthor of Chapter Fifteen)*

NOEL W. BARKER, *Department of Psychiatry, University of Chicago (coauthor of Chapter Seventeen)*

EVA MARIA BLUM, *Institute for Public Policy Analysis, Stanford University*

GAIL A. CRAWFORD, *Department of Psychiatry, University of Chicago (coauthor of Chapter Seventeen)*

EMILY GARFIELD, *Institute for Public Policy Analysis, Stanford University (coauthor of Chapter Twenty-Four)*

MARK GARFIELD, *Institute for Public Policy Analysis, Stanford University (coauthor of Chapter Twenty)*

DAVID GARVIN, *Institute for Public Policy Analysis, Stanford University (coauthor of Chapters Nineteen and Twenty)*

PATRICK H. HUGHES, *Department of Psychiatry, University of Chicago (coauthor of Chapter Seventeen)*

Jerome H. Jaffe, *Special Action Office for Drug Abuse Prevention, the White House; Department of Psychiatry, University of Chicago (coauthor of Chapter Seventeen)*

Peggy Joseph, *Institute for Public Policy Analysis, Stanford University (coauthor of Chapter Twenty-Four)*

Edward Lewis, Jr., *U.S. Bureau of Narcotics and Dangerous Drugs (coauthor of Chapter Twenty-Five)*

Thomas Martinez, *Department of Sociology, Stanford University (coauthor of Chapter Twenty-Two)*

Nicholas Munson, *San Francisco Police Department (coauthor of Chapters Twelve and Twenty-Eight)*

Lee Ross, *Department of Psychology, Stanford University (coauthor of Chapter Twenty-Two)*

Suzanne Schumann, *Department of Psychiatry, University of Chicago (coauthor of Chapter Seventeen)*

Jean Paul Smith, *Center for Study of Narcotics and Drug Abuse, National Institute of Mental Health (coauthor of Chapter Five and coauthor of Chapter Twenty-Six)*

Robert Spaan, *Institute for Public Policy Analysis, Stanford University (coauthor of Chapter Twenty-Two)*

Alan Sutter, *Department of Sociology, University of California, Berkeley (author of Chapter Sixteen)*

Jonathan Wolfe, *Institute for Public Policy Analysis, Stanford University (coauthor of Chapters Twenty, Twenty-One, and Twenty-Five, and author of Chapter Twenty-Seven)*

THE DREAM SELLERS

Perspectives on Drug Dealers

PROLOGUE

*M*uch in print bears on our inquiry, some of it in the form of scholarly work presenting important findings on drug dealing, some of it on the milieu in which drug use occurs, and some of it focusing on or demonstrating broad economic and cultural factors of which drug use and sales are but aspects. The literature, then, contains both objective and partisan material. We here emphasize the scholarly forms, although we draw briefly on the others to illustrate points. Readers interested in detailed bibliographies on modern illicit drug use are referred to literature reviews presented in our earlier work (Blum and associates, 1964, 1969a, 1969b; Blum and Blum, 1967; White House Conference on Youth, 1971).

Illicit-drug dealing is not learned only clandestinely, without benefit of "public" support. To the contrary, the underground press and campus newspapers which serve the youthful audiences who so often constitute the drug scene offer advocacy and, inherent in that, moral support and also lessons on how dealing ought to be done. Let us quote from a student newspaper published on one of the campuses where we have done drug research:

> *For students plagued by rising tuition costs and expensive patterns of escape, "scoring" a key of marijuana on campus has become a sure way of making an extra buck, with the added incentive of enjoyable working conditions. . . . Increased marijuana usage . . . has created a gold mine for dealers. An investment of about two hundred dollars . . . will yield almost twice that much when sold. . . . Increased usage appears to have legitimized the avocation of dealing. . . . Grass is accepted by students and sought by them as is the dealer. . . . One large dealer*

> *traces his business from 1967, when "I sold three keys a week; . . . now I'm selling fifteen."*

The article goes on to describe the friendly aspects of spreading around "people's dope." It assures the reader that there is "no police problem . . . because the enforcement of possession of marijuana laws on campus is impossible"; notes the minor risk of theft, violence, and cheating; observes that those of radical, moderate, and conservative persuasion deal; and concludes with a quote from a dealer: "As long as I can get people dope and make a little money on the side, well, that's OK, right?"

The article has a teaching or propagandist function, for it assures students that everyone deals, that it is safe, profitable, friendly, in vogue, and highly approved. The same message is also found in the underground press. Consider the following from the April 1970 *Berkeley Barb:*

> *Dope dealers. There's plenty of them around, that's for sure. . . . They supply much needed goodies to the community. No complaints about that. But the money and the profit is a different matter. . . . Dealers make good profits. . . . It's not that they don't deserve making some. . . . However most dealers don't take any responsibility for their customers or their products, and that's not fair. . . . It's time the dealers assumed some responsibility.*

The article proposes a "people's tax" for dealers to pay to a Legal Defense Fund for people arrested on drug charges, and observes: "If people become responsible citizens of their hip community by sticking together, the man [the police] will have a tougher job getting away with all this busting shit. He is getting away with it now because people are unwilling to care." The message here is not only supportive of dealing but undertakes to say how it should be done: humanistically, with solidarity, and with taxation to assist the suffering.

A London underground paper, the May 1970 *Friends Magazine*, observing the increase in cannabis prices and enforcement activity and an influx of American buyers, counsels action. "London's heads are, after Amsterdam's, possibly the best served in the West . . . . They have come to accept this as a matter of course . . . . It's time heads realized that London is no longer a dealer's haven . . . . Unless heads —all heads, consumer and dealers alike—get it together quite decisively, this privileged position could be lost." The article goes on to complain that the consequence of President Richard Nixon's antidrug action was to increase the transit of drugs through London to the United States:

> *American dealers have introduced American techniques. . . . They come from a hard, tough scene, and they are out to make big money. They are prepared to do things that English dealers don't even have fantasies about. They are also unreliable. . . . In short, Nixon's fatuous reaction to drugs is being felt here: it has landed us with a number of people we could well manage without.*

The article argues against selling to Americans and reminds the reader "that bringing one hundred weight of righteous shit to London is a revolutionary act; it is a bulk shipment of 'mind-change' and as such qualitatively better and infinitely more revolutionary than exploding one hundred weight of TNT under the arse of authority." Discussing hash (hashish, a stronger form of cannabis than marijuana), the article contends:

> *Hash . . . is more than just a turn-on and more than just a social scene to make with friends. . . . It's the main economic artery of the underground, of our subculture. . . . Hash is the one form of capital . . . which is primarily under our control. It represents the strength, the power of our subculture. If we do not maintain our control of it, we not only lose a vital economic strength . . . but also lay the "underground" open to total economic dependence on the "straight world."*

While accepting the possibility that there should be drug control laws, the piece condemns the unfairness of present laws, which visit stronger punishment on dealers than on robbers, who make considerably more. It asks the reader to "get it quite straight and appreciate the dealer's role in the community. He's doing something for us that no one else can. If he's any good he's an experienced, cool, and honest cat who does a tense but rewarding job well, . . . [not] mean and evil men running a mean and evil racket." The article, after inveighing against British government policy (which it describes as granting that smokers are harmless but dealers are evil), pleads with the heads not to make the same assumption and warns against gangsterism if the dichotomy is maintained. Moreover, a monopoly is proposed; the English heads must stick together to control the hash traffic. If the heads fail to appreciate their own dealers and not "buy and sell British," fear and disaster loom.

The foregoing messages of support and moralizing are pale compared with those from the pen of the master, one of the spiritual fathers (but we think not the sire) of the drug movement. Timothy Leary's underground press syndicated article (December 1969) includes the following:

> *There are three groups who are bringing about the great evolution of the new age. . . . They are the DOPE DEALERS, THE ROCK MUSICIANS, and the underground ARTISTS AND WRITERS. Of these three heroes . . . the dealers are the most essential and important. In the years to come . . . he is going to be the Robin Hood, the spiritual guerrilla, a mysterious agent who will take the place of the cowboy hero or the cops-and-robbers hero. There is nothing really new about this. Throughout human history the shadowy figure of the alchemist, the shaman, the herbalist, the smiling wiseman who has the key to turn you on and make you feel good has always been the center of the religious, esthetic, revolutionary impulse. I think that this is the noblest of all human professions and certainly would like to urge any creative young person sincerely interested in evolving himself and helping society to grow to consider this ancient and honorable profession. . . . The righteous dealer is . . . selling you the celestial dream; . . . he is peddling . . . freedom and joy .*

Leary goes on to speak of an Arab dope dealer he met in the Middle East: "Here was a magician . . . telling us that he was not a businessman but sent by God to turn people on." Leary argues that only one who is himself pure, radiant, not lusting for power or wealth can succeed as a dealer: "I can say flatly that the holiest, handsomest, healthiest, horniest, humorest, most saintly group of men I have met in my life are the righteous dope dealers. They have got to be that way because they have to continue to use their own product." Strongly criticizing "psychedelic liberals," who are for use but against dealing, Leary suggests instead: "I think it is a moral exercise that every one of the thirty million who are using psychedelic drugs should take a turn at dealing." He goes on to talk about some dealers he knew:

> *A group of clear-eyed, smiling, beautiful dealers. They were young men in their twenties, as all dealers have to be young. They were living together with their families, . . . and there*

> *was no reason for them to leave the country on one of these thrilling missions. They were planning another. . . . I asked them why they were doing it. . . . Their answer: . . . "We believe that dope is the hope of the human race, it is the way to make people free and happy. . . . We wouldn't feel good just sitting here smoking the dope we have . . . knowing that there are thirty million kids that need dope. . . . Our lives have been saved from the plastic nightmare because of dope. . . .* [*And regarding the police network?*]. . . . *We are smarter and wiser than the FBI, the CIA, and the Narcotics Bureau put together."*

Leary concludes, "Don't ever buy grass or acid from a dealer who doesn't lay a prayer on you while he takes your money. It's powerful medicine, it's magic. And it has got to be treated that way."

The American public, perhaps not having read Leary, takes a different view. A Gallup poll (*Washington Post*, April 10, 1970) found that the majority of Americans believe convicted heroin dealers should be given stiff sentences, 67 per cent calling for more than ten-year sentences and 4 per cent for the death penalty. Sixty-three per cent want minimum ten-year sentences for marijuana pushers, 2 per cent favor the death penalty. Users are seen differently; although 52 per cent ask for prison for heroin users, 12 per cent propose treatment. Fifteen per cent propose no penalties for marijuana use, although 62 per cent favor some prison term. Young people in their twenties take a softer approach, as do women. Comparing the campus and underground press with Gallup's findings makes clear the dramatic differences among Americans in their views of what the drug dealer is like and how those around him should respond.

Let us look now at some of the available facts on drug commerce. We begin with the obvious. There is money in the illicit-drug trade. In New York City alone the upper estimate of the total revenue accruing to the heroin distribution system is $463 million per annum (Moore, 1970). Even if this one-drug, one-city estimate is too high, one wonders what an all-drug national figure would be. It must surely be at least hundreds of millions of dollars.

This illicit traffic is but one facet of the total trade in pharmaceutical preparations affecting the central nervous system. The estimate for the sale of prescription drugs in 1967 was about $882 million (U.S. Department of Health, Education and Welfare, 1968). In 1969 more than 200 million prescriptions were filled—the majority refills (Lennard, Epstein, Bernstein, and Ranson, 1971). We have calculated the dollar volumes of over-the-counter (nonprescription) drugs, which are primarily psychoactive (ranging from aspirin to sleeping preparations), liquor, and tobacco. These sum to twenty-five billion dollars ($25,000,000,000). In addition to these direct revenues, advertisement costs for prescription and over-the-counter substances are also considerable. We have no total estimate but cite C. W. Weinberger (quoted by Johnson, 1970) to the effect that TV ads for sleeping aids alone in 1969 cost twenty million dollars. The pharmaceutical industry spends three-quarters of a billion dollars annually just to advertise to fewer than 200,000 physicians (Lennard, Epstein, Bernstein, and Ransom, 1971).

Thus, the production and traffic in drugs which affect the mind is one of the major businesses in the United States, and the traffic in illicit drugs is part of this larger attraction to and regular use of psychoactive drugs by Americans. Like the legitimate trade, the illicit one is likely comprised of efforts both to respond to existing demand and, when supply exceeds demand, to enhance it.

The New York City heroin trade is the only illicit marketplace which appears to have been systematically studied; economic and sociological investigations have been conducted, supplemented by scientific observations on the characteristics of at least some of the persons involved in that traffic. Moore (1970) proposes a pyramid of dealers in the city with the distribution system consisting of small marketing units and a centralized organization at the top.

In regard to the dealers themselves, Moore (1970) proposes that, on the basis of an economic model, there is little reason for them to quit since the skills they need are not applicable outside and because they lack skills valuable in other jobs. Preble and Casey (1969), looking at what dealers do from day to day and applying both social and economic concepts, also conclude that at least lower-level dealers in the heroin system do not voluntarily leave it, not just because of income factors but because it provides them a meaningful way of life, allowing them to escape from the monotony of slum life and to get "revenge on society for the injustices and deprivation." Observing that jugglers, sellers from whom the street addicts buy, are always addicts and street dealers sometimes so, Preble and Casey argue that the heroin they and other consumers get is insufficient to sustain physiological addiction or to account for their dedication to the life. The addiction, they suggest, is to "taking care of business," that is, to "accomplishing a series of challenging, exciting tasks every day of the week."

Since at these lower dealing levels, dealers are users, it may be useful to sketch briefly some of the relevant findings on users. A complex discrimination among users is offered by Brotman and Freedman

(1968), who identify four kinds of heroin addicts. One is the conformist, who is conventional and not involved in criminal activities; another is the hustler, who is heavily involved in the criminal life but not in straight world activities; a third is the two-worlder, who is both conventional and criminal; and the fourth is the uninvolved, who is engaged neither in conventional nor in criminal activities. The point these investigators make is that conventionality and criminality among heroin users are not opposite ends of one spectrum but two quite discrete sets of activities which may be engaged in simultaneously. As we see later in our own data, this observation extends to the youthful dealer elsewhere in the drug scene. These two sometimes independent sets of activities both constitute continua so that within a large population of users one may place people as more or less conventional or more or less criminal. The criminality of the user need not include dealing but may show much other delinquency, either before or after onset of illicit drug use (Ball and Chambers, 1970; Chambers, Moffett, Moffett, 1970; Grupp, 1971). Preble and Casey's work, for example, showed that the hustling addict is busy with burglaries, robberies, fencing, shoplifting, and the like.

Analysis of the case histories of addicts provides illustrative data. The excellent epidemiological and clinical work of Chein, Gerard, Lee, and Rosenfeld (1964) showed how neighborhood, racial mix, peer association, family, and individual personality factors all contribute to the development or nondevelopment of heroin use. Examining Negro opiate users who passed through United States Public Health treatment centers, Chambers, Moffett, and Jones (1968) found that onset of addiction is associated with prior marijuana use and with association with heroin-using peers. Continuous use of marijuana, compared with irregular use or nonuse, proved to be associated, in their sample, with its early use, with early arrest, and with becoming a narcotics dealer. Delinquency preceded the onset of heroin use; males more than females had criminal histories; and both males and females appeared less often to have held straight jobs than would be expected for the normal urban Negro population. Since early drug involvement, early earnings from crime, and reduced legitimate work characterized this group, not surprisingly about half the sample had been drug dealers, an activity which nicely combines these early propensities. That dealing had, at one time or another, provided nearly three-quarters of their income.

In another study of a group at high risk of addiction, Puerto Rican males, De Fleur, Ball, and Snarr (1969) identify two major patterns among opiate addicts. One is characterized by high school education, steady employment followed by addiction, then arrest, and, ultimately, after incarceration or treatment, a good chance for abstinence, reemployment, and an honest life. The other pattern is of elementary education, little likelihood of straight work, early delinquency and arrest, then addiction, and, following incarceration or treatment, no chance for abstinence, reemployment, or an honest life. Among this criminal group are found the drug dealers, 65 per cent of them having dealt as opposed to none in the employed group. (A study by Bates, 1968, showed similar results.) Between these two extremes is a middle group, those with sporadic employment who are intermediate on most measures. The investigators suggest that they are transitory in their life style; that is, they are moving either toward employment and abstinence or toward increased involvement in opiates, in crime, and, by extension, in drug dealing.

Heroin users have generally been drawn primarily from young urban slum males, often minority group members (1967 Task Force Report on Narcotics and Drug Abuse). Dealers among them have been, as the foregoing studies suggest, the less employable, less educated, and earlier delinquent. That such youth—perhaps "unemployables"—should engage in crime rather than legitimate work is considered by Banfield (1970) as partly due to the fact that illicit enterprises set an "informal minimal wage for unskilled labor that has no relation to the market value of such labor and that other employers cannot afford to pay. As a result the young dropout loses face and self-respect unless he is either a 'hustler' or an idler, the suggestion that he be paid what his work is worth is tantamount to an insult." Banfield goes on to discuss such youth's attitudes to work, observing that foresight, diligence, and self-discipline may not be found and that they may prefer excitement and nonwork (Doeringer, 1968, cited by Banfield, 1970, p. 112).

> *Resistance to steady work on the part of able-bodied persons is especially strong in the slums. A study of the ghetto labor market in Boston in 1968 showed that about 70 per cent of the job applicants referred by neighborhood employment centers received offers. More than half of the offers were rejected however, and only about 40 per cent of those who took jobs kept them for as long as a month. "Much of the ghetto unemployment appears to be a result of work instability rather than job scarcity."*

Another report cited by Banfield (U.S. Department of Labor, 1967) shows lack of employment interests among 10 or 20 per cent of slum youth and attributes this disinterest to inferior education, lack of skill, police records, discrimination—age more than race—family inadequacy, drug addiction, and a sense of hopelessness. It concludes, "The problem is less one of inadequate opportunity than of inability, under existing conditions, to use opportunity."

These points are supplemented by the theoretical propositions advanced by sociologists concerned with crime. For example, Merton (1957), Cohen (1966), Cloward and Ohlin (1960), and Matza (1964) emphasize—although not without disagreement—the function of delinquency as a solution primarily to career barriers associated with poverty, to cultural-social stresses, and to personal frustrations as these are perceived by the young slum dweller. Given this mix of economic, social, and psychological factors coupled with the availability of drugs and a demand for them, one can see how slum drug dealing appears as a desirable pursuit. It offers wages above those available for unskilled labor, provides excitement and rewards for delinquent tendencies and records, requires no self-discipline or bending to institutional requirements, and allows a fairly discreet delinquency (as opposed to bashing heads) to coexist with normal social values—for example, money-making independence.

The foregoing may contribute to criminality and to drug dealing. But for slum dealing to occur—at least at the lower level, where organizational skills and self-discipline are not required—involvement in the drug life is a precondition. For those individuals who suffer some psychological deficit arising from any source—family inadequacy, genetic liability, character-warping early experience—and who are in association with drug-using peers and outside of moral control through institutional structures (family, school), the attractiveness to that life and particularly to heroin is great. The studies cited show us that over half these drug-centered users—the hustlers and two-worlders—become dealers at one time or another.

The foregoing discussion applies to the slum dealer and his conditions, but it is not an adequate picture of all youthful dealing. Heroin use occurs outside the slums in connection with other illicit drug use among middle- and upper-class youngsters and persons in their twenties. These groups also generate dealers. As 60 per cent of some public school classes are now estimated to have had heroin experience, slum origins are not now necessary preconditions Densen-Gerber, Murphy, and Record (1970). Heroin use outside slums is not accounted for in terms of concepts such as pervasive clinical psychopathology or various theories of poverty-linked frustration. Densen-Gerber, Murphy, and Record (1970), after studying school-attending New York City teenagers, suggest that middle-class youngsters who are not psychiatrically ill can respond to peer pressures which include heroin use as a fad (or ritual experience). The correctness of that observation was clearly demonstrated in the English town of Crawley, where peer experimentation led to heroin use by De Alarcon's (1969) and De Alarcon and Rathod's (1968) samples. These subjects, male and between fifteen and twenty, did not differ from the nonusing population; all were living regularly with their parents, were employed, were not part of visibly delinquent groups, and ranged across the socioeconomic scale. Insofar as this group began use simultaneously, sharing heroin with one another and turning on their friends, most appear to have been heroin distributors in the technical sense, although not sellers.

Another English study (MacSweeney and Parr, 1970) learned that all users had sold at one time or another; their heroin dealing itself was irregular and connected to their need for money to buy drugs. As with the Crawley sample they were not from low-income groups; when seen by MacSweeney and Parr they were separated from their families and were very mobile (gypsylike). They had also been involved in nondrug delinquencies prior to selling heroin. On personality tests heroin dealers in this group did not differ from a larger sample of users. All heroin users were, however, significantly more hostile and neurotic than normal youths. When the dealers were divided into those who had sold for six months or less and those who had sold for more than six months, the trend was for the regular dealers to be more heavily involved in drug use and to have more unusual motives for selling; those motives included self-aggrandizement, "idealism" (recall the underground press), and dealing to create obligations in others. The latter action we consider a form of manipulation.

Data from San Francisco show a chain of events similar to those on the East Coast and in Great Britain. Characterizing 1971 as "the year of the middle-class junkie," Bentel and Smith (1971) and Sheppard and Gay (1971) describe the growth of hard drug use among the middle class and the associated growth of ill health and criminality. They emphasize how drug explorations leading to stimulant use can then lead to the further discovery—in response to felt necessity—that uppers such as amphetamines require in turn downers such as the opiates or barbiturates. The cost of such discoveries can be high, medically and socially as well as economically. One way to meet the monetary cost for maintaining a habit, as well as to ensure supply and to remain in the swing of things, is to become a dealer.

The fact that heroin use is (slowly) becoming middle class suggests an interpretation for the growth of much other drug use and of dealing: As part of the melting pot process in America the values of classes intermingle, and such diffusion is in itself deemed worthy. As Banfield (1970) notes, just as middle-class concepts dictate "appropriate" levels of income and support for the poor; so some of the styles of the slum poor, in particular of the delinquent slum, spread to the middle and upper classes, and become appropriate there. Banfield observes that the "youth culture somewhat resembles lower-class culture" in respect to work attitudes. "Lawful, safe, and well-regulated jobs" are unattractive when excitement, casual styles, and—with regard to drugs—immediate pleasure and chemical escape may be gained elsewhere. Marijuana may be another and earlier example of the same diffusion; and the adoption and popularization of criminal cant seems to be a particularly good example. A parallel illustration is the accommodation and integration of the styles of the psychedelic scene to mass media advertising, a process which we take to demonstrate the absorption of deviance into the larger culture as part of democratization. We assume the function of such democratization may be to reduce intergroup conflict and increase the number of acceptable styles of conduct, while at the same time normalizing these styles so that pluralism is ultimately reduced. If this interpretation is correct, middle-class youthful drug dealing, with which our work is most concerned, can be viewed, in part only, as one form of the democratization of delinquency. Such a movement by no means implies that middle- or upper-class youth were without delinquency prior to the popularity of drugs and dealing. It does imply that new and more prevalent expressions of delinquency, along with justifications for that conduct, become idealized despite what the law says is criminal. We assume that this cannot occur unless drug use—and its inevitable dealing facet—is intrinsically satisfying to the youth involved.

The upward class diffusion of drug use and its correlates is by no means limited to the United States. D. U. Bueno (in Harris, McIsaac, and Schuster, 1970) describes how marijuana, until recently considered lower class and criminal in Mexico (indeed marijuana as an adjective implied criminal or soldier status), has climbed the social ladder. Bueno observes that in climbing it has jumped a rung, moving from the lower class to highly educated and wealthy groups but bypassing working-class and lower-middle-class folk. Bean's (1971) observations in London show a similar distribution of arrested users (who also have associated delinquency) among the higher and lowest socioeconomic groups with underrepresentation of the lower-middle and working class. From observations of the families of college drug dealers (Chapter Nineteen), we have similar evidence that democratization of drug dealing moves from low to high but does not easily penetrate the conservative bastion of clerks, hard-hats, and others in the working class and "petty bourgeoisie." Perhaps these bastions of convention will respond to the innovations of the upper-middle class when the latter's children, some of whom are now explorers, dissidents, and deviants, have become leaders of wealth and prestige to be emulated by others striving for respectability. This process is by no means a new one, history has seen it before (Blum and associates, 1969a) as the drug discoveries of the intelligentsia were dedramatized and diffused in society. Over time present definitions of drug delinquency will probably change dramatically.

There are several other more immediate implications of the current democratization of drug dealing. One is that conscience has not disappeared, otherwise exhortations and assurances of Leary's sort would not be needed. The sources of conscience are changing and are, for children of less excellent families (Blum and associates, 1972), increasingly based on peer values—inherently less stable and possibly more hazardous (think of William Golding's *Lord of the Flies*)—rather than on the authority of traditional institutions. Possibly the acceptability by that more insulated youthful peer society (itself stratified by age) of what is for most adults criminality is part and parcel of a larger set of changes in our society. The symptoms include an ever increasing rate of juvenile and adult street crime, the challenge to traditional authority and establishment norms (which expresses itself in a variety of movements and ferments), and the advocacy of a pluralism which, in its extreme aspects, is anarchistic. All these developments are accompanied morally by denunciations of the positive law—the regulations passed by legislatures and the edicts of those in power—in favor of the natural law as determined by man in communion with God or his conscience or both. Indeed, we propose that there cannot be widespread changes in what youth does in areas charged with emotion and moral values, as drug use and dealing are, unless other important changes occur in a society. These larger social changes allow, give impetus to, and are, in turn, affected by innovations which the youth propose or practice.

But there is more to middle-class dealing than emulation of the slum scene. Indeed, the denunciation of heroin use by the dominant voices of the psychedelic-marijuana scene demonstrates, if not wisdom alone, a conflict between middle-class youth and slum users as to what constitutes a good drug or, perhaps better said, a good drug life. What nonslum drug life is like, what role dealing plays in it, and what is implied are now considered. We draw on the work of Carey (1968) and Goode (1970). Carey describes the Berkeley "Colony" of ten thousand to twenty-five thousand students, parastudents, and associated street people who are the drug scene in and next to the University of California. With regard to dealing—basing his descriptions on a sample of eighty users, including ten middle-level dealers—he observes that dealing is common if not universal. He quotes from a dealer: "Everybody I know deals on some level." The movement from experimenter to user to dealer is rapid if the user enjoys his drugs, if his friends are regular users, if he likes being in the center of drug transactions, and if he has leisure time and is willing to take risks. (As measured by the Kogan Wallach test, according to Evans and Kline, 1969, consistent drug users score higher on willingness to take risks than do nonusers.) Since many users meet these conditions, the street pusher resembles his customers; one man's customer is another man's dealer. However, a regular dealing role seems indicated if the user also likes money, is friendly, wants peer approval and prestige, wants to be the center of action, wants proof of his personal identity as drug-centered, and is willing to violate the law. Carey (1968) quotes a knowledgeable participant: "Most people who deal are lazy—they won't work. Dealing is the easiest thing for them to do. . . . Or they deal strictly to build up the ego. . . . They like being in an in-group—looked up to and respected." Dealing is satisfying, "not a desperate last-ditch effort to survive. The pushers like what they are doing and where they are."

But dealing has its problems: it is time-consuming, and competition is heavy; there is a "vast leakage of drugs, thefts occur, overhead is considerable, and enormous risks are required to get ahead." In consequence, most dealers work for very little, "less than a decent wage." Carey says that an efficient street pusher could, from 1965 to 1967, expect to make a profit of only twenty-five to thirty dollars per week. Success—defined as good money, few hours, little hassle, and low risk—also requires that certain rules be followed: dealing only with trusted people, engaging in regular (efficient, reliable) transactions, being cautious and deceptive (that is, concealing the dealing role well). Carey calls attention to the discrepancy between the rules for pushing and the motives of most Colony pushers. "The format for success is to be a cold fish," and yet the average Colony member is frivolous and not serious and for these same reasons he refuses straight work. Consequently, most Colony dealing is "love dealing" and not hard business. When a Colony dealer does make some money, he is likely to spend it staying high and retire from work.

Because of the difficulties in being a success and the incompatibility between doing that and the motives that brought one to the scene in the first place, "the turnover among street pushers is very high. Either they step up their operations and move up in the distribution system or they decide to quit." Those who remain are part of the estimated 250 pushers who directly serve an estimated five thousand customers in the community. Of these 250 "very few make a decent living, but that's not as important as the fact that many make some living off illegal work, and they willingly try on this identity as an outlaw." A dealer is quoted: "Hell, I don't know what I want to be. I know I don't have any—uh—image of myself as an adult pusher. I don't want to knock it. Like, it's a nice place to visit, even if I don't want to live there." Some deal only for a few weeks. For those who stay on, moving up or losing out to the police, Carey finds a deep attachment to the life and increasing isolation from the straight world.

Thus, the street pusher is in it for little money and lots of satisfactions. Ordinarily he is not stable personally, is experimenting with being a pusher, is similar to the user, is not employed by a "mob," and values being independent and enterprising. In background middle class, likely to be in his twenties, rarely getting rich, not involved with criminals, not violent, not prone to cheat customers, otherwise rarely delinquent, he is always a user. That is Carey's picture of the soft drug dealer (cannabis, hallucinogens, possibly amphetamines) in Berkeley, circa 1966.

Accounts by Goode (1970) tell us about dealing among 204 marijuana smokers in New York City in 1967. (In his sample, as with most samples of regular users of illicit drugs, the pattern is one of multiple drug use. The emphasis on marijuana occurs because this drug is the most widely used of the illicit psychoactives, and while users of other drugs rarely have not also used marijuana, some marijuana users do not regularly use other substances.) They were mostly university faculty and students and employees in a publishing firm and in a market research firm. Goode likens drugs among users to food among us all; sharing and hospitality are the themes, not sale to one's friends and guests. Nevertheless, there are sellers of marijuana, and Goode's observations on what factors are related to selling are very important.

His first finding is that the most important factor associated with whether a person sells is how much he uses. Among those using every day, 96 per cent had sold; among those using less than once monthly, 29 per cent had sold. A continuum connects these two extremes. Selling marijuana is also linked to the extent of multiple drug use (or, in our view, involvement with a drug-centered subculture). Persons who had taken only marijuana had sold it in 13 per cent of the cases. Persons who had taken three or more other illicit drugs had sold marijuana in 64 per cent of the cases. A third point is that selling is linked to the number of close friends who are regular smokers. Among those who claimed 60 to 100 per cent of their friends were users, 68 per cent sold. Among those claiming 0 to 29 per cent of their friends used regularly, 21 per cent sold. Also, the amount of selling is distributed over a continuum, from selling once to selling frequently. These are fundamental points.

We think that Goode's statistically supported findings coupled with Carey's informal reports provide excellent insights into selling soft drugs. Selling is a matter of use of and involvement with drugs, of being part of—and wanting to be central in—social relations centering on use. It appears to be related to personal characteristics such as risk-taking, willingness to do something illegal, and need for prestige. Selling is also a function of the group and situation; among Carey's street people selling seemed linked to not wanting straight work, to a transitional or experimental life style among those who were young, immature, or suspended in career, whereas with Goode's regularly employed sample these factors were not cited. The duration and the direction of the selling career are also likely results of personal and situational factors. In Carey's sample, street dealing was short-lived and was a stage on the way to businesslike (bureaucratic) dealing or to arrest or to quitting. Perhaps in Goode's sample, especially among those who were older and established smokers holding respectable jobs, such transitional or fluid developments among dealers would be less common. In neither sample did dealing appear to be linked to violence, the Mafia, street crimes, or other such unpleasantness.

In sum, then, among people in the drug scene strong advocates take public stands in favor of drug dealing as a friendly, useful, and virtuous activity. In contrast, most adult Americans oppose drug dealing and would impose prison sentences on sellers of either heroin or marijuana, although this punitive approach is less prevalent among young people even when they do not use drugs. A conflict in public policy formulation is apparent here. One can predict that as long as strongly opposing views exist, any policy on dealers will be unstable—subject to debate—and limited in its deterrent and corrective capability since dealers will not accept the inherent moral dictum that they are in error.

Any policy based on incorrect assumptions about dealing is also likely to be unstable. Present beliefs are that dealers are different and can be handled differently from users; legislation and action are based on this view. Yet studies among slum heroin users, middle-class heroin users, middle-class marijuana and multiple drug users, and street people of the psychedelic scene offer consistent findings that dealers are users, that most regular users deal at one time or another, and that both using and dealing are satisfying activities which can serve many social and personal needs. Among young, urban, male slum dwellers dealing is associated with other factors predictive of delinquency and unemployability—poor education, delinquency prior to drug use, failure to respond to arrest or treatment, probable disinterest in or unfitness for straight work, and so forth. Among young middle-class illicit users studied through 1967, delinquency proneness was not identified, and among employed groups no factors adverse to employment could be found. Among middle-class street people aversions to straight work similar to those found in the lower class were present. Regarding persistence in dealing, for young middle-class user-dealers, low-level dealing was likely to be a transitional activity, leading to involvement at higher levels or to arrest with its consequences or to quitting. For slum heroin users transitional activities were also found (although these may occur at a much later age) leading, as before, either further into the drug life and correlated criminality (street crime) and dealing or, alternatively, to employed status (Winick, 1962). (Other outcomes such as alcoholism, hospitalization, and death are not to be excluded.)

We speculate on some broad correlates of dealing seen as an indicator of social change. We propose that these factors may include an absorption of slum styles by the youth of the middle class, a shift from traditional authority to peer authority as an anchor for conduct codes, a heightened appeal for pluralism (many different life styles allowed within the society with none dictating to the other), and a justification of individual- or group-centered, rather than nation- or community-centered, conduct based on appeals to the ascendency of the natural law over the positive law.

We also call attention to the fact that illicit dealing is part and parcel of the larger accepted pattern of drug production and sales in the United States, the latter a multibillion dollar commercial activity. In that large sense Americans approve of doing business in drugs. We see no reason to doubt that among the young—or others—who have shucked conformance to particular aspects of the culture, this principle remains in acceptance.

On the basis of observations, we suggest that drug dealing is by no means removed from the mainstream of American life and that, for people using illicit drugs and being unable or unwilling to accommodate either to legitimate work or to ordinary social relations, dealing provides an acceptable and enjoyable activity, income, access to drugs and supporting situations for their use, and partial resolution for various personal inadequacies and needs. But because it is a job which is the object of disapproval and subject to external stress and internal conflict and because its pursuit—we believe—ordinarily provides only a partial resolution of personal problems or an incomplete experiment in growth and living, it is likely to remain a short-term activity subject to much ambivalence. One would expect that dealing is transitional, that being a dealer will lead either to going deeper into drugs and crime (including the criminal organization of the drug business) or, especially as one gets older, to getting out and looking for somewhat more harmonious ways to live.

The crystal ball aside, let us now turn to our results to see what they reveal about dealers, the development of their careers, dealing as an activity, and relationships between dealing and the institutional settings or life situations in which it occurs or which are concerned with its control.

Chapter 1

A VARIEGATED POPULATION

We sought to identify drug dealers representing as many different levels of activity, kinds of people, and types of drugs trafficked as possible. We wanted to be able to compare one type of dealer with another, but since we did not know what the "real" population of all dealers is like—for they are a concealed group—we could not use ordinary census-type survey procedures to gather our sample. Instead, we set sampling goals based on population diversity, which we knew to exist. We could not estimate the actual size of these diverse groups within the total population of illicit drug dealers; so we did not set quotas of the sort which, in ordinary surveys, aim to get proportionate representation. Our diversity sampling, for example, did require that we obtain some young and some old dealers, some who had been arrested and some who had not, some in jail and some out, some selling LSD and some selling heroin; some from the Haight-Ashbury, some from the Tenderloin, some from suburbs, some from communes, some from each ethnic group in the Bay Area, some who had quit as well as those still in the business, and so on. We also set sampling limits; for example, after we had interviewed ten street hallucinogen peddlers in the Haight-Ashbury, we stopped seeking any more of this breed and shifted to a different place, dealer level, or user population. When we did know something of a population's real size—for example, the percentage of blacks in the Bay Area—we tried to be sure that the number of dealers drawn from that group would be roughly proportional. Thus, 9 per cent of our sample is black; blacks constitute about 8 per cent of the Bay Area population, where most of our work was done.

Our work-a-day procedures were simple. We had been studying drug users in the Bay Area for nearly ten years. We had studied hippie, student, patient, professional, and other groups of illicit users. We had been involved in various education and treatment endeavors. We had colleagues working in diverse settings, ranging from detoxification centers, vice squads, church counseling services, prisons, and the like, to free clinics, poverty programs, neighborhood centers, and user self-help enterprises. Finally, from prior work, we knew a number of dealers. To begin our work, we turned to all these sources. We asked those who were willing to join us—and whom we thought reliable—to become interviewers. We pretested, for several rounds, an interview schedule which, when judged satisfactorily by interviewers and interviewees, we adopted along with a detailed set of instructions for use and a set of standards for behavior. The latter were to assure the safety and anonymity of dealer subjects and the safety and reputation of interviewers. From the standpoint of cooperation, clarity, and safety, the procedures worked.

One basic and bedeviling problem was never solved. Since we could not identify subjects by name, we could not reinterview them for reliability; nor could we independently assess them to test the validity of their replies. For the most part, dealers were interviewed by interviewers who already knew them and thus were in a position independently to judge the truth or falseness of what was said. Even so, we accept the possibility that we were told lies and that the data do not entirely reflect the state of affairs of some of our dealers. We did ask each dealer what questions he believed other dealers would not answer truthfully. Almost half (45 per cent) of our sample thought that dealers would lie about something—mostly how much money they made; that is, they would brag about and exaggerate their income. (Four per cent of this group believed that other dealers would lie about everything.) In our study of deception among normal citizens (Blum, 1972), 18 per cent of our subjects said that they or their neighbors were also likely to lie about their incomes. In this matter—as, we shall see, in some other matters—our dealers reflect American status and values. Indeed, exaggerating income and personal worth ranked first as the kind of lie reported by respectable (randomly sampled) American families as they spoke of lies told to neighbors, lies told to casual acquaintances, and lies between good friends. The relationship between the dealer and his interviewer was usually that of friends or acquaintances, and so the dealers' surmise about lie-evoking questions is compatible with the normal citizens' pattern.

We estimate that several thousand nonincarcerated dealers in the Bay Area were identified during over two years of field work, 1968 to 1971. Among these, 480 constitute that sample which we refer to as the variegated dealer and which occupies our attention in these early chapters. These were dealers who met our sampling goals and who cooperated with us.

Sample Characteristics

Our dealers range in age from 12 to 70 years old. The median age is in the 19 to 23 bracket. About three fourths are male, and 65 per cent have never been married. Nearly 10 per cent eschew the conventional marital categories (married, separated, divorced) and spoke of homosexual, group living (multiple partners as in a commune), or other unconventional sexual arrangements. Over half of the sample have had some college education. Ten per cent have college degrees; one fourth have some high school education; about one fifth hold high school diplomas. Nearly all of those reporting incomplete schooling—65 per cent of the total sample—said that they were dropouts.

Most of the dealers in the sample were already known to our interviewers or were introduced through friends or acquaintances. About one fifth were sampled via a formal police contact (that is, they were in jail or on parole). At the time of the interview half held a straight (legitimate) job; half did not. Half of those working held white-collar or professional positions; half held blue-collar positions. Businessmen are represented among the dealers as are civil servants, artists, and others. In fact, the only major urban work levels or styles not represented in the sample are clerics, housewives, or major corporation executives. As we have already noted, most (84 per cent) of our dealers are white; about 9 per cent are black; the rest are Oriental or classified themselves as racially mixed. On old-fashioned anthropological grounds we classify Mexican-Americans as Caucasian, even though young Mexican-Americans in California now often identify themselves separately—on social-ethnic grounds—as "Chicano."

Families

Fifty-five per cent of the dealers' fathers hold white-collar or professional or business positions; and more than 5 per cent work in religious or supervisory civil service occupations. Thus, over 60 per cent of the dealers came from upper- or middle-class families. (U.S.

Census figures show that approximately 47 per cent of California families have heads of households in these upper- or middle-class jobs.) The single most frequent occupation for mothers is that of housewife. Less than 15 per cent are employed as domestic servants or in working-class jobs. Mothers and fathers (45 per cent mothers, 36 per cent fathers) are most often Protestant, with Catholics (29 per cent mothers, 26 per cent fathers) second. About 10 per cent of the families profess Judaism. Excluding those families with one or both parents deceased, the majority (58 per cent) of the parents are married and living together; one third are either divorced or separated or (in a few instances) were never married to each other.

The drug-use and criminal histories of the parents were of interest to us. Alcoholism is described in one or both parents by 28 per cent of the dealers, with the father more often alcoholic. Three per cent describe one or both parents as opiate addicts. Felony arrests are noted for their parents by 23 per cent of the dealers. As with alcoholism and addiction, fathers more often than mothers have felony-arrest histories.

We cannot be sure that the dealers' characterizations of their parents as either alcoholic or drug-addicted are correct. If we accept them, it is apparent that the alcoholism occurs more often in the parents of dealers than would be expected to occur among married adults; problem drinkers occur among the total adult population at a rate of approximately 6 per cent (Blum and Blum, 1967).

Similarly, a drug-addiction rate of 3 per cent—even presuming that barbiturate dependency as well as opiate dependency is included—is many times greater than would be expected from a representative adult population; estimates of narcotics addicts in the United States at any point in time do not exceed 200,000. The dealer parents' addiction rate does, however, come closer to the 4 per cent rough-estimate figure in the Bay Area normal population study (Blum and associates, 1969a) of overall illicit-narcotics experience. One wonders whether the dealers believe that their nonaddicting parents' experience with narcotics really constituted addiction; or whether dealers are reporting "real" addictions at a rate so much higher than past studies estimate because there really is much hidden addiction; or whether dealers are simply inaccurate in describing their parents—for example, projecting their own drug habits, justifying them, and the like.

We inquired about the dealers' brothers and sisters. The average number of children in the dealers' families runs between three and four. Fifteen per cent of the dealers are only children and one third are the eldest; altogether, about half of our sample are first-born children. Given the average family size of 3.6 children, there are more first borns than would ordinarily be expected. Ordinal position in the family may be a factor in becoming a dealer. (See Schacter, 1962.)

When we examine the reported delinquency pattern among dealers' brothers and sisters, we find that the older siblings have had more frequent arrests than the younger ones. On the other hand, reversing the positive age and delinquency association, there are more juvenile than adult arrests for dealers' siblings. Among the oldest siblings, vis-à-vis the dealer, one fifth had at least juvenile arrests. Among the dealers themselves, 62 per cent have had juvenile and/or adult arrests. Analysis of age and delinquency reveals that the differences between dealers and their siblings in reported delinquency are not due to artifacts arising from sex or age differences. Individual (idiosyncratic) propensities are clearly operative.

Among the arrested siblings at all ages (here again their siblings are contrasted to the dealers) narcotics offenses are far and away the most common reason for arrest. Among oldest siblings, that is, the oldest in the families excluding the dealer, these narcotics offenses occur at least ten times more often than the next most common offense, which is drunkenness—and that too is a drug offense. However, the actual number of arrests for narcotics violations among siblings of dealers is small compared with the prevalence of illicit use that is not revealed by arrest; for instance, among oldest siblings the ratio of narcotics arrest to prevalence of illicit use, as described by the dealer for his sibling, runs one to three. This ratio of arrests to illicit use remains constant at one to three for all siblings down through the fifth sibling. Drug peddling also is found among siblings, but not as often as illicit use. On the other hand, peddling among siblings occurs at the same rate as moderate or heavy illicit-drug use. As with overall delinquency, siblings' drug commerce is less common than that of the dealers. For example, among the older sibs (who deal the most) about one fifth are said to deal; among these dealers about half are very active dealers (that is, those who peddle regularly). Drinking problems, as identified by our dealers, occur more rarely among siblings than among their parents. About 11 per cent of the oldest siblings are said to have alcohol problems. This estimation rate decreases to 5 per cent through sibling 5. As a proportion of siblings with alcohol problems, this rate is fairly constant.

The sibling data—and here we focus on the oldest sibling, since that is the one with the greatest chance of having used drugs—show that the rate for overall illicit drug use by eldest siblings is 31 per cent. This figure, given the oldest sibling's median age of 24 to 35, suggests that the dealers' siblings rates are "average" for California urban resident (under 29) illicit-drug use.

We asked whether the dealer's siblings had ever initiated him or her into the use of drugs. Nearly one fifth of the dealers say that they were first given at least one illicit drug by their oldest sibling. There is a gradually decreasing role for younger siblings as initiators of an illicit drug experience; for the very youngest, no teaching role at all is described. We asked whether siblings had also introduced the responding dealer to criminality other than illicit-drug use. Although this did occur, again with decreasing frequency the younger the sibling, it was rare; for example, only about 3 per cent attribute to the oldest sibling any role as a criminal leader or teacher. As a final question we asked the dealer whether he likes his siblings. Most, between 80 and 90 per cent, like all of their brothers and sisters. There is no indication of any greater affection for those who had taught them drug use—or were themselves users—than for the younger, straighter, siblings.

Interests and Social Relations

Aside from drugs, and drug-related sociability, what leisures do the individuals in our sample enjoy? Although many are mentioned, there is a striking theme: 90 per cent list activities that are solitary. Only 7 per cent enjoy team sports and athletics; about 12 per cent mention nondrug social activities. (Double coding accounts for a sum > 100 per cent.) As for their risk-taking propensities, most of them like fast cars, but only 40 per cent like gambling.

What about preferences in other matters? In school the most favored subjects are arts and humanities; technology and hard sciences are second; the social sciences are third. In politics the great majority prefer liberal Democrats; some prefer the radical left; Republicans are far behind. In religion the preference is for "nothing"; only a minority claim Catholicism, followed by Protestantism, mysticism, and Judaism. These preferences mirror those reported by drug users in general (R. H. Blum, 1969).

As far as family relationships are concerned, most claim that they get along well with their parents; only 9 per cent state that they emphatically do not. As for teachers, half claim that they were liked by their teachers; a strong minority say that they were both liked and disliked; one third claim that their teachers either disliked them or were indifferent to them. Being liked was not enough to keep them in school. We have already noted that many are dropouts; further, the majority (60 per cent) were truants before they quit. We presume that the truancy was in high school; for whereas most (72 per cent) enjoyed elementary school, a lesser number (63 per cent and 61 per cent, respectively) enjoyed junior high and high school. Among those attending college, most (79 per cent) report enjoying it; paradoxically, however, most did not complete it (although a few are still there). In school most claim that they were either average or above average in popularity, although over one fourth say that they were either unpopular or loners. The majority had many or some close friends, but one third had no friends or only a few.

In discussing present friendships, 71 per cent indicate that they have close friends who are not drug users. Two thirds say that they have close ties to someone of the opposite sex: spouse, boy or girl friend, or mistress/lover. As for settling down to enduring relationships such as marriage (only 13 per cent are now married and living with their spouse), about half think well of that; many are not sure or are antipathetic.

Asked about spending patterns, 40 per cent say that they are spenders, not savers; only 17 per cent confess to being thrifty, parsimonious, or otherwise "saving" without a spending goal. Even so, 40 per cent report investments; most do not use charge accounts (85 per cent); half have no present debts, and the debts outstanding average under $500. They are also lenders—although not so many of them as are borrowers—with the average debtor owing them under $500. More intend to pay their creditors back than say they expect to see themselves repaid. As for their individual income requirements, these are modest indeed compared to their actual incomes, the median being between $200 and $300 per month. We conclude that ours is not totally a spendthrift sample and that they are capable of self-control in financial matters.

Self-Descriptions

Turning to their own person, we asked each dealer to describe himself. In analyzing these responses we coded for the tenor of that description—whether self-approving or self-rejecting—and for the substance of it; that is, we tried to discern an underlying set of values or orientations linked to particular traits, and we classified dealers by the most-used terms (or traits) in their self-descriptions. We set one theme as that of the Protestant ethic; terms linked to this theme are "hard-working," "competent," "self-controlled," "foresightful," and the like. Another theme is the naturalist-humanistic one encountered so much these days in the drug scene; traits linked to this theme are "loving," "relaxed," "pacifist," "sincere," "natural," and "friendly." A third theme is that of the modern psychological ethic; words here cover the range of diagnoses, adjustment, and insight such as "aware of myself," "uptight," "nervous," "paranoid," "at peace with myself," "self-realized," "intelligent," "open," and "honest with oneself." Another theme is that of the artistic ethic; self-description classifications here include "creative," "artistic," "musical," "flamboyant," "intense," and "emotional."

The theme of the conventional religious ethic also appears, although conspicuous by its rarity. Self-descriptions linked to it include "I believe in God," "Christian," "religious," "pious," and "God-fearing." Another theme is that of the uncertain soul. Here are classified those who use terms such as "seeker," "searcher," "trying to find myself," "unsure," or "I don't know." A final theme is that specific to drug use—as, for example, "junkie," "head," "freak," and "ex-addict."

The self-descriptions reveal considerable self-acceptance; in their descriptions of themselves, 51 per cent of the sample use only words that we judge to be benign. Thirty per cent offer a mixed, indifferent, or negative view; 4 per cent have only bad things to say about themselves.

As for the descriptive themes, the naturalist-humanist one prevails two to one over any other. The most common traits offered are "free," "natural," "sincere," "unspoiled," and "friendly." In second place is the psychological ethic, with the uncertain soul a close third; indeed, some may prefer to place these inner-state-concerned and adjustment-oriented themes together (in which case that combination equals the naturalist-humanists). Psychological terms popular are "aware," "realizing one's own potential," "honest with self," and "no hang-ups"; favored items of the uncertain souls are "I don't know," "haven't found myself," and "searching." The Protestant ethic runs a very weak fourth (outranked three to one by psychological or naturalist folk); the artistic ethic behind that; the drug ethic next; and, by less than 1 per cent, the religious man or woman.

Descriptions by Interviewers

"O wad some power the giftie gie us, to see oursels as others see us!" Perhaps it exists, for our interviewers rated the dealers. The interviewers were diverse in outlook and untrained in rating; their ratings were not checked for reliability and not subjected to validation. Consequently, these ratings have only the same poor virtues as the self-descriptions: words used by humans to describe other humans without assurance of agreement. The rating-list words and the percentages so described are as follows: (A) friendly (85), reliable (58); (B) angry (5), domineering (6), suspicious (13), unreliable (4);

(C) businesslike (20), good salesman (58); (D) nervous (12), confused (8), slowed or overactive (14), ill at ease (11).

If we take A (friendly and reliable) to reflect approval in two areas, immediate social relations and trustworthiness, we conclude that most of our interviewers (85 per cent) approve of the dealers as social beings but that fewer (58 per cent) are confident about their trustworthiness or consistency. If we take B to reflect disapproval in aspects of interpersonal relations and, again, trustworthiness, we again find that the majority of our interviewers enjoy or approve the dealers' person, as in A. Fifty-eight per cent of the raters check the positive rating "reliable," but only 4 per cent check the negative rating "unreliable." There is clearly a discrepancy in the raters' behavior and, we infer, the certainty with which they view the trustworthiness or predictability of dealers they are rating. Let us assume that C estimates aspects of work competence. If so, our dealers impress interviewers more as salesmen than as hard-headed and matter-of-fact business types. Let us treat D as a diagnostic device. The results imply that a fairly consistent proportion of the dealers suffer at least visible strain and possibly worse —disorders in thinking, affect, or mood. Let us return to C and reconsider "businesslike" as a Protestant virtue. Our interviewers rated that ethic, then used it twice as often as the Protestant ethic theme emerged in the dealers' own self-descriptions.

Interviewers also rated dealers on their dress, hair style, and hair grooming. In dress the descriptions and ratings were as follows: casual (60 per cent), conventional (29 per cent), high style (8 per cent), shabby (8 per cent), flamboyant (5 per cent), and dirty (3 per cent). Hair styles are, for males, collar length (46 per cent), conventional or crewcut (37 per cent), shoulder length or below (17 per cent). For females, the long, smooth, below-shoulder (hippie) style is the most common hair arrangement. Hair grooming for 91 per cent of the males and 93 per cent of the females was described as clean, combed, and well kept.

History of Drug Use

Each dealer was asked to complete the drug-experience profile we used earlier. (Blum and associates, 1969b). Because this history-taking device was generally used in informal settings, and because dealers sometimes showed a casual disregard for the definitions of amount of use, the results obtained are general, not exact, indications of the dealers' drug-use histories.

With regard first to the approved social drug *alcohol,* 27 per cent of the dealers report that they began drinking during childhood (up to age 13), with 12 per cent of those who did drink doing so regularly (more than once a week) or considerably (more than four drinks a day). Alcohol consumption increases sharply during the teen years, with 88 per cent reporting any alcohol use and 10 per cent of these users describing considerable use. The prevalence pattern continues during the early twenties, when drinking by the 87 per cent reporting shows increases to include 37 per cent who drink regularly to heavily and 14 per cent heavily. Among the older dealers (26 or over) a decline in use occurs; but among those (66 per cent) still drinking, "considerable" drinking is proportionately greater (22 per cent).

A similar pattern occurs for *tobacco.* We find that 27 per cent began smoking in childhood, with 34 per cent smoking regularly (more than once a week) or considerably (one package or more per day). A sharp increase occurs in the teens, with 77 per cent smoking and, among these, 70 per cent smoking regularly (38 per cent of the regular smokers smoking considerably). A further increase has occurred by the early twenties; 82 per cent now smoke, and 86 per cent of the smokers are regular or heavy smokers, 57 per cent smoking one pack or more a day. A slight decline in prevalence (to 77 per cent), occurs with age; but the incidence of heavy use among smokers continues as before.

With regard to *tranquilizers* we find use prevalent among 26 per cent of the dealers during their teens and 39 per cent during the early twenties (19 to 25 bracket); after 25 a decrease in prevalence is reported (30 per cent). However, among those who continue to use tranquilizers, the incidence of regular (more than once a week, but less than seven times weekly) and considerable (daily use) use rises—from about one fourth during the teens and early twenties to two fifths among dealers 26 and older.

Thirty-seven per cent of the dealers reported that they used *sedatives* when they were teen-agers; 53 per cent in their early twenties; and only 43 per cent later (25 years and older). From age 13 on, the incidence of regular (more than once a week, but less than seven times a week) and considerable (daily) use remains constant (about 30 per cent); but an increasing proportion over time become daily users (from 12 per cent in teens to 14 per cent in twenties to 18 per cent of those 25 and older).

The histories show most *amphetamine* use beginning in the teens, with a prevalence of use of 50 per cent. By the early twenties prevalence has increased to 69 per cent, followed by a decline after age 25 (back to 52 per cent). There is a constant incidence of regular (more than once a week, but less than seven times a week) and considerable (daily) use, averaging about 40 per cent from age 13. If one singles out the heaviest use, the incidence pattern (20 per cent considerable) remains unchanged with age. With regard to manner of use, nearly half (45 per cent) report intravenous use of (mostly) methamphetamine.

Cannabis (marijuana and hashish) ranks third behind alcohol and tobacco in its use during childhood. Six per cent of the dealers report cannabis experience before 13. A sharp increase occurs during the teens, with 65 per cent reporting use; 90 per cent of the dealers say that they used cannabis by age 25. A slight decline after age 25 is reported, with 82 per cent of those 25 and over reporting cannabis use. The incidence of regular (more than once a week, but less than seven times a week) and considerable (daily) use increases from the teens to the early twenties (from 68 per cent to 80 per cent) and falls off somewhat after age 25 (70 per cent). Heavy (daily) use remains constant for about 44 per cent of all the users from age 19 onward. As for the type of cannabis used, most dealers report experience with both marijuana and hashish. However, 28 per cent of the users say that they have had only marijuana.

Hallucinogen use is reported by 36 per cent of the dealers during their teen years and had increased to 69 per cent for those in the 19-25 bracket. Dealers over 25 are more likely to abstain from hallucinogens than the 19 to 25 group, for only half of those over 25 report any hallucinogen use. About half of the using sample (46 per cent and 49 per cent) report either regular use (once or twice or three times a month) or considerable use (four or more times a month) from the teens through early twenties; but only 41 per cent of those using after age 25 report regular or considerable use.

As for *opiates,* 1 per cent report childhood use: 35 per cent during the teen years, 66 per cent during the early twenties, and only 57 per cent in later years (25 or older). Heavy use (defined as regular or considerable; that is, more than once a week to daily) characterizes most childhood users: 30 per cent of those in their teens, 35 per cent of the early-twenty group; 66 per cent among the 26-and-older dealers.

Cocaine experience is described by 1 per cent in childhood, 15 per cent in the teens, 39 per cent in the early twenties, and 26 per cent in the older group. Heavy use (regular or considerable; that is, more than once a week to daily) is reported by 18 per cent in the teens, 14 per cent in the early twenties, and 36 per cent in the older dealer group.

The use of *special substances* (gasoline, glue, nitrous oxide, etc.) began for a few in childhood, peaking in use (to 26 per cent prevalence) during the teens and early twenties, and declining thereafter (15 per cent using after age 25). Heavy use declined from a high proportion of 17 per cent of the teen users to 7 per cent in the early twenties and then rose again after age 25 to 18 per cent. However, the teen users most often used glue or gasoline and the over-25 group, if they used at all, most often used more esoteric substances such as nitrous oxide, atropine, or amyl nitrate. Multiple special-substance use occurs more often in the 13 to 18 age group.

Index of "Favorite" Drugs. We thought an index for drug dealers' enduringly favorite psychoactive drugs would be interesting. We created an index by ranking each drug according to the greatest number in any age bracket who had ever tried it, the least absolute decline in use with increasing age, the greatest heavy use (for alcohol our "considerable" category, for all others our "regular" or "considerable" category) in any age bracket, and the greatest increase in intensity of use from any early years to the post-25 years. Arbitrarily we gave equal rank to drugs when percentage-point differences were less than 5 per cent between them. The overall ranking of enduring favorites places tobacco first and cannabis and opiates a close second. Classifying favorites (drugs of enduring demand in three major groups), we find, in order, (1) tobacco, cannabis, and opiates; (2) tranquilizers, alcohol, cocaine, hallucinogens, amphetamines, and sedatives; (3) the special substances (least in demand).

Shifting emphasis now, let us compare our dealer sample with a "normal" population. We can do this only crudely, since data on "normal" drug use are limited; and, ideally our dealers should be matched with controls from the same age, background, and so forth. As things stand, it is apparent that compared with a normal population drawn from the Bay Area in 1966 (Blum and associates, 1969a) and again in 1969 (Manheimer, Mellinger, and Balter, 1969) the dealer group's overall rate of use for all psychoactive drugs is considerably greater than that of adults drawn randomly from the same region. Comparing dealers with special samples—for example, college students —again one sees much higher use among the dealers.

Summary

It appears that dealers' parents are more likely than ordinary parents to have serious drug-dependency problems. The parents are also likely to have more visible (publicly recorded) criminality than ordinary parents. Dealers' parents also come more heavily from high socioeconomic levels than lower levels. A bimodal distribution, one of middle-class and one of disordered lower-class families, is implied within the variegated dealer population. As for the brothers and sisters, they appear to use illicit drugs at approximately the "normal" rate for the region(s) in which they live. They appear to have escaped illicit-drug involvement, including dealing, as well as the delinquency which characterizes the dealers. The foregoing suggest that family factors (drugs and crime) are predictors for drug dealing (see, for example, Robins, 1966) but, in addition, personal or idiosyncratic features within the youth (or adult) himself will have to be invoked.

The histories of the dealers shows that nearly all (476 of 480) are themselves involved in illicit-drug use; that the majority of dealers have at one time or another used a variety of psychoactive substances (including alcohol, tobacco, sedatives, amphetamines, cannabis, hallucinogens, and opiates); that some dealers decrease their drug use as they grow older, whereas others continue to use at least some potent substances with increasing frequency. A hierarchy of drug preferences, measured by an index of enduring favorites, ranks tobacco, cannabis, and the opiates first and sedatives and the special substances (glue, thinner, and so on) last.

Most dealers report that their favorite nondrug leisure activities are solitary ones. They claim good relationships with parents and teachers, reasonable popularity among peers, friends, and heterosexual ties. On the other hand, most had been truant from school, a third are without close friends, only 13 per cent are married and living with their spouse (compared to an estimated California average of 66 per cent for that age group), and half are dubious about ever settling down.

Half of the dealers describe themselves in self-approving terms; only 5 per cent are solely negative in their self-appraisals. Most of the self-descriptions reveal an adherence to the naturalist-humanistic ethic prevalent in the drug scene, or the modern psychological ethic, or the theme of the uncertain soul. Words most used in self-descriptions illustrating these self-views are "free," "natural, "aware," "honest with self," "friendly," "realistic," "I don't know," "unsure," and "haven't found myself."

Dealers were rated by the interviewers. The ratings suggest that the interviewers liked most of the dealers but saw a small but consistent minority as, at best, ill at ease and, at worst, suffering mental and emotional upset. In their appearance, most dealers were well groomed and neither flamboyant nor hippie types. Their appearance is in keeping with their own counsel not to attract attention and be discreet. It is also compatible with their avowal of many values of the dominant non-dealing, nonusing society.

Chapter 2

EVOLUTION OF DEALING

During the interviews we inquired further into the circumstances of initiation and development of illicit use and dealing itself. We learned that most dealers (72 per cent) had tried an illicit drug by age 18; indeed, 37 per cent had done so by age 15. Friends (peers) were most likely to be the source of drugs for 71 per cent of the dealers. Siblings (for 7 per cent) ranked a far second, equal in rank to self-initiated and presumably nonsocial drug seeking (for example, a youth is trying a drug on his own initiation, without being urged; or its being given to him, as in solitary buying or stealing). Parents accounted for 2 per cent, and physicians and teachers provided the forbidden fruit on rare occasions. Initiators are either age mates or older. It is very rare (in 2 per cent of the cases only) for a younger person to introduce an older one to drugs. This higher-status older-age variable has been observed before in drug initiation (Blum and associates, 1964).

The settings for initial use were most often private homes, although 13 per cent of the dealers received their first illicit drug in jail or some other institution, such as a psychiatric ward. That inaugural drug use was a social if not a festive event is illustrated by the fact that 80 per cent of the dealers describe the first occasion of use as a "party." Nearly 10 per cent of the dealers experimented in their own homes. With the previous data on siblings' giving drugs to dealers in mind, it appears that brothers and sisters who do give or take drugs together do not do it as an at-home activity.

It is not surprising that youngsters who begin illicit use in their teens would also meet drug dealers during the same period (70 per cent had done so by age 18). These first-met dealers are described as friends or acquaintances; only 6 per cent were strangers. The moral reaction to the first dealer was, for the majority (59 per cent), one of approval; only 16 per cent said that they disapproved of someone who dealt in drugs.

The first transaction with a dealer was, for most (73 per cent), a later and different event than their first drug use. Even so, that first transaction with a known drug dealer occurred within the framework of a social rather than a commercial (profit-making) activity; for 62 per cent state that the drugs provided by the dealer on that occasion were a gift or were shared by the dealer. Twelve per cent say that they bought the drug at cost; 26 per cent engaged in commerce on their first "buy," purchasing at a price which they believed brought the dealer a profit. The amount of money involved was small—for 77 per cent, less than fifteen dollars. About 5 per cent started as big spenders, paying more than one hundred dollars at the first drug purchase. The first drug purchased was, by 76 per cent, marijuana. LSD ranks second, 8 per cent first buying it; 6 per cent bought amphetamines, and 4 per cent bought opiates.

This first venture into the dealer's world—through getting a drug from a dealer—was not without its emotional significance: only 15 per cent claim that they were indifferent or otherwise unmoved by the occasion; the majority recall feeling nervous (39 per cent) or excited (19 per cent). Some felt "good," a few were "high" or felt "important," less than 1 per cent admitted to feeling guilty. Immediately following the purchase, emotional shifts occurred. Almost two thirds (62 per cent) of those who had been nervous or excited now were calmed. On the other hand, the majority (57 per cent) now experienced euphoria—presumably pharmacological but quite possibly also linked to the successfully completed buy. Afterward twice as many buyers as before just buying felt "important," almost half as many claimed indifference, and almost none admitted feeling guilty. As for their opinions of their supplier, these differed in no way from their earlier opinions of dealer acquaintances: most approved of him, some were neutral, and a few had misgivings about him.

The next step in career development was their own first illicit distribution of a drug. (Under the present California and federal law, one who gives away a drug is subject, theoretically, to the same penalties as one who sells.) Again, the transaction was not likely to be a strictly commercial one. Most of our sample first distributed a drug to another by giving it away or sharing it. A few sold at cost. Only one fifth (21 per cent) were merchants from the first, selling at a profit. As in their own initiation into use, so in their becoming a drug distributor, the occasion was social, a party, for 75 per cent of these users-turning-dealer. The sharing and giving of drugs on these sociable occasions was not a one-to-one encounter but a group affair: 67 per cent said that they distributed to a group of friends and acquaintances; only 3 per cent distributed drugs initially to strangers. Those who were receivers on the inaugural illicit distribution were, for the most part, age mates. How did the distribution come about? The most common theme (39 per cent) is that the budding dealer himself sought out recipients, either to share the drug experience (46 per cent), to consolidate friendships (16 per cent), or to feel important (4 per cent). Nineteen per cent say that they wanted to make money. Their friends also sought drugs from them; 33 per cent of the dealers report that the initiative on the first distribution occasion came from others.

As with their own initial drug use, the most widely distributed first drug was marijuana, 76 per cent supplying it; 8 per cent provided amphetamines, 7 per cent hallucinogens, and 5 per cent opiates. By the time the first distribution took place, many of the dealers in our sample were in regular touch with other dealers. Many (53 per cent) indicate that the drugs they shared, gave, or sold on this occasion had come through commercial channels, not from friends or acquaintances or relatives.

We asked our dealers to recall how they had felt on this first occasion when they had supplied drugs. Forty-nine per cent say that they felt happy. Some (17 per cent) were nervous or excited; 11 per cent felt important. Indifference was claimed by 18 per cent, guilt by only 1 per cent.

For most dealers in our sample (67 per cent) the occasion of first drug supplying was not the same as the first sale. We therefore asked the same questions about the first action as a commercial trafficker, as opposed to the earlier stage of being a strictly sociable trafficker. We again find that social occasions—parties—were the most common setting for the first selling of drugs at a profit. Most of our dealers on that occasion sold to many persons rather than to one. Unlike the first distribution, however, most of our dealers (57 per cent) say that other people played a major role, seeking drugs from them. Under these circumstances, there was also a shift in "motives"; for whereas earlier supplying had been done mainly for various personal-social reasons, the first sale included money making as a motive in over half (53 per cent) of the cases.

As for the emotional tone recalled, while half were still feeling "good" about what they were doing, only one person was supplying while "high" on drugs. Furthermore, nervousness and excitement had abated considerably compared to the occasion of their own first use or buy, so that only 9 per cent recalled being nervous or excited about selling. On the other hand, indifference—perhaps better called matter-of-factness—was becoming more common, with 28 per cent reporting this emotion-free condition. Even so, many of our subjects did have second thoughts, or at least some disturbing feelings, about embarking formally on a career as a drug dealer. For example, half did reflect that they could be arrested for what they were doing, one fourth acknowledge that this possible consequence did worry them, half (of those willing to discuss it further) note that the combination of awareness and concern altered their behavior insofar as it made them, even at that first sale, more cautious. Eleven per cent admit that they were bothered by their consciences because they were, in a sense, formalizing their roles as drug dealers.

Dealers were asked whether any set of events could have intervened to prevent this illicit career—specifically, the movement into regular dealing for profit—from developing. Some (34 per cent) of our dealers say that they would have been deterred by an arrest very early in their careers; 16 per cent say that they would not have continued if their money problems could have been solved without their having to get straight jobs; 4 per cent say that they would not have become dealers if, when young and in need of money, they could have obtained straight jobs; and 2 per cent would not have become dealers if a fellow dealer, supplier, or customer had been arrested.

We inquired about the further development of our dealers' careers. Most of them describe a fairly similar pattern. They sought to expand their income by getting more customers (which usually required little or no effort). Then, primarily through their drug-using friends and acquaintances, they learned of new and varied sources of supplies for their own trade; and they established a pricing mechanism, most using flexible prices, charging customers whatever they were willing to pay (above dealer's costs). Some established a fixed profit/cost ratio, and about 10 per cent either inquired of or joined with other dealers to establish prices. Most claim that they derived the necessary precautions to prevent arrest from their own wisdom; only one fifth mention "tutelage" in the sense that they sought or received advice or instruction from others in learning security methods. A few sadly admit that they never did learn such criminal security; and they attribute their later arrests to just this failure. Among the precautions taken, selling only to friends rather than strangers ranks first. Also mentioned are being discreet (not talking about dealing), behaving and dressing unobtrusively, conducting all business in private, not being noticeably aggressive as salesmen, and not carrying drugs. Only a few tried to identify narcotics agents. No Bay Area dealers (but two living on the Mexican border) say that they learned early to bribe policemen in order to stay in business.

We asked whether our dealers had had any troubles at the beginning of their careers. About one third deny any problems; among those who did have them, the most common was being cheated, arrested, or in trouble with parents and authorities; being too generous and giving drugs away; and having difficulty in finding wholesalers to supply them. For most of the dealers some particularly helpful associate—most often a drug-using (and we presume dealing-experienced) friend—had helped to solve or prevent these problems. Second ranked (by 23 per cent) in this role was the first drug supplier—which suggests that about one quarter of the dealers had something like an apprenticeship, whereby they learned techniques from their first dealer-supplier.

The final question in our interview was "Is there anything we can do to be of help to you?" We were prepared to honor, as best we could, calls for help and toward this end maintained a file of service personnel, agencies, and other sources of succor. Requests for anything were minimal; in this setting the dealers were—as they often were in dealing too—prepared to give (of their time and suggestions) rather than to receive. Some few asked for money, some for drugs, some for our help in changing social policy. A few interviewers were invited to get high. One dealer asked for medical service, none for psychological aid or counseling.

Summary

Most of the dealers in our sample began to use illicit drugs in their teens, and the majority made their first sale while also in their teens. The sequence—which includes the visible events of first meeting a dealer, making the first buy, and first supplying drugs (without profit to others)—is part of the larger context of social activity among drug-using peers. The profit interest enters only after experience as a supplier has been gained. There are a number of gratifications which dealers report as part of the development of drug use and distribution. These include sharing the drug experience; good feelings about oneself and others as part of group activity; and a sense of personal importance, linked to the status of being a provider of welcome commodities.

The evolution of a dealer involves what we believe to be strong emotional components, not the least of which are excitement and nervousness associated with beginning illicit use and both euphoria and reduction in nervousness and excitement as an immediate response to the drug most often associated with the entire sequence—namely, marijuana. As the budding dealer moves from first user to first buyer to first distribution to first sale, he becomes less nervous, more matter-of-fact, more profit-oriented, and more cautious. Nevertheless, the general aura appears still to be emotional in that personal and social satisfactions continue to be met. The compelling features of this development appear strong; and almost none of the dealers in our sample describe internal restraints, competing internal values, or external alternatives sufficient to interfere in their career evolution. Instead, when they discuss interventions which would have effectively prevented the crystallization of their early drug use and exchanges into a regular business, they speak only of external forces that would control and/or frighten them and supply gratifications without requiring them to go to work.

Although the majority of our dealers were assisted throughout their early drug involvement by others who gave generously of drugs or advice, only a few were apprenticed to a successful dealer or otherwise systematically learned the trade. An impression of casualness rather than training-for-crime or economic purposefulness is conveyed in the descriptions of the youthful onset of drug dealing.

Chapter 3

DEALING LIFE AND COMMUNITY

At the time of the interview 65 per cent of our sample were dealing actively, the majority on a regular basis. A few (15 per cent) of those who had quit planned to resume; a larger proportion (39 per cent) were not sure whether they would return to the business; and, among those still dealing, 71 per cent had considered quitting. There is, obviously, considerable ambivalence about dealing within the sample; for a majority of those "retired" are thinking about resuming, and a majority of those in business are considering quitting.

Whatever has contributed to their doubts about dealing, it has not been old age or growing stale in a rut. The average length of time selling (since that first event) has been, for almost half of the dealers (47 per cent), two years or less. Only one fifth have been dealing for six years or more. On the other hand, arrest—which for the neophytes had been recalled as a distant and unobtrusive force—now looms large. Sixty-three per cent fear jail. Jail is the major reason behind either quitting or thinking about quitting for 52 per cent of our dealers. Other negative aspects of the dealing life include, in order, the hassle (time and trouble—8 per cent); disenchantment with drug users or the drug scene (4 per cent); and addiction or the fear of it (4 per cent). On the positive side, as attractions or alternatives outside of dealing, less than 2 per cent quit primarily because they could get or did get legitimate jobs; a few (5 per cent) quit because they either made their fortunes dealing or found a more successful criminal enterprise than drug peddling.

When asked about the "now" of dealing life (in their last active period), half (52 per cent) of the sample report dissatisfactions; half report none. The overriding distress appears to be a general mental state rather than any specific worry, for *fear* (in general) and *paranoia* are the words they use. Among the dissatisfied, 14 per cent no longer like their associates; 14 per cent feel that dealing is too much trouble; 10 per cent no longer like themselves. Furthermore, 40 per cent are worried about their own drug use; 59 per cent of these worried ones, almost one fourth of the total sample, worry primarily about being dependent or addicted. In addition, one fourth worry about their own possible—or known—alcoholism (alcohol-related problems). These concerns began as early as childhood and continue through the teens and twenties. The other major worry is about physical ill health associated with drug use (hepatitis, abcesses, and so forth). One fifth now complain of poor or only fair health.

Also, 38 per cent of the dealers report external pressures, not from the police, to quit. These pressures come mostly from parents, but wives or husbands or girl friends or boy friends or other social friends also push the dealers to give up the life. Another type of pressure, mentioned by one third of our sample, is fear of associates: the irrational acts of people on drugs; customers angry at having been cheated or robbed by the dealer; revenge from other dealers who were informed upon (or believe they were); interference in the drug business by gangsters. Three fourths of the dealers are also troubled because their actions can bring misery to people they care about. For example, if they were arrested—or killed by another dealer—they realize that their families would be distressed.

Our dealers have been in the life long enough to observe what has happened to others in their same position. Three fourths describe changes in other dealers which they would prefer not to see occur in themselves. Personality changes observed include psychological problems presumably due to drug use (described by 33 per cent); obsession with drugs (23 per cent); egotism, including self-preoccupation (22 per cent); and "paranoia"—usually meaning paranoid character or thinking, not classical paranoia of the psychiatric nomenclature (16 per cent). A second category of change is in health. Twenty-nine per cent say that they have observed the development of addiction in their fellow dealers, and 15 per cent attribute illness or death either to drugs or to associated life styles. A third category, emerging criminality, concerns some: 11 per cent describe a growth of violence in dealers they have known; 9 per cent allude to involvement with nondrug criminals or crime. However, most dealers do not believe that other dealers have become unfit for straight work; only 19 per cent suggest that a person who has once been a dealer cannot make a living any other way.

Discussing whether it is hard to get out of dealing, half state that it is—mainly because dealing keeps one supplied with drugs and with money for drugs (mentioned by 31 per cent). People with a habit cannot leave. Obligations felt toward one's customers—satisfying their need for drugs—ranks second (19 per cent), whereas liking the money for its own sake is noted by 17 per cent. Money is underemphasized in this context; but in another context, when asked about the attractions of dealing (which also make it hard to leave), 62 per cent reply that they like the tax-free money. Third ranked among attractions for these experienced dealers is liking for the people in the life; 15 per cent mention this social aspect.

Business Development

Dealers were asked about changes in their business methods from the time they began until now or until the time they had quit. Almost all of the dealers report that they have become more efficient businessmen. However, they have also become more apprehensive and they are now more often robbed (ripped off) than in the past.

Perhaps the best overall index of improvement is in profits. Even though the median monthly profit remains in the $100 to $499 bracket, there is a shift from low to medium and from medium to high income. For example, 8 per cent of the dealers claim incomes of over $1,000 per month when they began dealing; none claim over $5,000 per month. Now (or upon quitting) 31 per cent claim incomes over $1,000 per month; and, of these, 7 per cent report incomes of over $5,000 per month. If these figures are accepted,[1] one sees rapid income growth in the few years that they have been in business. For an initially casual group, many of whom had dropped out of school, these dealers are (or were) doing very well indeed.

As a consistency check, we asked about profits in the year 1968. The median profit level reported for 1968 remains the same ($100 to $499 per month), but the number claiming incomes of $1,000 and over is reduced to 16 per cent. However, since one third of the former

[1] We were able to check the report of one high-income dealer by comparing what he told us ($1,000,000 gross, $400,000 a year net) with what BNDD agents told us on the basis of their investigation (he was arrested a year after our interview). They estimated $1,000,000 a year gross and $600,000 net.

dealers (including those in jail) had quit, some of the reduction may be attributable to 1968's being a no-dealing, no-profit year for them. Even with the introduction of a correction for exaggeration, it is clear that profit increase has occurred as part of dealing experience.

Other changes which attended the development of a dealer's business career include considerable increase in travel within the United States and internationally; a much reduced reliance on friends or relatives or acquaintances as suppliers and a movement to wholesalers (a fifteenfold increase in that direction); a marked reduction in students and friends as customers, with an equivalent increase in sales to other dealers (a fifteenfold increase); and an increase in sales to addicts and to "straight people."

There also appear to be changes in the drugs traded, mostly in the direction of an expanded line and an increasing emphasis on the more profitable items. For both early and present (or termination) sales, cannabis has been the most widely traded drug. As their careers have developed, there has been an increase in the number carrying hallucinogens (from 9 per cent to 36 per cent) and opiates (from 4 per cent to 7 per cent). There has not been much expansion in carrying amphetamines, stimulants, or sedatives; but there has been a drop in cannabis trading (from early 73 per cent to a later 60 per cent).

The preferred drugs are not always those carried, suggesting that some of our dealers still do not have the sources they would like to have. Most noticeable, more dealers would like to trade in opiates than do so, whereas some who now trade in the sedatives and tranquilizers would prefer not to do so. Along this line, 80 per cent of the dealers refuse to handle certain drugs. Opiates are boycotted by 46 per cent of those practicing self-restraint in trade. Amphetamines and other stimulants rank second on the boycott list, with 32 per cent refusing to handle them. The reasons offered mostly (by 46 per cent) are health ones; dealers describe these drugs as harmful. However, some dealers offer simple moral judgments; the opiates are "bad."

Customers

It is, in the drug business for the experienced man, a seller's market. That is perhaps why dealers can be choosy about their customers. Just as there are preferred and rejected drugs, so there are preferred customers. Preferred customers are safe customers, ones already known and trusted—and therefore unlikely to be "narcs" (narcotics-law-enforcement officers) or "snitches" (informants).

Among the nonpreferred are, in order of antipathy, "uncool" people—those who are nervous or unsophisticated and are likely to be dangerous if narcs are around. The same is true for opiate users, who, as addicts, are believed vulnerable to arrest and to being "turned out" as police informants. Casual acquaintances are anathema, as are the people they may turn out to be—informants or undercover officers. Children and youth are also suspect on the same grounds as the uncool and the addicted. Some few dealers also suspect "straight" people, and some distrust or dislike those of a different race.

Most dealers, instead of outrightly refusing an unpreferred customer, prefer simply to avoid him. Those who are most often refused (as opposed to being nonpreferred) are "teenyboppers" and other foolish young who can get the dealer in trouble or who, in the dealer's opinion, just "ought not to use drugs." Among dealers, 36 per cent refuse sales to customers.

The age considered "too young" to be a customer varies. The median age bracket for the youngest customers ever sold to is 14 to 15; but 11 per cent of the dealers have sold to children under 10 years, and 14 per cent have sold to children from 11 to 13 years old. As for the "oldest ever" customer, the majority have not sold to persons over 49 years old. In day-to-day business the youngest customers generally are 16 or over, whereas the average customer, for over half of the dealers, is between 19 and 23. For no dealer in our sample, even those few who are themselves over 50, is the average customer over 50 years of age. Given the age distribution, it is not surprising that many of our dealers (39 per cent) say that many or most of their customers are students.

As for the sex of customers, the majority of dealers supply mostly men; one third have about equal numbers of men and women as customers; and only 4 per cent supply predominantly females.

The number of customers supplied is (or was at termination) as follows: 15 per cent of the dealers have fewer than ten customers; 33 per cent supply ten to twenty-four; 33 per cent have twenty-five to ninety-nine customers; and 19 per cent have one hundred or more.

Asked to characterize their recent clientele, two thirds of the dealers describe their customers as white; half cater to casual users and half to habitual (or dependent) users. Social groups to which customers belong include, in order, hippies, students, straight people (businessmen, teachers, workers), criminals (habitual or professional), entertainment folk, and deviants (homosexuals, outlaw motorcyclists). Those who supply students say that most are college undergraduates, with the next largest group being high school students; 3 per cent of the dealers supply primarily junior high or elementary school children. Most of the students attend public schools.

Dealers' Views on Drugs and People

Dealers were asked why, in their opinion, their customers use drugs. The primary reason given is enjoyment. Second ranked is escapist use (to suppress tension or to avoid facing the world). Third is exploratory uses; that is, curiosity, trying to expand the mind or to achieve religious experience. Fourth ranked, but no doubt overlapping the first, is use to facilitate sociability and interpersonal relations ("to be more loving").

Dealers also speculated on the characteristics of our society that make drug use both possible and important. In this area there is little agreement among the dealers (no more than 10 per cent on any item). Indeed, as many deny that society or social conditions cause drug use as claim that any particular cultural factor plays a role. Among the factors proposed are the following: the isolation of the individual (see Riesman, Glazer, and Denney, 1953), the depersonalization of the individual, hypocrisy (conflicting deeds and values), limitations on individual freedom, and the pressure for achievement. A few of the dealers mention the felt impotence of youth in obtaining desired changes or goals. Poverty and affluence figure as explanations for only a few.

Asked to compare drug users with nonusers, most dealers cannot specify differences. The others describe their customers and associates as less conforming, more aware (more sensitive to sensory stimuli, more insightful into one's own personality, with a finer appreciation of what is worthwhile in the world—in contrast to establishment goals and activities or presumed values), more paranoid, less aggressive, more adventurous, and more dissatisfied with society than others. These personal traits are linked to what the dealers see as the major effects of the drugs themselves. Facilitating interpersonal good feeling ("loving" is the word most often used) is most often described, followed by increased awareness and escape from reality (including inner tensions and disabilities). Fun and excitement again are noted. The following effects of drug taking are described: loss of motivation, depression, loss of inhibitions or control, increased activity and/or agitation, paranoia, personal withdrawal, and social isolation.

We asked dealers to discuss both the best and the worst effects of drugs seen from their vantage point. For cannabis the greatest benefit (most often mentioned) is relaxation—getting high and having fun. A remote second is increased self-awareness; third is social facilitation—

feeling friendly. For the hallucinogens, increased self-awareness ranks a strong first; euphoria ranks second. The amphetamines, at their best, help one to be active and get things done (included here sometimes is the observation that amphetamines counteract depression or lassitude); the amphetamines are also said to increase self-awareness. The opiates are also for fun and relaxation. In spite of the specific effects attributed to particular drugs, most of the dealers mention primarily general effects. Indeed, for the four classes of drugs above, one finds only four major outcomes noted—all of which, except for "activity," can be produced by several or all of the substances specified. What are the worst effects? These parallel the observations on adverse effects described earlier. About half of the dealers emphasize psychological damage; and half emphasize physical damage. Almost no dealers argue that drugs produce only good effects—or only bad ones.

The extent of bad results within the drug-using population served by these dealers was of interest to us. We asked our dealers to estimate—among the people they knew personally—what proportion had suffered serious ill effects or damage. Nearly one fourth (24 per cent) state that no one known to them has suffered serious ill effects from drugs. The most common estimate (by 56 per cent), is that from 1 to 10 per cent have suffered bad effects. One fifth give estimates ranging from 11 per cent to 100 per cent.

We also asked for a benefits estimate. What proportion of their acquaintances have gained from the use of drugs? Thirteen per cent declare that none have; at the other extreme, 13 per cent state that every user has gained. The median estimate is that 51 per cent to 75 per cent benefited.

In further discourse, dealers were asked to express their own personal drug preferences. The one substance acclaimed by the majority is cannabis. The order of preference is then LSD, the opiates, amphetamines and other stimulants, alcohol, cocaine, and sedatives or tranquilizers. What about drugs they would not use? Thirty per cent are catholic in taste; there is no drug they would not use. For the rest, there is no drug that a majority agree they would not use. Their list of drugs that are dangerous and addictive (these being the major reasons for nonuse) follows, in order of frequency with which dealers state that they would not and do not use the drugs: opiates, amphetamines and other stimulants, LSD, sedatives and tranquilizers, cocaine, alcohol, and cannabis.

What is not good for oneself may be good for business. But only a few (10 per cent) say that they have sold dangerous drugs which they would not take themselves. For the rest, there is reported perfect correspondence between what they would be willing to use (not that they necessarily use it) and what they in fact sell. More dealers, however, follow the rule "What is good for me may be too good for the customer." Thirty-two per cent say that they use drugs which they do not sell, most often because the drug is too hard to obtain but sometimes because they consider the drug unsuitable for their clients (and here we find a few dealers protecting their younger clients from dangerous drugs to which they themselves have succumbed) or because selling is too dangerous. The most often used-but-not-sold drugs are heroin and opium. LSD and other hallucinogens rank second, and amphetamines-stimulants third. As for new drugs coming on the market, or new batches of old drugs, as with gourmet merchants, so with dealers. Most dealers (84 per cent) try out new products before they sell them.

A different problem from that of safety or short supply attends those drugs that might be enjoyed but whose effects are deleterious to business, because a dealer who uses them ceases to work effectively. Eighty per cent indicate that there are indeed drugs in this category. Some dealers wistfully recall the good old days when they could enjoy using and rapping over (socializing, chatting) a favorite chemical now discarded in the service of efficiency and ambition. Others base their personal-use rules on what they have seen of other dealers on the drugs in question. Among the ranks of pleasurable "no-no's," only the opiates are mentioned by a majority. The others are, in order, amphetamines, hallucinogens, and cocaine. Alcohol, cannabis, and the sedatives and tranquilizers are not ordinarily believed to interefere with one's performance as a dealer.

Have the dealers seen, among dealers they know, any consistent progression from one set of drugs to another? About half say that they have—most of them claiming progression from marijuana to the hallucinogens; second, from marijuana to the opiates. Others observe that "progression" is simply a matter of what is available for sale at any given time.

We asked the dealers what, in their opinion, America would be like if prohibited drugs became freely available and the United States became a "stoned society." Half of the sample anticipate consequences which they consider good; half are opposed, saying that the outcome would be bad.

As a final inquiry related to drug effects and the future, we asked the dealers whether they would allow their own children to use certain drugs. Eighty-one per cent would allow use of cannabis, 56 per cent LSD, 19 per cent speed (methamphetamine), and 14 per cent heroin. Comparing the drugs they would deny to their own children with those that they themselves refuse to take, we see a consistently greater protectiveness toward their children on every class of drug than for themselves. For example, only 3 per cent reject cannabis as dangerous or unwise for themselves, whereas 19 per cent refuse it to their children. The order of magnitude of this child-protection over self-protection stays roughly about four to one except for the opiates, where there is more correspondence in protective behavior between one's child and oneself. The big question was "Would you want your children to be drug dealers?" Eight per cent say "yes," 38 per cent are "not sure," 54 per cent firmly say "no."

With respect to their policy views, only a minority (29 per cent) would see all drug laws abolished; most believe that only cannabis should be legalized but that government intervention should be limited to the treatment of users harmed by drugs. In discussions about justice as they see it, the great majority feel that contemporary law enforcement is unfair—specifically, the inappropriate harshness of cannabis penalties, the use of law as a means of harassing groups with different values from those of people in power, and the discrimination against the poor. Penalties for all "street crimes"—from burglary to assault to vice—are considered too harsh and inflexible; and the behavior of the police themselves, as they engage in narcotics enforcement, is criticized as a violation of constitutional guarantees or of the criminal law itself.

Which drugs, we asked, should be controlled by regulation or criminal statutes? Most of the dealers call for control of opiates, amphetamines, barbiturates, hallucinogens, tranquilizers, alcohol, and tobacco. Only with cannabis is this pattern reversed, so that a call for legalization emerges. The main reason offered for control: All of the drugs except cannabis are potentially harmful. In addition, a few dealers mention the need for regulations to assure purity of preparations.

Control by law does not mean, for our dealers, the maintenance of present penalty provisions, although there is some diversity and contradiction within the group on this matter. A minority (38 per cent) hold the line on present penalties for at least some drugs—opiates and amphetamines in particular; the majority propose lighter penalties and expanded treatment. Asked whether they themselves would ever actively work to cut down the use or distribution of illicit drugs, one third say that they would. The targets for this paradoxical dealer-backed antidrug campaign? Opiate addiction and drug use by children. Also, given their emphasis on amphetamine control, they probably would work against amphetamines as well. How would they go about cutting down drug traffic in these cases where they cared? Education and persuasion are the means they would themselves employ.

At the end of our interview, in keeping with our promise to serve as a channel for their views, we asked what recommendations to their fellow citizens and to their government they would like to see in print. These, amended by us for the purpose of clarity and organization, are as follows in order mentioned:

Major recommendations (by 10 per cent or more): (1) Education should be emphasized and more research conducted to provide information for dissemination. Education implies communication to young and old, and it implies an unbiased presentation of what is known. (2) Treatment and rehabilitation should be emphasized. Problems associated with drug use should be handled as medical-psychological matters. As a matter of policy and tactics as well as philosophy, the emphasis should be on the welfare of human beings, including those in trouble with drugs. Those not in trouble do not, by implication, require outside interference in their affairs. Treatment also implies that some (trouble-prone) young people may need help prior to their drug experimentation as a preventive measure supplemental to education and persuasion. (3) Marijuana and hashish only, among presently illicit or controlled psychoactive drugs, should be legalized.

Minor recommendations (by fewer than 10 per cent): (4) All drugs should be legalized. (5) Those who make judgments about drug use should first use the substances whose effects they are evaluating. (6) Everyone should use (the presently illicit) drugs. (7) Only cannabis and the hallucinogens should be legalized. (8) A discriminating penalty structure must be devised which provides lesser penalties for sale of less harmful (nonaddicting) substances.

Activities of Dealer Community

Trying to assess the fraternity of dealers as such, we asked our dealers how many "brothers" they are acquainted with. The median estimate of sellers known to them is about thirty-five. Only 12 per cent can identify fewer than ten sellers known to them. On the other end of the spectrum, 11 per cent estimate that they have known more than 500 during their lifetime. Our dealers, then, are well acquainted with many others who have sold drugs. This group constitutes a portion of the drug takers who constitute the dealer's business and social world. We venture that, whatever the magnitude of correction for double counting and erroneous description, there are a lot of drug dealers in California.

There are three times more male than female dealers in our sample—that, in spite of the fact that studies (Blum and associates, 1969b; San Mateo County School Studies, 1970) indicate that female drug use among the young, while less intense, approaches in prevalence that of males. Our dealers confirm that among their acquaintances more men than women sell drugs. Asked for the reasons, the dealers suggest first that women do not have the personality for it, that they are too paranoid. They also say that women are victims of the double standard; their being in the dealing business is generally disapproved. Some observe that women are less business-oriented in general and so are less likely to be entrepreneurs in peddling drugs. Some contend that women are in general less competent; others hold that women, as the girl friends or sexual partners of dealers and users, can get their drugs free and need not worry about drugs or money. Finally, some of our dealers point out that women cannot do as well in dealing because men, who comprise the majority of the business network, are not comfortable dealing with them or do not trust them.

How do dealers classify or rank one another? There are two ways, one based on volume of business and the other by the kinds of drugs sold. In the first system, the categories are big dealers and small ones, or retailers and street dealers versus wholesalers and manufacturers. In the second system, sellers of hard versus soft drugs are most readily distinguished. Some discriminate between speed, opiate, and psychedelic dealers—with cannabis sellers in the psychedelic group. Alternative descriptive systems employed in the trade include those based on customer characteristics: "He supplies blacks . . . or hippies . . . or hypes." Another one—based on business practices and implied personal characteristics (or vice versa)—discriminates between honest-reliable and dishonest-unreliable dealers; or between high quality and low quality drugs sold; or between dealers who have not been arrested and those who have. In addition to honesty and carefulness, other personality traits linked to success are friendliness, generosity, and intelligence.

Prestige and status are built into the descriptive systems, for the descriptions reflect matters of value and concern to the dealers. In ranking, business practices (the honest and reliable dealer) come first. Closely following is the volume-success factor, sometimes personalized as "business competence." Product quality ranks third, but this may be a variant of business practice. Fourth is that competence associated with avoiding arrest. A status hierarchy associated with stock-in-trade does not appear very important, although psychedelic dealers do demean speed and opiate dealers, and the latter occasionally deride the former.

Giving Away Drugs. Dealers may stay in the life for money, drugs, and the companionship of like-minded people; but additional satisfactions exist. One "kick" comes, dealers say, from the special pleasure which attends giving, not selling, drugs. Another is the knowledge that one is admired and important. Having money helps achieve this. Others describe "kicks" associated with opportunities in the social situation and in the dealer-client relationship. Access to sex ranks first among these. Another "kick" is described as the pleasure that a dealer in drugs gets from manipulating people who want or need those drugs; that is, the user's desires make him vulnerable to the power ploys or power needs of the manipulative dealer.

Since more dealers observe that kicks come from generosity than from anything else, we explored that practice further. Almost half (45 per cent) of our dealers say that all of their dealer-acquaintances occasionally give drugs away, whereas only 6 per cent do not know any dealers who give away drugs. Few can explain this widespread practice beyond saying that it gives a dealer personal pleasure. A few say that dealers give away drugs in order to obtain new customers, or to have someone to get high with, or to prevent illness or withdrawal symptoms in addicted customers—a development that would be untidy at best and possibly dangerous for all concerned. Some speak of gift giving as anthropologists studying peasant societies have described it—that is, as a reciprocal arrangement signifying a continuing relationship, a form of insurance or banking, or a means for building up obligations in the recipient. A few dealers, conscious of the role and the tradition of turning others on for free, say simply that it is their duty or obligation to do so.

Introducing Others to Drugs. Whether or not they have given drugs away, dealers do introduce the uninitiated into illicit use. The median for our sample was to have turned on five other people. One fourth had turned on, for the first time, twenty or more. Summing the estimates and assuming accuracy of recall as well as identification of drug virgins (that is, assuming that no two of our dealers had both turned on the same initiate, each thinking it was the novice's first experience), we arrive at the figure of 8,000 people, most of them in their teens and twenties, having been introduced to an illicit drug by our 480 sample members. We obtain, then, an overall average of sixteen initiates per sample member. To speak of averages may mislead, for a relatively small number of dealers have been very active in initiating many people.

These figures should not be interpreted to mean that the drug dealer has persuaded or induced otherwise uninterested young people to take drugs. Three fourths of our dealers state that such a thing never or rarely happens; only 7 per cent claim that it happens often. The majority claim is supported by extensive data on high school and college drug use; these data show that people begin drugs, once their peers set the fashion and the opportunity arises, because they want to, not because someone else insists. This does not exclude the coercive operation of youthful fad or of peer-group pressures, but it does rule out—as a frequent occurrence—the seduction of the uninterested innocent. The exceptional case does, of course, exist. We have elsewhere (Blum and associates, 1964) described a zealous proselytizing in which people not interested in drugs have been persuaded to take them. In talking to dealers we found them also admitting to such missionary or manipulative tactics.

Major Business Activities. We constructed a chart of business activities in which dealers might be expected to engage and asked each dealer how much time he spends, if any, doing each. The following activities are engaged in, to some or a large extent, by the majority of dealers: giving drugs away, rapping and/or turning on with customers, selling drugs at cost, retail trade, wholesale trade. The following activities are engaged in by an important minority (20 to 50 per cent): national trade (transporting across state lines), information gathering for source location or marketing, acting as an agent (for sellers, not buying for resale oneself), logistical support (providing premises, equipment, transport), banking and insurance, farming, manufacture for retail markets, manufacture for wholesale markets, international trade. The following services are used or provided by 10 to 20 per cent of our dealers: cover (providing legitimate fronts, concealment), protective services (bribes, threats, guarding), professional services (legal, accounting, chemical-pharmacological).

On the premise that sustained business requires regular structured relationships with others, dealers were asked about working agreements that constitute organized business. Two thirds report that they have continuing agreements and arrangements, including those with steady customers; about half of this group appear to have agreements with others than customers—suppliers, wholesalers, fronts, cops—which would better fit a definition of an organized business. Thus, about one third of our sample can be described as engaging in systematic business or, put another way, a form of "organized" crime.

Included in the concept of organization is the notion of specialized functions, planning, special relationships, and the like. Only a minority of the dealers describe these aspects of organization. Mentioned, in order, are the following: reserve funds set aside for special needs (purchases, bail, protection when needed); the services of a lawyer (employed for criminal defense, advice on operations, negotiations with others); arrangements with straights (for rental of premises, transport, purchase of chemicals); Mafia ties or agreements; contracts with manufacturers for supplies; arrangements with the police.

If we were to take organizational arrangements with the Mafia, with manufacturers, and with police as signs of criminal sophistication, we would conclude that 10 per cent (±5) of our sample qualify. If we return to the activities roster and look for those who spend their time primarily in hard-headed business—not often giving drugs away, selling at cost, chatting, or turning on (except when necessary for business itself)—we judge that about 40 per cent qualify as serious street (retail) dealers. If we look for activities bespeaking higher organizational skills, we estimate that about one fifth are involved in such activities. These estimates are in general agreement with the stated vocations of the dealers. Fifty per cent have no straight jobs; 22 per cent receive no income from legitimate sources; 13 per cent receive less than half from straight sources; 7 per cent receive half from such origins. All in all, 42 per cent rely heavily on illegitimate activities for their major revenues. However, only one fourth deal routinely, whereas almost three fourths are periodic or episodic dealers.

Problem of Supplies. We have already had strong indications that dealers cannot get all of the drugs they would like to have—for personal use as well as for trade. Opiates and perhaps cocaine seem in shortest supply. With only four exceptions, our dealers acknowledge that continuing supplies are a problem for them, although half maintain that the difficulty is infrequent rather than chronic. Of those facing a chronic difficulty, about two thirds have been forced temporarily to give up dealing in the unavailable drug. Under such circumstances about half of the dealers, at one time or another, begin selling other illicit drugs that are available; the others look for a new source. Where do they look for sources if they are unacquainted or unreferred in a new town? The geography of likely connections places hippie neighborhoods first, followed by college and high school campuses; black, Chicano, or lower-class areas; and white slums or criminal areas (such as San Francisco's Tenderloin). A few optimists said "Anyhere."

A national perspective on the "best places to meet like-minded people" shows a certain provincialism. The West Coast ranks first, followed by the eastern and the northeastern sections of the country. Almost none of our dealers (half of them experienced in trafficking across state lines) speak well of heartland America—the massive area between California and the Eastern Seaboard. This ranking of favorite watering places parallels a ranking of the safest (and presumably best) drug markets. We do see, however, an increase in the number who speak of midwestern urban centers as drug markets, even if these cities are not spoken of warmly as hospitable to the drug scene.

As for an international view (more by hearsay than experience, since only 29 per cent of our dealers have themselves trafficked across international boundaries), the best countries or regions for buying drugs are said to be as follows, in order: Mexico; Mid-Asia (Nepal, Afghanistan, India, Pakistan); the Far East (Hong Kong, Bangkok, Singapore, Laos); the Near East (Turkey, Lebanon); Europe; Canada; Africa (Morocco, Tunisia, Nigeria).

Views of Police and Drug Laws. Given the near universal problem of supply, which we attribute to law-enforcement interdiction (although crop failures or laboratory breakdowns can also intervene), we focused on the role of the police and the criminal law in interdicting the drug trade. Three fourths of the dealers express their conviction that the police cannot force them out of business—mainly because drug traffic is extensive and well established but also because (according to 12 per cent of our dealers) the police do not want to stop the traffic. One fourth of the dealers, however, say that the police *can* force them out of business—and in some instances have already done so.

One way to change things would be to legalize certain drugs. Discussing the consequences of such hypothetical (but now strongly advocated, see Kaplan, 1970) developments for cannabis, most dealers believe that it would ruin business. Others suggest that dealers would find other illicit drugs to sell or would manage to undersell the legal price, thus continuing a bootleg traffic. A few say that they would become legal pot producers or sellers. Only 4 per cent consider the possibility that dealers would go looking for legitimate jobs.

How would they go about reducing drug traffic? Half of our dealers observe that legalization would accomplish that; others propose the removal of major suppliers. Some believe that there is no way to reduce traffic. In assessing the competence of various narcotics police, our dealers give federal officers (Bureau of Narcotics and Dangerous Drugs, and the U.S. Customs) the award for outstanding performance [2] four times more frequently than any local or state narcotic-vice squads or patrol-detective forces. The least competent police, judged by the dealers, are those in local city departments (nominated by 62 per cent

[2] We propose this as an annual award rivaling the Oscar and Emmy. It shall be called the "Jackie"—after John Ingersoll, whose BNDD agents received this first year's poll acclaim.

of those specifying incompetents). As for the average "narc," one fourth of the dealers adopt a tolerant view—regarding narcs as just people doing their job. A few dealers express some sympathy for the narcs, speaking of the difficulties of the job—its demands on time, the emotional strain of undercover work, the unpleasantness of being feared and despised. The majority of the dealers, however, disapprove—sometimes strenuously—of narcotics officers, citing their mistaken value systems and their oppressive or illicit methods, or demeaning their intelligence, or suggesting power hunger, or offering unkind diagnoses of their sexual interests or prowess. This derogation of narcotics officers extends, although somewhat less extensively, to views of the police in general. Two thirds of the dealers describe the average policeman in disapproving or unflattering terms; one fourth say that they are ordinary guys doing their jobs. About one fifth say that they themselves would or might be willing to become policemen. As an item for police selection, two fifths of these dealers ought to be ruled out for police work because they declare they sometimes break laws for the sheer pleasure of doing so.

Arrest Records. Discussion of police intervention to reduce drug traffic usually leads to a dealer's own experience with the police. Three fifths of the sample have been arrested for either drug or nondrug offenses. Among those who have been arrested, about half had drug arrests, 12 per cent had only drug arrests, and 20 per cent had only nondrug arrests. The majority of those with drug arrests had multiple such arrests. The average number of drug arrests per dealer arrested for drug offenses is 2.2. Three fourths of those who suffered arrest also have a record of convictions. There were three convictions for every four arrests or, counted differently, an average of 1.4 convictions per arrested dealer. The major reasons offered for a failure to convict are the police's lack of evidence, competence of the defense lawyer, or a deal made with the police (including informing). The majority arrested for nondrug offenses also had a history of multiple arrests. The average number of nondrug arrests, per arrested dealer, was four. Two thirds of those arrested had convictions. The rate of convictions over arrests was about one to two, or an average of almost three nondrug convictions per convicted dealer. For our sample, drug convictions seem more easily obtained than convictions for other offenses. As for the types of crimes involved, these were (in order of frequency) burglary, drunkenness and assault, larceny and auto theft, robbery, forgery, curfew and loitering, liquor laws, vagrancy and runaway, prostitution, and disorderly conduct.

Nondrug Offenses and Profits. The foregoing statistics represent known offenses. We asked about less public ones. Thirty-nine per cent of our dealers admit that they regularly commit nondrug offenses —among them, weapons offenses; one fourth state that they carry or have carried guns, and one third of this group say that they have used the guns. Asked about income taxes, about half say that they regularly file returns; 14 per cent sometimes do. However, only 1 per cent declare their income from drug dealing. This income, based on figures given for the year 1968, approximates $10,000 net per dealer per annum. The total profit not declared by these dealers over the years of their selling is estimated by them at approximately $28,000 (which is in good agreement with the earlier figures on both income and probable income increases over the one to five years typical dealing time span).

In spite of these relatively high profits realized over a short period of time, however, most dealers are, in terms of volume, small-time—as their single largest transaction for each drug illustrates. For example, most of those dealing in marijuana have never sold more than ten or eleven kilos. The distribution here is essentially L-shaped. Four per cent deal in lots over one ton. A U-shaped distribution characterizes hallucinogen dealers; half have never sold more than one thousand doses (pills, caps, etc.) at a time; however, one fourth deal in lots of ten thousand or more per transaction. The amphetamines are still different, with more dealers at the upper end (a reverse-L distribution). Here, nearly two thirds deal in ten thousand doses or more at a time. Hashish deals are like marijuana, most at the lower end; three quarters of the very few who deal in hashish sell in one-pound lots or less. Opiate transactions in our sample are also mostly small and the distribution L-shaped, two thirds never having sold more than ten ounces (the average addict dose varies from one or two grains daily to as much as one hundred or more grains daily).

In current practice (or most recent practice for those no longer dealing) the majority of those dealing a given drug usually buy marijuana in kilo lots; LSD by the cap; and hashish, amphetamines, and opiates by the ounce. Ordinarily, marijuana is sold by the lid (about one ounce); LSD by caps; hashish by the dose (grams); amphetamines by the dose; and opiates by the dose (grams). These amounts again reflect the mostly retail trade of the dealers.

Other Aspects of Business. Four fifths of our dealers guarantee their drugs, with a policy of return of poor-quality merchandise or money-back refunds for all or at least better customers. Cash and carry is the major policy, with some requiring payment before rather than at delivery. One third advance credit upon occasion. Delivery practices appear to favor customers' going to the dealer (or to a prearranged meeting place) rather than the dealer's delivering to the customer.

As for sources, most dealers maintain several simultaneous suppliers, three on the average. Many dealers keep trying to find new suppliers; they rely on other suppliers as well as other dealers and users for such recommendations. Some, about one sixth, have stolen (ripped off) their supplies (recall those who have carried and used guns). This is an occasional rather than a regular practice for most of those doing it, although about 13 per cent of these (2 per cent of the total sample) steal their supplies often or "as often as possible." The victims are predominantly other dealers, followed in order by drug supply houses (warehouses, legitimate wholesalers), legitimate retailers (drugstores, clinics), and illicit suppliers. Younger dealers have stolen drugs from their parents and siblings.

With reference to competition and aid, we asked dealers how many people they have helped bring into the business and how many they have put out of business. Over half say that they have helped new dealers get started, but only one fifth have tried to eliminate others. Elimination methods—and results—range from underselling others, or getting better suppliers, to killing them (13 per cent admit to violence in eliminating competitors). In regard to this kind of competition among dealers, we note that among older, better-established, more competently criminal dealers homicides are alluded to but appear to be, for the most part, undetected as well as unpunished. Murder, it seems, not only will out, but it will put others out, and it will remain out of the public purview as well.

The presence of violence is not new to criminal enterprises and is not unexpected in the drug trade, where there are high stakes and no ordinary constraints or routes to redress. Nevertheless, the drug scene has itself become more violent, according to 68 per cent of the dealers (see also R. Smith, 1971), in the years (1964–1971) in which they have been involved. The majority of our dealers also report more criminal organization, some of which is allegedly Mafia involvement or Cosa Nostra. Over half of our dealers contend that the Mafia is involved at some level of the traffic in which they deal on the West Coast.

These developments may contribute to the overall assessment by the majority of dealers that the drug scene is worse now than it was before. It is also worse because drugs are "tighter" and more costly, the police busier, and "burns" (cheating) more common. Some dealers look back to the golden years, when the drug scene itself was a friendly place full of love and flowers. Others (16 per cent), however, think that things are better now—possibly because (as most of our dealers admit) there is more money to be made now than in the past.

Do our dealers think of themselves—regardless of what we may think—as professionals? Two thirds do not. In their own eyes they remain amateurs, casually involved in dealing or still learning the ropes and not yet skilled or committed enough to think of themselves as professionals. Most say that they are not yet professionals because they are not making enough money or do not have enough customers to justify the title. Some say that they do not consider themselves professionals because dealing is not their most important activity, and a few (less than 1 per cent) abjure the title because they think of themselves as holding legitimate roles instead.

What about seeing themselves not only as professional dealers but as professional criminals? Few (less than 14 per cent of the sample) do—only half as many as see themselves as professional dealers. Most often the criminal label is renounced because "dealing is not criminal," or, second, because "drugs should be legal," or because one is not a professional dealer and therefore cannot be a professional criminal, or because dealing does not hurt anyone, or (last and mentioned by only a few) because one is not a professional criminal until one has been arrested. Do the dealers think that the police are wise to what the dealers are up to? Over half think not, over one fourth are certain that the police do know, and about one fifth are not sure.

Finally, we asked the dealers what the future holds for them, what they expect to be doing in five years. Half of them say that they expect to have new occupations, either straight jobs as such or in the arts or as mystics or students. Ten per cent expect to be doing just what they were doing now, dealing. Six per cent expect to have made their fortunes and to be retired. We also asked what they think their dealing colleagues will be doing in ten years. Two thirds think that their colleagues will be out of business; almost one fourth think that some will be dealing, some not; only 10 per cent feel sure that most of their associates will still be selling drugs. Among those who expect their colleagues to be out of business, most dealers believe that the colleagues will be in jail. Almost one fourth expect them to have gone straight, about 10 per cent predict that most of their associates will be dead, and 8 per cent expect them to have retired as wealthy men.

Summary

Two thirds of the dealer sample were actively dealing at the time of interview, but most of those still dealing had considered or were considering quitting, whereas most who had quit were contemplating returning to the business. In the course of their relatively short business careers, most having been dealers for five years or less, a number of experiences have occurred to contribute to ambivalence about the trade and about their lives as dealers. Negative experiences have included an increasing awareness of the risk of arrest, observation of unhappy outcomes in the lives of other dealers and of users, and increased worries in relationship to their own drug use. Positive experiences have been increasing business competence, with subsequent income growth, and, for the drug-interested dealer, assurance of a drug supply.

There is evidence of an increasing interest in money-making, with associated emphasis on efficiency; there is, in addition, a decline in the importance of earlier friendly social relations. The customers served are primarily in the teens and twenties, but extend to children and the elderly. Hippies, students, criminals, and deviants constitute the major visible groups served, but outwardly straight (older) people are also customers.

Dealers believe that illicit psychoactive drugs are widely efficacious in producing euphoria, in assisting escape (tension reduction, shutting out reality, blunting emotion), and in improving social relationship (or at least the feelings about others held by drug-using individuals). Regarding long-term effects, the majority estimate that 1 to 10 per cent of the people known to them have suffered serious harm from use, whereas from 50 to 75 per cent have become happier or better people.

The effects of particular drugs, or classes of drugs, are differentiated. The most widely used, preferred, and sold drug is cannabis, which is also considered the safest substance. LSD and other hallucinogens rank second. Opiates are considered unsafe and are disavowed by many; nevertheless, they are widely used, rank high in preference, and are viewed as worthy stock-in-trade.

Dealers' recommendations for social policy on drugs are both liberal (in the sense that current heavy penalties are criticized and increased education and treatment are recommended) and conservative (in that controls over all psychoactive substances except cannabis, but including alcohol and tobacco, are advocated). Recommendations for the administration of justice are in the democratic tradition, calling for elimination of harassment, discrimination, and violation of constitutional guarantees. The dealers apparently do not question the importance of criminal law for controlling conduct harmful to others, nor do they question the responsibility of government to regulate drugs and conduct in association with their production, traffic, and consumption. One third of the sample would lend themselves to active efforts to reduce drug traffic, primarily in pursuit of prevention of opiate and amphetamine abuse and of drug use by children.

Dealing is an occupation imbedded in a network of acquaintances; dealers know large numbers of drug users and people who, if not dealers, occasionally sell drugs. The dealer community is composed of males more than females, and is ranked by status based on money-making success, competence in avoiding arrest, reliability, and the quality of drugs sold. Although dealers are known by the kinds of drugs they handle, and some pride in the line handled is inferred, this is not the basis of the pecking order.

Dealing brings many pleasures associated with its social aspects. These include being admired and having power. Giving away drugs is an important part of being a dealer, especially among younger and less hard-headed folk. This generosity has several functions, not the least of which are being appreciated for largess and providing partners for oneself in sharing drug effects. Most dealers have played a role in introducing novices to use, but only rarely can one speak of the seduction of the innocent.

As far as activities are concerned, drug traffic requires enduring sets of agreements and relationships as well as specialized functions. These are, for most, performed in casual and inexpert ways; however, this is a form of "organized crime." In our sample about 10 per cent are organized in an expert way and 40 per cent qualify as serious street dealers. For this latter group and all the rest, dealing has a large component of sociability, drug use, and other pleasurable and undisciplined activities.

Although supply problems have affected most dealers, only a minority have had to suspend dealing because of these. When supplies of one drug are short, dealers shift to trading in other kinds. Most were convinced that law enforcement cannot interdict drug dealing. Fewer than half have themselves been arrested for any drug-law violation, although a majority have been arrested for one or another offense. Not only are multiple arrests common but many indicate that they regularly commit nondrug offenses—including weapons offenses, compatible with what dealers report as an increasing trend toward violence in the drug scene. Income tax law violations are universal but are not mentioned as offenses. Given the estimated average annual net income for each sample member of $10,000, a considerable revenue loss to state and federal government is indicated.

Although earlier years of the flower children are harked back to as better days, profits are greater now and drug "futures" are quoted as bullish. Dealers are busier now, not only making money but committing or defending against robberies, cheating, and occasional homicides.

Most of our dealers deny that they are professional dealers or professional criminals. Consistent with this noncriminal self-concept of most of the dealers whom we studied, many predict (if somewhat vaguely) that they will leave the dealing world and take up honest although not necessarily conventional activities. A few, perhaps between 10 per cent and 20 per cent, are without such expectations or illusions and qualify for consideration as committed and professional criminals. The importance of recognizing the amateur or transitional status of many young dealers is emphasized.

Chapter 4

CAPSULE CASE HISTORIES

It may be helpful to shift levels of presentation, now moving from statistics and speculations on their significance to something real, the case of a dealer. In thinking of those I knew whose development was in the mainstream, I reflected quite naturally on those who are, in a dramatic sense, interesting people (not "classical" cases). They summoned themselves before my mind's eye, a roster of seekers, sad sacks, respectables, and rogues; and their faces there serve as reminders that, for all of the effort to weave a consistent fabric of the data, dealers *are* a variegated lot.

Lobo

Let me speak of Lobo, a Yacqui Indian who became a United States citizen, now a dealer in a border town and a federal fugitive. As he said,

> *I was on a work party outside Leavenworth's walls one day and I fell into this river passing by. Try as hard as I could, I couldn't swim upstream and next I knew it carried me here across the border again. That's not escape, is it? That's fate.*

Lobo is almost 70, uneducated, born and raised in abysmal poverty but of good Catholic parents whose other children are straight as Yacqui arrows (the Yacqui, by the way, are cousins of their Apache neighbors to the north). Lobo began using drugs and earning a criminal livelihood in his teens. He has never done anything else, and for all his smiling dreams ("Ah, if only I could find an honest job") he is in dealing for the rest of his life. He knows nothing else, and besides he enjoys the excitement and loves the freedom—when he has it, that is. He has served two prison terms and is now in a Mexican jail for marijuana sale and possession (a charge arising, ironically, after a drunken brawl in which he had the egregious poor taste to hit a Mexican policeman, who—even though in Lobo's pay—would not stomach insult to his machismo or a bloody nose). Lobo probably does not have the tenacity to put up with the irritations that go along with straight work. An addict, to be sure (although he depends on no particular drug and gets in trouble mostly when he is drunk), Lobo must be a part of the drug world in order to supply his own needs, which are compelling ones.

But Lobo is far more than a reasonably competent drug dealer, suffering from a pervasive dependency on drugs. He has been a rip-roaring bandito in the old border tradition—one third Robin Hood, one third Pancho Villa, and one third Al Capone. Among his men he is a stern and commanding figure, even awesome. Among his Yacqui people he is respected for having been to the outside world; but among them he is primarily a medicine man, a knower of herbs and of the gods who dwell within. (See Castaneda, 1968.) His knowledge of plants is broad, his folk-healing skills are much admired, and the breadth of his interests and self-taught knowledge—botany, folklore, politics—is impressive.

But for a picture of Lobo the dealer, imagine a dirty side street in a small Mexican town near to a larger one which is a major border point. Lounging around, chatting and smoking, are his friends and colleagues. Occasional tourists come by; once in a while a pair of Americanos in their twenties stop and chat with one of Lobo's crew and then disappear with him to make a buy. Lobo stands straight, stoney-faced, a revolver in his pocket, watching that all goes well; in his hands is his reading material for the morning, last week's *New York Times*. Lobo would have done better at another time and in another place. Perhaps with help as a child he was once a salvageable soul; his present life is a tragedy.

Guillermo

Guillermo is another one—handling half a million, one million, two million dollars a year. Mexican-American, he was born in California and is a fugitive in a border town, running one of five major rings. He is blind from gunshot wounds inflicted in retaliation for what he did to one of his competitors. This competitor got into his car one morning, turned on the ignition, and, as Guillermo puts it, "had his arms and legs fall off." The competitor's colleagues took their revenge in spite of Guillermo's bodyguards. Simultaneously an alcoholic and a heroin addict, he finished off a bottle of cognac—one of a set dutifully carried by his bodyguard, along with a tommygun—during our interview session. Later he was robbed by his own bodyguards, sought by others for the reward on his head. He lives in a fortress, his gross profits depleted by payoffs to officials (summing to hundreds of thousands of dollars annually); through it all, struggling with a derelict body and empty holes for eyes, he stays cunning enough to live. Caught, sold out, and now in a penitentiary (after our meeting), he survives still.

Frank

Consider Frank, a straightforward case. He was a business student in a good college, a casual drug user who came to like his grass. And having an economic bent, he soon learned the marketplace. He did very well, quit school and made dealing a full-time business. Now twenty-four, he is a likeable fellow, neat, with crew-cut hair and clear eyes that look straight at you while he talks, all in the best business tradition. He is a conservative dresser, and he has a good but not flashy car. He speaks of the irony of his giving up his drug use almost entirely in order to stay clear-headed for his business. Careful and serious, he avoids opiates and amphetamines and their users. His parents, wealthy suburbanites, know he is doing well but think he is in "merchandising." Yet success is not enough, and he confesses that he really doesn't like being a criminal. When last we talked, he planned to quit and return to school. Did he? I have no idea.

Otto

Otto is a brilliant chemist with a Ph.D. He is well paid as a professional; but, long involved in the psychedelic scene, he has a side business. In his personal laboratory he creates new hallucinogenic substances and sells formulas to illicit drug manufacturers. The operation is legal, since he does not traffic in drugs already known and does not himself sell or administer them for use with humans. But he is a dealer among his friends, for, as in the days of bathtub gin, once in a while he will turn out a batch of LSD or mescaline.

Colin

Colin is a lawyer who used to work for the Internal Revenue Service. He quit to practice on his own as he was getting involved in the early hip scene. That involvement grew, and he became a full-time advisor to one or several drug syndicates. He takes their cases before they get caught, so that they can plan either to stay within the law or to anticipate enforcement countermoves when they cannot. He has no shingle, no listed telephone. He is a bright fellow, but thoroughly unreliable. Of all who worked for or with us, he is the only one who cheated us. We wish him an early arrest and conviction.

Marybeth

Marybeth is blonde and lovely. She is twenty-one and works in a large stock-brokerage firm in San Francisco. She dresses handsomely and supports her wardrobe by drug dealing. She loves the swinging scene, which is for her quite a ball, much better than her awkward adolescent days when she felt wallflowerish. She buys and sells in the hub-bub of the big city financial district and uses these same occasions to flirt with those she meets (not all of them users). One has the impression that sociable excitement is a strong component in her activities. It is our guess that she is likely to get married one day and settle down with some conventional banker in the suburbs, where they will both smoke marijuana but lead otherwise unremarkable lives.

John

John, an unstable fellow from a wealthy family, found himself more at ease when with drug dealers and when he himself used drugs heavily. He went to a university but had difficulty there. Again, his best times were when he was with the "heads" and not the books. He does have a flair for things, a rather breezy style coupled with a bit of grandiosity. Sometimes the combination works. When last we heard of him, he was importing heroin in many-pound lots, using his father's corporation airplanes to do so in an arrangement which required the complicity of a few select employees.

Ishi

Ishi is no Indian but a blond and bearded hippie who, now over thirty, is an emigrant from the Haight-Ashbury to the greener commune pastures of California and Nevada. He has been a commune chief himself and, like some early Mormons in this and no other way, boasted a covey of wives. A restless roamer, he uses and deals wherever he goes. Affable, intelligent, fast-talking, tangential, circumlocutious, totally unreliable, he is often strung out on speed or freaked out on acid. The difference is not too great, for when "clean" he is verily like a paranoid schizophrenic. One suspects he is, therefore, delusional off as well as on drugs.

Metamorphosis of Gentle Jim

Gentle Jim, like the others, is a vignette; but at least he can be brought up to date, which will be seen to make all the difference. He is my selection as an illustration of one subgroup of dealers whose shadows were projected in earlier chapters.

Jim was twenty-three when interviewed. I had known him for three years, since the time he had begun living with Frances. The two had a baby, Ilene, but neither wanted to marry. Frances was no longer around during our talks; she had left Jim after a series of rip-offs in their pad, when guns had been drawn and drugs had repeatedly been stolen. A few days before, he had had a shoot-out, the results of which were inconclusive—no one was dead. Now Jim was lying in wait with a shotgun ready, which he planned to use at closer range. Frances, concluding that this was no environment for a baby, left.

Jim, whose parents were school teachers in San Francisco, had begun his use at the suggestion of his sister, a student, who had in turn been initiated by the older psychedelic crowd in her university. She had no record of arrest, although Jim says she used to shoplift and tear up traffic warrants when she was in her teens. He himself had been arrested once for stealing beer from a neighbor's house. After first turning on, Jim quickly became a heavy user of both marijuana and LSD. Within a year he had begun dealing:

> *A friend, a dealer, gave some grass to me. After my first real high I immediately wanted more—that's when I asked him for more. That's when you are a head, get a craving, become a Mary Jane addict. As soon as you like weed, then you get into dealing right away. That dealer, by the way, went insane from speed. . . . He taught me a lot about dope . . . and he gave me my first acid.*

His first supplying was to a group of slightly younger friends at a get-together. He gave them cannabis. Soon, "I started selling after I took acid and dropped from school." On that first occasion:

> *I had acquired some acid to sell—I went East—sold to Brooklyn hoodlums with guns, but they were nice, not hip, just heads. I met them through guys I knew in school. I conned them,*

felt superior to them, gave them a big line. It was an ego thing for me.

Would anything have prevented him from beginning dealing?

I suppose if I had a decent job I wouldn't deal, but I don't like to work. No, nothing would stop me, I guess, unless you just gave money away . . . a guaranteed income—but no, I'd still deal.

Jim worked irregularly, took unemployment insurance, and decided to try to make money more regularly through dealing. Customers were easy to find:

There's a tremendous demand. I hung around the college where the kids were hard up for drugs. So I just went up to people and asked them—since I knew there was no heat on campus. But it was a bad deal, to commit a felony for a five-dollar profit. I would have gone out of business if I hadn't made the link to blacks at that time. A guy had taken me aside and explained the business aspect to me—to move to bigger deals to make the money and avoid the hassles, match the risk to the money. I read the lawbooks too—I'd wanted to be a lawyer. My biggest problem was learning what size sells best, people won't pay fifteen dollars for three fourths of an ounce, but they'll pay ten dollars for a half ounce. It's a merchandizing problem, but since they all want bargains they don't care about quality—on the other hand, I had to learn to spot quality. But it was Walter, an older black, who helped set my organization for selling drugs to the blacks. I'm a middleman. I've learned to avoid hippies or blacks as suppliers; they'll burn you. That's one of the things I like about dealing—learning about people and business in a hurry. Working [straight] I'd not learn as fast. You get harder and tougher in this business.

But I've thought about quitting. It's a lot of trouble for the money, it's very competitive with so many other dealers. I'm under-capitalized because I get ripped off so much I need more capital—lack of capital is a big problem in a squeeze, just like Lockheed. Another problem is your hustlers—they're too loose, not serious enough.

Still, it's a good thing for me to become harder, better than having your back broken. I grew up in that soft, liberal tradition. But things are getting worse in our society so I'd better get hard. The liberals are mistaken. My parents raised me and they were wrong. They had the wrong impression of the world. Now I've got to go out and learn what the world is really like for myself. You can bet most people will take advantage of you if you're soft —they'll walk on you. If you're down they'll take over. If you want to be somebody's flunkie, don't learn; otherwise learn. I was never told this once as a child. I've learned more being a dealer than making money—it's all made it worthwhile. My main problem in life is other people's screwing me around. You have to learn to size people up, whether they're bad, bullshitters or what. Now I take people seriously. Now if a guy steals I know he's a psychopath and I don't associate with him or I take damn good care. You've got to be up, aware.

The dealing life is good. On the other hand, all my family and friends want me to stop, but I'm on my own now. They're more paranoid than I am. I went into it to learn and it's my bag. Of course, I'm only learning the drug trade. I ought to learn something else. I do worry about getting hurt though because dealers are outside the law, some of them want to take over your operation, some want to rob you, and they burn each other. Besides I owe too much money . . . [*maybe that's why*] *dealers get nervous or paranoid.*

But the life is good. Loose, I like the hours. Lots of leisure and you're not stuck indoors. It's entertaining too; you meet and enjoy a lot of people. It's an activity and gives my life purpose; you know, it's important to be involved in the world and to be a part of it and dealing is a job, an activity which gives that involvement. And you do learn for yourself to stand on your own two feet; it's good for me to find how not to be beaten by others, not to be soft inside.

When I began, I retailed lids, but I've found it safer and more profitable to wholesale through an organization of street men working for me. Now I've got regular sources, regular organization; and I handle only the middle, which is safe. I've learned to be less greedy and satisfied with the organization I've got— and I deal in larger amounts than I used to. Even so, my profit isn't any bigger—I've had so much stolen, make about $75 a week. I sell grass because it brings no trouble. I'm tempted to sell cocaine and reds [*barbiturates*]*—the blacks want them, but you bring in* *bad clients and heat. Also morally, I don't want to pump cocaine and reds into the ghetto, where there's enough trouble anyway. Grass cools the ghetto. Even so, my customers rob me.*

I've had a big problem learning to keep my mouth shut; it takes a lot of self-control. I want to talk about what I do, I'm a big-mouth, and you have to talk a little to generate business. The other problem I haven't solved is that I sell to blacks. I don't want to, but I haven't the capital to deal with whites. Working-class people in general will rob you—I guess I'm getting prejudiced.

I like clinching a deal—accomplishing your business. I like the thrill—arranging it all, setting up connection, the illicit side. And I do like money.

I would have become an alcoholic but I got onto weed. I'm as compulsive about weed as I was with alcohol. Generally drugs make people more relaxed, open-minded. Grass is the best; it's but a passive drug. It's the best intoxicant there is. Speed gives intense pleasure and an ego trip, but it's a false one. Acid deconditions you, relieves you of your past training and beliefs. It frees you, but I don't think I'd use heroin, I'd never shoot anything; well, I might just try smack but not get into it. You can't use anything, though, when you're dealing. I can't even use marijuana if I want to deal actively—you have to be free of drug effects for that. . . . It's hard to say how many people have drug problems because they don't tell you when they have them, and it's all relative; you disagree on what a drug problem is. Anyone who craves a drug shouldn't use it. Even marijuana makes you listless; you can't take care of yourself if you overuse it. As for benefits, well not many people gain. I'm the only one I know—yet it's beneficial to enjoy drugs even if they don't make you better or happier. As for myself, I'm sure I'll get off marijuana some day as I grow older and find something I want to do.

As for narcs, they're my natural enemy. Nothing personal about it, you understand; but they're worse than cops—insidious, low people. It's psychopathic to go around lying all the time as they have to do. They make their money by lying. That's why they're so unpopular with most people, even cops. Worms! They're conservative to the point of paranoid. Imagine to be that young and uptight. That's why they're easy to spot—because they're full of shit. The average cop, on the other hand, is a good man. Sharp, clear-thinking. Rough having to take their lives in their hands like that. I'm in the vice business, that's all. I want no trouble with [*regular*] *cops. I'm not contumacious. I'm not sharp enough to go to work for the police myself.*

But I will go into legit business when I grow up. I'll get some money together to do it. I'm learning business now.

Jim describes himself in the following way:

I'm too good-natured. I'm honest and generous. I'm lazy and I'm impulsive. I'd say I'm a typical middle-class offspring for these times. In a word, I'm an average guy.

Jim speaks for himself. For him, drug dealing is a way to grow up, an exciting and self-proving way, with the added advantages of money and access to and involvement in that drug use which he himself admits is compelling and sometimes disabling. It is a toughening process for a child of the liberal era who, he says, was brought up by kindly parents whom he loves but who fed him on milk and honey in a world where others are nursed on thistles and iron. He sees nothing exceptional in what he is or what he does, expects to outgrow his current experiment in living and, through it, to learn how to get along in the real world. That toughening, that movement from weak to strong, is his metamorphosis.

Did it work? No. A youth who recognized his weaknesses, it appears that he did not master them. Someone trying to become active, mean, aggressive and alert cannot do so by compulsively using a drug which, he claims, makes him chronically passive, euphoric, and inattentive. Those blacks to whom he was attempting to sell robbed him of all his capital—coin and cannabis. And when the moment for the final shoot-out came, he, child of peace and anger's suppressor, could not kill. The others had killed and would have killed and walked away winners. Where is he now? Returned to the milk and honey of home, unemployed, still drug involved. A life of crime might pay, but not for Gentle Jim. Growing up didn't work.

Cobra: A Verbatim Account

Let us seek authenticity via another route—by hearing what one concerned ex-dealer himself has to say by way of autobiography, observation, and social commentary. The setting is California, the dealer is Cobra, the interviewer is Enquirer. The town is Discomfort. The interview is followed by the remarks of Commentator, another dealer from the same scene. Changes in the transcript are deletions of actual names of people, and insertions are clarifications.

Enquirer: How many drug dealers did it take to supply your community?

> Cobra: *There was only one big dealer and he is still active. He has anywhere from twenty-five guys working for him, and they have guys working for them with occasional outsiders. The street workers work for the middlemen.*

What does the big dealer make a year in profit?

> *Hard for me to say but it's way up there. I'll make a guess, let's see—I don't think I would miss it much, say $60,000 or $70,0000 a year or better.*

The twenty-five middlemen, what do you think they will make a year?

> *Not too much because on the average they're using up a lot of their money on the stuff for themselves. If they'd stay off it and just take care of business, they'd make $30,000.*

If each of these middlemen has four men working for him, that's about one hundred street dealers. How much do they make?

> *On the average it has been my experience that they would only get money to deal and money for their own habit. I worked myself up to being Number-3 man, among the middlemen. I know some white guys who have 15 and 16 year olds running for them.*

How much of that sort of thing goes on?

> *Quite a bit of it. Most of them don't care—if the kid is old enough to come in with the money and if he's reliable, they give it to him.*

What is the average age when a kid starts dealing?

> *About 17 years, when they can sell in enough quantity to make a profit. The other kids look up to them.*

Is there any part of the community where a bunch of kids do not look up to drug dealers?

> *Yes, that would be the Christian kids who come from homes where people take time and explain the pitfalls, as compared to kids whose parents are doing the same kind of thing the kids are doing. There are quite a few people over there running shooting galleries, whose kids are down with it—who know everything that is going on—the kids know people are shooting—know what type of dope it is. I know "J" has a shooting gallery where people get down with it right there in the kitchen—his kids 13, 14 years*

old are right there. Couple of occasions his daughter helps to bag it up.

When did you first start to use illicit drugs?

I got turned out on weed when I was 15. I fooled with weed from then right on up. After I went to the joint and got out, I did my parole. My first wife got a divorce and I took it pretty hard. I turned alcoholic at first, but it didn't agree with me—I kept getting in fights. Then I got together and was going to work. My new wife was using dope—at first I didn't know she was on any type of dope, but one day I came home and found a big crowd of people, three or four teacups and spoons. Then we had a talk. It didn't work out too good. This was the first time a cop ever came into my pad behind dope. They didn't find any and left. I was disgusted. I wanted to try it but I was afraid of the needle. I tried to swallow some but it came right up. She said, "Come on, it isn't going to hurt, it's a nice new point." Finally I took it and it was pretty nice to me. I started dealing about the same time. I used coke, heroin, but I was afraid about heroin—about getting the habit.

Do you have the habit now?

No.

You are clean now. Do you drink?

No, I haven't had any drink since '58. I guess you could say I'm cleaning up my life.

Do you have a job?

No. But I'll get along—I won't have to get off into the bag.

Would you be better off going back to burglary or dealing?

I made out better dealing than in crime. I never had a narcotics bust, which most of the good suppliers consider a good thing. If you know the different types of dope and have never been rousted by the police, you have no jacket on a dope charge.

How did you know where to go and get a supply? How did you set up in business?

I met all these people at this particular time through the big local supplier—it took sixty-five dollars to get an ounce of speed; then I could trip with him to the city and cop.

Then gradually you acquired more sources?

"A" approached me. By this time I had built up a good reputation for getting rid of dope and other stolen merchandise.

You were fencing—taking orders for fur coats, etc.?

Yes, I knew who wanted a stereo and who had one, and I'd pull a profit on both of them. After going to the joint, I gave up burglary and changed my m.o.

Becoming a drug dealer was a way for you to avoid going to jail?

Yes, they had me down for burglary.

You are still out of jail?

Just barely.

What would you do yourself about drugs if you were in charge of this country? If you were President, what policy about drugs would you set?

I got to be honest, there is no policy that a President could set to keep drugs out of this country, but there needs to be some type of special fund set up to get the money they need to bust the people from dealing. The police need a lot of help finding these people. I know three or four people could have been popped but they didn't have the money. It's just not what's happening.

If drugs were made legal, what would happen?

Depends on what drugs.

Let's say we made grass legal?

I could dig it.

What would happen in our community if you could buy grass at the grocery store.

Sales would fall off. There wouldn't be any thrill in selling it.

What about hash?

That's more powerful—I don't think I would legalize it.

What happens to people who used hash?

I think they hallucinate—they trip out.

Can you trust them in that state?

I would not.

What about barbiturates—would you make them legal?

No, I'm more afraid of a person on reds than on speed.

Give me an example of a kid on barbs.

Kids get full of those reds, it's just like the Wild West days. Everyone has a gun and with the slightest argument, everyone starts shooting.

Do you think their judgment is bad?

Yes, I think it's the reds.

How old are your kids?

My son is 14.

He's just right.

That's one of the major things that helped me think the way I am thinking. He was living here with his mother. It's easy to get the stuff here.

How do you instruct him?

I don't hide anything from him. I tell him the consequences, how my life was, how I would like his life to be better than my life. I don't want him going to jail, using dope. I'd like him to have some of the things I did not have as a kid. I don't want him fooling around with dope.

Does he believe that? Does he want things to be that way? Does he have confidence in himself?

Yes. He was a summer teacher in the Head Start. He has a paper route. Right now there is this Honda Trail Blazer he wants. I told him I have no job—no money right now, but when I get to work I'll start saving and help him get one. When I get a few bucks ahead, I'd love to go fishing—take him along, do things together.

Do you think you can keep kids off dope that way—with an outdoors healthy life?

Yes, I do.

We've heard about drugs being only a white man's problem. What do you think about that?

I don't hold with it.

What do you know about guns?

On the average, all the street people are armed (all the people who use dope except maybe those who use weed and drop bennies).

That did not used to be so.

No. When I was coming up we had fights, but it's not that way now.

What do they do?

If they don't have a gun, they'll slip up behind and brain you.

It's more violent now?

Yes.

Where do they get their guns?

Steal them. You can buy a 32 automatic for twenty-five or thirty dollars.

Did you ever deal in guns?

No, but I knew several people who did.

Was there an overlap between guys who dealt in drugs and those who dealt in guns?

No, it's a different problem. Usually one of their friends would have knowledge of a place where guns are stored; and the first time they catch people with their guard down, they pop it.

What about machine guns?

They used to have quite a few around. I knew about ten or twelve. Then I got out of contact for about sixty days, and when I got back out they had these Eagle Brand type automatics they were selling—they call them machine guns but they are not really machine guns.

Have you seen any of the dealers you know armed with genuine automatic weapons?

Yes.

Why do you think a guy like that has a gun?

It's his intention to use it if he is raided. A lot depends on how the police hit a place.

Is it true that drug dealers are willing to use their guns on police?

Sure, why not? There is no fear of the death penalty. You are going to do the same amount of time no matter how many cops you shoot. That's the way they look at it.

Did you carry a gun?

Yes, a 32.

You didn't use it?

I'm not violent.

Why did you have a gun?

Mainly for my associates—to keep from being ripped off. They did rip me off and kidnap me. I owed them eight hundred bucks, and I was so far in the bag I wasn't doing much. They took me up to the city and kept me locked in this house. Every day they'd whammy me [mix up a big batch of speed] and leave me dingy for about two weeks. Then they let me come back. Rather than do that again, I was willing to leave the stuff alone and come back to work. It's common practice. Either I do it or they drop me in the bay. Actually this is what led up to my bust on the forgery. I was getting them their money back.

You were working off your debt?

I feel it was a setup. They had all their money but a hundred dollars; they didn't need me any more.

Why do you think guns are so attractive? Is a machine gun a status symbol?

There are so many radical organizations teaching hate and revolution, my personal opinion is that everybody feels important, bigger, if you own a lead.

When you say you are a professional criminal, are you saying you take pride in your work?

Yes, you would have to take pride in anything you did, in order to be successful at it.

How much did you make a year as a dealer?

Let's see, when I was working for "A"—on the average about 3,000 dollars a day.

That's gross proceeds. What were you selling?

Everything.

What was in your kit?

You would sell whatever the people would ask for. They would tell me what it was they wanted, how much they had to spend, and I would call "A," give him thirty minutes' notice, and he would have what I needed.

What risks were involved, other than the police?

Being ripped off—by people who never buy anything. They catch a dealer going down the street, and they rip you off. I was ripped off twice.

When did you first get involved in dealing?

From '64 or '65 until a year ago, 1969.

But you did other things also; you were involved in burglary?

I was more of a procurer. If you needed something, I could get it.

You weren't a pimp?

No. I can't stand that. It's the only thing I never made any money off. I always valued women more than that. That's how I really got hung up in the dope racket. The girl I was associated with was hooked on speed; in order to get her to stay home, I would get it and store it up for her. Then, since I had it on hand, I started selling it to get some of my money back, and she still had it when she needed it.

Did it work?

Yes. At that time I was working for "K" Company, but a couple of weeks after I started selling it, I quit my job.

What about the girl?

Eventually, it ended up with her going to Corona [California's Narcotics Rehabilitation Facility].

Were you supplying her?

I was for a while. This was in order to keep her away from some of the people she had been associated with.

What did you get out of being a dealer, other than money?

It taught me something. Deep in my heart I always wanted to, and when I had the experience I would never go back into it. It's not a life I cared for.

While you were dealing, were some good things happening?

You had plenty of money—you could afford things you normally could not afford.

What was the first thing you bought?

A car. A new Buick Electra. New clothes. I had the air of a pimp even though I wasn't one. I went to the finer clubs, dressed well, went with the high society of the dope business. In a sense you are limited to people that are in the dope business because you have something in common. You are afraid if you step out of this circle you might be informed on.

In that set you were making good money and could be proud of it. In what town was this?

In and around San Francisco. I made a couple of trips, buying and selling. I got to know people transporting.

Were you dealing with Mexican stuff mainly?

Yes, one guy I got to meet on the other side was Mexican. He was a big wheel over there. Had cabs and restaurants in Tijuana. He had a warehouse with so many reds—they would be that thick on the dirt floor.

Six inches thick? How big a floor?

Larger than the jail—bigger than the Safeway. He had a big place and everything was uniform. He had reds in the back, all cased in their bottles; then, after reds, bennies, heroin, cocaine, weed.

How much heroin did he have?

Oh Christ, I couldn't sit here and tell you. There is no one man could buy out his warehouse. I know "J" and "H" whenever they would go down they would buy anywhere from 180,000 to 200,000 pills plus weed and heroin and what not.

How did you get it back over the border?

There are a number of ways. One of the best ways was the newly-wed game; where you have a guy and a girl, just married, it has a tendency to relax the border patrolman. In cars it varies—the '69

Chevy, right over the fender wall in the trunk you got a drop that's hollow—you push the pills in that one at a time; and you can carry over 200,000 in the tailgate of a pickup truck.

Did you hire your own newlyweds?

They usually have their own people who will do it—they pay $800 for the trip and a third of whatever you get over.

Are they mostly Mexican, white, blacks?

Mixed; quite a few whites, quite a few blacks.

Are most suppliers black?

About half.

Did you retail or did you wholesale—that is, supply other dealers?

Most of the time I just dealt to street people.

Blacks only?

No, mixed. In fact I used to say from Hell's Angels on down. The hippie set—I had quite a few of them sewed up.

Local hippies?

Right.

How many street users do you think there are in your community [population 18,330]?

Out of the young people, I would have to say a little over half of them are using narcotics of some kind, or barbiturates.

What do the kids 13 and 14 use?

They use mostly a little acid, and weed. They drop quite a few reds. By the time they are 16 I would say maybe 5 per cent of them are shooting stuff, speed.

How about coke?

They sniff coke a bit. The coke set is quite a close set. In my area, other users have a pretty rough time getting into that particular set. They have a tendency to get paranoid.

Did you supply coke?

No, the fellow who has been supplying coke is still loose.

What is the youngest age that is using any of the illicit drugs?

I would say 13.

Why do kids begin to use?

I think it's an influence of the young adults, especially with the black kids. They see them with new cars. "He's always clean," they say; "how is he able to do this? My old man never has done this well; but this guy's a dope dealer." So automatically he wants to be a dealer.

Do they think of being dealers, and is that how they get to be users? After all, they see some pretty strung-out users as examples.

Yes; but people, when they start out, never think they'll end up like that—but you never know until you get into the bag what will happen.

Can people control it?

There is no control past weed.

What percentage slip past weed?

Nowadays there are so many different forms of narcotics—ways to get loaded—it's hard to say, but reds and acid seem to be the big thing.

How long before you begin shooting?

There's no age level. It's just a matter of somebody being low enough to introduce the kids to it; and if they like it, they continue.

Do you see any difference in the kids that go past weed to reds and stuff—difference in background or personality—against those who don't?

I would say most of the guys and gals who just stick to weed will eventually cut it out and go on through school and maybe become lawyers or doctors or what not. The others—by the time they reach 17, they are so strung out they have no way but one to go. Some will turn out to be pimps, prostitutes, boosters, any phase of the game—whatever they happen to be skilled at. If they have sleight of hand, they could become pickpockets.

Among those who are on grass and go on to other stuff versus those who stop using it—is there anything you can use to describe or predict which they will do?

Well, yes, I guess you could say there is a difference in their background because usually those that go on got parents—I have to be honest—they are the kind of people that never have time for their kids. When they are not working, they are in some bar or in the street cussing and fighting—the kids raise themselves; they grow up to be hustlers from an early age. It has been my experience they will take a chance of five to life, with a gun.

Do you see any difference or the same difference in those kids that don't use and those that begin to use?

They have this problem, parents being out in the street, clubs. Then, it has to do with fear. I know back when I was a youngster I was scared to death of the reds. I can use anything else. One of my school buddies died from an overdose, and I have never been able to take reds—shoot or swallow them. I have seen people mix up seven or eight of them and shoot it.

Have those kids never seen anyone in trouble? What accounts for their not being afraid of reds?

That's kind of hard for me to explain. It could be they have never seen anybody who O.D.'d [*overdosed*]. *It could be a lot of people will try anything. There are some who don't want to be called chicken and they will try it. No one user can say that he likes stuff before he has shot it the first time. There has to be someone somewhere to entice them to take it.*

What would you tell a guy to entice him?

If he is weak and he probably is, I'd say "Why don't you try a little stuff, it's groovy" or "Don't be chicken"—it depends on the individual.

How many people do you think you have turned on for the first time to stuff?

None.

What about grass?

Quite a few, about fifteen or twenty.

While you were dealing what were you using?

Some of all of it. I like bennies. First time I tried speed, I couldn't swallow it. I was afraid to let anyone else shoot me; I finally ended up letting my old lady do it. They got me to lay down on the couch.

Kind of an initiation ceremony.

Yes. I was afraid, so they told me to lay down. I was feeling pretty groovy, and after I saw it wasn't going to hurt me, I could enjoy it.

Did you take it often after that?

Yes, I did. It almost cost me my life.

What happened?

I got off for about four months on speed really heavy. I stopped taking care of business. I would take these people's dope and rather than make money I would party it up.

Can anyone deal and use at the same time?

Nobody that I have met can use and deal too, because you will end up giving it away or shooting up more than selling.

Can a guy get to be a heavy user and still make the grade? In other occupations—burglary, etc.?

Yes, these are the best thieves, the ones who are strung out; they aren't going to work, so they have to have some way of getting money to obtain their narcotics.

Why don't they work?

It's too slow. The drug money is too slow in coming in—when you have to work forty hours for a fix.

What does it cost a day in your area to maintain a heroin habit?

Some guys are shooting better than a hundred dollars a day.

What about the trippers?

I'd say no more than fifty dollars.

How much for grass?

I'd say about twenty dollars a week.

What about the average kid—LSD, etc.?

Depends on how his system is built up to stand reds. Some kids drop eight to fifteen reds a day and still stumble around; some people take just one and are out like a light.

What would a red cost?

The last knowledge I had they were three for a dollar; some places two for a dollar.

Somebody who takes five to six reds a day would be spending two dollars?

Yes.

Do they take every day?

Yes, every day, as long as they're awake.

So when you say 50 per cent of the kids use, you mean they use grass every day?

Right.

Does anyone ever get tripped out because he can't get supplied?

Yes, supplies get short.

What drugs have been in short supply?

All of them but acid and coke. You can always get those. Some people up in the hills make acid.

What's the longest period ever without any?

Never any long period—just a couple of days. They will jack the price up—ten to fifteen and twenty-five dollars.

Would you try to drive the market up so you could make more money?

Yes.

Was that good?

Yes. What they will do—the chemist will run off a bad batch of speed and flood the streets with it. Put all the good speed back, for a week or two. Won't let any of the good speed show up. They then let two or three guys turn loose of the good stuff, they're the only ones who have it and only so much. So a nickel paper won't do it. One individual will have to spend ten or fifteen dollars for what he would normally get in a nickel paper.

If we could take a minute, could you tell me about the drug-distribution system in your town—not in terms of anyone's last name. Let's say we have 18,000 in your town, two thirds of whom are kids—say 12,000 kids—half of them over 12, half of them, say 3,000 kids, using something.

In [*my town*], *just being honest, it's hard to find someone who is not using some kind of something.*

About guns—how many people in your community, would you say, have guns?

In a black community, they say every black man should have two guns—the one he keeps and the one he has at home for his wife when the revolution starts.

Gives him a feeling of potential—power?

And the youth, they got 'em just cause everybody else has them. When they get loaded they got a tendency to show off with them. Lot of times things get real serious. Most times a lot of shooting and hell raising and nothing happens.

But someone could get killed accidentally.

Right. I saw this guy shoot his best friend with a 22 pistol. Guy never went to a doctor, there was never a complaint. They stretched him out on a pool table in the bar, and someone handed him a fistful of reds. He downed them, someone took the bullet out with a pocket knife, put some gauze on, and he's walking around today. Said it was an accident.

What would you say is the age when kids start carrying guns?

When they get big enough to steal one and keep it hidden from whoever they have to hide it from—14 or 15.

Happens the same time as they might start using drugs?

Yes. The younger ones have a pocket knife or something.

The sixty-four-dollar question is "What happens to all those kids in your town who are using drugs, not the ones that are using just grass, etc., but the guys who have gone on to acid, reds, carrying guns?"

Most of those who don't get killed will end up getting arrested. Those who are not arrested will end up being strung out, addicts.

What is it like to walk through the streets of your area with a crowd of 15 and 16 year olds on drugs?

You are on guard all the time.

You don't mingle with your own customers? Why don't you?

> *You know the effect the stuff has. It depends on what you're selling, and you know just about what their reaction will be. You are in a sense jeopardizing your freedom, possibly your life and business, by mingling with them. Eight out of ten of those street people who are using will be on a police blotter of some sort, and when you start being seen with them, if your name crops up over a couple of times, you got the cops breathing down your neck, wondering about you, what your connection is.*

So you are better off insulating yourself from them?

> *You graduate up to the class of people who like to stay home and have their private parties, pot parties, freak parties.*

How do you teach kids discretion?

> *You don't.*

How do people learn discretion?

> *Run-ins with the police.*

Are there some people who learn discretion an easier way?

> *I never seen any. Nobody can tell you anything 'cause you already think you know it all and if you attempt to tell them something, it's going in one ear and out the other. They got to learn it the hard way—and some never learn it. I got to think about when a man goes all out doing everything he can to make something out of his son, but his son just don't have it.*

What's the future for the black community? You describe your town where half the kids and half the adults are using drugs and where some portion are going to be continually using something besides grass; and you say there is nothing the police can do to stop that drug use or interfere—and these don't change that pattern—those that aren't jailed become addicts. What's the future of your town if that is what's happening?

> *Well I tell you, myself and a lot of people have been looking forward to this—especially since the Watts riots. It's going to blow up and a lot of people are going to get hurt and a lot killed before it's over with. This is something you can just about stake your life on, without being able to put your finger on it.*

When you say "blow up," you are describing a lot of people who are on drugs, have guns, are not working, lead street lives, whose lives are not safe with one another. When will it blow up and how?

> *I don't know. If I did know I would probably be one of the first ones to try to do something about it. But you really don't know. You take like last year, after midnight it wasn't safe to be riding down the street. One time around 2 a.m. places were closing up, and at X and Y Streets this guy comes out of a bar and starts shooting across X Street—he doesn't know who he's shooting at, just blasting away; and when he empties his gun, he ducks back. Right there at the Z Street apartment house—you were afraid to go up in there after dark.*

That's where you live?

> *No, but I know people who do; these people are so paranoid—they didn't have just one shooting incident—all this kind of stuff; two or three people got shot on X Street—it's pitiful.*

What proportion of the shootings get reported?

> *Ten per cent, if that many.*

What proportion of the murders are identified?

> *Not very many. There're a lot of them never even reported.*

Give me a guess—in your town how many murders do the police find out about?

> *I know of two cases out of seven or eight that came to police attention.*

Is there anybody in your town who leads a life of reasonable satisfaction, optimism, and relaxation?

> *The Christian people; of course, I don't know how they feel deep down but they don't have any association with all of this; I imagine the biggest portion of them don't realize what's going on around them.*

Will they be robbed and shot at?

> *They'll be robbed now and then, homes burglarized, and what not; there's nothing they can do about it. All they can do is tell the police "My home was broken into, my stereo and color TV was taken."*

Well, back to the big question then: If this is the way it is going, you foresee it as an explosion where everybody simply picks up his six shooter, and his ten reds and lets go at once; or even if it's just a fizzle, everybody takes his heroin or his bag of reds, and goes down the tubes. Either way, as you describe it, one doesn't get a sense of hopefulness, or perhaps half of the black people in your town must think their future will be a dreadful one.

> *I don't.*

Is there anything society can do about it?

> *I can't say there is anything you can really do about it. What has to be done is going to have to come from the people of the community, and I say this because they are going to have to knock down two or three of these largest dealers who have the place sewed up. The community was, on a whole, better off when they had a whole bunch of little dealers who were going to the city, buying their stuff. It wasn't organized; there was no attempt at organizing the dealers. The users were in groups. When the Big Man got in there, he commenced organizing; then he pulls out all these small-time dealers. This is how "J" got shot—he was going around pistol whipping people—I happen to be one who he pistol whipped. But them being stronger, they won out because the Big Man was able to import gunmen. There was a time when "J's" house was an arsonal—he had ten to fifteen guns there.*

So when a dealer tells me he wishes the city were organized, he may not mean it.

> *No. He don't mind, the money is good, the life is easy. Those that were chippying along, that got froze out, they will naturally resent it—there's always animosity. First chance they get, they'll always inform; but where does it end up? Just a big mess in court, when they are all equally guilty.*

They are all part of the life.

> *They all have done something to each other and ended up trying to kill each other.*

Some say that when the Negro gets involved in organized crime, he is on the way out of crime because he is learning how to do business, learning how to organize, how to deal on a systematic basis.

> *He is learning to organize, true, but I can't say on his way out of crime.*

Why not?

> *Although he may be able to make the money, he still hasn't got it up here—how to hold on to it. You go back to education and sense of business. This isn't something you learn out in the streets.*

Didn't the Big Man learn?

> *Yes, he learned—he is one guy who learned. I think he is from back East somewhere. Came up in the gladiator school.*

What is that?

> *He was a young gunman—gangster. He learned through hard knocks; no one handed it to him on a silver platter.*

Does he have kids?

> *I don't know, I know very little about him.*

Where does he live?

> *He has any number of places, all in the Bay Area.*

It would be interesting to see if his kids will go to college or pursue a life of crime.

> *I would say if he could he'd probably get 'em to go to college, but if there are any boys involved I would be inclined to believe that they'll end up following his footsteps.*

And some day he'll end up dead?

> *If different organizations that are after him don't get him first, he has a lot of young people out there would like to pop him. It's a thrilling life if you like danger.*

Do you like danger?

> *To be honest, yes.*

Part of being a dealer—part of this whole business—is the thrill?

> *I have a reputation of sorts. I am not known as a violent individual, but not many guys can say they have downed me.*

You are tough but not violent?

> *I have never shot anybody or anything like that.*

Maybe that's one of the things that makes it hard to give up dealing—the thrill.

No, you have to reach that stage of life when you really get a chance to look at yourself and look at what you are doing and think about it. In my particular case I think how close my kids came to turning out that way—my oldest son was well on the road.

The 14 year old?

Yes, this is what made me turn around—my concern for my kids.

This is the difference between you and "F"?

He was shooting heroin as much as he could get his hands on. Doesn't care about his kids. Deep in his heart all he thinks about is his next fix—that's what he lives for. Once you get hooked that's the way it is.

For these people there's no way for people to help their kids—they're too far down the tube. As you describe it, we must just let it go—there is nothing we can do?

You can't just let it go. You have to keep chipping at the old block until you find a way to knock down the tree.

You mean as a nation?

I mean as a nation, as a whole. This thing is not just localized in my town. I can start from San Francisco and run right on to Mexico, and I can buy as much dope as you got money to give me to buy it with.

Whenever you hit a town?

Yes, the biggest portion of your really big dealers now—Arizona is wide open. The kids got plenty of money—they are constantly looking for dope. People leave California with their supply, go into Arizona, unload and come back, cop again, go back. This is a running business now.

And even the Customs and the Bureau of Narcotics have been unable to make a change?

No, every time they bust somebody, and find out one way somebody is getting it across, somebody else dreams up a new way of getting it across. You can never completely stop it. But you will never be able to curb narcotics in this country. It is out of the question. You're fighting a rear-guard action. You slow it down when you pop a few people, but those people have people work-

ing under them who did not get popped who step into their shoes, and they, in turn, have learned quite a bit and know the mistakes the other guy made.

Well, from the standpoint of a cop it's a sad note to end on. That's where we are, but you at least are out of it and your life will be not as sad.

I don't intend for it to be.

You are not going down the tubes.

In fact, I think I am on my way up out of the tube. Before they eventually catch up with me, I will probably have quite a few people [dealers] down the tubes in this state. Out of connections I had and can make, I will knock down a whole lot of dealers. I am somebody who had time to think and I would like to make something good out of my life, and do as well at it as I did when I was doing bad things.

Commentator's Remarks. From reading Cobra's answers, I would say that he obviously had made the scene and knew what he was talking about. However, there are some inconsistencies that don't quite add up and make me wonder if he was bragging or just what. Mostly I wonder about the money he said he made, because if he was making as much as he says, he wouldn't have been busted; he would be too high up and have a legitimate front for himself.

The scene probably has changed since Cobra's interview, at least as far as what drugs are dealt now and who handles what. The guys who deal in pills will probably deal in acid, but there seems to be a trend away from the pill bit. The guys who handle heroin also probably have coke—there's a lot of snorting going on now. The grass dealers seem to stay with grass mostly. 'Course, there are some guys who will deal in anything. You tell them what you want and they'll get it for you. I don't know about speed lately—haven't heard anything about it. Mostly the scene is becoming more and more a heroin-coke route, and I really don't like to see that.

Chapter 5

PSYCHOLOGICAL CASE STUDIES

About the turn of the century, de Tocqueville observed that Americans have a penchant for turning social problems into legal issues. Our purpose here is to turn this trenchant observation around by examining dealing (the illicit sale or distribution of drugs), heretofore viewed as a legal problem, from the perspective of the lives of three people who do not share our society's commitment to restricted availability of drugs. We focus here on three individuals—examining some of the forces that shape their personalities and influence their lives.

The case-study method is most congenial to our probe of feelings and life styles of these dealers against the backdrop of their peer groups, families, social norms, and environments. Rather than viewing their dealing as simply an expression of personality needs or traits, we seek to picture the adjustive personal strategy of the individual first and then see how illicit dealing relates to it. By this approach, we hope to reduce the negative "halo effect" (which is present, more or less discernibly, in most of us) against our three dealers.

A further word about our use of the case-study method is in order. Using it, we hope to generate hunches and understanding, not generalizations about personality factors which predispose people to become dealers. Focus on the individual, with a naturalistic rather than an experimental aim, arises from the intent to explore behavior rather than to verify hypotheses.

Selection of Cases

No sampling in the usual sense was involved in the selection of these three cases. They were chosen from ten available subjects on the basis of diversity and the ease with which dealing could be seen in the perspective of their total personality. We have not followed the temptation to seek striking, flamboyant individuals who are making enormous profits and living in high style. Such persons fit too neatly the old stereotype of a dealer; and, although they are colorful and exciting, their numbers are few and they are less amenable to change than the rest. In short, since big dealers are more committed to dealing and are likely to fit into a diagnostic type of social deviant (such as sociopath), they were not selected for these observations.

Our subjects may be termed "marginal dealers." They are not engaged in dealing primarily for the money, but neither is it irrelevant to them. They are not otherwise a threat to society, nor have they become members of a large network of dealers.

Since knowledge for the prevention and intervention in dealing is our ultimate aim, these marginal persons are of special interest. From the perspective of containment of drugs within approved channels of distribution, big-time operators are a far greater threat to society. Yet marginal dealers occur in vastly greater numbers; they provide the entry point or recruitment pool for larger operations; they are often the end point in the distribution chain; the impact they have on other persons as visible models of dealing is significant. We currently lack promising techniques of intervention for that group.

Of the three dealers studied here, two are from a high school in the mid-Peninsula area of the San Francisco Bay region, and the third is a college dropout living in the same area. The two high school students were located as a result of contact with school officials in a large high school. The nature of the research was explained to a knowledgeable vice-principal, who assisted in setting up informal meetings with many students. His help was invaluable.

Techniques used to obtain information were both traditional and innovative: interviews, projective tests (the Smith Drug Stories adaptation of the Thematic Apperception Test and the Rorschach), group discussions, walks in the woods, family interviews, home visits, and beer drinking in local taverns.

All three subjects gave information about themselves on the basis of the relationship established between them and myself. Their cooperation and confidence depended upon their seeing me as a friendly or neutral person who wanted to learn something from them about drug use, dealing, and the "whole scene." My affiliation with a university was indispensable to creating a relationship of trust, providing an appropriate setting for some of the interviews and testing sessions. A commitment was made to protect their anonymity.

We now turn to the case studies themselves, remembering that they are intended not as definitive statements about the personality of each subject, but rather as attempts to gain insight into their feelings and attitudes toward themselves and their involvement with drugs and dealing. We ask: How does dealing fit into the adjustive life style of the individual, and what is the meaning of illicit-drug dealing as an expression of or functional component in the personality of the three individuals?

George

George is a short, stocky lad of 17 with long blonde hair framing his face and falling over his shoulders in floppy curls. Regarded by his schoolmates and family alike as easy-going and good-natured, he nevertheless has an air of heaviness, even defeat, about him. He takes his poor grades in high school in good humor despite the disparaging remarks from peers and staff about his achievement and prospects for graduation.

Born in San Francisco, George has lived his entire life in California, starting off with a secure place as the middle child in a family of five. He had no major problems in early development. He participated in athletics to the extent of breaking local YMCA swimming records while a 10 year old. When his father encouraged him in the direction of competitive and physical-contact sports, he lost interest in athletics.

An extreme disparity existed between the mother and father in their relationship with their children. The mother, in her fifties, was a jolly woman, accepting, encouraging, and understanding of her children—to a fault. George's father was born into a wealthy family that later lost everything. The manager of a retail chain store, he was distant and demanding with his children, wanting perfection in everything from mowing the lawn to school grades without taking the time to help them learn the requisite skills.

The only comments George would make about his father were critical. Several years after his father left the family and a divorce was final, George said: "The son-of-a-bitch doesn't give a damn about his family." In the wake of the father's leaving, the family was faced with unsurmountable medical, legal, and money problems, which George saw as forcing him to grow up faster than he should. "I'm 17 and I feel like I'm 24," he remarked.

George's older brother, Ted, resembles his father. A straight-A student with interests in books, music, and art, he works in a grocery store and writes term papers for college students in his spare time for spending money. With both an allergic and diabetic condition, he regularly injects himself with insulin and has developed a hatred of needles. Both George and Ted smoke marijuana regularly, George having started at 14. Living in his brother's shadow for many years, George began dropping acid at 15; and when he was 16, he shot "speed" for four months, losing 28 pounds. Whenever his friends were without drugs, George would share his with them, bragging about his "good grass." At 15, he started selling joints and lids of marijuana to acquaintances to recover his money and found it exciting and socially rewarding, claiming a good reputation as a dealer in grass, barbiturates, and mescaline, occasionally selling speed. He regularly sells lids and kilos of marijuana, obtaining his supply from several friends who live in the mountains close by.

Since George was neither the protegé nor the accomplice of other dealers, he learned the ropes painfully by trial and error. On three occasions he was burned in his purchases of drugs. Once, in an attempt to purchase five hundred dollars worth of marijuana, he met his contact and they proceeded to the house where the promised amount was to be picked up and handed over. His contact then persuaded George to give him the money, or "the man inside" wouldn't hand over the marijuana. George gave him the money and waited outside for twenty minutes, believing that the big-time dealer inside was simply protecting his identity, until he went inside and found that the middleman had skipped out the back door with his money. Michael Douglas (1971) describes a ritual which portrays the sophistication necessary to successful dealing:

> *Dope dealing, especially when buyer and seller are acquainted, involves a primitive ritual which can be described in terms of I Am More Hip Than Thou. The object, if you are buying, is to let the other cat know (never directly but as forcefully and significantly as possible) that (1) you have bought a lot of dope in your time and are not to be messed with; (2) you know what dope goes for in the area; and hopefully (3) you are a very big dealer yourself and can provide the seller with a lot of business if he measures up to your standards.*

George was not gifted in the arts of dissimulation, being a more accepting and nonsuspicious person than his fellow peddlers. Although he was aware of the unspoken rules of dealing in dope, he could not convincingly carry out the ritual of Being More Hip Than Thou.

His sales were mostly to friends or acquaintances, practically all of whom were young males. Although he was outgoing and enjoyed being with girls socially, he never had a steady and had not engaged in sexual intercourse. Occasional heavy petting was as far as George would go, the fear of "getting into trouble" holding him back. Group parties with wine, marijuana, and rock music were his preferences—with forays into student action on one occasion, when he bought bumper stickers for his drug-using peers to protest an illegal search by the police for drugs.

On a visit to George's home and extended talks with his mother, we found her to be happy to discuss the family. She repeatedly made the point that "George is a good boy." She hoped that the trouble over the drugs would make men of her sons.

Except when she became angry or defended her children, she vacillated back and forth—the uncertainty being, we infer, an outward expression of the sense of incompetence she felt about her family and herself. She admitted in passing that she drank too much but would not say how alcohol had affected her life. After her husband left their modest three-bedroom home in a lower-middle-class neighborhood, she went on welfare and worked part time, rarely discussing family problems in any depth with her children, even Ted, George's 21-year-old brother, who in reality managed household affairs.

When we raised the question of George's involvement with drugs his mother angrily replied, "It's mostly just a social thing. The kids pass the stuff back and forth. There may be one kid selling five dollars' worth of speed to another—but there is no dealing or anything. Just selling it back and forth to each other."

Although pretending to take the parental view of "boys will be boys," she recognizes in fact that her son engages in dealing but denies that it is serious. Her rationalization of her son's dealing matches George's perception of his activities, illustrating that she has become a satellite in the world of her children. Although she was unable to set limits on her children long before the appearance of their drug problems, her security as a parent depends heavily upon the satisfaction of her emotional needs by the children, especially George. Maintaining the psychological fusion between herself and her son has helped her to avoid facing her own helplessness as a parent, especially after the pivotal events of her husband's withdrawal and separation.

The degree to which she can maintain an indealized and unreal picture of her son is indicated by her immediate reaction to George's arrest for illegal sales in January 1970. When she found out, she became extremely angry but felt impotent, allowing Ted to handle discussions with their attorney. She said, "George is goddamned bitter because other people are doing really big-time things and just when he was getting better, they drag him in. It's just terrible to see kids in juvenile hall." Whether the conflict was between George and the police, school, probation officer, or employment agency, his mother showed the degree of unconditional acceptance of her son's behavior and attitudes that, in effect, prevented her from offering independent guidance and advice which the children—and especially George—needed badly.

George attended school in the mid-Peninsula region south of San Francisco. "A darling boy who never liked school. He didn't like to be cooped up," according to his mother. In their grammar school years, both George and Ted went to Sunday School; but religion has meant little to any member of the family except Ted, who reads books about mysticism. The father, of the Jewish faith, did not attend services.

In 1968, the high school certified that George was a habitual truant, missing over 100 days of school out of 140. He was placed on probation for six months. In October 1969, at the time his father was leaving the family, George cut more classes. Records show that when in class he was "sloppy in appearance and fooling around in class. He makes resolutions to change and sometimes shows a sulky attitude." As an industrial arts major, George earned two Cs, two Ds, and one F (in English) as a freshman; in his junior year, he was given incompletes for everything except crafts and food service lab. Tested in 1967 on the Lorge-Thorndike, which measures the ability to work with ideas and the relationship among ideas, George scored higher than average. In verbal areas, he functioned at the seventieth percentile level on national norms and at the sixty-sixth percentile on district norms. Comparable scores for reading are the twenty-fifth percentile and twenty-fourth percentile, respectively. The above-average potential shown by George was not matched by his day-to-day performance.

In January 1970 George and his brother were picked up by the local police and charged with sale and possession of marijuana. Although there was suspicion of possible involvement of his mother and 13-year-old sister, no charges were brought against them; and charges against Ted were dropped. In a four-month period of time beginning in September 1970, George was arrested, put on probation, and arrested again (the January sale charge). During this time, his mother's problems intensified, and she had several accidents. Internal hemorrhaging from an ulcer required eleven blood transfusions; a broken foot laid her up for several months; she drank excessively; she said vaguely she had "blood problems" and that she lacked money to support herself and her children. In family discussions, she relied on her children to remember both recent and distant events and, when interviewed, showed no real thread of continuity in her ideas.

When he was interviewed in the detention facility, George's reaction to the arrest and detention was one of helplessness, resignation, and impotent anger. With the kind of insight that comes during stress, George remarked, "Maybe I need probation" because "I've screwed myself up several times just as I was ready to get off it. Maybe I'm not ready." He worried about his mother, thinking that his arrest might make her ulcer break open.

Contact with their private lawyer brought the disheartening news that he wanted a thousand-dollar advance retainer before accepting the case, money the family did not have. In order to provide money for a more reasonably priced defense attorney, Ted dug up one of his ten-pound caches of marijuana buried in the yard and peddled it to obtain money for George's defense. On the advice of his attorney, George pled guilty at his hearing—feeling that "They're gonna get me some day for something." Recommendation by the probation officer was for rehabilitation in a special youth facility away from home rather than a jail sentence or individual psychotherapy. The recommendation was followed by the court. At last report from the director of the rehabilitation facility, George was responding well to their work and group-counseling program.

Mary

An outgoing, dark-skinned girl with coal black hair, Mary is a high school senior with a wide circle of friends of both sexes and, at 17, has a rather sophisticated style, circulating primarily with a "hip" group in school and out. Full of vitality, she shows an easy enjoyment of her friends and acquaintances, especially their antics and clowning, without mindless following of group whims. Although she is spontaneous with her peers and adults, she shows a caution in her relationship that gives her the distance from others that she prefers.

Socializing with a group experienced in the use of drugs, she has not become a "confirmed doper" herself, although she has experimented with all kinds of drugs: marijuana, peyote, amphetamines, and opiates. Her use of this experience is clear. She lets people know that she has been to the drug mountain and earned the badge of experience that comes from being into drugs: "I know because I've done it." Her use of drugs began at 15 and is now restricted to occasional joints and wine; she apologizes for her cigarette smoking. After they had been through several bad trips together, Mary and her group spoke out against drug abuse, especially speed, opiates, and LSD, christening themselves the Non-Droppers Society. The school attempted to use this informal student-organized antidrug effort but found that to include it in a formal drug program did not work. By drug "abuse" the Non-Droppers meant avoiding harmful effects ("don't use a drug unless you're ready for it") whereas the school was attempting to prevent use of any drugs.

Our interest in Mary stems from the fact that she was ripe for entry into a career of dealing but did not enter. Her family was split by marital strife and divorce; in addition, there were constant relocations, medical problems and shortage of money, no professed religious belief or involvement, exposure to a heavy drug-using group and personal acquaintance with over twenty illicit drug dealers, and intense conflict between her mother and herself over her freedom to run her own life. Add to these the fact that Mary once had sold a small quantity of amphetamines, thus crossing the legal and symbolic dealing barrier, but she refrained from such further activities. The question is: What aspects of her personality and social environment account for this resistance to becoming a dealer?

Mary was born in October 1952, in a medium-sized town in Kansas. She is the second of four girls, all spaced within five years. When Mary was five, the family moved to San Diego to be near her mother's relatives. Later moving to the San Francisco Bay region, the family was constantly on the move, changing residence over twenty times before Mary was in high school because her father always became "restless." Mary's mother did not believe in divorce, but when her husband began to work less and less, she had to support the family. Continued strife led to his leaving. Later—in 1965, when Mary was 13—the mother filed for divorce. She was awarded the divorce and child support by the court, some of which she began to collect in 1967, when her ex-husband began working. Mary's mother wanted her children to have respect for their father, so she did not "mention her husband's weakness in front of the children." She remarried in 1969. Her children, especially Mary, are ambivalent about their stepfather.

Mary's mother is an attractive dark-complexioned woman in her late thirties, who lives in a lower-middle-class neighborhood close to the railroad tracks in a town south of San Francisco. Of Jewish and Indian grandparents, she spent her early years on a reservation in the Southwest, from which she ran away at 14. A bright, determined person, she found a family to take her in and she finished high school at 15. She obtained some technical training in electronics, although she has never been able to use this background to get a job, working now as an inventory-control clerk. She describes her politics by saying, "I'm a member of the disgusted party"; her preference in the 1968 Presidential election was Eugene McCarthy.

The family situation has been financially shaky since the father left the family. Since then, the mother has barely been able to keep them together, making less than $5,000 per year and bearing the brunt of serious illness, the last one causing a nine-month period of disability due to a slipped disc, arthritis, and bursitis. The family has been on county relief for the last three years, making Mary an "underprivileged child."

A moderate to heavy experience and exposure to drugs occurs in the family. Mary's mother extensively used prescribed sedatives and tranquilizers when she could no longer cope with her husband's leaving the family. For intense pain from medical problems she relied on morphine, demerol, codeine, and glutethimide—needing to switch medication and increase dosages at times to get relief. Severe personality distress in the form of troubled thinking, hallucinations, and a suicide attempt convinced her of the necessity "to get counseling and to pull myself together" again. She is not worried about hippies or her children's joining them; she feels that communists and black power advocates are far greater threats to our society than student activists, hippies, or the indifference of suburbanites.

Acknowledging marked conflict and, to a lesser extent, competition between them, Mary's mother described her child's early years in the following manner:

> *It's hard to know what a child thinks. There's always been resentment between Mary and me. She has been a difficult child. She learned to read and write before going to kindergarten but in the first and second grade she didn't fit in, taking her chair to a corner and sitting there. She's a very moody child and very smart. If she liked something, she'd turn on the personality and be just great. She's a very, very planful person. Deliberate.*

And her comments about Mary's older years reveal her style of parenting:

> *In many ways, Mary is like me. And there has always been resentment between us. Parents have a big fat question mark hang-*

ing over their heads today. You really have to haggle to keep the rules even though at times you're incapable of it. Once Mary said to me that all the other kids were going to a rock festival and I was the only parent who wouldn't agree. So I asked her for a list of the names of her friends and their mothers' names and said I'd talk with them about it. "If I'm the only one, I'll change," I said. That ended that discussion in a hurry.

When she looks back on her early years in elementary school, Mary thinks of herself as a problem child and a "creepy little kid." She almost "flunked kindergarten" but recalls that "after they began to give me harder lessons, I did better." It wasn't until the fourth grade that she recalls making friends. After the school began to recognize her ability, she blossomed, gaining and holding the reputation all through school of being a superior student. In spite of taking extra classes in singing, making her own clothes, and working in a restaurant to earn money, Mary maintained a 3.9 (almost all A) average. In 1967, she was tested on the Lorge-Thorndike and was over the ninetieth percentile in both verbal and reading areas for national and district norms. College Entrance Examination Board scores were 667 for verbal and 623 for mathematics. Strong Vocational Interest testing showed highest scales in art, music, and teaching (73, 71, and 64) and lowest in technical supervision, merchandising, and sales (27, 36, and 38). After she graduated near the top of her high school class, several scholarships to college (all of them small) were awarded to her.

Showing a tendency to operate at the extremes, Mary is usually wound up psychologically—running for classes, which start at 7 a.m. with singing lessons and last until mid-afternoon, when she goes off to her restaurant job. The long hours and heavy demands on her time and energy are crucial aspects to her style of living because they allow her to accomplish far more, showing mastery over both assigned and self-selected activities; furthermore, the race through the day from one thing to another tests her stamina, dissipates the intense bursts of energy, and wards off periodic mild depressions (which she terms "being sick").

Her attitude toward drugs reveals the balance she has struck between having fun and maintaining control of herself. "I never want to get addicted to anything, so I'm careful what I take or try." To her, frequent use of drugs would threaten a "chemical takeover" of her mind at a time when she is still not sure she is in charge of herself. Not yet completely free of overt parental domination and not yet comfortable with adult self-direction and responsibility that she is building up inside herself, she fears anything that threatens the freedom she has already fought for and won. In consequence she rejects drug use that would be that "chemical takeover."

In one of our group sessions, Mary complained bitterly that her mother did many things that she, Mary, was not allowed to do. Instead of agreeing with her, a perceptive student asked her why her mother had to keep such tight reins on her. That led Mary to reflect for a moment on her mother's reasons for setting limits on her freedom. That she is capable of such reflection and objectivity portends well for her judgment and growing autonomy.

Because she had a strict mother and a passive or absent father, Mary developed the feeling that women are stronger than men but fickle and that men are nicer but lose out when they compete with women. This surmise is consistent with interview material and confirmed by her responses to projective testing. She was given the adapted version of the Thematic Apperception Test (J. P. Smith, 1971). In response to Card 18BM and the accompanying drug story which concerns alcohol, Mary said:

> *Yeah. He's having horrible trouble. His ex-wife is hassling him for money. After every hassle he gets super drunk so his friends have to help him home. He wakes up and still there is this horrible hangover.* [*What happened to lead up to this?*] *Between him and his wife?* [*Yes.*] *She socks him for all the bread that he has. Since drinking is his habit, he does it every weekend and friends help him home.*

Feeling a deep but not immediately visible sense of inadequacy (the "creepy kid" lives on), she is dedicated to the need to improve herself with education, music, and crafts as vehicles to carry her out of her deprived family situation. While she places very high value on education as a means of mobility and a way of obtaining recognition, she seriously doubts its value to her in personal terms but is unwilling to test out any other avenue as a way out of her underprivileged status. Her dislike for authority operates primarily within her immediate family, expressed in direct conflict with her mother, but does not reach sufficient intensity to require displacement onto police, political, or educational figures.

For Mary, an early sense of inadequacy was later overcome through academic and personal achievement. She seized an opportunity to interest teachers and friends in her abilities, impressing her mother and gaining recognition from peers and school staff without losing her friends through competitiveness. Illicit dealing offered her an opportunity to try out a new role; no real personal gratification followed it, but her reasons for not dealing go beyond that. She had developed from early childhood the feeling that she was "on her own" and had learned to anticipate what situations might be a threat to her freedom and self-esteem.

The fact remains that her use of drugs has also been illicit, as was her one act of dealing. Her mother's strictness did not prevent either. It is Mary's perceptions of the significance of the two acts—the difference between personal use and dealing—that is crucial to understanding her behavior. She felt that using drugs is a matter of individual choice but that the prohibition against dealing is legitimate, a matter on which she and her mother agreed.

She felt guilty over the one act of illicit sale, and she was sophisticated enough to give instrumental reasons ("It's not worth the hassle") rather than moral reasons ("It's against the law; it's wrong") for not dealing. She thereby avoided taking a position vulnerable to peer pressure, which could push her to prove herself to the peers through dealing. Her proffered instrumental reasons for not dealing were not her real reasons—which were partly moral. Her unwillingness to risk her hard-won achievement and self-esteem by dealing had been born out of a conflictual family relationship dominated by a perceptive and strong mother with whom she has much in common.

Monte

Monte is a cautious man in his early thirties who would never stand out in a crowd. With hair that barely covers the tips of his ears, he dresses in a style that may be described as "field jacket casual" in California, but in other regions his taste and his manners would be termed moderately conservative. He is Caucasian; but with the reddish look to his face and with his dark hair, he could be mistaken for part Indian or Spanish. Contacts with people, "the right people," are important to him, although he does not drop names to impress people. Monte is the son of a retired lawyer who formerly held a high position in a financial institution in the Bay Area. One of Monte's close relatives is a Presidential appointee to a federal agency.

Contact with Monte came about in an unusual way. As an adult dealer, he became involved with the teen-age son of a university acquaintance of mine. The son knew of my interest in illicit dealing. When his mother, my acquaintance, became aware that her son was keeping company with a real dealer, she was angry and wanted to intervene, blowing the whistle on Monte. After we discussed the problem, the mother agreed instead to talk directly to Monte, warning him and at the same time asking him to participate in a psychological study of dealers.

Monte accepted that blackmail-tinged invitation and we began our work together. At a later date he told me the reason he agreed to participate was that "Mrs. Jones had been so nice over the phone. It just takes a feeling of trust, that's all. My friends tell me I'm crazy. If I get busted, I just get busted, that's all." We should not discount entirely the reason he gave for participating—since it expresses a style of thinking and interpreting emotions and motives; yet it is patently clear that Monte's cooperation was strongly influenced by his desire to avoid an angry mother turning him into the police, even if she lacked concrete evidence to make a charge against him stick.

The terms of our relationship, which took three weeks to work out, were a commitment from me not to reveal any information about him. He agreed to provide information on the local drug and dealing scene and to provide a picture of himself and his drug-related activities. As with all our data, information on Monte was stored in such a fashion as fully to protect the identity of respondents. The manner in which our contact with Monte originated and progressed must be understood, since the way an investigator finds his cases definitely influences the results of his study. In contrast with the two high school dealers, Monte even after ten sessions together never gave up his cautious reserve or really relaxed.

Monte was born in San Francisco, attended Catholic elementary and junior high schools, graduating from high school in 1955 with a college preparatory curriculum under his belt. He describes these school years as "the best years of my life because of the good friends, the neighborhood crowd," some of whom he still sees. He immediately went on to the (Catholic) University of San Francisco at his parents' expense, earning a 3.0 (B) grade-point average. After two and a half years as a political science major, he dropped out. "College came at the wrong time for me. I just couldn't stay with it."

Liking intramural athletics and writing for a local newspaper, he decided on his own to leave college because "the mental readiness was not there." His draft board ordered him to active duty in the Army, where he spent two years as an enlisted man. His fellow enlisted men were not interesting to him, and so he fraternized with the officers because they had graduated from college. The Army experience was "a waste of time, but you can get used to anything." Monte's father and mother were college educated, and his acceptance of their upper-class status was not ambivalent. His ideal future was to become an independent manager of a business firm or the director of research for a corporation, neither of which he had training or experience for. He felt that his father would highly approve of this type of career.

Monte maintained a conventional view of his family as successful, accomplished people. With only himself and a sister four years younger, a housewife who lives in San Francisco, remaining of his family, he was at first unable to remember anything about his childhood and then shortly afterward gave this highly conventional description:

> *My parents raised me in the normal fashion—the traditional value system. They taught me the difference between right and wrong. I had no hassle with them. If I did something wrong, I caught hell. I got spankings as a child, and then later they withheld privileges. We had normal American values and were careful about our money.*

He got into fights occasionally as a young boy but "doesn't remember the details." He has better recollections of puberty and early teens, spontaneously but sparsely describing his first sexual encounter:

> *What do I remember vividly between 9 and 15? That's when I first balled a chick. I was a sophomore in high school, about 15. It was late in life compared to other kids. We were by ourselves. I was really scared. I kept thinking, what will happen if my parents find out.*

Monte came close to being engaged to a steady girl friend but she moved away. Parents and relatives ask him when he is getting married, but he views bacherlorhood as synonymous with freedom: "As long as I'm happy and enjoying myself, what's the difference; but my freedom is not the hippie type of thing."

In high school, the effort of studying and taking tests did not set well with Monte. Teachers could control him in class by asking him difficult questions, embarrassing him by his ignorance. When his whole group got together in one class, "We made life miserable for the teacher. We were always loud mouths." Monte has mellowed since the emotional storms of adolescence into a quiet, reserved person whose outlook shows a curious blend of traditional and conventional American values and a hedonistic philosophy of life.

Oriented toward material things, he places an extremely high value on the dollar. "If I have money, I can get what I want—cameras, record players, TV equipment." Rather than build new relationships with people, he prefers to maintain his past friendships—not only because they offer less threat to a dealer in illicit drugs but also because fewer constraints are placed on him in the company of people whom he knows well. His hobby is going to musical concerts, ranging from classical to rock depending upon his mood. His ideal picture of himself is the omnicultured man. This is in contrast to his actual materialism. "If I pay money to go to a concert, I really try to enjoy it." A surprising feature about Monte is that he feels his parents are more liberal than he is. "They voted for Humphrey and I voted for Nixon. I liked what he was saying and I thought we should give him a chance."

As a person with above-average intelligence who has reached maturity, Monte has learned to describe his drug interests in his own way rather than accept current rhetoric about dealers. He sells to his friends or the friends of friends, with occasional contacts outside this circle. He is often passive in the transaction, waiting for others to call him. Not a big operator relying on dope trade to provide his sole or major income, he rejects the label of "dealer" in describing himself. After we discussed different meanings of pusher, dealer, peddler, and trafficker, he admitted to being a "social dealer." When he was challenged on the inconsistency between his preferred values, which are traditional American, and his social dealing, he minimized the difference by contending that his dealing was not really that important to him.

Monte began to use and sell marijuana in his early twenties. He has used LSD and mescaline occasionally. These drugs are drugs he handles casually; "selling comfortably," he calls it. He does not know what his monthly net profit is but sells several thousand dollars' worth a year without making his dealing a visible, easily recognized activity to neighbors and relatives. His own suppliers are a stable base of four or five people whom he knows intimately. Several are college students and all are Caucasian. Monte has a deep mistrust and fear of black dealers, since one tried to steal his money at gun point in the Haight-Ashbury after promising to deliver "really great stuff." Monte says that he learned early in dealing "never to keep the money on me and never front it [show it]," but the incident "really shook me up. I never carry a gun."

He uses marijuana several times a week, and alcohol and tobacco on weekends or at parties. He has given up cigarette smoking since the Surgeon General branded cigarettes as hazardous to health. Initially afraid to use LSD, he read a great deal about it and became so curious that he took it in early 1967 with a knowledgeable friend. The trip "seemed like a mystical fairyland, but when you come down you realize that life is not like an LSD trip. You have to make the best of life as it is, and that's better than depending upon a pill."

Monte's dealing reflects his cautious and guarded life style. Copping areas at universities are dangerous because "student-type narcs are there; and in the city the police watch everything. So I stay away from both of them." He uses his car and makes pickups and deliveries where other people ordinarily stop their cars, such as the parking lots of grocery stores. He does not work at expanding his illegal operation, merely taking advantage of opportunities when they arise.

His present straight job is clerking in a small appliance store. He says, "I like getting paid for being there and doing a job rather than working for a commission—a basic laziness you might say. But I don't consider myself a really lazy person."

Although he regards current drug-control laws concerning possession and use of drugs as unwise if not immoral, his conscience is not bothered by dealing: "It is strictly a financial angle; and people I sell to, I know. My stuff is guaranteed. If it's no good, they get their money back. They are level-headed people. I don't give it that much concern."

Personal assurance of good drugs is more important to him than questions concerning guilt or wrongdoing. His actions are more suggestive of an adolescent's rebellion against his family than a sociopathic character acting out against society. In areas of conduct not concerned with drugs and dealing, Monte shows a conventional sense of propriety and concern for wrongdoing.

Since family and peer interviews were not possible, we used projective tests to provide additional information concerning Monte's personality on the assumption that the depth of his psychological involvement in dealing is not determined by the amount of money or drugs he buys and sells. Monte has developed an awareness of subtle aspects of dealing that reflects his past experience. He easily spots amateurish attempts at selling drugs and expresses disdain for them, as illustrated in his response to the Drug Story for TAT Card 20 [1] (a picture of a dimly illumined figure of a man in the dead of night leaning again a lamp post):

> *What went on before? Obviously they had made a connection. The pusher here doesn't know his customer very well. He made arrangements over the telephone. They don't know each*

[1] The Drug Story which was read to Monte while he looked at the TAT card was: "A pusher has his supply of heroin ready. He is waiting for an addict to pick up the drug." The quote in the text is Monte's response to both the card and the drug story.

other and that's why they are at an outdoor meeting place. The drawing looks like it's old. Looks like a street light and it's foggy. He is waiting on a lonely street. He can spot the guy from anyone else. He is waiting and waiting and waiting. The customer doesn't show up. It's a casual deal. The guy just goes by him and nobody comes up to buy the stuff, so he is left with it. The pusher doesn't have too many smarts, meeting a person he doesn't know out in the open like that. [*And what does the pusher think?*] *Only that there's foul weather. He wants to get this deal over with and wants to get out.* [*What does he think about the other guy?*] *Bad vibes. What the hell is he? The bastard doesn't show up. He doesn't let this feeling linger. He has his freedom and the stuff. He is pissed off because he is waiting in a bad area.* [*The outcome?*] *He'll do it again in another time and place.*

Summary

What we learn about Mary, George, and Monte warns us of the risk inherent in accepting labels and typologies—such as "drug peddler" —without close examination of behavior. While trite, it is nevertheless true that people are incredibly complex creatures. Our scrutinizing these three people points to the conclusion that dealing is an ill-defined form of behavior; as a description it is likely to be misleading if it has connotations that go beyond the simple fact that an illicit exchange of drugs has taken place.

Recall now our cases. Mary, whose "personality glue" is the strongest of the three, made her first and only sale when external pressure momentarily lowered her resistance. George shows how a male adolescent in the struggle to overcome confusion and turmoil may assert himself against society's drug code when a crumbling family structure places him at the mercy of constant, powerful peer influences and a dependent, sick mother. Our confirmed but casual dealer, Monte, became involved in pushing dope as an adult. Beginning with a desire for excitement and adventure in an otherwise conventional life, he continued his part-time dealing when he found it provided an easy, comfortable means of making money that was quite consistent with and even increased his neurotically tight relationships with people. Not facing the glaring discrepancy between his self-picture as a "conservative conventional person, like everybody else" and his real self, including his illicit activity, he nevertheless harbors a deep-seated feeling that when he disagrees with others he is above the norms and rules which apply to them.

The most powerful techniques to prevent illicit dealing are the standards set by society, which are taken over—built into—the individual from an early age in the pattern of child rearing. These techniques have been most successful with Mary, primarily because she has had the strong even if conflictual support of a mother who, in spite of a broken marriage, did not allow a psychological vacuum to develop. Mary's own talents and intense desires to better her life are, equally, assets.

The helping agencies—government or private—interposed between the needy individual and society could not provide the necessary constant and close support required to buoy up George, who most needed outside assistance in lieu of weak family support. As a result of his inability to handle a momentary problem—lack of money for gifts at Christmas time—he reverted to the street, where he was caught selling drugs to an acquaintance who had become a police informer.

Monte presents the most difficult problem—both for those who advocate prevention and those who espouse increased law-enforcement pressure to curb dealing. Fear of detection and arrest disturbs him, but his whole life style is consistent with containing and rationalizing his feelings without altering his behavior. He points to the suspiciousness and paranoia found throughout the illicit-drug scene but is not aware of the fear and alienation inside himself which are part of his dealing, since these reactive feelings fit into his basic style.

In none of our cases was a direct drug effect responsible for dealing, nor was any search for relief from symptoms caused by the absence of drugs involved in their continuing practice. If we distinguish between situational motivations and more enduring strategies of adjustment, we find a vast range of immediate motivations present. Money, excitement, a desire to impress or please, protest, intrigue, power, sex, or ego—any of the interpersonal games that express or symbolize the engines of man are found in the hearts and minds of dealers. The modern plagues of our land—poverty, racism, unemployment, crises of ecology—make all of us more vulnerable to pathology; yet these disorders of the entire social system must touch the individual in personal ways to carry their impact. As unelaborated "causes" of individual behavior, they are totally insufficient.

For both George and Monte, we find nothing distinctive in their personalities or backgrounds that sets them apart from other persons who perform comparable acts of delinquency. Given a different time and other surroundings, they might well be involved in other illegal or socially disapproved activities. The current lack of agreement on social policy concerning the possession of drugs for personal use contributes to the climate in which many Montes and Georges grow up and live today. And it must be remembered that the subculture in which these persons live provides approval of their activities, even if the larger society does not.

Our brief excursion into the lives of three dealers who periodically get high from drugs points up the fact that neither they nor society ultimately holds a trump card. For dealers who go undetected, like Monte, the suspicion, fear, and self-imposed loss of freedom may over a period of time lead to rigidity, estrangement from people, and paranoia. For those who do not elude the law, the ponderous intervention of the system for the administration of justice takes over with its high social costs and likely emotional ones to the individual.

Study of the lives of dealers highlights the need for prevention of illicit dealing by nonpunitive means, in addition to current use of threats of arrests and incarceration. To instruct or otherwise counsel individuals as to the unrecognized costs arising from dealing may assist those involved in it—especially ones capable of making rational decisions—to abandon conduct which, however immediately gratifying, carries risks which outweigh the gains.

Chapter 6

COMMENTARY ON DEALERS

In this chapter we consider some of the implications which may be drawn from the data in the preceding chapters. The intention is not to identify major conclusions at this stage or to note, much less underline, all findings which are important. Rather we dwell on possibilities which suggest themselves but which might otherwise be overlooked.

Preference Patterns

In the first place we derive from the drug histories in Chapter One a major developmental pattern. We see a rise in the proportion of dealers using (any) drugs through the teen years and early twenties followed by a decline in the prevalence of use—that is, by increased abstinence on the part of former users—from age 26 on. The degree of abstinence with increasing age varies according to drugs but is constant for groups of drugs. Over time there is a consistent falling off, measured by abstinence on the part of one fourth of the sample, for alcohol, tranquilizers, amphetamines, hallucinogens, and cocaine. The least reduction occurs for tobacco, the opiates, and cannabis. Midway are the sedatives, the use of which is abandoned by about one fifth of the older dealers.

As for the frequency of use (incidence), three developmental patterns suggest themselves. The most common one is that an increasing proportion of those who use certain drugs (alcohol, tranquilizers, opiates, cocaine, and to a lesser degree tobacco) use them more often. A second pattern (which can be applied to sedatives and amphetamines) is of a plateau; the proportion of heavy users among all users appears stabilized. A third picture is of a decline in intensity of use with age, as occurs with cannabis and the hallucinogens. These patterns are tentatively set forth here, for, given the youth of our sample (only 5 per cent are over 35), insufficient data exist for characterizing middle-age drug-use changes, and, in some cases, the shifts in incidence are but slight.

The change in prevalence of use noted for all drugs, rise-peak-decline, suggests that some dealers reduce their use of at least some—if not all—illicit drugs as they grow older. Since our dealer sample includes those who have quit dealing as well as those still active, we wonder whether there may not be a three-way association among growing older, becoming more abstinent, and giving up drug dealing. Analysis of data presented later shows a significant difference in dealers' ages, with the more active concentrated in the 19 to 25 group, and a trend for the older men and women in the sample to have given up dealing. Thus, our expectation is supported and deserves later consideration.

A second development is that of increasingly or chronically intensive use among some dealers who continue to use one or several psychoactive drugs. What label best describes this most often increasing incidence of heavy use for some dealers is uncertain. One may speak of involvement in the drug life or centering on drugs; one may argue for increasing tolerance, which requires heavier doses; or one may invoke the terms *dependence* or *addiction.*

If we consider the index of favorite drugs, the construction of which embraced measures of prevalence and incidence and gave weight to large increases in intensity of use over time and to the absence of abstinence over time, we see that the all-time hit drugs for our sample were tobacco, cannabis, and the opiates. Second ranked were tranquilizers, alcohol, cocaine, hallucinogens, amphetamines, and sedatives. Least in demand were the special substances. These preferences certainly do not conform to any current pharmacological classification scheme. That fact should not however lead us to ignore a different classification which may tentatively be entitled one of enduring (or compelling) attractiveness for youth. Such a concept is independent of any requirement of consistency of probable drug effect or of consistency in ease of access, legality, manner of administration, and the like. Given our limited data and the arbitrariness of the components in our index of favorites, we do not argue that tobacco, cannabis, and the opiates (heroin primarily) are demonstrably those which have the greatest enduring attraction for youth. We do propose that one might entertain this index finding as a device for predicting which drugs those youth heavily involved in illicit use will most likely want to continue using and which, consequently, there may be greatest resistance to abandoning if measures either for control or persuasion are employed for intervention. Given our current experience with tobacco smoking among the young, the growth in cannabis use rates, and the reluctance of heroin users to change their brand, there may be something to this claim. Obviously the inference from the index about compelling attractiveness is not in harmony with current use patterns of alcohol, which nationally clearly remains our most prevalent drug of "abuse" defined in terms of the number of people suffering visible drug-related problems.

Dealing as a Personal Adjustment Solution

Throughout the interviews our dealers spoke of the social settings in which their drug use began and continued. They spoke of the importance of being together, rapping with one another, and turning on together. What they said is compatible with what one has learned elsewhere of drug use as a social activity. Yet we must offer a reservation based on an unobtrusive item: the statement by the great majority of dealers that their favorite nondrug leisure activities are solitary ones. This statement is supplemented by a minority report of a fourth that in school they were isolates or loners and the claim by one third that they now have no friends or very few. It is further supplemented by the fact that not only are 87 per cent of our sample not married and living with a spouse (with 80 per cent of that sample being between 19 and 35, and the California figures showing that 42 per cent of young people between 18 and 24 are married as are 88 per cent between 24 and 35) but half are not at all sure they ever wish to settle down to such stable relationships. Our reservation is that this sample of dealers must contain a large proportion of individuals who, like Monte of the case history, are at least introverted, possibly shy, and perhaps awkward or maladapted in establishing and maintaining relationships with others, certainly those requiring enduring sexual ties.

In contrast, we accept their own reports about the large number of people they know and deal with and the social context and interpersonal gratifications of dealing; and we accept the interviewer ratings suggesting that most dealers are at least superficially friendly and at ease. What is to be made of the contradiction? Might it be that the age-old use of drugs for their major purpose—the pleasurable facilitation of social relations (see Blum and associates, 1969a)—is especially important to people in our sample simply because without that boost they might not enjoy such relationships? Whether the speculation is in terms of euphoria, dampened anxiety, the release of inhibition, a set of shared expectations that chemical grease on the ways will ease the ship of sociability, or these together and more, possibly for dealers the heavy involvement in drugs is a means to enjoy with others experiences which they would not have without drugs.

This possibility raises others. Might it be that the evolution into the dealer role not only reflects an evolving adjustment to drug-using needs (continued access, supplies in case of tolerance, money to make buys) but constitutes simultaneously a special solution for these young people for several other problems? Dealing solves an economic dilemma. One can make good money without a good education and without having to engage in straight work, which does not appeal. Moreover, in spite of one's own appraisals of oneself as fit for such work if it is wanted, one may not be so fit from the standpoint of an employer. If dealers are, as the interviewers suspected, unbusinesslike and of uncertain reliability, if their work does involve a great deal of chatting, giving away of produce, and being high on the job, they are not cut out for diligent, circumspect, and nose-to-the-grindstone enterprises. "They" of course remains a speculative "some" or "many," never all this variegated group.

Might not dealing do more? Might it solve, temporarily, the problem of finding a role in life, an identification (a much overused term), or something to build a day around? Preble and Casey (1969) argue well that heroin use among slum dwellers in New York City—including their hustle of buying, selling, and using—provides "a motivation and rationale for the pursuit of a meaningful life, albeit a socially deviant one. The activities these individuals engage in and the relationships they have in the course of their quest for heroin are far more important than the minimal analegesic and euphoric effects of the small amount of heroin available to them. If they can be said to be addicted, it is not so much to heroin as to the entire career of the heroin user." Preble and Casey quote one 15-year heroin user: "Drugs is a hell of a game; it gives you a million things to talk about."

Perhaps for our otherwise possibly searching, shy, and uncertain souls (many of them preoccupied with their adjustment, their inner states, and "finding themselves") to be a dealer is to be one of the few things that fits: one's kindness expressed in generous drug giving; one's leadership seen in turning on new faces to new light; one's prowess seen in access to sex and admiration; one's power felt, if the need arises, as one plays with the vulnerability of the drug needy who come, dependent, seeking supplies; one's capabilities and prestige confirmed by that proof of success, the dollar; one's dependence on others (when there is such) mercifully put aside in the knowledge that one is not dependent as long as one has a fine supply; and one's uncertainty about what to do or how to do it put on the back burner of the mind as one busies oneself with each day's activities.

For some, in addition, dealing supplies the adventure and risk-taking they seek, the flouting of law that self-proof and perhaps some early infantile rage at restraint demand, and a raft of confederates who agree that delinquency is not immoral, that crime is not criminal, and that the natural law of one's peers supersedes the positive law of one's larger community. For some whose flattering self-portrayals are sheerest balderdash, dealing is also an opportunity to exploit and be aggressive: to carry a gun, to rob, to cheat, and sometimes to kill. Is this not violent pie to set before the would-be delinquent king? Do keep in mind that this group had quite a set—an average of four per dealer—of nondrug arrests, of which assaults ranked second. Add to that the unprosecuted homicides plus two official ones—acknowledged to interviewers—and one detects anger and destructiveness in the social-psychodynamic picture. Interviewers noted such tendencies among 5 per cent of the sample.

We propose that being a dealer satisfies one more important urge in that complex person—or the complex composite—being presented here. Consider how much like the rest of us the dealer is, how he values American virtues, how reasonable his policy proposals are, how surprisingly conservative he can be, and how fair an appraisal he can make of the consequences of drug use or the dealing life. Consider how he seeks social and career goals common not to the radical revolutionary or the bombed-out acid freak, but to the ordinary businessman. Keep in mind the values and practices of getting ahead; being intelligent, honest, reliable, friendly; offering a good product; giving money-back guarantees; and so on. Think how fiercely independently the business is done—not being part of any large and suspect corporation—how the dealer sets prices in best free-enterprise style according to what the market will stand or what the merchant's association agrees upon as a fixed price, giving preferential treatment to good customers, disdaining the dangerous expansion of credit, keeping profit without bowing to that monster federalist intervention the income tax, and turning to the government only for regulation not coercion. Is this not the platform of a small-town Chamber of Commerce or a conservative political group? Add to those views the flavor of the western frontier—

each man unto himself defending his homestead (plus his stash of grass), hoping to strike it rich in the lawless land—and one has the drug dealer in heroic posture. To be a dealer, then, is to be a frontier American laissez-faire entrepreneur with the values of that vanishing species. Whether the dealer is this stereotype in fact, or at least a reasonable facsimile, or whether the image is chimerical, an American myth which he is acting out, is another matter. Clearly dealing is a form of business which, done (mostly) by the young, for the young, and to the young, allows those who do not fit into regular molds to feel virtuous and to move toward a kind of respectability through irregular channels.

That dealers are not fit for regular channels may be noticeable early, not in their drug use, which is common enough, but in that curious pattern of running away even from the things they liked—or say they liked. Here are included both families, with whom they claim they got on well, and school, which most of them claim they liked. That latter liking, although it decreased with age (which we presume represented increasing dissatisfaction with educational institutions), was still a general feeling, yet it did not suffice to keep them from either being truant or dropping out. Similarly, parental relations were mostly good ones just as feelings toward brothers and sisters were positive; yet the dealers moved out into the drug scene, against what was likely to be parental desire. (Recall that most say their behavior hurt their families. Certainly dealing is a far cry from what ordinary families cherish for their children.)

Since in giving their reasons for drug use, or those ascribed to others, they do not condemn either schools or parents, a further puzzle is posed as one wonders then how it was that families and schools failed to attract and hold them. Except for the psychological case studies of George, Mary, and Monte, our interview material in this part provides no in-depth evaluations of the dealers or direct observations of their families. (For a study of the family etiology of drug-risk behavior see Blum and associates, 1972.) It is clear from George, Mary, and Monte and from our family studies that drug involvement does rest on developmental and psychodynamic processes and events. Thus the failure of families and school to attract and hold can be understood only in terms of the larger context of the relationships between the child and his parents and between him and the school.

Yet one developmental feature is worth proposing. We believe it may be stated as the capture of the youth by the peer culture when the family ceases to exercise the affection and control necessary for maintaining the child integrally within the family bosom. To a lesser extent the same may be said of schools or, more exactly, of teachers. If as institutions, both family and school become so weak, so uncompelling (a nucleus without charge by which to attract and hold its particles) that neither commands nor generates attraction or duty, then why should children not drift off to the semiautonomous culture (or nonculture) of peers, an environment studded with attractions, few of which make demands on the superego or even ego? An alternative guess is that the reasonably cool picture presented by dealers of relations with teachers, parents, and siblings (with notable exceptions) was a denial of hotter feelings. Were that so one could posit various psychological stresses within family and within child which, although operating to lead to his estrangement from conventional institutions and from affectionate parental relationships, were, like much else in the dealer's life may be, unacknowledged. Such speculations are supported by work such as that of Keniston (1960) and Eva Maria Blum (in Blum and associates, 1969b).

Dealing as Career Development

Drug dealing has partial origins in social activities among peers—activities involving illicit drugs and centering initially on desires to share an experience, to consolidate friendships, and to prove one's importance (implying that the drug-dealing role is an important one among the using community). These activities occur in situations which are, for the most part, outside parental control, for the parties where so much dealing begins occur in homes other than those of the dealers. We guess that no parents are present at the time. Getting acquainted with dealers, which we take to be essential for later dealing, begins easily and early in these drug-using social circumstances, for the first dealers met are already friends or acquaintances, not strangers. The first drugs taken are gifts or shared pleasures rather than purchases; and later, when buying begins, prices are low.

The process of becoming an illicit user and then a dealer does not occur in an emotional vacuum. Although initial and later approval of dealers met was the mode, some of our sample do admit to an initial moral disapproval, one partly but never completely attenuated over time. The emotional mix on the critical occasions—first illicit use, first distribution, and first sale—was heavily positive. Our then young dealers were enjoying conviviality as well as (probably pharmacological) euphoria, and we infer that their friends affirmed the goodness of drugs and their sharing. Even so, we take it that the venture as perceived by the doer is partly perilous, for the majority were nervous and excited before their first buy. However, that phase passes; only a third of those nervous when buying initially were in that state when first distributing, and half of them were calm by the time they initiated selling for profit. Simultaneously and expectedly, matter-of-factness increased, although slowly and never in the majority. We thus conclude that through the early stages, including the commercial ones, dealing has emotional gratifications for most as well as emotional drawbacks (guilt, worry) for some.

Dealers link initial drug use, as well as the mastery of the illicit and whatever it all symbolizes psychodynamically, to a reduction of nervousness and an increase in euphoria. This observation is by no means surprising in view of the probable pharmacological effects of the drugs in use, but we note it here as part of the sequence of events which dealers themselves recall from the before and after pictures in their minds; this recollection does suggest a series of gratifying (positively reinforcing) events which may serve both suppressive functions (nervousness and guilt reduced) and pleasure-giving ones. We do note the marked reduction in being high, however, which indicates the shift from sociability to commerce. As the economic motive is introduced, the era of good feeling, specifically intoxicated good feeling, is abolished as part of the immediate aura of the supply transaction. Likewise, rationalism (or at least procedural concerns) is introduced because of the need to protect against arrest.

Another shift is reduction in the immediate prominence of the dealer's social and emotional needs as a trigger for supplying as he moves from the sharing or give-away to the profit stage. Once our dealer had supplied drugs freely and enjoyed that, he also became known as a source. As such he was approached by others in those settings where he had already played the supplier role. By this time our dealer had come to a decision which was at least partly economic, so that when the desires of others could be turned to money-making advantage the budding dealer did so; at the same time, he was able to play the part of the supplier, which he had initiated early without profit —presumably gaining the same social and emotional gratifications as before from that position. The budding dealer, then, enjoys a situation in which he may have his cake and eat it too.

For such individuals the prospects appear so compellingly attractive that even though many hypothesized events might have prevented their commitment to dealing, almost none suggested a sense of internal restraint or counterforce. Thus, if external authority had stopped them through arrest, teaching them early what many of them learned late, they believe they would not have continued dealing.

Similarly, if someone had come along with money but had not required labor, some would not have gone on to deal further. Indeed, less than 5 per cent of the total discussing prevention and intervention came up with any hypothetical conditions which involved their own activity or self-restraint. All other proposals were passive—that is, if drugs were legal, if there were no drugs available, if their suppliers were all caught, if they were stony broke and so could not buy drugs, then they would not have gone on. These orientations reflect what might variously be called a high demand quality, an approach-approach situation, a compulsion, a passivity, or simply a lack of awareness of any pleasing alternatives once the then young dealer had experienced both the satisfactions of drug use and of the role of the supplier and the economic advantages to be derived.

This developmental process is a remarkably speedy one, considering the theoretical constraints which ought to be operating in young people from largely middle-class families, having mostly non-delinquent and non-drug-using siblings, and knowing both the illegality of and the risk of arrest associated with dealing. Consider that the majority began to use and began to supply within the same three-year bracket, ages 15 to 18. There is a lag, to be sure, since the sequence goes in steps; 16 per cent who had started using by age 18 had not started supplying until some time between ages 19 and 23, and 22 per cent of these 18-and-under users did not sell until ages 19 to 23.

This youthfulness and the middle-class origins of many dealers probably account for their informality and lack of professionalism (in the criminological sense). Ever since Sutherland (1937), sociological studies have emphasized the learning of criminal careers and the discrimination between professionals who know what they are doing—and how to get away with it—and various other groups of habitual, amateur, emotional, and other ne'er-do-well or sad-sack offenders. Professionalism implies tutelage, planning, skill, connections, and strong economic interests. Although some of our dealers do become professional, few start out that way. The consequences of such naïveté for some are thoroughly discussed by R. Smith (1971) in his study of speed dealers in San Francisco.

In spite of their lack of skills, our dealers appear to have gotten along rather easily in the early stages; at least most report no problems in the business—most likely because their drug use and trading took place in a familiar and friendly social environment. Such an environment, protected from pervasive law enforcement threats and no jungle in itself, did not reward carelessness or naïveté with disaster. The casualness of early dealing may also be linked to the general style of the California drug scene, which proclaims the value of relaxation and recreation (Goode, 1970) or of being easy, hanging loose, or staying cool (as opposed to being up tight, which implies anxious carefulness). Casualness can also be linked to personality components (remember our speculation about passivity) and to possible chronic drug reactions. With regard to the latter we must not forget that, by the early twenties, the majority of our dealers were heavy users of cannabis, and many intensively used hallucinogens, amphetamines, or opiates, or all three.

Dealing as Disharmony

Except for the older minorities at either end of the spectrum—those who have quit drugs and dealing for good and those who are fully committed to addiction or professional criminality or both (see Chapter Eight)—our dealers are, we believe, somewhat unsettled—that is, not of one mind, not in harmony with themselves and their environment. That imbalance is not apparent from their actions. However, when one listens to their reflections, observations, concerns, and plans—above all, perhaps, their hopes for their children—the evidence for doubts about the wisdom of their life course to date is compelling. To resolve these doubts, three major courses are open. One course is deeper immersion in drugs—the solution of Nepenthe. Another is movement into the straight life. The third course, imposed from the outside, consists of arrest, prison, disabling ill health, or, for some, death. Both arrest and ill health contain possibilities for change—either through treatment or spontaneous shifts in goals. The data, however, to date (see Blum and Blum, 1967; Blum, 1967) are only modestly encouraging for either of these.

When we saw them, the most salient experience among our dealers was their growing realization that people do get arrested and do go to jail. This realization was evidence of the overthrow of what may variously be called fantasies of infantile omnipotence, adolescent foolhardiness in believing they cannot suffer harm, or simply learning in the face of experience. Compared to the threat of arrest, all the other specific sources of expressed dissatisfaction with their lives were mild. Of course, this focus on arrest as a reason for felt apprehensions may be simply a convenient, understandable, acceptable—but in fact psychodynamically incorrect—hook on which to hang anxiety arising from inchoate, internally generated conflicts. We suspect, for example, that the very infrequent reporting of guilt (in Chapter Two) in association with early drug use and supplying does not square with the high levels of nervousness or excitement described on these same early occasions. A conflict of conscience may exist and does not disappear, even if denied, as one grows from teens to twenties, so that the emotional tax on dealing is chronic. Such a strain, augmented by other buffeting forces associated with learning one's way in the world, might well generate internal distress that would be, as is normal for most humans, blamed on (projected onto) external circumstances.

Our dealers have had some unpleasant experiences other than arrest or fear of arrest (38 per cent have never been arrested): ill health, personality change, disenchantment with the scene, fear, violence, growing criminality, addiction, and the like. Also, most have had some personal experience with "bad trips," and nearly half fear becoming—or believe that they have become—drug dependent. All these experiences have happened to them rather quickly. After all, the average dealer in the sample is now only in his early twenties, has been dealing for only a few years, and began his illicit use just a few years ago in his teens. These young people must have some difficulty in accepting all the unhappy external events and in coping with the frightening internal ones. Even if there is an ethic of being cool, which likely pervades what was told the interviewer, even if chronic drug use has itself blunted the sharp edges of distress, we believe that the painful components of living are sufficient to account for dealers' negative reactions to the life.

Yet ambivalence remains. Most of the dealers are still in the life; those out want to return; and many of those in deny that they are dissatisfied. That denial is, we believe, more than simply playing it cool for the interview. We suspect that it is linked to the remarkable lack of interest—on the part of nearly all our dealers— in alternatives. Consider, for example, that almost none of our dealers are attracted by straight jobs—not because they feel unfit for work in the straight world but because the straight world is not their cup of tea. When discussing the pressures to quit dealing, few mentioned pressures from within. Even the knowledge that their life involves risks to others whom they love (an admission made blandly, sadly, or hostilely depending on the person) is not any reason to want to quit. A few exceptions spoke of moral qualms which moved them to quit; others, in discussing their own dependence and inability to straighten out, implied—perhaps—a desire to clean up, but we cannot be sure.

As ambivalence has sharpened over the years, other less equivocal changes have taken place as well: less interest in and pleasure from others, greater wariness and suspiciousness of others, more emphasis on money and business, more preoccupation with one's own inner states, more dependence on drugs. In short, dealers have become more egotistical, paranoid, and obsessive; more self-centered, more work-oriented, and less easy-going and friendly. With the exception of drug use, are these not major characteristics which youngsters in the drug scene abhor among their establishment elders? Ironic if by a different path our friendly and well-intentioned dealers have come to the same fate. (For a provocative exposition of this development in a similar group, see John Weakland in Blum and associates, 1969a.)

Dealer as Businessman and Criminal

Our dealers are part of a much larger California group with whom they have social and business ties. This group contains thousands of users and a large but unknown number of regular dealers as well. Within it status hierarchies for dealers are functional in the sense that conduct or traits for which a dealer is commended or admired are, in part, those which make it easy and safe for others to do business with him. We noted in Chapter Three that some of the same conditions apply to the dealers' selection of customers; reliable, predictable, mature people are preferred. These functional virtues are not unique to dealers but are part of those of the larger society; so it is that men are admired for intelligence, friendliness, and generosity as well as reliability and the like. In being in business at all, in valuing success, in building organizations, and in being sociable while they are at it, we believe that dealers reflect the society of which they are a part. Thus, while deviant or different in various ways—and along a many-hued spectrum—they are also much the same as the rest of us in what they hold dear. Insofar as they place special emphasis on values held generally by modern youth—the goodness of pleasure, freedom, and relaxation—these dealers are likely closer to other youth than are their harder-working, pleasure-denying elders.

The fact that women do not participate as fully as men in the risks and profit of dealing too is a national, indeed nearly worldwide, phenomenon. Dealers seem no different from others in accounting for or justifying it. (We add here only that the suggestion of women's not being trusted, in the absence of evidence that women are either more paranoid than men or more dishonest in business, allows the suggestion that some of the paranoia attributed to women may be a projection of the distrust of the paranoid man.)

However busy and successful these young people are in selling drugs, the majority are amateurs not fully committed to the dealing life, not convinced that they are themselves real dealers (professionals), and sure that they are not criminals. Most are making money—good money, for many—but their dealing is not just business, even if the longer they stay in the more businesslike it becomes. That business is just an aspect of the scene itself, where the pleasures of drug use and socializing, of sharing drugs and experiences are paramount features. Indeed, one of the definitions of a professional (having one's primary interests allied with dealing) enters here; many of them do not have their primary interests so allied even if, by now, most are deeply immersed but, as we have said, ambivalently so.

Their lack of professionalism, or perhaps better put as their lack of a strict vocational role or trade identification, may be seen in their ideological stance vis-à-vis the police and the law. Other workers, whether plumbers or old-fashioned professional criminals, do not usually derogate the police as an immoral force. Most of these young people do. Young dealers do not accept being labeled as criminals. In the same way Goode's (1970) sample rejected society's judgment of their marijuana use as wrong because to them it was right. Our dealers explain that they are not criminals (even if they can be executed in two states for activities such as sales to minors) because drugs should be legal and because selling does not hurt anyone. Their lack of commitment in an active sense to a life of crime may be deduced from their expectations for themselves for five years hence; the majority look forward to some kind of honest activity, even if not in conventional ways. Most also look forward to their associates' going straight.

At this point two qualifications must be entered. One is the reminder that the sample is variegated, not homogeneous. There are professionals in it—professional dealers, professional criminals: full-time, money-making, tough, competent characters who have no illusions about their job classification as judged by society and about their future intentions. Whether we use the complexity of their business activities, their arrest or addiction history, the amount of money they earn, their age, or their statements of their intentions and their self-descriptions as professionals, from 10 to 20 per cent of this group are not part of an amorphous drug-powered fellowship but are at the hard end of the criminal spectrum.

The second qualification is a reminder not to believe everything we are told. Especially, young dealers ought not to believe what they tell themselves. We have earlier met in this sample the denial of guilt accompanied by what was at least a very odd nervousness over what one was doing. We have heard thoughtful and profound discussions by dealers themselves concerning the hazards of drug use and of the dealing life. The past was the golden age, the present is money. The past was flowers, the present is increasing violence. The past was childhood, the present is involvement to the point that almost none think of quitting the life for anything in the straight world. And tomorrow is more money as well as trying to assure oneself a supply of drugs because in many cases, one fears, one has to have them. It is only the day after tomorrow five years hence that "I will have a straight job, but in the meantime straight people are not for me." And in the meantime half our sample are making their only income from dealing, two thirds are becoming skilled and developing organization, and an unprofessional 40 per cent qualify as serious street dealers.

We affirm that most of these young people do not seek a criminal career in any purposeful way, that many would like to enjoy honest lives later on as a way out of the stress and strain which pervades dealing, and that most subscribe to the larger social values of honesty, peacefulness, trustworthiness, and the rest. They are transitional people or, in Erikson's (1950) sense, are enjoying an extended moratorium in the uncertain sanctuary of the youthful drug scene. Whether aging will bring with it another significant shift, opposite to that observed so far (which has carried them into more businesslike dealing and more intensive drug use), we cannot say. For some it clearly will, for our data show that some have become more abstinent and some have left dealing. For the others, given the course on which life's river has carried them so far, given the unattractiveness of any immediate goals in the straight world, given the satisfactions of their drug scene, and given the dubious resources of many to gain those same satisfactions in the rigorous world of the straights, one must wonder whether the dreams of a straight life will ever come true.

Voice of the Dealer

With regard to the policy recommendations made by dealers, those who imagine dealers to be bomb-throwing radicals, fanged monsters, or Martians will be surprised by the degree of compatibility between their drug policy proposals and those made by reputable and responsible citizens: continued government control of production, traffic, and consumption; increased education, research, and treatment; penalties (milder) for drugs, sales, or other conduct with demonstrable harmful effects; reduction of traffic in harmful substances or sales directed toward the child consumer. Indeed, one may see signs of public interest coming before self-interest in their recommendations, for some of those same dealers who ask for cannabis legalization expect that event to ruin their business. Some even call for stronger controls on drugs which they themselves employ—whether these be alcohol and tobacco or hallucinogens, opiates, or amphetamines. As for their general view, they express the need for more justice in the best tradition of a constitutional democracy and for alleviation overall of our criminal-law approach, which has made United States penalties often heavier than those in other Western lands without any increase in efficacy by way of either deterrence or prevention of recidivism; these and other proposals are neither radical nor unthoughtful. To be a deviant, in the sociological sense, does carry with it a host of correlations suggesting a certain generalizability of being different (Berg and Bass, 1961; Robins, 1966); but we should not overlook that, perhaps in most ways, even those who are very different are much like the rest of us after all.

Chapter 7

ARRESTED AND NONARRESTED DEALERS

*I*n this chapter we begin to present information based on comparisons of various groups found within the larger sample of 480 dealers. We had set out to assure diversity in that group, with an eye to comparing subgroups divided according to features that we considered important. We expected that such features would be keys to a whole set of differences, the identification of which would give us a better understanding of the different groups of dealers. These expectations proved to be correct. We found that when a diverse group of drug dealers are classified according to some important feature in their persons or dealing career, those in one class will differ in many ways from those in another. So it is that dealers who get arrested are different from those who do not. Furthermore, those who get arrested for only drug offenses differ from those who get arrested for nondrug offenses (but who may also have drug arrests as part of their record).

The basis for our comparisons were the replies to questions and the ratings which constitute the data for our 480 dealers. We ran two statistical tests for each set of comparisons. One is the test of differences between proportions. It tells us whether proportionately more dealers in category A gave a certain reply to a question or were rated in a particular way than dealers in category B. Since we used three classifications in every comparison, the statistical test indicates whether or not Group A differs from Group B and from Group C. It also tells us whether Group B differs from Group C. When the probability of the actual difference observed would have occurred by chance fewer than five times out of one hundred ($P = < .05$) or fewer than one time out of one hundred ($P = < .01$), our computer so noted. The other test which we ran was the F test. It does not compare one set of responses (that is, one code category) for Group A against B, and so forth, but rather examines the total distribution of replies for Group A to a given question; that is, it looks at all of the different answers given to that question and coded as separate and indicates whether there is improbable variation in overall distribution comparing Groups A, B, and C. That analysis was also set to identify the .05 and .01 levels. Significance here indicates that the groups differed on question or rating *in general* regardless of whether any subset of replies (any code category) comparing any two groups revealed a significant difference. This test contributes nothing to our understanding, but underlines the fact of differences in how the various dealer groups respond or are rated.

There were 576 questions put to the dealers, or ratings made on which replies were possible. This number is inflated over the actual replies given, since it includes a repeat set of questions for siblings up to the number six. Thus, dealers who had six siblings could reply, but those who did not have so many could not. The N of 576 for items does not refer to the number of actual tests for differences made, for a test was run on each type of reply as it was coded. For example, on the single item age, there were eight codes or possible entries: one for those who did not answer or where the interviewer failed to enter a response (we exclude these DK/NA codes for our summaries of statistical differences), and the remaining seven consisting of frequency classifications (namely, age under 12, age 12 through 15, age 16 through 18, age 19 through 23, age 24 through 35, age 36 through 49, and age 50 and over). For each item, appropriate codes reflecting the distribution of replies were set up; and in each case a statistical test, comparing the proportion in each group replying to that item, was run.

Given the fact that many hundreds of items had one or more significant differences in the comparison of replies or ratings coded therein, our presentation of the data necessarily required a considerable amount of boiling down. We inspected the items and noted those which (a) contained the largest number of significant differences and/or (b) contained the higher level of significance (.01 as compared to .05) and/or (c) occurred in an area worthy of discussion as a separate entity, rather than being a visible correlate to a larger set of differences that had already been presented. Thus, if we had already noted that Group A contained more opiate addicts, we would not repeat that observation in the many different contexts in which it could be made (drugs preferred, drugs carried, drugs sold, amount of opiates sold, biggest opiate deal, etc.). Notice that we have said "worthy" of discussion. This means that we exercised our judgment—and our interests and biases—in selecting items which contribute to our discussion of differences. Other items as significant, statistically, have gone unmentioned because they seemed less important for an understanding of the major characteristics of the groups being compared. It is possible that another person scanning the computer output would have selected these items for inclusion. Yet selection there must be, not only for the sake of developing a picture but simply because space does not allow analysis of every difference.

Nonarrested, Drug-Arrested, and Other-Arrested Dealers

There are 180 nonarrested dealers, 57 with drug arrests only, and 235 with arrests for offenses other than drugs. Among those 235 experiencing nondrug arrests, 139 (60 per cent) have also had drug arrests. These are self-reports, not rap sheet counts.

On the 576 inquiry items there were 231 where significant differences in replies or ratings occurred between drug dealers who had never been arrested and dealers who had been arrested only for a narcotics offense (possession, selling, conspiracy to sell, and the like). There were 400 significant differences between the nonarrested dealers and those dealers who had experienced arrests for nondrug offenses (covering the gamut from homicide to sit-ins). Sixty-six per cent were major offenses including homicide, robbery, burglary, and aggravated assault. Thirty-one per cent were general delinquency including disorderly conduct, and vagrancy. Three per cent were minor offenses such as traffic offenses (other than alcohol related). Dealers arrested for nondrug offenses may also have had drug arrests. When dealers with only drug arrests are compared to dealers with arrests for other than narcotics-law violations, 271 significant differences are obtained. The F test results show 400 significant differences in the between-group comparisons of patterns of replies to the 576 items.

The foregoing findings are interpreted as demonstrating that nonarrested dealers differ in many ways from those arrested for drug offenses and from those arrested for nondrug offenses; that dealers arrested for nondrug offenses differ in many ways from those arrested only for narcotics-law violation; and that nonarrested dealers are more similar to those arrested for narcotics-law violation than to what seems a generally delinquent or criminal dealer group (indeed, the nonarrested and drug-arrest-only groups share many characteristics in common in contrast to the delinquent dealers). The criminal dealer, then, stands most apart from those dealers involved only in drug delinquencies (arrested or not).

Nonarrested vs. Other-Arrested Dealers

Let us compare the major characteristics of the nonarrested dealers and the criminal dealers. First of all, there is no age or race difference, but there is a sex and educational one. The criminal dealers are more often male, and they are less well educated than the nonarrested dealers. Criminal dealers are more often in frankly illicit occupations; nonarrested dealers, in professional, white-collar, or student positions. The latter are more often from intact homes, but are themselves single. Unskilled or blue-collar jobs, alcoholism, and criminal histories more often characterize the parents of the criminal group; so do larger families.

In their drug histories, the criminal group began heavy use of alcohol, tobacco, amphetamines, sedatives, opiates, cocaine, and special substances at an earlier age than the nonarrested group. As adults they also drink more; smoke more; and use more speed, barbiturates, tranquilizers, opiates, and cocaine. They do not differ consistently from the nonarrested group on marijuana and hallucinogens, except that the nonarrested group use marijuana more at early ages and the criminal group more in the teens and after 26 years of age. An earlier age for initial illicit use occurs for the criminal group, with amphetamines and opiates more often the first drug, compared to initial marijuana use by the nonarrested dealers. The criminal group began drug supplying earlier (under 15) and sold to younger customers (their young peers) and to strangers or to fellow inmates or patients in institutions. More dealers in the criminal group recall the moment of the first supplying and of the first sale (if these were different) as one making them feel important, "big time," or otherwise proud and prestigeful. At the same time, this group look down on their customers; in contrast, the nonarrested dealers, supplying more to friends, think well of their customers.

Early arrests for drug-law violations were experienced by the criminal group, as were other nondrug arrests. Also, this group has been dealing longer than the nonarrested group; for example, 29 per cent of the criminal group but only 12 per cent of the nonarrested dealers have been dealers for six years or more. At the time of interview, 45 per cent of the former group were not dealing, as compared to 18 per cent of the nonarrested dealers. Thirty-four per cent of the criminal group were in a correctional institution or on probation or parole at that time. Among those not dealing, significantly more of the nonarrested group were contemplating a return to drug pushing (68 per cent) than were the criminal group (52 per cent). Similarly, among those still dealing, more who had experienced nondrug arrests said they were thinking of quitting (73 per cent) than were dealers in the nonarrested group (63 per cent).

Fear of arrest or the past fact of arrest looms as a significant discriminator in the reasons offered for having quit or thinking about quitting the dealing life. The criminal dealers are more often dissatisfied with the dealing life; have been or are under pressure from families and others to quit; but continue (when they do continue) because of their need to support their drug habits or because they resent or are otherwise negatively affected by persuasion and coercion applied to get them to quit. Given their stated need to support their habit, from which we infer addiction, it is not surprising that more of this group are worried about their own drug use than are the nonarrested dealers (50 per cent to 30 per cent). The criminal group are more alert to undesirable changes they have seen in the dealing scene: violence, personality deterioration, and the like. It is, nevertheless, apparently more difficult for this group to quit dealing on their own than it is for the nonarrested dealers. It is, partly at least, a financial matter; more of the criminal group rely on dealing for their sole income.

Perhaps because of their longer dealing careers, the criminal dealers report more changes over time: a shift to the greater sale of amphetamines and opiates, increased volume and profit, increased travel, more businesslike arrangements, a shift to customers who are themselves confirmed users or diversified sales to all comers, increased concern with police informants, and the like. With regard to profits, it is the criminal group who report the highest profits during the peak of their (sometimes now defunct) careers; 22 per cent of them, compared with only 4 per cent of the nonarrested dealers, claim monthly net over $1,000. On the other hand, when figures for the prior year are gathered, one finds that only 15 per cent of the criminal dealers are still in the big money, whereas there has been no change in the proportion of nonarrested dealers in the higher income bracket.

In their current or most recent (prior to incarceration or retirement) dealing, criminal dealers serve customers who are more often male, addicts, comparatively older in age, black or Chicano, nonstudent, and themselves criminals. They have more customers—21 per cent claiming one hundred or more, compared to 6 per cent of the nonarrested group. The criminal dealers are more widely acquainted with other dealers; 15 per cent claim to have known more than five hundred other dealers in their lifetimes, whereas only 4 per cent of the nonarrested group so claim. In explaining the pleasures of dealing, the criminals more often include the manipulation or exploitation of others; they give away far less of their stock-in-trade; they have introduced larger numbers of novices to drug use; and they acknowledge more than do the nonarrested dealers that peddlers do often induce (that is, seduce) novices into taking drugs for the purposes of creating new customers. On the other hand, more of the criminals also claim never to have turned an innocent onto drugs. (The criminal dealers claim, in general, that dealers seduce the innocent, but compared to nonarrested dealers, the criminal dealers *personally* more often disclaim that they themselves have persuaded someone to take drugs who was not already interested in doing so.) The criminal group also contains more dealers who believe that business success requires the dealer to avoid certain drugs even if he would like to use them; opiates figure most strongly here, but cannabis is also mentioned. It is in the criminal group that one also gets frequent reports of a progression in use from marijuana to heroin.

The criminal dealers—more organized by far—spend more of their time in serious retail and wholesale activity, in the manufacture of drugs for retail and wholesale outlets, and in international traffic; they are more likely to act as agents for others and to provide muscle (protective services) and money. They more often have lawyers (after all, they have needed them) and quiet arrangements with the police, with the Mafia, and with straights. They are generally not hostile to the police; they respect federal narcotics-law-enforcement personnel but are critical of the competence of local and county narcotics enforcement.

Among the criminal group, those who have had drug arrests have had multiple ones, just as their nondrug offenses are multiple ones. Gun carrying and gun use are primarily found in the criminal group, but some of the unarrested dealers are also violent. The criminal group likewise is much more likely to engage in the theft of drugs. Furthermore, they are more often the people who consider themselves professional dealers and professional criminals; even so only a minority of the criminal group consider themselves "professionals." The criminal group report, in contrast to nonarrested dealers, getting more new dealers started in the trade and putting more competitors out of business. The criminal dealers less than nonarrested ones expect dealing colleagues to still be in business ten years from now; instead, they more often expect them to be in jail, dead, or in straight jobs or to have retired wealthy.

In their interests the criminal dealers, more than the nonarrested, enjoy sports and team activities, preferred vocational or physical education courses while in school, and are affiliated with traditional churches. In their personal feelings and status, members of the criminal group more often report poor relations with parents, worry over alcoholism, poor health, dislike of school, truancy, dropping out, few close friends, and enjoyment of gambling.

As for drugs and their own children, the criminal group are significantly more conventional, disallowing the use of illicit drugs and not wanting their children to be drug dealers. In their view of the drug laws, they call for more controls and they are less in favor of drug use in general and, specifically, use by children.

In their appearance they are more often dirty or casual, not well groomed, slowed or overactive rather than normally alert, and are described, more than nonarrested users, as ill at ease.

Nonarrested vs. Drug-Arrested Dealers

We have indicated that nonarrested dealers do not differ as much from drug-only-arrested dealers as both of these groups differ from the dealer arrested for other than drug offenses. This observation, coupled with the analysis of the content of differences, allows us to posit a middle-ground position for the drug-arrested dealer. He is more like the nonarrested dealer but is moving in the direction of (that is, also shares characteristics with) the criminal one. Let us highlight this briefly.

There are no important age or race differences; but the drug-arrested dealer, compared with the nonarrested one, is male, not a student, a former school truant and dropout, and comes from a family where the father does not hold a high-status position and where the parents have criminal histories. Drug-arrested dealers, compared with nonarrested dealers, have earlier alcohol use; earlier heavy tobacco use; and earlier amphetamine, sedative, marijuana, hallucinogen, and opiate use. Neither drug nor family histories, however, differ as remarkably between these groups as between the previously compared nonarrested and criminal groups.

First distribution and first sales were later for the nonarrested group. The drug-arrested dealers were, at the time of the interview, less likely to be dealing (46 per cent not dealing among arrested persons; 18 per cent among nonarrested ones). Only 10 per cent were in jail or under probation or parole supervision at the time. Of those who have quit, fewer (52 per cent) contemplate the resumption of dealing among the arrested group than the nonarrested group (68 per cent). There is no significant difference between the groups in the proportion still dealing who were, at the time of interview, thinking about quitting, although the trend is for more arrested dealers to consider getting out. The two groups do not differ significantly in the total time they have spent dealing, but again the trend is toward a longer time in dealing for the arrested group. More of the arrested group earn their full keep from dealing. They are earning more money than the nonarrested group, prefer to sell opiates, show less aversion to opiate dealers, and are more often engaged in wholesale trade and manufacturing.

As a group the majority of drug-arrested dealers have had only one drug arrest and one or no conviction. They more often carry a gun —but no more often use it—than the nonarrested group, and are less likely to file tax returns. They more often classify themselves as professional dealers but not as "criminals."

Drug-Arrested vs. Other-Arrested Dealers

The differences between these two groups are, as we have indicated, greater than between the nonarrested dealer and the drug-arrest-only dealer. The differences between the criminal group and the drug-arrest-only group are of the same general order—in the same direction and with the same substance—but of lesser magnitude than between nonarrested and criminal dealers.

"Psychedelic" vs. Criminal Dealers

There are two major groups within our sample who can be identified by their arrest histories. Both are familiar groups. One, our criminal group, tend to be from poorer origins, to have early histories of drug use and sales, to be heavily involved in nondrug offenses, and to be deep into the criminal subculture (if it may be called that). They are fairly conventional morally—in what they profess if not in what they do. These are simultaneously the successful dealers—measured by their business skill and income—and the failures—measured by their frequent arrests and incarceration, their lack of resources by way of skill or education, and their own personality problems as measured by drug dependency and reported parental relations. Dealing for them provides primarily personal gain, drugs, power, and money. All-round dealers, they are, nevertheless, much more in the hard-drug business (opiates, cocaine, and amphetamines) than involved with marijuana and hallucinogens. We infer that their lives are not joyful, their options narrow, and that they are much like many others who, sharing their traits, comprise the clientele of our nation's jails, prisons, and drug-treatment centers.

Since some of them are addicts, habitual offenders, and professional criminals, it is likely that the harsher forces in society have shaped their behavior. Given their school histories, their health and personality problems, their lack of vocational skills, we cannot assume that they have benefited much from the helping institutions, schools or medical care, or from straight employment. How have they responded to those tougher legal-penal experiences which they have had? Over half are out of business, including one third in prison or juvenile hall or on probation or parole; and three fourths of them (or rather of those who replied) indicate that they may quit dealing.

If all dealers do what they are now doing, we see that arrest interdicts dealing in slightly less than half the criminal sample. If all go on to do what they say they have considered doing in the future (or are not sure they will not do—whether quitting or resuming), about one third of the criminal dealers would remain in the dealing business. Were we to consider ours a fair sample of all criminal dealers with backgrounds and arrest histories like theirs, we would conclude that arrest does make a difference. It is an intervention which works; or, qualified more, it is an intervention which, in association with other life correlates, does lead to changes in conduct. It puts many dealers out of business temporarily, and the fear of it stays on the minds of those who continue to deal. On the other hand, law enforcement and resulting processes can be sure of keeping dealers out of business only as long as they stay in jail (and not always even then); for even the knowledge of likely future arrest, coupled with the experience of multiple past arrests, is not sufficient to keep one third of these diversified delinquents from heading back to those green but bitter pastures where they feed on kinky money, dangerous drugs, bad company, a life of crime, and related fodder. If we add a correction factor for fond hope and white lies, the figure staying in or returning to the dealing business among this criminal sample would be even higher. Given current recidivism rates in the nation, such a correction for pessimism is not out of place.

The second major group of dealers is comprised, to a large extent, of middle-class, educated, skilled individuals whose drug involvement—using and dealing—began later and remains more casual and social as opposed to businesslike and criminally organized. These dealers are mostly involved with the use and sale of marijuana and the hallucinogens; they believe that drugs are good things for themselves and their children, and they pit themselves emotionally and ideologically against the police and the current drug law, and sometimes against the middle and the right in politics. This group is not composed solely of hippies, radicals, or noncriminals; however, in comparison to criminal dealers, these (let us call them psychedelic) dealers are more conventional in what they do—avoiding violence, theft, and opiates, and affirming in practice the Christian ethic—and less conventional in what they say—renouncing church, drug-control laws, the police, middle-ground politics, ordinary views about the dangers of drugs, and what-have-you.

This psychedelic dealer group, like the criminal group, is heterogeneous; and those dealers within it who have had a drug arrest may be moving in a more criminal direction, even if their own backgrounds provide restraining features. The relative infrequency of arrest in the psychedelic dealer group as a whole can be attributed to a variety of features. First of all, because of shorter dealing histories, and because they generally deal with friends, avoid strangers and criminals, and stay in the more protected or insulated world of the campus or commune, they are less exposed to the penetration of police agents. Their middle-class background, often conventional dress, educational skills, and other assets may enable them to avoid detection as dealers as long as they remain in the "cover" of the straight world—working part time, being students, avoiding drug dependency. What can happen if psychedelic dealers do begin to move more drugs to more strangers for more profit is indicated by the presence of a first-arrest group within the psychedelic sample.

Comment and Summary

Dealers with histories of arrest for crimes other than drugs (but including drug offenses), dealers with only drug arrests, and dealers with no arrest history were compared. Each group differs in many ways from the other, but the nonarrested dealers and the drug-arrest-only dealers are most alike in contrast to the dealers experiencing arrests for other offenses. We have described the latter group as the criminal dealer. We have combined the two others, the nonarrested dealers and the drug-arrest-only ones, into the one descriptive category of the psychedelic dealer.

The criminal dealer is characterized by lower-class origins, poorer education, earlier and greater involvement in illicit drugs, later movement to more businesslike, organized, nonsociable drug dealing with higher profits and risks and with increased likelihood of opiate use and addiction. The psychedelic dealers, on the other hand, are more likely to be middle class, to be involved primarily with cannabis and the hallucinogens, to be more sociable in their dealings and to be less criminal in the sense of involvement in organized criminality. They are less likely to project an image as a professional dealer or criminal, less likely to be violent, to produce high profits, or to maintain businesslike approaches to dealing.

Paradoxically, the criminal dealers are more conventional in their stated morality—church, disapproval of drugs, acceptance of the police and the law—even though their conduct is clearly more threatening to the persons or property of others and they are themselves in greater trouble with the law, and drugs, and they suffer greater health, and (inferred) adjustment problems. The psychedelic dealers, on the other hand, present an ideological position which is more unconventional in terms of conduct norms—although their conduct itself is rarely as harmful to others or to themselves as is that of the criminal dealers.

Examining the impact of arrest, we find that unarrested dealers are more likely to be dealing—and to expect to continue to deal—than arrested dealers. Arrest—when it does occur—interdicts drug dealing at an equal rate among the criminal dealer group and the more middle-class psychedelic group. Evaluation of the impact of arrest must be considered in the light of arrest vulnerability and the set of life-style correlates thereto. The evidence is clear that not all drug dealers are equally liable to arrest. The effects of law enforcement are but short for some portion of the arrested dealers sample; for among those arrested or fearing future arrest are dealers who are still active. We interpret our data as showing that the impact of arrest, while striking, is also limited. Consequently, even the effective enforcement of the criminal law will not eliminate the phenomenon of illicit drug dealing.

Chapter 8

ACTIVE AND INACTIVE DEALERS

In this chapter we examine some of the characteristics of dealers who were dealing at the time of interview as opposed to those who had quit. We have already seen that dealer groups differentiated on the basis of an arrest record differ also in a variety of background, career, drug, delinquency, and personal variables. Among other significant differences, dealers with arrests were more likely to have quit dealing by the time of our interview with them. Disenchantment with the drug scene accounted for 23 per cent of the terminations, fear of arrest accounted for 70 per cent, addiction and physical danger accounted for 4 per cent, and those who retired after having made enough money accounted for 3 per cent. We expect that a corollary analysis, comparing dealers who have quit with those still in business, will show considerable overlap with the characteristics identified in the past—characteristics associated either with the general middle-class psychedelic pattern or with the multiple-offense lower-class criminal pattern.

A summary of the number of significant differences shows that for 287 of 576 inquiries those now dealing actively differ from those not dealing at all. Comparing those dealing actively with those dealing irregularly, we find 176 significant differences; comparing the irregular dealers with those who have terminated, we find 335 differences. Significant F tests number 416. So in many ways the regular dealer (N = 159), the irregular or sometimes dealer (N = 148), and the terminated (disenchantment, fear of arrest, etc.) dealer (N = 169) are different types of people.

To illustrate the differences, we note first that the regular dealers—compared with terminated dealers—are better educated (college graduates), have parents in the professions, have not engaged in bizarre or other criminal occupations, do not come from broken homes, do not have parents with a history of addiction or arrest, and do not have an early and heavy opiate-use history. So far, then, it appears that the terminated dealer comes from the more disadvantaged home, where both parents and child may share opiate use and general criminality.

The active dealer is more likely to have early and heavy hallucinogen use, to have begun other illicit-drug use later, and to have been "stoned" on the occasion of his first act of dealing. As a dealer he concentrates on cannabis and hallucinogen sales. He is unlike the terminated dealer in that the latter has, as a primary reason for expanding his dealing career, a need to get money to maintain his own habit. Interestingly, the terminated dealers have had less total time selling than the still active ones. This finding differs from the arrest-versus-nonarrest comparisons made in Chapter Seven, where increased dealing time was associated with increased arrest vulnerability. Here, then, is a discriminator of special importance; for it suggests that there is a group of well-educated middle-class nonaddicts who stay in the business for a long period of time without hazard of arrest. At the same time, these data reveal a sample of quick losers—early heroin users who are arrested shortly after they begin dealing. This is substantiated by data on dissatisfactions with the dealer's life; the terminated dealers but not the active ones speak of fear of arrest. The former also speak of their own addiction as salient in their lives. This addiction, we posit, accounts in part for the finding that the terminated dealers think it harder to quit dealing than those who are actively in the life. (It may be like cigarette addicts: only those who have tried to stop know how hard it is to do so.)

As is to be expected, the active dealers rely far less on legitimate sources for income than do terminated ones. On the other hand, a majority of the terminated dealers—as well as active ones—report that they do not now have straight jobs. Since less than one third of the terminated dealers are currently in prison, we must assume that welfare or illicit income from other than dealing brings in money to terminated dealers.

Active dealers report considerably greater pleasure from the drug-sharing, proselytizing, rapping activities in their dealing life. Consistent with this, and with their having been in the business longer, is the finding that active dealers have turned on many more people for the first time. Consistent too is the disfavor with which the active dealers view alcohol and opiates. Not surprisingly, the existence of progression from marijuana toward other drugs is reported by the terminated dealers, who have themselves gone this route; it is denied by the psychedelic dealers, who have not. A subsequent pessimism on the part of the terminated dealers is found; they are likely to deny that the use of psychoactive drugs gives any benefits, whereas the active psychedelic dealers claim that most people gain from drug use.

The terminated dealers have reason to be pessimistic on other accounts; for they are, of course, the arrest-prone ones, both for narcotics and other violations. On the other hand, one third of our active dealers have also had drug arrests (compared to two thirds of the terminated ones) but have not been deterred by the arrests. Multiple drug arrests are more common among the terminated dealers. The active dealers have also experienced nondrug arrests—indeed, more of these than drug ones; but again the prize for frequency of busts goes to the terminated dealers. Finally, the nonaddicted, relatively immune active dealers make the biggest money, at a rate of about nine to one. These dealers seem justified in the greater extent to which they refer to themselves as professionals, both dealers and criminals. No wonder that they expect still to be dealers five years hence. No wonder, too, that the terminated fellows—when asked about the best times for dealing—look to the past, the good old days before arrest and addiction. These same terminated dealers have a bad opinion of themselves. For all of these reasons one may think of the terminated dealers as including a large number of chronic losers.

For leisure activities, the active dealers prefer getting high and making love; the others prefer outdoor and team sports. The active fellows liked the humanities and arts in school, dislike Republican politicians, embrace atheism or agnosticism, and liked college—all in contrast to the terminated dealers. Moreover, active dealers are not interested in settling down to the conventional life and more readily would allow their children to use illicit drugs and to be dealers. The active dealers are more often rated by the interviewer as flamboyant, high-style, nonconventional dressers with long hair, and as friendly and domineering. Given all of this, let us call them more than active dealers; let us embrace them with an image: the cool-man-hip-on-the-big-dealer-trip. And for the terminated one, let us say he is the poor-man-sick-of-a-bum-drug-kick, the loser who has lost his ticket and his way.

The sometimes dealer differs from both the cool-man-hip and

the loser; indeed, in magnitude of difference, the sometimes dealer is more different from the terminated one than is the active dealer. We shall highlight some of the characteristics in telegraphic style. The sometimes dealer, compared with the active one, is

More often female

More often a moderate as opposed to a heavy pot smoker

Less likely to have tried a variety of opiates

Less likely to be a heavy hallucinogen user

More likely to have begun supplying drugs for fun and sociability

Less likely to have been apprenticed to a knowledgeable dealer

Less likely to rely on dealing for a source of income

Less likely to sell more drugs or make more profit now than when first beginning

Less likely to have changed suppliers or customers from the onset of dealing to the present

More likely to sell only to friends and to avoid strangers

More likely to sell to women as well as men

More likely to sell to casual users than confirmed heads

Less likely to know many dealers

Less likely to have introduced others to illicit drugs

Less likely to have observed people becoming hard-drug users

Less likely to be involved in wholesaling, regular retailing, manufacture, international traffic, or specialized or organized dealing activities

More likely to have stopped dealing because of an interruption in supplies (i.e., sources went dry)

Less likely to have opinions about narcs as people or to be able to estimate competence of law-enforcement agencies

Equally likely to have suffered drug or nondrug arrests

Less likely to commit nondrug offenses as part of living

Less likely to carry a gun or to have used one if carried

Less likely to be informed about informers and their characteristics

More likely to deal in marijuana by the lid or ounce

Less likely to consider self a professional dealer or a professional criminal

Less likely to expect to be dealing five years hence (expects instead to have a straight job)

Less likely to focus on drugs and sex as leisure-time preferences; more likely to enjoy solitary activities

Less likely to be worried about own alcoholism

More likely (if a female) to have a steady boyfriend

Less likely to be thrifty or to make investments

More likely to have a bad opinion of self

More likely to be rated as casual, clean, and well groomed and as not a good salesman

These statements summarize themselves; the sometimes dealer is involved in his (or her) drug scene, but dealing—even if regular by our definition—is not a central part of life. These casual dealers are not on the way up in the dealing world; nor are they, we would guess, on the way out via arrest, drug dependency, violence, or the like. They are likely to outgrow dealing if their own plans come true and if their own psychological limitations (which, we infer, include some lack of self-esteem and a need for drugs to induce conviviality) do not hinder them from developing more conventional life styles.

Although we have focused on the differences between the active and casual dealer, in most ways these dealers are not far apart; that is, in all the features of the psychedelic (which includes use of the amphetamines, and occasional hard drugs) life and in most of the views and activities associated with being a dealer, the two styles are closely linked. The typology which we have created here is only a convenience by which to separate positions on what is likely to be a continuum.

Let us now compare the casual dealer with the terminated man. Again we highlight. Compared with the terminated dealer, the casual dealer

Is better educated

Comes from a middle- or upper-class family

Comes from a smaller family

Has less early heavy alcohol and tobacco use

Has less heavy amphetamine experience

Has less opiate and cocaine experience

Began illicit-drug use later

Received less of a self-esteem boost from becoming a user

Began selling drugs at an older age

Believes that nothing could have intervened to prevent his movement into the dealing life

Has been dealing a longer time

Is not dissatisfied with the dealing life

Is not under pressure to give up dealing but also is not obliged to continue it in order to support a habit

Is not worried about his own drug use

Is not aware of the growth of violence in the scene

Is not aware of personality deterioration—or other disapproved changes—in fellow dealers

Is not aware of changes in social relations among dealers or in consequence of their being in the life

Would not find it hard to stop dealing

Earns more of his income from legitimate sources

Has not shown an increase in sales volume or profit from the time dealing began

Has not changed suppliers or customers from initial to current dealing and prefers to sell to friends and nonaddicts who are part of the drug scene

Does now sell and prefers to sell marijuana and hallucinogens and rejects amphetamines and opiates as stock-in-trade

Has hippie late-teen and early-twenty white customers who use for pleasure; does not have many customers

Has not observed progression from marijuana to hard drugs

Is more optimistic about the good effects of drugs and less pessimistic about frequency of bad outcomes

Is in favor of a "stoned" society

Deals at a lower level of organization and activity

Has had few arrests for drugs or other offenses

Is not acquainted with characteristics of narcs

Believes that he has not been identified by the police (informally) as a dealer

Thinks the drug scene is getting better, not worse

Prefers liberal Democratic candidates, atheism or agnosticism, and, in school, arts and humanities

Will allow illicit-drug use in his own children and will allow them to become dealers

The foregoing characteristics of casual dealers versus terminated ones provide but little additional information, given the earlier comparison of the active dealer with the terminated one. Both of the dealers who are primarily involved in the psychedelic scene differ from the loser addict; both have social advantages over him. Even so, it is well to bear in mind that the loser does not differ totally from cool-man-hip and the sometimes fellow or gal. All are or were in the drug life, and most in the delinquency "bag" as well.

Comment and Summary

Dividing dealers into three groups—the active, the casual, and the terminated—and comparing these groups with one another, we conclude that three separate constellations are identifiable. The first two bear close resemblance to the psychedelic dealer described in Chapter Seven. The terminated dealer overlaps with the arrested dealer, although there are some very important distinctions to be made between the arrest classifications and those presented here. The arrested lower-class or criminal dealer group, for example, would seem to include two subgroups: the short-time down-the-tubes dealer, described here as the loser; and, by inference the remainder who are those criminal dealers who do not terminate and who remain long in the dealing and criminal life.

Among our psychedelic user-dealers it is clear that there is a big difference between being a casual dealer—one who is in the scene for pleasure but probably not to stay and certainly not dealing to make money—and the active dealer, whom we call cool-man-hip-on-the-big-dealer-trip. This latter is the middle-class success story in youthful drug crime; for he is relatively immune to arrest, makes good money (not always, of course; for our typology obscures within-group differences for the sake of a conceptual scheme), is a businessman but still enjoys a degree of (self-centered) sociability—indeed, is a swinger for drugs and sex. And for all his hardening in learning criminal organization, in seeing ill effects of drugs, and all the rest, he remains a consistent optimist who expects to stay right where he is—swinging on top of the cannabis-hallucinogen heap.

Chapter 9

BIG DEALERS AND MAFIA DEALERS

In Chapter One we learned that some dealers make big money. We would expect these dealers to have much in common with our previously identified serious and successful dealers, the cool-man-hip and those residual members of the criminal dealer group who are not losers. Since, however, both of these groups were identified on the basis of criteria other than money (that is, on the basis of arrest histories and extent of dealing activity), the congruence is not perfect.

In order to learn about the big money, we have analyzed our data by dividing the sample of 480 into those who state that, for the year 1968 (or, if they had quit dealing, the last full year they had dealt), they averaged a monthly profit of less than \$100 (N = 117), a profit between \$100 and \$1,000 per month (N = 170), and a profit of over \$1,000 per month (N = 53). That criterion of monthly profit is only one of several possible ways of grouping; for, it will be recalled, as a consistency check we asked several times about income—and learned, as we had been warned, that inconsistencies do emerge in the direction of the expected exaggeration. In another question we asked for estimates of total profits from dealing. Had we classified our sample according to these responses, there would have been a different grouping; for example seven dealers in the other-than-big-money category estimated total profits of \$75,000 and over, and three dealers in our big-money group reported total profits under \$15,000 (but none under \$1,000). The association between monthly income in 1968 and this other total-profit estimate is, however, significant on six out of eight money brackets beyond the .01 level. Another grouping could have been based on the dollar amount (gross) of the biggest transaction. For example, three dealers not in the present big-money group reported single transactions of $50,000 and over. Indeed, the single biggest transaction, one where over $500,000 cash changed hands, was claimed by a dealer who was in the middle-money category in 1968. Eight of our 1968 big-money men reported that their biggest transactions were in the $100 to $999 range. Nevertheless, there is a significant association between being a big-money man and being at the extreme end of the distribution in reporting large single cash transactions. We believe that our sample is reasonably consistent in the various measures of income and that our big-money criterion, one of monthly profit over a year, is a reasonable basis for grouping.

In comparing the three groups, we find 313 significant differences out of 576 areas of inquiry and rating when the little-money dealers (less than $100 per month) are compared to middle-money men and women ($100 to $1,000). There are 257 significant differences when little-money men are compared to big-money dealers. There are 236 significant differences when middle-money and big-money dealers are contrasted. There are 387 significant F tests.

We shall, in this chapter, ignore the middle-money men and contrast the groups that are most different—little-money and big-money dealers. We begin by observing that there is no significant difference in the number in jail at the time of interview, although the trend is for big-money dealers to be in prison (19 per cent compared to 11 per cent). Overall, more big dealers were referred to us via official channels than were little ones.

There is a significant difference in arrest histories; more big-money dealers have suffered both drug and nondrug arrests; 27 per cent of the big dealers have never had a drug arrest (compared to 75 per cent of the little ones), and 34 per cent have never had a nondrug arrest (compared to 63 per cent of the little ones).

Fewer of the big dealers are students and professionals in their vocational roles, although no differences in actual educational level exist. One does find an interesting difference in cover jobs (the work a dealer pretends to do or may in fact do but which is not his major income source and which is used—by the big-money dealer—to provide an acceptable role). Big dealers more often are in the arts (musicians, painters, writers) than little ones. The little dealers, on the other hand, when asked what they would like to be, want to be in the arts. The big dealers more often are, then, where little dealers would dream of being in terms of "legitimate" vocational roles. Big dealers are also less often single but more often divorced, less often white, less often from upper-middle-class homes (defined by occupations of both parents). No significant differences exist, however, in the criminal or alcoholism histories of the parents. Indeed, more little than big dealers reported addiction in a parent. To this point, then, it may be said that big dealers are not drawn from the less educated or markedly lower-class groups; in this respect, they differ greatly from the losers and some others in the group of multiple-arrested, opiate-using, lower-class dealers described in earlier chapters.

In regard to drug-use histories, much greater use of tobacco, amphetamines (including intravenous), sedatives, tranquilizers, marijuana, hallucinogens, cocaine, and opiates is found in the big-dealer group. The majority are heavy users of marijuana and the opiates. There are also more big dealers worried about present alcoholism.

Big dealers get an earlier start in illicit use (often age 15 or younger), and when they meet their first dealer, approve of him and what he does. Little dealers, on the other hand, reported more nervousness and were upset in association with their first drug purchase. Big dealers got off to an early business start; for, more than little dealers, they reported that from the first they dealt to make money. They were also more impermeable to prevention, at least by their own accounts; for whereas the little dealers said that they would have stopped had someone close to them been arrested, the big ones said that their embarkation on the career could not have been prevented. That career was aided, for big dealers more than for small ones, by some friend.

In spite of the income, not all is joyful with the big money. Big dealers, not small ones, said they were considering quitting the trade; and big dealers, not small ones, were the most dissatisfied with the dealer's life. They were also under more pressure to quit; since they were older (usually in middle or late twenties, some in middle age) and often married, we can understand that the pressure to quit comes mostly from their wives—but also from parents. It was not just others who worry about them; they worried about themselves. Many more big dealers than small reported that physical injury and death were real risks of the trade; they saw these dangers as coming most often from their customers—their irrationality or criminality. Big dealers more than little ones are sensitive to negative changes that have occurred since they began their dealing—changes in the dealers themselves and in the social scene, including a growth of violence. All in all, we can see that, in spite of big money, there are reasons for big dealers to want to quit the life. But, as we learned earlier, those who are most in it find it hardest to get out, and so it is with the big dealers—mainly, of course, because dealing is profitable for them.

In their career evolution, big dealers—in contrast to little ones—experience important changes in the business itself; they can now control who their customers are—a very important step to assure safety and income. They now (or most recently) sell primarily to other dealers rather than to students and the like. Their volume, profits, and travel all have increased. The drugs they now sell are more often opiates and cocaine, and these are the preferred stock-in-trade. The reason is simple and unromantic; these are easier to handle, and they bring in more profit. The big dealers are more likely, in contrast to little ones, to refuse to handle cannabis and the hallucinogens, because these drugs are bulky and bring low profits. These big-money dealers stated they did not wish to sell to students, friends, or other personable folks; what they wanted in a customer was money, good credit, and maturity. Their customers tend to be older (average age, 24 to 35), whereas the little dealer handles the kids. Most of the big dealers' customers are male, regular users (including addicts), and more likely than those of the little dealer to be criminals (pimps, whores, burglars, hustlers, and what-have-you). The big dealer is less likely than the little dealer to believe that his customers use drugs for pleasure; more often he believes that his customers are escaping pain and/or reality and that they are paranoid, emotionally disturbed, suspicious, and selfish. Furthermore, the big dealer believes—in contrast to the little one—that drugs and the drug life can bring about paranoia, fear, and anxiety.

The big dealer, as a successful businessman, is immersed in the dealer community. In consequence, he knows many more dealers than does the little fellow. What makes the larger dealer a success is not friendliness and honesty but shrewdness and good business practice. It is not good business practice to spend time chatting with customers, to give drugs away, or to induce or seduce customers to take drugs (as little dealers tend to do). It is good practice (or is at least associated with being in the big money) to be a wholesaler or a manufacturer; to be in international or interstate traffic; to provide or buy protective services; to concern oneself with logistics, supply, and equipment; to offer or use specialized or professional services; to operate using cover; to ignore federal income tax returns; to keep a lawyer and bank funds for business use; to have working arrangements with the police and with straights; to carry and use a weapon; to steal drugs; to put other dealers out of business; to work in a systematic way that resembles the operation of a legitimate business; and to have ties with the Mafia.

The big dealers are most likely to be regular dealers—although most of them also stop periodically for cover or rest, to wait until the heat cools, to serve sentences (but no more so than little dealers), or because drying up of sources has interfered with their work (although the majority have never suffered such interference). The estimates of the market differ for big dealers compared to small; the big-money boys say that the action is found on the East Coast (a statement compatible with usual estimates of where most opiate-cocaine importation and consumption take place; the little boys prefer the West Coast) and that Mexico is the best place to buy. As would be expected, the majority of the big-money boys described themselves as professional dealers; although significantly more big dealers than little dealers also considered themselves professional criminals, most big-money dealers have not considered themselves professional criminals (only about one quarter do). Big dealers, compared to small, more often expect to be dealing five years hence or to have retired wealthy. Little dealers, on the other hand, expect to be students or to have legitimate jobs.

With regard to personal and interpersonal matters, the big dealers more than little ones reported poor relationships with their parents, truancy in school, few close friends, being a dropout, but also, as adults, more often enjoying a current and at least moderately stable heterosexual relationship. They are no more often in debt than little dealers but owe their creditors considerably more. Their standard of living is considerably higher than that of little dealers. The big dealers are more conservative if we use as a measure the lesser desire on their part for changes in the drug laws which would reduce punishments; indeed, big dealers support control of marijuana, tobacco, LSD, tranquilizers, and opiates. As far as the ratings are concerned, the greatest difference was that big-money men are often described as "good salesmen" in contrast to the little ones.

The Mafia

It will be recalled that the big-money dealers more often than others claim Mafia ties; indeed, almost one fourth of them say that they have had something to do with La Cosa Nostra. Yet, smaller dealers too say that they have had such ties. It is natural, in this age of concern with organized crime and with the Cosa Nostra in particular, that we would want to know more of these dealers claiming Mafia involvement.

Before venturing to the analysis, let us immediately disclaim competence in that folklore and mythology, or journalism and politics which constitute so much of Mafia commentary appearing these days.

For a body of testimony on the Mafia we refer the reader to some earlier data, Senate Hearings and old Federal Bureau of Narcotics reports (1963, 1964). For a more recent view we recommend the material in the reports of the President's Commission on Law Enforcement and the Administration of Justice—and, much better, a sparkling commentary and criticism contained in the *New York Review of Books* (September 1969).

Whether the Mafia, as conventionally described, exists as a force in California crime is still hotly debated. *Life* magazine (1969-1970), in its Mafia series, has said—with names, dates, and places—that the Mafia is involved in crime in California; *Look* magazine (September 1969) also has said so and has accused the mayor of San Francisco of being tied in. The mayor has vigorously denied the allegation and is involved in litigation with *Look* authors over that charge. We have asked the heads of various vice squads and police departments in California whether they believe that there is an active Mafia involvement in the Bay Area. Most have thought not, certainly not in drugs. On the other hand, one independent Bay Area Commission and one county's sheriff's department are not so sure and have inquiries under way into the Mafia in general in the Bay Area and into the Mafia in drugs in particular.

Given this uncertainty among law-enforcement personnel, as well as the disagreement among other observers, how are we to handle the fact that our big-money men say that, as part of their business operation, they do have Mafia ties? We could claim that they are simply ill-informed, having been sold a bill of goods by distant business associates, or that they are status seekers, exaggerating not just income but the bogey man as well. It is also possible that our dealers have converted the term "mafia" into a generic one, meaning any organized international trade in cocaine and opiates but no longer alluding to a Sicilian-American involvement. They may simply assume that anyone they meet who has an Italian (or Corsican) name is a Mafioso. It could also be that our dealers do have Mafia ties but that these ties are on the East Coast and abroad, where our dealers travel, buy, and sell and where the Mafia are said to be ensconced. Finally, the Mafia really may be operating in California, in the Bay Area, and in the drug business. We think any of these possibilities within the realm of reason.

Do the dealers—not only big dealers but middle and little ones as well—who claim Mafia ties differ in any significant ways from those who do not claim ties? Yes, they do. Excluding those not replying ($N = 14$), we found 337 significant differences in one or another coded reply to the 576 inquiry or rating areas between the 42 claiming Mafia involvement and the 424 denying it. There are 340 significant F tests.

We shall be brief in our data analysis, calling attention only to differences that seem surprising, given what we already know of the characteristics of big dealers and their greater stated Mafia association. First, we call attention to the fact that the total "Mafia" sample—compared to non-Mafia and, retrospectively, to the big dealers—tends to contain more individuals not now dealing actively, and worried about their own drug use. The "Mafia" dealers are least likely to feel that they will ever be forced out of business by law-enforcement crackdowns and are more likely to contend that the police, because of corruption, do not in fact intend to stop drug traffic. The "Mafia" dealers also have many more customers than others.

Even though they more often describe themselves as professionals, it is worthwhile noting that in absolute numbers only half of the "Mafia" sample consider themselves professional dealers and only one fourth consider themselves professional criminals. We note also that there are no differences between "Mafia" dealers and others on their own avowed religion or that of their parents (one might expect those Mafia themselves—if of Italian extraction—more often to be from Catholic families).

And that is it. None of the findings differ importantly from our earlier-identified group of big-money dealers, complemented in this analysis by the addition of a few smaller dealers whose characteristics might well be random ones and whose "Mafia" ties are indeed hard to believe. The lack of professional identification as dealers and criminals—common throughout our sample—and the particular lack of Catholicism make it seem unlikely that our self-styled "Mafia" associates are themselves old-fashioned Mafiosi, and we wonder whether the smaller dealers can be anything but misled or Braggadocio. The latter word is particularly appropriate since it is false Italian, being derived, after all, from the English.

We leave by the same door we went in and hope that some amongst our readers can shed more light than our data, our dealers, or we have—on the role of the Mafia in California drug dealing.

Comment and Summary

There is big money in drug peddling, but to earn it requires organization, tough business practice, and the taking of risks (which include arrest and violence). Also, heavy drug use—especially opiates and cannabis and possibly alcoholism—characterize big dealers more than little ones. For both drugs and money making, the big-money men (13 per cent *are* women) appear to have got off to an early and determined start, compared to those who earn but little. There are also signs of early personal maladjustment in family and in school; we interpret these as individually pathognomic rather than simply a general socioeconomic problem, since big dealers do not differ in major ways from the low-income dealers in social class or educational achievement. Unlike the earlier-encountered losers, the big dealers do not report as much addiction as such (whatever we may infer to the contrary from their heavy drug use), even though they do describe dangers in their lives as a consequence of being a dealer. As older men with family obligations, they are under pressure from their wives to quit dealing, but the lure of big money is a hard-to-beat attraction. The big-money man appears to be unromantic and not a drug idealogue; indeed, he tends to think that the drugs he sells—more often opiates and cocaine—do bad things to people and, with most other psychoactive substances, ought to be controlled by criminal law.

Arrest appears ineffective among these men in contrast to lesser dealers, for although three fourths had been arrested for narcotics offenses, only a minority consider quitting the business. The rest expect to stay on or retire early *and* rich.

The Mafia dealers tend to be more concerned about their own drug use and less concerned that they will ever be forced out of business by law-enforcement crackdowns than the non-Mafia dealers. They have many more customers than the non-Mafia dealers but only half consider themselves professional dealers and only a quarter consider themselves professional criminals. They are not easily categorized by religion (or the religion of their families). Otherwise, they resemble closely the non-Mafia dealers.

Chapter 10

PUSHERS

We have, in the past, had occasion to examine proselytizing in some detail (Blum and associates, 1964). In earlier chapters our population of dealers have described the gratifications from dealing. Now we shall see whether there is more to be learned about those pushers who have the most impact as far as the spread or diffusion of illicit-drug use is concerned—impact here defined as introducing the greatest number of heretofore nonusers to illicit drugs.

We have already presented some data on the motives and characteristics of these proselytizers, whom we shall refer to as "initiators." Most dealers, as we have seen, deny the accuracy of the popular belief that dealers, in order to create addicted customers, often purposely trick or seduce nonusers into becoming users; on the other hand, some —especially our so-called criminal dealers—do admit to this practice. Within the dealer group that we have characterized as criminal (lower-class, opiate-using, multiple delinquency), however, there are two subgroups: an experienced professional group who turn on many newcomers (more than psychedelic dealers in general do) and a group of noninitiators, who claim that they never turn on novices. These noninitiators bear close resemblance to the terminated dealers, whom we compared with active dealers. In that comparison, it will be recalled, an especially active group of initiators were those active dealers whom we called "cool-man-hip," whereas the terminated dealers in general were noninitiators.

Findings from these comparisons suggest that initiators can be predicted on the basis of their dealing style and history or on the basis of typologies (conceptual conveniences designed to label a cluster of characteristics that are shared, to a lesser or greater degree, by an identifiable portion of our sample). What we have learned so far indicates that there is a significant association between being an experienced serious dealer—whether in psychedelic or harder drugs—and being primarily responsible for the spread of drug use to new people. We do not here imply that the dealer is the sole cause; we know that drug use "spreads" because people are curious about and then come to enjoy or need drugs, because there is a social milieu in which that use is accepted and encouraged, and because there exist neither internal nor external barriers sufficient to prevent people from engaging in this conduct. Nevertheless, there is an immediate human instrument who transfers a drug from one place into the hands (or mouth, veins, nostrils) of the novice. The dealer is this instrument, although he comes in a variety of forms, including the form excluded from our sample—the nonregular nonprofit-making fellow who, evidenced in the work of Goode (1970) and Carey (1968), is simply a regular user trading drugs back and forth with other regular users.

In our sample of 480, we have 74 dealers who contend that they have never sold drugs to someone who was not already a user; 270 who state that they have introduced between one and nineteen people to their first illicit-drug experience; and 124 dealers who say that they have "turned on" twenty or more people. These groups form the basis for our comparisons. A summary of the frequency of statistically significant differences shows that the greatest differences are between the extreme groups; these differences occur in 325 out of 576 inquiry or rating areas. Between the affirmed noninitiators (none turned on) and the small-impact group (one to nineteen turned on), 313 differences occur which are significant beyond the $P = < .05$ level. Between the small-impact and the major initiators (twenty or more turned on), there are 236 differences. The 387 significant F tests affirm a difference in the distribution of ratings or replies between groups, as contrasted with within-group distributions. We shall limit our analysis here to a comparison of the extremes.

The initiator group, more than the noninitiator group, came into our sampling net via either police or prison referrals (the official criminal group) or via referrals from another dealer; that is, through serious business channels. The noninitiator dealers were introduced to our interviews via a social chain; that is, as part of friendship networks.

In comparison to the noninitiator dealers, the initiators are older, better educated, less often employed in straight jobs (but less often in bizarre or other criminal ones), single, and not black. Individual cases indicate that initiators—compared with noninitiators—have had less early exposure to alcohol and less heavy later alcohol use, less later-life tobacco use, more intravenous amphetamine use, more cannabis use, more hallucinogen use, less opiate and cocaine use, and less special-substance use. At the beginning of their dealing careers the initiators less often were involved with hard drugs, more often sold to make money and did so without qualms, were aware of risk of arrest, and expanded their business on their own initiative. They enjoyed the guidance of a more experienced dealer and were, at the time of interview, more likely to be those active dealers we examined in the preceding chapter. They are less likely, in comparison to the noninitiator dealers, to have considered quitting; they have been dealing for a longer period of time, state that they do not fear jail, and are not dissatisfied with the life of the dealer. Not worried about their own drug use or addiction and thoroughly committed to drugs and dealing, they make most of their income from illicit sources. Their dealing career has brought them increased profit over the years and increased business travel; and they have increasingly emphasized cannabis and hallucinogens, both for sale and personal preference, and avoided addicts and speed freaks as customers.

The initiators have had the younger customers and, at the time of interview, concentrated their sales in the late-teen and early-twenty group; most of their customers are white. Unlike the noninitiator group, whose customers are believed to seek escape, the initiators believe that their customers want enjoyment and excitement. The noninitiators are the more sensitive to paranoia and upset in their customers; the initiators extol the tranquility, sensitivity, openness, and nonconformity of theirs.

There are no differences in the number of customers, but the initiators know many more dealers than the noninitiators. The former speak of their enjoyment in turning people on. The initiators are far more optimistic about the effects of drugs on people than are the noninitiators; no wonder the initiators are in favor of a "stoned society" and the noninitiators are opposed. The initiators are also less businesslike, if nonbusiness is taken to include giving drugs away, spending time chatting, and selling at cost. On the other hand, the initiators are more often wholesalers, farmers, manufacturers, national and international traffickers, agents, bankers, and otherwise specialists in other than street trade. Even so, they have experienced more supply problems than the noninitiator street dealer—which suggests that they are not the best of businessmen. They are more emotionally involved in drug ideology, if their negative views of narcs and a variety of proposals for changes in drug laws are taken as measures.

The initiators have experienced fewer drug arrests (36 per cent vs. 63 per cent) but do not differ markedly from noninitiators in nondrug arrests. This is a paradox, since more nonarrested dealers than arrested dealers have turned on large numbers of novices. We conclude, after scrutinizing the data, that there is a trend toward lesser criminality (defined by nondrug arrests) among the initiators than among the noninitiators.

The initiators more often than noninitiators admit to breaking the law for the sheer pleasure of it. They also more readily describe themselves as professional dealers, but not as professional criminals. They have helped more new dealers get started than have the noninitiators. Also, the initiators describe their relations with parents as not good ones; and they seem not to have enjoyed elementary school or high school, sensed themselves as disliked by teachers, and were truant. While they claim many close friends, fewer of these are not users—compared to the friends claimed by noninitiators.

Comment and Summary

The comparison of dealers who claim never to have initiated novices into illicit use with those who claim they have frequently done so reveals that although there is overlap with the groups described earlier—the initiator having characteristics akin to the active (cool-man-hip) big dealer and the experienced criminal dealer—there are also important special features which set initiators apart. They are, primarily, psychedelic dealers whose careers and self-descriptions suggest special psychodynamic features.

There is an early verbalized history of family and school maladjustment, of social relations which depend upon drugs for their existence (not just their facilitation), and of "acting out" of rebellious sentiments (breaking the law for the fun of it). There is also, as part of what we might guess to be the "empty extrovert" syndrome (external socialibity with inner loneliness), a rather singular rationalization of drug selling from the beginning as a money-making enterprise—when, in fact, the history of the dealer suggests that psychological rather than economic needs are pushing him to push drugs, and his involvement in the drug scene is emotional and ideological. The initiator is optimistic about drugs for others and for himself, and he makes special efforts to draw others into his own drug world—not just by turning on novices but by recruiting new dealers as well.

It is well to distinguish the proselytizing dealer from the more serious active and criminal dealers; for among the initiators, dealing retains a strong social component and has not developed into as highly specialized, criminal, and successful a business—even though it contains these elements. Its evolution appears to be more horizontal, embracing more people, than vertical, an upward movement to hard business practice. It appears to be, at all times, a self-initiated development. We infer that the proselytizer has embarked on his dealing consciously; he is not simply swept along the stream of life to accidentally find himself in the role of the supplier.

The drug dealer who does not initiate others is rare, most like the criminal dealers, especially the losers in that group; he has comparatively little optimism about what drugs can do for himself or for others. He is as busy and successful—he makes as much money and has as many customers—as the proselytizer; but he does not involve himself with the young, with being sociable, or with drug ideology. For all of his involvement with opiates, crime, arrest, and the like, his compulsion—if it be that—is for drug ingestion and not for making the world over into one large drug scene. One can argue that the initiator acts to bring others into his world to relieve his own social distress. That is a speculative proposition, for one could also argue that the nonproselytizing dealer is far worse off, having never had dreams or enthusiasm, lacking the push to do anything but chemically assuage himself with private rather than social solace, and not enjoying the benefits of a supporting ideology.

Accompanying these characterizations and speculations, there must be the caution that there is no one classic proselytizer or pusher. There is variety within the group and at least two clear subgroups: one, part of the psychedelic scene; the other, part of the hard-drug scene (and the twain do meet). In the proselytizer we have detected few signs which support the myth of the purveyor who sets out to create drug slaves or to build his fortune on drug-wrecked minds and bodies. To the contrary, the dealer who initiates most believes he is doing a good thing for his clients and honors his clients with complimentary views of their persons and philosophies. It is the noninitiator who—himself perhaps bitter about what drugs do—abstains from introducing newcomers to them. Nevertheless, behind the generosity and chemically aided conviviality of the proselytizer do lie some strong needs which are not those based upon an objective diagnosis of what is best for his clients. We suspect that the heavy purveyor wishes to recast his world in shapes more like the molecule of delta 9-tetrahydrocannabinol or lysergic acid diethylamide-25, so that he can be more comfortable socially and psychologically and so that he may vent, in his action, some of his unresolved conflicts about discipline and authority. We suspect he is like the driven missionary who must have converts lest he himself lose faith.

Chapter 11

SINS OF THE FATHER

It is an agreeable proposition that, for the development of the child, parents do matter. In the body of folk wisdom and in findings from sociology, psychiatry, and related systems, there is always posited a correspondence between the position of the parents (viewed either in terms of socioeconomic or cultural conditions or psychodynamically) and that of the child. One of the best sets of discoveries along this line—and most depressing in its implications—is the work of Robins (1966), with its demonstration that the best predictors for childhood and adult generalized disorder (sociopathy)—ranging from poor work histories to drunkenness, mental hospitalization, and frequent arrest—are parental histories of alcoholism and of criminal arrest. These predictors function independently of social class, although both alcoholism and visible criminality are found to be concentrated in lower-class urban groups.

Parental drug habits in general are contagious, teachable, copied, or otherwise shown to be significantly associated with what drugs their offspring use, as our earlier work on correlates of young people's illicit use has shown (Blum and associates 1969b).

Given these facts—and data from Chapter One showing rates of reported alcoholism, addiction, and criminality for dealers' parents higher than would be expected from a normal population—it would seem valuable to compare those dealers whose parents reportedly have such histories with dealers who do not report such social and psychological disorders or difficulty in their parents.

That the two groups do differ is clear. However, the magnitude of difference, as measured by the number of inquiry areas for which significant differences obtain, is considerably less than for the comparisons in previous chapters. In 197 of 576 inquiry or rating areas, one or more significant differences obtain between coded responses or descriptions for the two samples. There are 383 significant F tests (including the "don't know" codes, which are excluded from the comparisons of coded items reflected in the 197/576).

Examining areas and items, we find that the 197 dealers whose mother or father (or both) has a history of any one or any combination of alcoholism, illicit-drug use, addiction, or criminal arrests (excluding traffic violations and "political" offenses such as sit-in arrests) differ from the 268 dealers not reporting such histories (fifteen "don't know" or "no reply" dealers excluded) in a variety of ways. Before describing these differences, we note that the parental package of being troubled and making trouble is strongly associated with being separated or being divorced. Thus, when we speak of dealers whose parents are in trouble with drugs and the law, we may also conclude that these parents are in trouble maritally.

The children of these troubled and trouble-making parents differ from dealers with more stable parents in that the former are less well educated and less often single (they also marry earlier and have higher rates of separation and divorce), and engage in early heavier use of alcohol, tobacco, amphetamine (including intravenous), sedatives, tranquilizers, marijuana, hallucinogens, opiates, and cocaine. Very much greater marijuana use from childhood through later years is apparent. Moreover, these dealers from troubled families, unlike those from stable families, often were first introduced to illicit-drug use by their own parents. The age for this "germinal" experience was considerably younger for the troubled-family dealers, some having been introduced as children and the majority before they were 15 years old.

These troubled-family dealers met drug dealers earlier in their lives—again, the majority before age 15 (much earlier for those whose parents were themselves drug dealers, as was sometimes the case). They also began supplying others earlier—nearly two thirds doing so by the age of 18. They less often recall feeling "guilty" as they began their dealing. At the time of interview they had—inevitably, given their earlier start and age match—been dealing longer than the others. They express more dissatisfaction with the dealing life and more often say that they have been under pressure to quit—the pressure emanating not from parents (as is true for other dealers) but from friends.

One aspect of unpleasantness in their lives as dealers is a fear of getting hurt. Again, the troubled-family dealers offer a reason not previously discriminating between dealer groups; in this case they are afraid of retaliation from other users or dealers because they, the troubled-family dealers, have been robbing, cheating, and otherwise exploiting these acquaintances. As far as career development is concerned, in this group one observes an odd shift—in comparison to dealers from stable families—from earlier opiates, which they prefer to use, to later use of sedatives and tranquilizers. In absolute numbers this shift of choice involves only a minority. There is no general profit increase for the troubled-family dealers, although a few do become significantly higher earners over time than do the stable-family dealers, more of the former than the latter reporting current (or, if they have terminated dealing, most recent) profits at over $5,000. The troubled-family dealers are more likely to be widely acquainted with other dealers and are less likely to supply students, especially college students. More often than stable-family dealers, troubled-family ones are engaged in full-time street dealing. They also more often manufacture and show partial specialization. More Mafia ties are reported by them. The troubled-family dealers are more likely to have experienced both narcotics and nondrug arrests (a minority report narcotics arrests; a majority report nondrug arrests) and to demean the personality of police officers. These dealers also more often report breaking laws for the fun of it. They are also more likely to carry and use weapons and not to file income tax returns. More often the troubled-family offspring considers himself a professional dealer and criminal; but even so, only a minority so identify themselves.

In their interpersonal relations, the troubled-family dealers more often report that they did not get along well with their parents, that they were truants and school dropouts, that they are not in good health and are worried about being or becoming alcoholics.

Comment and Summary

We summarize by saying "Like begets like." Drug-using, unstable, and criminal parents rear children who go in the same direction. Indeed, some parents make sure of it by introducing their offspring to illicit drugs and, we must presume, other delinquency as well. Certainly the early age of onset for illicit use and for dealing bespeaks, in this sample, either very early parental abandonment of offspring to delinquent peers or being taught in the bosom of the family.

We should also remark, "Like supplies like"; for in this sample, as elsewhere, one sees a strong tendency for suppliers to supply persons close to them in socioeconomic or life-style conditions. Here, for example the closeness is not just familial but is more general; these lesser-educated dealers do not supply better-educated users any more than, in other chapters, we found psychedelic dealers supplying junkies or big-money men doing petty peddling on the streets. The affinity of drug dealers for their "likes"—or, put differently, the immersion of illicit-drug-learning, drug-using, drug-trading conduct within a larger framework of shared familial, age, educational, socioeconomic, and drug preference frameworks—is important.

There is no evidence that, for all his early start in drugs and crime, the child of troubled and trouble-making parents is better equipped to be a success in a life of dealing and crime. With the notable exception of a very few, who at the time of interview said they were in the big money (but who did *not* report total lifetime profits greater than others), most follow careers not very different from the sample at large. There are some oddities, one of which is the shift for a few over time in personal preference for and in sales of sedatives and tranquilizers. Keeping in mind that most dealers eschew these in favor of the middle-class "ideological" drugs—cannabis and hallucinogens—or the lower-class and big-money favorites—heroin and cocaine—we can only term the shift remarkable. It may reflect simply failure: if one cannot afford the "better" drugs—euphoria-giving depressants—then one moves to cheap ones. The worry about current alcoholism in this group may be evidence in support of such a proposal. That proposal implies self-medication; that is, the use of depressants commonly associated with "escape," mood suppression, or anxiety reduction. It also implies an addiction liability in the troubled-family dealers.

Is this psychodynamically idiosyncratic or familial, at least in a general sense? We cannot say, but we can return to the data to look at the reported use of drugs by these dealers' siblings—keeping in mind the data from Chapter One showing a much greater tendency on the part of dealers than their oldest siblings to be involved in drugs (and crime). We do find a consistent tendency (fifteen out of eighteen code categories in the relevant inquiry areas but each code itself not significantly different for the two groups) for the oldest siblings of troubled-family dealers, more than stable-family offspring, to have reported histories of juvenile and adult arrests, drinking problems, illicit-drug use, and drug peddling. The same is true for the second-oldest sibling, with sixteen out of eighteen individual reply items showing trends in the direction of greater delinquency and drug use for troubled-family as opposed to stable-family offspring. The same trends are found for sibling three and four as well, but the N is too small for the fifth-youngest sibling to allow comparison. We conclude that the impact of the parents—and/or of forces which have also shaped the parents—is generalized within these troubled and trouble-making families. In affirming a generalized familial "trouble" factor, we also affirm, as with the dealer sample as a whole, an idiosyncratic one for the dealer as the special child; for while over half of our troubled-family dealers have had arrests, as have about half of the stable-family offspring, no more than one quarter of the oldest siblings in troubled families and one fifth in the stable families are described as having such histories.

With regard to their personal adjustments—whether measured by their heavy drug use, alcoholism worries, poor family and school adjustment, or simply by their lack of success in crime and in dealing —we infer greater disorder in this sample than in dealers coming from stable families. Clearly, having troubled and trouble-making parents is not good for children (or for parents). We believe that such parents play a special role in the genesis of delinquency, drug use, and dealing in their children.

Chapter 12

VIOLENCE

In this chapter we shift gears. We include a comparison of the dealers who admit carrying guns, and those who admit using guns, with those who do not report such behavior; but we go beyond that to consider other information which bears on drug dealing and violence.

Because most drug dealers are drug users, the conduct of the dealer as dealer cannot be disassociated from his conduct as a user, including his personal history leading to drug use, his behavior when under the influence of or being withdrawn from drugs, and his conduct in pursuit of drugs or the wherewithal to purchase them. His being a dealer, of course, gives him more than ordinary exposure to violence; for dealing implies heavy involvement in a delinquent group and subjects the dealer to extraordinary needs, stresses, and demands. Consider the elemental fact that dealers are trading in valuable products in a situation unprotected by conventional laws, codes, or other safeguards. They are exposed to being cheated and robbed in the course of their work, and some of them do that cheating and robbing themselves. Theirs is a more fluid and unstructured life—indeed, that is partly why they are in it—but it is also a much more uncertain life. If we add to that mix the availability of weapons and pride in their possession, a national history of violence, and a host of psychological familial factors associated with child-rearing and civilizing failures, we cannot but expect that drug dealing is and will be an unstable and often violent scene.

We cannot, in this chapter, review the complex and interesting literature of aggression and violence or of violence and drugs. We refer the reader to Berkowitz (1962), Tinklenberg and Stillman (in Daniels, Gilula, and Ochberg, 1970), Wolfgang and Ferracuti (1967), Sanford and Comstock (1971), and to Blum (1969). We think it helpful to quote at length the summary of our 1969 report:

A brief survey of history, current social practice, and recent laboratory work with humans and animals has shown a variety of links between drugs and violence. Employed as releasers or facilitators, psychoactive drugs can, in some individuals and in some settings, release assaultive or self-destructive behavior and can be important components of accidents. Drugs can also be used as tools of violence, as weapons in homicide, as devices to control or exploit others, or in warfare to incapacitate or kill. In terms of available data, the demonstrable correlation in the United States between illicit-drug use and criminality is a function of a larger syndrome of acts which are at best shortsighted and immature and at worst hopeless and savage but which express life styles in which both criminality and drug abuse are but a portion. These actions, criminal or drug-using, have their own effects on lives. Most of these effects are not salutary, so that for many persons with chronic histories of drug abuse or crime, there is increasing social disability. This disability need not be violent in the sense that others are harmed. There is also impressive evidence that most youthful illicit-drug use is not associated with ill effects and much of it appears to be self-terminating —certainly violent outcomes are rare indeed when calculated in terms of their prevalence among populations of otherwise nondelinquent persons who do use illicit drugs. In absolute terms, the drug most often implicated in violence is alcohol—these findings pertain to homicides, to assault, to suicide, to traffic accidents, and no doubt to other offenses. Alcohol does not stand alone; its abuse is usually associated with a variety of psychological and familial disabilities not the least of which is predeliction in exposed delinquent populations for the abuse of other drugs.

There is also evidence that the drugs which people use illicitly, and in doing so may become violent, are nevertheless drugs capable of benign effects. Thus almost every substance for which hurtful or violent outcomes are claimed is also claimed to have benefits. These benefits have led to widespread approved use of psychoactive substances in medical practice. An exception are the hallucinogens, which, while claimed as beneficial by illicit users, have not yet been demonstrated to be actually beneficial. Cannabis is currently in this status. The benign effects claimed for most classes of psychoactive drugs—and for drugs used as weapons—include the control of violence. The contradictions in effects are more apparent than real; powerful agents can effect behavior; how they affect it depends on how they are used, by whom, in what settings, and in what amounts. Effects are also specific by drug and class of drug so that in refining predictions, one must say which drug family and which particular agent is under consideration. There appears to be no potent psychoactive agent which cannot be abused by its users or others administering it for their own ends. Yet on a scale of values, the tranquilizers seem least associated with unpredictable and undesirable behavioral outcomes and most associated with reductions in agitation, tension, and other feelings and behavior which are presumably linked to interpersonal distress. The amphetamines, while medically very useful, are not widely claimed to suppress violence—except the behavior disorders of some children and teenagers—and they do have, in illicit use in uncontrolled settings, the potential for unleashing bizarre and aggressive actions. The hallucinogens are also associated clinically, although not massively in terms of prevalence, with untoward reactions, some of which include suicide and assault. The opiates, widely used in medicine and rarely used illicitly, unless current trends continue, have received widespread attention, probably because of the correlative life styles which show many criminals using them and the likelihood of those who use them remaining criminal. Cannabis, the most widely used illicit drug, appears to suppress activity although the rare case will show a contrary assaultive response. The barbiturates do not appear to be widely used among delinquent populations and their use, among delinquents or others, is rarely linked to violence except for suicides in which the barbiturates play a major and frightful role. Some change in this pattern may occur as asocial persons inject barbiturates and amphetamines together or in sequence. There are a variety of other substances, such as volatile intoxicants (glue, thinner, etc.), which are in some use—especially among young and maladapted teenagers—but while these can be associated with accidental deaths, there is little evidence to show them implicated as violence precipitators.

On the whole, then, it may be said that the emergence of violence is rarely attributable only to the influence of drugs; and, indeed, with the exception of alcohol, the absolute number of cases in which there is even an association between acute drug effects and violent conduct is low. In larger perspective, there is certainly an association between illicit-drug use and criminality, including violence, and in looking at lives it must be presumed that chronic illicit-drug use does not facilitate rehabilitation or act as an immunizer against various kinds of destructive or damaging acts. Nevertheless, when one compares illicit-drug users as such as against other unskilled criminals, say assaulters as the extreme example, it will be evident that the user is not more violent and generally he will be found to be less violent than the offender with a chronic history of aggressive actions.

These generalizations apply, and only imperfectly, to populations of drug users as they have been studied to date. They do not apply to the special cases which constitute the combination of drug use and drug merchandising—the typical dealer. There is strong evidence that drug dealing is increasingly linked to violence, be this weapons carrying, weapons use, syndicate or other "protectionistic" associations, or robbing one's fellow drug users and dealers. Since much police action is directed at dealers, there are special dangers in the apprehension of the offender by the police. The evidence to date points to the concentration of violence by and against dealers within the drug scene and much less often, toward the square world outside. As drug use continues to expand and as more sociopathic individuals are attracted both to that use and to dealing, one must anticipate a continued increase in the violence risk within the drug scene and, insofar as present laws are kept on the books and enforced, an increasing risk to narcotics-law–enforcement personnel. Insofar as these personnel are armed, and to the degree they are precipitous, they present a violence risk to illicit users as well.

Arms Traffic

We became interested in the relationship between drug dealing and weapon carrying and arms traffic, for in the course of interviews with international traffickers we were told of well-organized trade patterns which involved the exchange of drugs for weapons, or the simultaneous smuggling of drugs and weapons between some destinations. This traffic was often described as related to political ends. Internationally, for example, our dealers report that arms are moved from the Near East (with arms origins in Eastern Europe especially) to Latin American countries, with drugs moving the further step into the United States or, alternatively, being acquired south of the United States border in exchange for weapons. A second pattern reportedly is the exchange in Western Europe of Near Eastern heroin for weapons which return to the Middle East. A third pattern, internal to the United States, involves the exchange of drugs for weapons to supply revolutionary groups within the United States. Such clandestine arms traffic, assuming the accuracy of our informants, is probably small in contrast to the legitimate arms traffic engaged in officially by industrial nations and perhaps even in comparison to the private arms traffic carried on by licensed businesses (Thayer, 1969; Ashcroft, 1970; Bloomfield and Leiss, 1970). These legitimate transactions do not, however, involve drugs.

After the researchers received several requests from drug dealers to supply to Latin states items ranging from military small arms to tanks, our interest was piqued sufficiently to seek funds to study the arms traffic itself more extensively, but in this we failed. We must say that institutional disinterest in the clandestine flow of weapons compared to much more dramatic institutional—and public—interest in the clandestine flow of drugs, whose dangers are less certain, stands itself as a paradox which is worthy of further inquiry.

In the Bay Area we conducted special interviews designed to gain information on local arms-drug trading. Discussions were held with federal and local officers, narcotics users, professional police informants, and with drug dealers (not members of the regular dealer sample). Three patterns were reported. The first was "political" in the sense that drugs were bartered for arms by members of groups who informants told us intended to use them for revolutionary purposes. A second pattern was ostensibly political in that the rhetoric of revolution was employed to explain drug-arms barter but in fact, that rhetoric merely exalted ordinary criminality, violent propensities, and individual drug dependency by delinquents flying political colors. A third pattern was clearly not political at all and involved only illicit money-making.

We have no data on the frequency with which any of the above forms of arms-drug barter occur, but we can illustrate from cases discussed with us the forms which it takes. We will limit our discussion to the third pattern—illicit money-making, which was the most common pattern reported. Consider that a user/dealer may carry a gun for protection or robbery, fall on hard times, and sell his gun for a fix. This puts the small dealer in the position of the "serious" businessman, and, beyond expanding his stock-in-trade of drugs, he sees the opportunity to sell other contraband as well. Since dealers carry guns, they are a market both as buyers and sellers, and guns are added to the inventory. A shrewd dealer can make more off of a bargain gun if he knows guns and their market than he can by taking cash. Our informants reported that it is easier and better business for the addict-burglar to fence stolen property to a drug dealer in a single transaction than have to go first to a fence and then to a dealer. We quote one in the trade:

> A dealer-fence will give a couple of $25 balloons (heroin) for a color TV, then sell it for $100. That way he turns 100 per cent on all his merchandise, guns, TV sets, whatever, over what he'd

> make on direct-cash drug sales. A real good gun might bring two $25 balloons unless the junkie is sick, then he only gets one.

or,

> Hell, there's one Black fence, a woman, who's rough on whites. She really makes them pay. Hype burglars have even complained to the fuzz that they brought her $2,000 worth of merchandise when they were hurting and she'd only give them a single fix and then throw them out on their cans.

or,

> Most of the guns coming into the drug trade come from nickel and dimer addicts [$5 and $10 small purchasers] who burgle houses and boost autos. They pick up hand guns that way to exchange for heavy narcotics. It didn't use to be that way ten years ago when a burglar wouldn't touch a gun because if he was busted, he'd go up longer for being armed, maybe give him three or five [years] more. Nowadays he'll pick guns up here and there until he has five or six. Then he'll go get one or two $50 balloons. If he's sick, he'll only get one balloon. That dealer will take the guns to his supplier and get about 50 per cent more heroin than if he'd paid for it in cash. That supports *his* habit and gives him a little extra to sell on the side. They [the guns] can pass through five or six hands until they end up in the laboratory and then they get into the revolutionaries' hands. Sometimes it's the same deal in reverse, these guys get the stuff [morphine or heroin smuggled in from Mexico] to sell to the lab.

It appears that problems of addiction, criminality, race relations, and politics all bear on the violence potential.

We wanted to see whether we could verify "with our own eyes" an arms-drug interchange. An associate with undercover experience (and a Lower East Side accent) was commissioned to find some guns in trade for heroin in San Francisco. Working cold—that is, without any knowledge of the drug scene and in the evenings only (he holds a straight job during the day)—he was offered, in exactly five days, 400 hot army 45s, all packed in original oil and cases, in return for heroin. He was also offered "select" shoulder weapons worth $36,000 which had been stolen from a salesman. These were for sale for $2,000 cash only, not in exchange for drugs. In another trial run, we sought, in one day on the Mexican border, to list weapons traded in the prior week to or from three drug dealers whom we knew. A list of some forty items, all hand or shoulder weapons, plus a case of new night scopes (U.S. Army), was obtained. Compared to the estimated traffic in drugs handled by these same dealers, these were incidental transactions. On the next day one interview was conducted while the bodyguard of a major dealer sat near, submachine gun in his hand. If nothing else, that was convincing evidence that dealing and arms do mix.

Our impression, to this point, is that the drug-arms link is real and that such transactions are increasing. Several developments could be responsible for this presumed growth: the expansion of the illicit market and subsequent dealing to supply it, the conditions of that illicit marketplace (as earlier described), and the growth of criminality. Additionally, nearby Latin markets and farther Middle Eastern ones for clandestine arms also happen to be cannabis-, cocaine-, and opium-producing or transshipment areas; furthermore there appears to be an expanded market—for drugs and for arms—within the United States in the form of revolutionary groups who simultaneously contain illicit users some of whom are also traffickers. The "amateur" status of the younger male offenders also plays a role. Unlike the older professionals, who took pride in their work and avoided guns and violence, the new young amateurs are more casual and too often aggressive and without foresight. They take risks that professional criminals would consider both foolish and dangerous. Specialization and caution develop skill over time (consider our big-money dealers). Nevertheless, a dealer as businessman, as criminal, and as opportunist will have his eye on the main chance. If a speed lab can double its take on a gun deal, why not? If a gun man can turn a fine profit by handling a shipment of heroin in payment for weapons, why not? If a "produce" truck crosses the border filled with marijuana, why return empty when a load of guns can occupy the same space? As far as the West Coast and Mexican border are concerned, the arms-drug link appears primarily to be of this opportunistic variety. We believe, on the basis of our inadequate information, that there are in addition a few individual entrepreneurs and several "systems" or rings which, catering particularly to Latin revolutionaries or banditos, routinely run smuggling operations with drugs and guns or with an exchange of the one for the other. Our police and undercover informants also emphasize the role of revolutionaries as recipients of guns-for-drugs in California. These reports require further evaluation.

Armed Drug Dealers

Our informants estimate that dealers carry arms more often than our interview data indicated. For example, one informant, who has been responsible for more than 2,000 drug arrests in six years, states that over 95 per cent of those whom he fingered carried weapons—about half guns and half illegal knives (concealed with blades over three inches long). The same independent estimates were made by narcotics officers credited with more than one thousand arrests each. On the other hand, informants, officers, and dealers agree that violence at the time of arrest (resisting) is rare.

We can compare the reports of our informants with quantitative data of three sorts: narcotics arrests where the subject was armed; arrests involving violence; and, from our variegated dealer sample, the proportion admitting gun-toting compared to those denying the use of weapons.

Narcotics Arrests. Federal Bureau of Narcotics and Dangerous Drug figures (Blum, 1969) from 1966 through 1968 show that 3 per cent of all those arrested for dangerous-drug offenses by Bureau agents were armed. About 10 per cent of the marijuana and opiate offenders were armed. We assume that most of these were big dealers, since street dealers are handled by local law enforcement. These figures of 3 per cent to 10 per cent fall considerably short of the 90 per cent estimate of our officers and informants and, even if knives are excluded, falls much below informants' estimates of 50 per cent carrying firearms.

Arrests Involving Violence. Violence at the time of arrest, ranging from resisting to assault or homicide, occurred among only 2.6 per cent of the federal arrest cases. In 1968 resisting arrest occurred five times more often among heroin offenders than marijuana violators. State of California figures (Bureau of Criminal Statistics, 1971) show that in 1967, 3.7 per cent of all drug arrests involved violence (resisting); in 1968, 5.4 per cent did; and in 1969, 5.2 per cent did. It is obvious that violence upon arrest is rare—although crucial enough to individuals concerned; in California in 1969 one agent was wounded and three violators shot to death, and in 1970 four officers were wounded in drug arrests. The low prevalence of violence is consistent with our informants' reports.

In the federal sample those who were armed were all male, more blacks than whites were armed, armed violators had prior criminal records more than did unarmed ones (85 per cent to 64 per cent), armed violators were slightly younger than the total sample average (27 compared to 29 years), and the rate of resisting arrest was higher for armed violators (8 per cent) than for unarmed ones (2 per cent). In the California sample (N = 500 drawn from 211,190 total drug arrests during the period 1967–1969) the drug arrestees, regardless of violence, were depicted similarly in probation reports as young men with early histories of unhappy family relations, incomplete school careers, abortive marriages, intermittent employment, and records of petty crime.

California's violent drug violators differed from a control sample in that they were more often 20 years of age or older, and proportionately more were 35 or older; were in the 140- to 200-pound weight range; were between 5 feet 11 inches and 6 feet 4 inches; had more prior arrests for crimes against person, more vehicile accidents, more driver's license restrictions or revocations; were more often known addicts; and were more often black. Wednesday and Thursday were peak violence days, as were the hours between 6 p.m. and 1 a.m. Alcohol and drug inebriation status could not be determined.

The apparent discrepancy between federal and state findings with regard to age is explicable on the basis of the average age of violators arrested. More than half of the California drug arrestees were under age 24, whereas most of the federal sample were over that age. This difference may be a correlate of greater criminal professionalism in association with age among federal enforcement targets. That is compatible with the hierarchy of resources and priorities among local, state, and federal enforcement agencies. The lesser rate of resistance among federal arrestees is also compatible with the notion of their greater criminal professionalism and, consequently, caution.

Variegated Dealer Sample. In our sample of California dealers, 351 said that they do not carry guns, 54 said that they tote them but have not used them, and 59 reported both toting and using in their dealing careers; 16 failed to give us information. We did not ask about knives or about incidents of violence. Summing the inquiry areas where one or more significant differences between coded replies or ratings occur, we find 339 out of 576 significant differences between those not carrying guns and those who report both having carried and having used their weapons. There are 353 areas where significant differences discriminate those who do not carry guns from those who do carry them, but there are only 136 such differences between those who have carried guns but deny using them and those who have carried guns and say they have used them. There is not much difference, as measured here, between those carrying and using a gun and those just carrying it without admitting use. There are also 387 significant F tests, signifying greater difference between these groups than among them in the distribution of replies and ratings in the inquiry areas.

Earlier chapters have given some evidence of personal and social differences between the violent (armed) and less violent dealers; armed dealers—in comparison with unarmed dealers—more commonly are big-money dealers with reported Mafia ties; come from troubled and trouble-making families; are active or at least casual rather than terminated dealers; have a history either of narcotics arrests or of nondrug offenses; and, with some qualifications, are proselytizing dealers. We conclude, then, that every measure of extensive dealing activity—whether viewed in terms of early involvement, specialization, success, official visibility, enthusiasm, or generalized delinquency— is also significantly associated with violence.

Analyzing our data further, we find that violent dealers were more often in prison at the time of interview. Violent ones—compared to less violent ones—have histories of narcotics or nondrug arrests, commit nondrug crimes routinely as part of their lives, do not file tax returns, break the law for pleasure, steal drugs from others (including, of course, robbery with their deadly weapon)—mostly fellow dealers and suppliers, and think of themselves as professional dealers and criminals. Their backgrounds are as expected: tending toward lower rather than middle class, uneducated rather than educated, and from pathogenic families (parents *and* siblings). As expected, their drug use, licit and illicit, is heavier, especially the use of opiates and cocaine. They are more worried about getting hurt themselves.[1] As far as their career development is concerned, the violent ones are the active criminal dealers who are heavily in the life, with heavy drugs, for money and not for idle pleasure.

Violent dealers are more pessimistic about their choice of vocations; more than nonviolent ones they expect to see their fellow dealers dead or in prison in ten years. That they are willing to take other risks, aside from gun-slinging, is suggested by their much greater affinity for gambling. They are seen by raters as more dominant, businesslike, and better salesmen but are less often described as "friendly."

Comment and Summary

We asked narcotics officers, long-time informants, and dealers (all supplemental to the variegated sample) about the relationship between narcotics and weapons traffic. Reports indicate that trader opportunism, coupled with weapons demands abroad in drug-producing or trans-shipping areas, does lead to frequent irregular and occasional systematic traffic, in which drugs are exchanged for arms or in which drugs and arms are carried together between limited points. Weapons and drug demands among revolutionary groups within the United

[1] One is reminded of a St. Louis study (Schultz, 1962) showing that knife-carrying Negroes were more worried about being assaulted than those not carrying knives.

States were commonly reported, but we did not gather any direct evidence or find hard data to substantiate these. At more casual levels, some drug users do steal and sometimes they steal guns. These can be traded for drugs to the advantage of the dealer.

How many drug dealers are, at one time or another, armed for business is uncertain. Officers and informants claim that half carry guns and most of the rest illicit (long-bladed or switch) knives. One fourth of our variegated sample admit that they carry guns; but only 10 per cent of the Federal Bureau of Narcotics and Dangerous Drug arrestees (opiate and marijuana violators) were armed at the time of arrest. The use of weapons varies with the occasion; most dealers use their weapons in defense against or to rob other dealers. Among federal arrestees violence at arrest occurred in only 2.6 per cent of the 1968 cases, as opposed to 5.4 per cent among California arrestees.

Review of personal factors shows consistently that dealer violence is predictable; that is, it is part of a life pattern which includes at least (drawing from the variegated dealer sample) (1) particular personality traits—for instance, those inferred from signs of pessimism, risk-taking, fear, and dominance; (2) early and heavy multiple-drug involvement, including concerns over alcoholism; (3) a cluster of activities that go with being an active, serious, involved dealer; (4) strong involvement in nondrug criminality (including significant association with prior robbery and aggravated assault); and (5) derivation from troubled (pathogenic) families. The federal and California state data, limited to violence at the time of arrest, also suggest racial and age correlates; the greater importance of heroin and/or marijuana as opposed to other drugs; and the relationship between prior violence, present violence, and being a dangerous driver. The California data on height and weight may imply particular body builds. If so, the work of Sheldon (1949) on the delinquency proneness of mesomorphs should be called to mind.

Most of these variables are likely not independent but rather constitute a constellation. Except for the dealing component itself, these matters of prior history, personality, alcohol involvement, pathogenic family life, and race and its criminogenic correlates are a familiar group. The setting variable (day and hour) too has been found in other studies (Wolfgang and Ferracuti, 1967). What one concludes is that the violent dealer is probably not very different from other violent offenders; indeed, given the prevalence of drug use and dealing among delinquents of all classes, the dealer role is only one element in the genesis of dangerous behavior.

Having focused on violence, we must not forget that most of

the dealers in our variegated sample deny it. Their denial is compatible not only with a somewhat exalted self-image but probably even with the facts. Most of our dealers are young, middle class, and in the psychedelic scene. Insofar as they are "sometimes" dealers, not serious, not otherwise heavily implicated in delinquent lives or attitudes, then one would expect them to be less violent than their older, poorer, sadder, and tougher peers. But even the most genteel of middle-class dealers are likely to be more delinquent than their own siblings and, we would guess, their less criminally commercial drug-using peers. Consequently, on the scale of dangerous potential, we would place any illicit dealer higher than his socioeconomically and neighborhood-matched nondealing age mates.

Chapter 13

DRUGS IN THE BUDGET

One way to look at drugs is to consider them as commodities bought and sold like any other. Since drugs are commodities much used in ordinary life by many ordinary young people, they can be considered in the same way as one considers purchases and sales of other household items or possessions, food or bicycles or what-have-you. What place do they have in the budget? Or, more basically, what is the family income, how is it earned, and what portion of it is spent on a given commodity, in this instance drugs? One can also ask, since we know that drug use and dealing often accompany each other, what portion of that budget is earned by drug sales.

With these and a few other questions in mind, we began a study of residents of the Haight-Ashbury in the summer of 1969. The Haight, you will recall, was the mecca for flower children and the mythical birthplace of the psychedelic scene. Kendall and Pittel (1970) review briefly the public image of that scene, calling attention to the rise (about 1967) of a concern not with the flowers or the Merry Pranksters of Ken Kesey (Wolfe, 1968) but to ill effects attending use and to a presumptive shift from marijuana and LSD to amphetamines and, by 1970, heroin. The golden age, it seemed, had passed and its originators gone from the Haight, leaving only predators, derelicts, runaways, strung-out speed freaks plus researchers, healers, and the like. But Kendall and Pittel contend that history is itself a legend and that, whatever changes in drug use and behavior may have taken place between 1964 and 1970, the people now living in the Haight differ little in background and personality from the ones living there earlier; indeed, a portion are the same people, showing more residential stability than the gypsy image would credit.

Kendall and Pittel (see also Pittel, Calef, Gryler, Hilles, Hofer, and Kempner, 1972) gave psychological tests to three Haight-Ashbury samples: (1) hippies representative of the early utopians, (2) their current grass-and-acid counterparts, and (3) a sample of young people hospitalized for psychiatric problems associated with drug use. The original utopians, tested in the summer of 1967, consisted of seventy-seven males and seventy females with a median age of 22 and median education of two years in college. The second group, examined from the summer of 1968 to the winter of 1969, consisted of one hundred males and seventy-three females with a median age of 21 and a median of one year in college. The in-patient group was tested at the Langley-Porter Neuropsychiatric Institute's Youth Drug Study Unit between summer 1967 and summer 1969 and comprises 70 per cent of all patients hospitalized on that ward. Their median age was 18 with a median high school education.

The results are striking. The test profiles on the Minnesota Multiphasic Personality Inventory (MMPI) are nearly identical for the early and later resident groups; no significant differences emerge. Both samples, insofar as they have "psychopathology," show predominantly character disorders (as opposed to neurotic or psychotic patterns): inadequate impulse control, lack of internalized values (tending toward the "psychopath"), and narcissistic (self-centered) tendencies. Such patterns have been found in delinquent adolescents (Lanyon, cited by Kendall and Pittel, 1970) except that the hippie samples from the Haight show much more "femininity" for both males and females, suggesting that they are much more passive, sensitive, gentle, and idealistic people than the ordinary delinquent. The psychiatric sample is also similar to the Haight-resident samples but shows greater depression, paranoia, and schizophrenia; the males also show scores high on "psychasthenia," which may be lassitude or obsessiveness. Kendall and Pittel suggest that these results may reflect drug-related psychoses on top of character pathology like that of the early and late Haight residents. Kendall and Pittel also note that these latter findings are similar to those of Cohen and Klein (1970), Frosch, Robbins, and Stern (1965), and Ungerleider and his associates (1968), who also found underlying character pathology in drug-related psychosis. They note also that the general character structure which they describe for residents (impulsive, psychopathic, self-centered, passive, idealistic) is much like clinical findings for the drug user's personality offered by other researchers—notably Barron, Lowinger, and Ebner (1970), Calef and associates (1970), and Welpton (1968). Kendall and Pittel conclude that the personality of the drug-using Haight-Ashbury resident has not changed, although his drug use has—encompassing now amphetamines, barbiturates, and narcotics. He has also become less utopian, having at least partially abandoned the dream of a beautiful community, and more suspicious of the world.

Another study, by Blacker, Jones, Stone, and Pfefferbaum (1968), describes some acidheads among Haight-Ashbury residents. Their sample, drawn for a neurophysiological study and found to be "uniquely sensitive to low-intensity stimulation" and "to modulate and organize sensory input in a different fashion" from normal, was composed of middle-class and upper-middle-class youth of conventional rearing whom psychiatric interviews revealed to be passive, frustrated, and angry at their parents and their own life situations prior to LSD use. They began use of the drug in an effort to reduce the unpleasantness of their own life emotions. Afterward they seem to have developed notions of omnipotence, faith in astrology, and a belief in their own power as mediums. These beliefs seem linked both to their drug use and to the beliefs of their neighbors in the Haight-Ashbury milieu.

Finally, Manheimer, Mellinger, and Balter (1969) studied a sample representative of all San Francisco adults. In their sample 13 per cent reported marijuana experience; among those 18 to 24 years old, half of the men and one third of the women reported use. Users are more often found among high school and college dropouts, among heavy smokers and heavy drinkers, and among those with nontraditional values—especially, no religious affiliation. We suspect that these characteristics would be especially frequent in the drug scene of the Haight-Ashbury district.

The foregoing studies tell us what the Haight residents we interviewed in the summer of 1969 were probably like as people. The original survey method that we attempted, a dwelling-unit sample, was abandoned because the interviewer was contacting mainly elderly shut-ins and not reaching the resident youth population, who were "on the street" during the day. Evening sampling produced suspicion, refusals, and threats to our interviewer and also had to be abandoned. In the sampling procedure finally adopted, our interviewer approached every tenth person that he encountered on the busiest block in the Haight-Ashbury and solicited cooperation until a total of one hundred was obtained. (People who were not local residents were screened out.)

We hope that our sample is a reasonable approximation of the Haight-Ashbury hippies.

Regarding background and current status, 4 per cent were under 15 (most likely runaways, although we did not ask); 51 per cent were between 16 and 20; 36 per cent between 21 and 25; 9 per cent between 26 and 40; and none over 40. Eighty-five per cent were single; 8 per cent were married and living with a spouse. Seventy per cent of our residents were male; 30 per cent were female. Eighty-six per cent were white; 11 per cent were black. There were two American Indians and one Oriental. Compatible with their age and Haight residency, most were dropouts (65 per cent); some 10 per cent were still in school and visiting for the summer. High school dropouts outnumbered college dropouts at a rate of four to three. Only 2 per cent had college degrees. Fifty per cent were thinking of returning to school.

Our respondents had lived in the Haight from less than one day to over six years. Thirty per cent had been there from one month to one year; 41 per cent from one to ten years. Most had been drawn to the Haight because of the place and its people. The majority were now living with from four to eight or more friends in a pad or small commune.

As for their expenses, 35 per cent paid nothing for housing (as spongers or guests); the others paid between $1 and $50 per month. Utilities were minimal, and no one was buying a residence; most felt, however, that their housing expenses were too high. Total weekly expenditures for the majority were between $1 and $25. A breakdown showed that during the previous week 77 per cent had paid between nothing and $20 for food; most had spent nothing on clothes; most had averaged less than $5 on transportation, nothing on medical expenses or books or art objects, and less than $1 to $10 on entertainment (rock concerts being the main choice); most of the sample spent between pennies to $5 on cigarettes and alcohol, nothing on insurance or bail or fines (with 3 per cent as exceptions), little on telephones, and nothing (except for 3 per cent) on weapons. Most had spent less than $1 on records or musical tapes, flowers or gifts. The majority had given pennies to $5 in handouts to friends or panhandling hippies. The only other notable expenditures were for pets or pet supplies.

With regard to drugs, 47 per cent said that they could not recall or would not say. Among those giving information, the range of expenditures for both licit and illicit substances was considerable—only 7 per cent spending nothing; 30 per cent between less than $1 to $5; 23 per cent between $6 and $20; 19 per cent between $21 and $50;

6 per cent between $51 and $100; and 15 per cent spending over $100 for drugs the prior week. Ninety per cent had spent nothing, and none had spent more than $3 for legal drugs (prescriptions and over-the-counter remedies). Headache remedies were the most commonly purchased item.

The breakdown of illicit-drug expenses shows that (in order of popularity) marijuana, hallucinogens, heroin, sedatives, speed (methamphetamine), opium, and cocaine had been on the shopping list. When the drug-expense question was asked differently a second time, in order to check consistency, more of the sample (50 per cent) reported no illicit purchases; and those who admitted illicit purchase (42 per cent) reported greater expenses—$20 or more during the preceding week. Discussing their total expenditures as well as their drug expenditures for the last week, the majority stated that these were about the same as for other weeks. They did complain that illicit drugs cost too much, although drug dealers were not criticized by most for their profits.

Inquiries about income and income sources revealed that 72 per cent had no legitimate jobs at the time but that most had done some straight work in the past, usually unskilled; the majority had never held a straight job longer than one year. When they were employed, their average income had been between $26 and $100 a month, with less than 3 per cent making more than $200 a month. Half stated that at the time of the interview they had no income from any straight source; one fourth reported noncriminal income of over $100 per month for the preceding month; the remaining one fourth of the sample had straight income of less than $100. Nearly half had received money during the prior month in the form of gifts or support or windfalls from parents or acquaintances. Among those receiving such monies, most got between $1 and $50. One fifth reported that they had received public welfare support, from $50 to over $250. Half earned money by panhandling (begging), with a range from $1 to over $260. Begging incomes here were, for the most part, in the $1 to $50 range. Two per cent earned money by prostitution, reporting between $50 and $100 during the past month. Eight per cent "earned" by theft, with incomes ranging from low to high; 3 per cent stated that they had made over $100 the previous month by stealing. Fencing (sale of stolen goods) returned income to 7 per cent of the sample; 2 per cent of this group had made more than $100 the prior month. A summary of illicit income, excluding drug sales, indicates that over half of the sample (55 per cent) did earn money illegally, that most received under $50 in this way, and that 6 per cent of the total sample had made over $250 illicitly the prior month.

Turning now to illicit income from drug sales, 50 per cent reported that they had sold drugs during the prior month; 45 per cent considered themselves dealers at the time of the interview, and 78 per cent said that they had at one time been drug dealers. The majority who sold the prior month had made under $100, the modal income being between $1 and $25. Higher incomes were not unknown, however. Eight per cent of those selling (4 per cent of the total sample) had earned between $250 and $500; 2 per cent had made between $500 and $1,000; and 3 per cent had netted more than $1,000. Also, 2 per cent reported income from the sale of false drugs (for instance, talcum powder in capsules sold as amphetamine).

Those who reportedly were not dealers at the time of interview were asked why they had quit. Of the thirty-one persons (31 per cent of our total sample) who responded openly, thirteen expressed fear of arrest or the fact of arrest; and four said that they felt they were becoming paranoid or constantly uneasy, a development linked to the arrest risk. Others indicated that they had lost interest because of family responsibilities, or had moved from drugs to yoga, or had decided that dealing is a degrading activity. Five had quit because dealing was not profitable for them or because they lacked the capital to resume buying for resale.

Those who were still dealing had, for the most part, been dealing for one to five years. The most common stock-in-trade was marijuana and hallucinogens, followed by anything and everything available. None in this group, however, had specialized in opiates, although a few had carried heroin or cocaine. Only 22 per cent of our sample had ever been arrested on any drug charge, but 65 per cent had been arrested for offenses such as begging, burglary, public drunkenness, and carrying concealed weapons.

We asked them what they would be doing in five years. Twenty-five per cent had no idea. Among those who did have plans, the majority expected conventional lives; 53 per cent of them (39 per cent of the total) mentioned marriage, straight jobs, school, farm work, and the like. (Recall that short-range plans for up to 50 per cent of the dropouts called for a return to school.) Only 8 per cent of the total sample expected to be doing the same as they were doing at the time of the interview. There was only one real pessimist. He expected to be in prison. When asked to select (from four possible categories) what they would do if they were ever in financial trouble, 37 per cent said that they would lean more on others for help, 21 per cent would remain inactive, 17 per cent would engage in criminal activity, and 13 per cent would engage in straight activity to get on their feet financially.

All of our sample disapproved of the current drug laws, and most proposed lessened severity or the legalization of some substances, particularly marijuana; but only 10 per cent proposed that all criminal sanctions be eliminated. We asked what major changes they would like to see in the United States in the distribution of wealth. Fifty per cent were in favor of socialism (the welfare state, equalization of wealth); more moderate proposals were for improved and equalized opportunities or reduced taxation for the poor. Fourteen per cent wanted no change in the economic structure.

Comment and Summary

One hundred Haight-Ashbury residents were interviewed in the summer of 1969. Most were young (16 to 25), school dropouts, single, white, and fairly long-term inhabitants of this hippie district. An analysis of their budget indicates that the major expenditures were for housing, food, and illicit drugs—with drugs the major item. Minor but consistent expenses in the $5 to $20 range monthly were for transportation, entertainment (rock concerts mostly), cigarettes, alcohol, and handouts (to friends and panhandlers). An estimated average monthly total expenditure was $160. At the extremes are 11 per cent who live on less than $40 a month and 9 per cent spending over $1,000 per month. Among those spending large amounts, only three items appear in the budget for the week preceding interview as having cost more than $100: drugs, bail, and fines. Among those willing to discuss their drug expenditures (and nearly half would not), nearly half spent more than an estimated $100 per month.

As for income, the majority (72 per cent) had no legitimate jobs at the time of interview, but 50 per cent did receive money legitimately (from parents or friends), with a median income of about $100. In addition, one fifth of the sample were on welfare, from which they received a median $100. Illicit income was reported by the majority of the sample—a few from theft, fencing stolen goods, prostitution, and the like, but half getting money from panhandling (a median $15 a month) and half realizing profits from drug sales. Illicit income, exclusive of drug dealing, appears to have averaged about $20. Drug profits are estimated at $75 (median) per month; one quarter of those who sell make less than $25, and one fourth make more than $250 a month—indeed, 3 per cent claim over $1,000 per month.

Most of the sample (78 per cent) had been drug dealers at one time. Those who had quit did so mostly because of fear of arrest. Only a minority (22 per cent) had ever had any narcotics arrest, but most had been arrested for other offenses.

Our sample is somewhat younger and less well educated than the volunteer samples seen by Rinker and by Pittel and his colleagues. Even so, given the extensiveness of delinquency, of drug involvement, and of passive solutions posed for stressful situations (the inactivity and dependency categories of plans or actions in response to our query about financial difficulty), we see no reason for assuming that their personalities differ much from those earlier described for Haight-Ashbury hippies. The sample contains many who are like the casual psychedelic dealers—and some active dealers—in our variegated sample described in Chapter One.

Since we drew our sample of pedestrians—not presented as users or dealers as such—from Haight-Ashbury residents in general, its findings serve to confirm the extensiveness of drug dealing, the importance of buying and selling drugs for the user's budget, and the presence of past and present nondrug delinquency in association with the drug-centered life style.

The findings here also tend to confirm the transitional status of the young dealer/user not from slum origins. Most of our Haight residents do see themselves moving onward and upward to rather straight lives. The question is whether or not they are fooling themselves. Given their delinquency, their drug use, their incomplete schooling, their lack of work experience, and their passivity, one wonders how many have the personality resources or vocational skills to achieve their own conventional goals. Given such difficulties, the direction of their transition may be socially downhill rather than up.

Chapter 14

A COMMUNE

The commune movement sometimes discussed as one form of utopian or intentional community, began to attract drug-using youth in the mid-1960s in the Bay Area, although for decades earlier Californians had been experimenting with a variety of communal or weekend retreats. Such developments are very much part of America—dating from the religious fellowship of the founding fathers through the various "brotherhood" experiments of the nineteenth century (New Harmony, Indiana, for example, or Free Love, or New Zion, Ohio). Popular descriptions of modern communes have been increasing (see *Look*, July 15, 1969; *Life*, July 18, 1969). Kovach (1971) distinguishes between the urban and the rural developments. In the urban areas, he finds mainly college-based, revolutionary, work-centered, and philosophical-religious collectives; in rural communes, he finds people with deeper commitments to spiritual utopian values, ordinary young people imbued with the self-support farmer's work ethic. He estimates that the average commune contains from five to fifteen members. Hartnett, in an April 1971 Associated Press series on "The Alternative Society," describes the cooperative and religious spirit common to many communes, as well as the divisive forces that lead to their failure.

Zablocki (1970) estimates that there are about one thousand rural communes of rural hippies; he and his students visited nearly one hundred of these communes. He describes a broad range of drug-use practices and observes that where there is no drug use a renunciation may figure in the ideal of the collective. Zablocki distinguishes communes not only on the basis of the degree of use or renunciation of drugs but on size. The smaller ones (with six to eight members), he suggests, have arisen out of a communion experience shared by these people, who are usually in their late twenties or thirties, often married, and whose communal life is stable and discreet. The larger communes (model size twenty-five) have more fluid structures, younger members, and a high turnover. The typical rural commune, according to Zablocki, is centered around the communal garden; garden cultivation, hunting and gathering, food stamp supplements, gifts from visitors, and occasional labor in nearby towns provide subsistence living standards.

Zablocki emphasizes that "an understanding of the phenomenological quality of the drug experience is crucial for the understanding of communal life style." One special feature of this phenomenological quality (namely, attending to inner experience and awareness) has been discussed by Krippner and Fersh (1971), who visited eighteen communes. They distinguish among secular unstructured, secular structured (administered), and structured religious communes, giving examples of each; and they specify the importance of paranormal (parapsychological) beliefs or experiences—telepathy, clairvoyance, and the like—in many communes. They suggest alternative explanations for these, ranging from post-psychedelic deconditioning and reorientations to regressive magical thinking to reduced ego boundaries subsequent to hallucinogen use. Whatever the sources, the emphasis on community, inner experience, and magico-religious conceptions is a critical feature of some rural communes, including the two upon which our limited observations are based.

Let us now describe one rural commune (a composite of the ones observed), which we call Consciousnesss III (see Reich, 1970). Consciousness III is in the coastal mountains near Santa Cruz, California. It has both stable and floating members, all of whom live in its one rambling old house. Our participant observer spent one summer in Consciousness III; although she became acquainted with all of the members, she was able to persuade only sixteen of the thirty there to sit down for our formal interview about the economic life of the membership. Those who refused to cooperate did so mainly because our preoccupation was with drugs, money, and the like, whereas the commune members actively deny the importance of many of our substantive concerns and, fundamentally, of social science research itself.

"Your approach is tangential" said one thoughtful resident, during discussion of budgets and survival. "We spend less than 1 per cent of our time concerning ourselves as a group with economic considerations." "You miss the point of spiritual growth and Gestalt harmony, which is the essence of our commune if not always the practice." The economic base is land gardening, but "that is linear, for . . . every commune has a center . . . an omnipresent now . . . metaphysically growing toward unification of Atman [singular karma], with Brahman [to create] one Ground of Being." To the members, then, our initial interests—mostly drugs and their budget—were simply irrelevant to what was in their minds. Drugs, for instance, are not particularly important in this commune; they are neither prohibited nor embraced. Marijuana is used, but life is centered on other things.

What did we learn by our tangential approach? Well, as to details, the people of Consciousness III are all between 16 and 25 years old except for the young offspring of these "elders." Most are single. There is one married couple, and two who have been divorced. All in the commune are white. Nearly all of the adults have had some college education. One member, of high school age, still attends school in a nearby mountain town. As far as budget is concerned, members contribute unequally to the house rental and to maintenance of the garden. Some do and some do not work outside the commune. Most provide no more than $25 a month toward the house; two give up to $50, depending on their wealth each month. Other expenses are minimal, since (at least during the summer of observation) food is grown in the garden. The average resident spends no more than $40 a month on all his needs. Most of the residents spend money only for cigarettes and/or movie admissions in the nearby mountain town. Four spend money on alcohol, two spend less than $3 on marijuana, one spends less than $1 on an illicit stimulant. All told, fifteen spend nothing on drugs, one spends 5 per cent of his total expenditures on drugs, and one spends his money on drugs only. Both residents and observer agree that these are average weekly expenditures for the whole commune.

Inquiry and observation regarding *income* and *income sources* reveal that eight members hold unskilled jobs, such as cannery work, where they earn a median of $50 a month. Some monies are earned from the sale of craft items and candles made in the garage. A few members receive small additional amounts from gifts, two are on welfare. No one, to our knowledge, sells drugs. In fact, the only "illicit" income known to us is $10 that one member received from begging.

In their past lives, however, most of our interviewees (fourteen of eighteen) were drug users and eight were dealers as well. All have quit—for various reasons. Two of them quit because of fear of arrest and one because of lack of profit; but most of them gave up drugs because of fundamental changes in their goals, interests, and self-conceptions—changes which brought them eventually to Consciousness III. Although one has been arrested on drug charges and three have a history of nondrug arrests, all residents are now engaged in lawful work (except for mild and infrequent incidents). In spite of their lawfulness, however, the commune members do not approve of current drug laws; indeed, most think that these laws should be abolished entirely. This view is part of their larger appreciation of freedom, expressed in their commune life.

Reviewing their financial status, we find no resident dissatisfied with his present status. Their wants are minimal; indeed, most claim that they need no more than $25 a month to supplement their self-sufficient and self-reliant communal farm. We can see that their actual income exceeds what they think they need but is, nevertheless, spent. Even though their aspiration level and income are low, the majority deny that they have ever been in financial difficulty. Asked what they would do if they were—or had done when they were—most (twelve out of eighteen) would go to work; none would opt for crime or inactivity; only two would become dependent on others.

We asked them what they will be doing five years from now. Only one expects to be engaged in more conventional activities; the others are uncertain or plan to remain with this or another commune or to be otherwise engaged in essentially spiritual pursuits. As for their economic-political philosophies, all want change, but only one is specifically political (Marxist); the rest call generally for equalization or enhanced opportunities; a few recommend expanded communal living as a solution.

Comment and Summary

An undergraduate assistant, under guidance, observed California commune members in the Santa Cruz mountains over one summer. We call their commune Consciousness III to reflect their intentions. Only half of the thirty people there (mostly young, single, with college experience) would respond to inquiry items expressing our interests: drugs, budgets, past history, and the like. Both observation and interview reveal that illicit-drug use is both unusual and unimportant; that commune members are spiritually concerned; and, even though ascetic and eccentric (even bizarre) by straight standards, they are self-reliant agriculturalists spurning conventional achievement or delinquency. They rarely use psychoactives (although half do smoke cigarettes, and marijuana is used casually), are content with their status, and do not plan to return to the traditional urban world. Their histories show them to be a well-educated nondelinquent group who, nevertheless, have had past intensive illicit-drug involvement—including, for half, experience as dealers for profit.

Their shift to this unusual and law-abiding life, while in a few cases attributable partly to the risk of arrest as dealers, seems to us much more associated with the failure of the drug-centered urban life to provide the satisfactions they sought and apparently found in Consciousness III. We also posit that these well-educated, religious, self-reliant and essentially nondelinquent youth could only be uncomfortable in environments such as the Haight-Ashbury or Telegraph Avenue, with their strongly psychopathological, drug-oriented, and delinquent life styles.

The people in Consciousness III may still be in transition, just as our Haight-Ashbury resident sample believe themselves to be, but the discrepancies so marked in the latter do not emerge in this commune. Many of the Haight residents are deeply involved in drugs and crimes and are personally and socially inadequate, if our reports and those of other investigators can be accepted. Without substantial work experience or educational assets, impulsive and undisciplined, and with a clear aversion to work itself, the Haight-Ashbury group nevertheless believe that their present dissatisfactions (with their income and living standards) will somehow disappear as soon as they themselves get straightened out and are working in the conventional world. These plans, however, do not match the interests or capabilities of the Haight residents. The Consciousness III group, on the other hand, probably could resume conventional urban living if they wanted to do so; but they do not. They seem to us well adjusted and realistic—particularly because there is little discrepancy between what they are doing now and what they conceive of themselves doing in the future. We consider this evidence for adjustment or realism, however eccentric a straight-worlder may consider their essentially ascetic collective or their "paranormal" rambling conversation to be. Even if their summer is but a transitory moment in the quest for a meaningful life and revealing world view, it is nevertheless a profound moment. It is also a constructive one measured by straight-world standards.

Chapter 15

ENGLISH DEALERS

Great Britain, like many other Western nations, has a population of illicit-drug users and, consequently, has its dealers as well. We are not aware of epidemiological or survey studies which indicate the prevalence of illicit use among British youth as a whole. It is known that occasional illicit use occurs among school children (Wiener, 1970); that opiate use has been on the increase over the last decade (Bewley, 1966); and that, at the beginning of 1970, there were 1,466 identified heroin cases (Home Office, 1970), plus approximately 1,400 using other opiates. Greater heroin use is revealed when other case-finding methods are applied (De Alarcon and Rathod, 1968; De Alarcon, 1969). The use of amphetmaines and hallucinogens also has been increasing slowly over the decade, judging from conviction figures—2,486 convictions in 1967 and 3,762 in 1969 (Home Office, 1970). And Clark (1971) has estimated that 60 per cent of university students have had experience with illicit substances—cannabis being the most common (Schofield, 1971)—and that regular cannabis use is engaged in by about 20 per cent of the university student population, more of whom are increasingly initiated into illicit use in preuniversity years.

Bean (1971) studied a census of cases appearing in London courts on drug charges over a ten-week period. Among these identified offenders, multiple-drug use was the pattern; the majority had used cannabis, amphetamines, heroin, and methadone. Most were regular (daily) users who received their supplies from dealers rather than from medical sources. Compared to national figures, these users more often came from very high or very low socioeconomic backgrounds. In spite of the absence, for most, of "deprived" backgrounds, the majority had a history of nondrug delinquency. Even so, delinquency was more common among offenders with lower-class, as opposed to middle- or upper-class backgrounds. Young (1971) has considered the English drug scene in its larger social as well as criminological perspective. In his view, current laws and myths rather than imputed delinquency require the primary examination. The most recent descriptions of English drug users, their characteristics, and their sources is to be found in I. P. James (1971) and Hawks (1971).

Laws

Britain, like the United States, is a signatory to the Single Convention on Narcotic Drugs, 1961. As such, Britain is obliged to impose legal controls on drugs covered by this Convention. Until 1971 the British law did not distinguish, in penalties applied, between dealing in drugs and possession of them. Indeed, the Advisory Committee on Drug Dependence (1968) decided that it would not be possible to do so. The Misuse of Drugs Act, 1971 (which was supported by both the major parties in Parliament), however, does change the law. The maximum penalty for dealing is at least double that for simple possession.

The law in force at the time of our interviews with the English dealers (later repealed by the 1971 Act) was contained in a series of statutes. The principal Act was the Dangerous Drugs Act of 1965, which controlled heroin, cocaine, opium, and cannabis, together with other drugs such as morphine, methadone, and pethidine (meperidine). The Act, and regulations made under it, made it an offense to import, export, manufacture, cultivate, supply, procure, offer to supply, offer to procure, or possess any of these drugs without authority, and also prohibited various other activities with respect to prepared opium, such as possessing a pipe for smoking opium. In addition, an occupier or manager of premises committed an offense if he permitted those premises to be used for the purpose of smoking cannabis, or of dealing in cannabis, whether by sale or otherwise.

Under the 1965 Act, all offenses carried the same maximum penalty, ten years' imprisonment or £1,000 ($2,600) fine or both.[1] At the

[1] Except where otherwise indicated, all maximum penalties refer to conviction on indictment. After summary conviction, the maxima are substantially less. There are no minimum penalties. A typical penalty for a first offense of possession of a small quantity of any illegal drug might be a fine of £25 ($60) on summary conviction. A dealer, if arrested in the course of a small commercial transaction (involving, say £100 ($240) worth of drugs) with a stranger, might expect to be tried on indictment and sentenced to eighteen months' imprisonment. The 1971 Act is not expected to affect this. The actual sentence would, of course, vary considerably with the circumstances of the offense and the court trying the case.

time of writing, the maximum penalty of ten years had been imposed on only two occasions: in 1965, on a 37-year-old Nigerian for supplying one grain of heroin to a 15-year-old boy; and in 1969, to a Canadian found guilty of importing a large quantity of cannabis. The 1965 Act has been critiziced as lacking adequate powers to deal effectively with trafficking (Lord Windlesham, House of Lords, 14 January, 1971). Although there is no difference in the penalties for them, British law follows the Single Convention in distinguishing between two varieties of cannabis. One, known simply as cannabis (or cannabis herb), is defined as the flowering or fruiting tops of any plant of the genus Cannabis from which the resin has not been extracted (that is, marijuana). The other, cannabis resin, is the separated resin, whether crude or purified, obtained from any plant of the genus Cannabis (that is, hashish). The seeds and leaves have never been within the Drug Acts, but intentional cultivation without a license is prohibited. Under the old law, amphetamines and hallucinogens (which were added to the Act in 1966) were controlled under the Drugs (Prevention of Misuse) Act of 1964. This Act prohibited the unauthorized possession or import of these drugs, but did not specifically make an offense of dealing in these drugs. A person accused of dealing in them may be convicted of possession or, alternatively, with aiding, abetting, counseling, or procuring someone to be in unlawful possession. The maximum penalty under this Act was two years' imprisonment or an unlimited fine or both. Barbiturates were not controlled by either of these Acts, but only by the Pharmacy and Poisons Act of 1933, which controls the distribution and sale of poisons. It has never been an offense to possess barbiturates, but unauthorized sale may be penalized on summary conviction by a fine of up to £50 ($130). There is no possibility of a prison sentence. Methaqualone, the principal constituent of Mandrax, a sedative-hypnotic which has recently been widely abused, was brought within the provisions of the 1964 Act in early 1971.

The Dangerous Drugs Act of 1967 made new provisions on the subject of searching suspected drug users in public places. The relevant section provides that if a constable has reasonable grounds to suspect that a person is in possession of a drug in contravention of any of the Drug Acts, the constable may stop and search him or a vehicle in which he is traveling. "Reasonable grounds" are at the constable's discretion. In practice it is difficult to prove that a search under this provision is unlawful. A search warrant is usually required before a private house can be lawfully searched (Advisory Committee on Drug Dependence, 1970). In any case, the British law on admissibility of evidence is not nearly as strict as in the United States, and evidence obtained in an illegal search may be used.

Until the Dangerous Drugs Act of 1967, any doctor could prescribe heroin to anyone dependent on it. However, in 1966 the number of known heroin addicts began to rise steeply, and for the first time in recent years exceeded 1,000. There was evidence, also for the first time, of a small number of doctors prescribing excessive amounts of heroin, a large amount of which was reaching the black market and was stated to be responsible for the spread of heroin use. The result of this (Interdepartmental Committee, 1965) was the Dangerous Drugs Act of 1967, which specified that only doctors who are specially licensed to do so may prescribe heroin, morphine, and cocaine to addicts. These drugs may be freely prescribed, however, for the relief of pain and for other purposes unconnected with addiction. In practice, these licensed doctors are usually attached to the drug-addiction treatment centers, set up following the 1967 Act, or to other hospitals with facilities for the treatment of addiction.

The result of this Act has been to reduce substantially the amount of heroin of legal manufacture being used by addicts since the treatment centers have tended to underprescribe rather than overprescribe. It has tended to be the policy of the treatment centers to replace heroin with methadone (dispensed in Britain under the name "Physeptone"), on which the user/addict is maintained. Syringes and needles are available in Britain both cheaply and legally.

Recently, the price of street heroin has risen from the 1967 price of about £1 ($2.60) to the present price of about £6 ($15.60) per grain (60 mg.). As the price has increased, some users—who have not been prescribed all that they feel they require—have turned to cheaper substitutes available on the streets such as barbiturates or the so-called "Chinese" heroin. In the course of such use, illnesses have developed, with a number of addicts suffering gangrene and subsequent amputations. "Chinese" heroin has been on the illicit market sporadically since 1967 and is powdered, impure heroin, sometimes brown, sold in packets of between ⅙ and ⅓ grain, for about £1 ($2.60) to £1.50 ($3.90) each. It is distributed principally through the Chinese community in London and presumed to come from Hong Kong.

It is in respect to such drugs as heroin that the British law differs sharply from American laws. Although possession of heroin not obtained under a valid prescription is a serious offense in the eyes of the British law, drug addiction is treated primarily as a medical condition and only secondarily as a criminal one. The desired effect is to make the country less attractive to a dealer in heroin, who might wish to expand his trade by getting users dependent on his supplies. In Britain anyone who is addicted is able to get supplies of his drug from a treatment center. Under the National Health Service a prescription for a day's supply of heroin or methadone costs the user not more than 20 pence (48 cents). There is, thus, no need to resort to crime to support one's addiction. The competition from legal heroin keeps the price of imported heroin down (despite contradictory contentions from foreign politicians), thus lowering potential dealer profits.

Another difference between the British and American scene is that in Britain hashish is much more common than is marijuana. It is easier to import, because it is less bulky and is the form usually produced in the Middle East and Asia. It costs about £10 to £12 an ounce ($26 to $31). Marijuana costs about the same when it is available, even though it is less potent. LSD is most commonly available in tablet form, although it has been on sale on gelatine, sugar cubes, blotting paper, and so forth. Its price varies considerably but is typically between 30 pence (72 cents) and £1. There have been no published reports of illegal importation or manufacture of barbiturates or amphetamines on a large scale. These sell at anything up to 15 pence (36 cents) per tablet.

The conviction statistics cannot be relied upon to yield an accurate picture of the relative popularity of various drugs; for conviction rates may reflect the priorities and outcomes of police activity and not the number of actual users of each drug. For example, Table 1 shows a lower proportion of LSD convictions than one might expect, considering the widespread use of the drug and the adverse public view of it. Perhaps arrests and convictions are infrequent because LSD is easily concealed, used only occasionally, and consumed totally. 1970 figures (Home Office, Drugs Branch) show a rise in convictions over 1969 for LSD.

It will be seen from the table that there are many more convictions for possession than for supply, this in spite of the expressed police priority for dealer arrests. One explanation is that dealing usually includes possession at some stage, and possession is far easier to prove in court. Under the old law, penalties were the same for both offences, and little would be lost if supplying could not be proved. Under the new law, the penalties for possession are still very substantial, and it is therefore possible that the same proportion of convictions for possession as against supplying will prevail.

Early in 1970, the labour government, then in power, introduced the Misuse of Drugs bill to replace the 1964, 1965, and 1967 Acts. The act sets out to consolidate and amend the previous law, and in particular to distinguish between the penalties for dealing and possession and to classify drugs according to their potential danger. It prohibits import, export, production, supply or offer to supply, possession with intent to

TABLE 1

1969 Statistics for U.K. Convictions for Drug Offenses (with acknowledgements to the Home Office)

	Cannabis Resin (Hashish)	*Cannabis Herb* (Marijuana)	*Opium*	*Cocaine*	*Heroin*	*Other* 1965 Act drugs including methadone, morphine, pethidine	*LSD*	*Other* 1964 Act drugs including amphetamines, methamphetamine, and mescaline
Possession	3,647	447	47	50	200	455	149	2,106
Import	74	48	2	0	1	3	2	8
Supply	132	15	1	1	36	73	1	29
Procuring	33	16	0	3	26	24	0	0
Premises offenses	200	25	1	0	0	0	0	0
Cultivation	0	5	0	0	0	0	0	0
Theft [a]	0	0	0	85	77	255	0	997
Other offenses [b]	37	4	2	1	1	68	7	463
Total	4,123	560	53	140	341	878	159	3,603
% of total	42	6	.5	1.5	3.5	9	1.5	37

[a] From authorized holders such as manufacturers, hospitals, and pharmacies.
[b] Including prescription forgeries.

supply, possession, and, if one is an occupant or concerned in the management of premises, knowingly permitting certain activities to take place there. These activities are producing, supplying, offering to supply, preparing opium, or smoking cannabis or opium. There are also the same opium offenses, and an offense of cultivation of cannabis, as under the 1965 Act. For all important drugs except barbiturates and methaqualone, the maximum penalties for any of these offenses is increased to fourteen years' imprisonment, with or without a fine.

The Act creates a new offense of possession with intent to supply. This is intended to cover a case where a person is found in possession of a large quantity of drugs where actual supplying cannot be shown but where the intent can be proved—as for example by the discovery of scales, or the packaging of drugs. The Act divides the drugs into two classes. Class A contains heroin, methadone, cocaine, LSD, mescaline, opium, and injectable amphetamines, among others. The maximum penalty for unauthorized possession of a drug in this group is seven years' imprisonment and/or a fine. Class B drugs include principally cannabis, cannabis resin, and amphetamines. The maximum penalty for possession is five years' imprisonment or a fine or both. In 1969 less than 1 per cent of those prosecuted for possession of small quantities of cannabis were sent to prison (Baroness Wootton, House of Lords, 14 January 1971). There is also a class C category under which the penalties are lower. Methaqualone is the only class C drug which is commonly taken recreationally. Barbiturates are not controlled under this Act—apparently because they cannot be included without interfering in the ordinary practice of medicine.

In addition, the Act provides that a doctor who is suspected of overprescribing a psychoactive drug be suspended for continuing to over prescribe it (after warning). Previously such a doctor could only be accused by the General Medical Council of serious professional misconduct and could continue to prescribe until struck off the Medical Register. Overprescribing is not considered a criminal offence. The powers of search and restrictions on prescribing heroin, morphine, and cocaine contained in the 1967 Act are included in the 1971 Act without substantial alteration.

The reasoning offered for the Act was that dealers pose more of a menace than users of drugs and therefore should be more severely punished for selling or distributing drugs. Elystan Morgan, the labour minister who first introduced the bill in Parliament, said, "The area of the pusher is the very area in which criminal sanctions can have their effect" (House of Commons, 16 July 1970). When the Conservatives came into power in 1970, they took over the bill; and one of their spokesman, Lord Windlesham, said that without this legislation "professional pushers and other criminals would be left to their own devices in exploiting, for their own gain, the weaknesses of human nature" (House of Lords, 14 January 1971). Another supporter of the bill had this to say:

"Most [traffickers] are utterly merciless. For money they are prepared to debase and degrade and ruin the health of people. They are prepared to see an individual die in the utmost misery having endured the most frightful agony" (Baroness Summerskill, House of Lords, 11 February 1971).

The feeling behind the Act is well illustrated by Lord Brook: "If a person is just taking drugs, the penalty should be small and effective, but it is doubtful if he should go to prison at all." However, "anyone trafficking in drugs is taking part in murder, not only one murder, but several murders, and it may be many murders. . . . I personally think the penalty should not be reduced from fourteen years to ten, but if anything should be increased from fourteen years to life." Scientific or other empirical evidence for distinguishing so sharply between users and dealers has not been offered. What is clear is that there is a widely held and strong opinion that a drug dealer intentionally profits from human weaknesses. The sentencing of the courts reflects this sentiment. On the other hand, the police—although they often claim to be concentrating on arresting drug pushers (*Observer*, May 2, 1971)—do not always see the dealer in as evil a stance as Parliamentary opinion. For example, the Hampshire Constabulary (1969) has said, "The common conception of a trafficker being some older person who manipulates the supply and demand from behind the scenes and whose identity is known only to a few is often far from true, although such types do exist. In many cases young people still at school or college are able to 'score' and they themselves commence to deal with their friends and associates on a profit-making basis."

Sampling Dealers

How does a sample of English dealers, self-identified as such and drawn from the "mod" drug scene of metropolitan areas, differ from our California sample? Release, a legal-aid group staffed by concerned young people, volunteered to seek information bearing on this query. During 1970, Release saw about 10,000 young people who wanted advice on legal matters, welfare or health counseling, or other community service. Through these Release clients, staff and their acquaintances, plus cooperating agencies, English drug dealers were identified. The sample selected contained (a) dealers contacted through the social chain of acquaintances, including already interviewed dealers; (b) dealers-users (mostly heroin) being treated in centers; (c) Release clients (usually cannabis users) receiving legal counsel for drug charges; and (d) dealers contacted without introduction in drug marketplaces (Piccadilly Circus, Kensington cafes, and the like).

The rate of cooperation varied depending upon the introduction, with (d) above proving least useful. It is estimated that, overall, two thirds of all those contacted agreed to participate, although only one third kept their later interview appointments, enabling them to be included in the study population. We had hoped to include a sample of imprisoned as well as free dealers, but permission could not be obtained for such interviews. The sample N of 96 is smaller than that intended, but the problems of case finding coupled with limitations of funds for interviewers proved insurmountable.

The case-finding method employed in the English study is based, like the California one, on sampling diverse populations. The English study does rely more, however, on dealers who have come to the attention of agencies—either Release itself or one of the several cooperating treatment centers. Over half of the interviews were from these "institutional" sources, even though it must be emphasized that Release is hardly an "Establishment" center. Whenever one rests a sample upon those cases known to agencies—however popular the agency maybe—some types of cases are almost certain to be missed. Morris (1957) has demonstrated that such self-selection as a bias source occurs in England (in health studies) as elsewhere. We must, consequently, expect that the English sample, both by dint of small size and the select dealer pools from which interview subjects were drawn, is not "representative" of all English dealers. Nevertheless, in age, drug histories, and ethnic composition we believe that it represents an important sector of English dealers serving a major population of English drug-using youth.

As will be seen, the English sample differs from the American one in some striking ways. We find 407 significant differences when inquiry and rating areas are compared by our test of the difference between two proportions, and we find 313 significant F tests. We shall be audacious enough to propose that these may be "real" differences between the two populations (London and California) rather than artifacts due to sampling error. These speculations—and they are that—shall imply that national (cultural) differences do affect drug use and dealing careers.

Examining the two sets of data, we find that the English dealers are less diverse in age, for all of them are in the 16 through 35 brackets. The majority are, like the California sample, 19 to 23 years old. There are proportionately more males in the English group, and there are more with advanced degrees. The arts (including musical performers) are more strongly represented among the English dealers, who are also more often single and white than their American counterpart sample.

Business managers are more represented among fathers of the English sample; parental marriages are more stable, and alcoholism among parents is less often described. Within the family the oldest siblings of English dealers appear to be less often arrested, less often to have alcohol problems, and less often to be drug peddlers than their American (more delinquent) counterparts. As is to be expected, then, siblings less often have introduced our English dealers to illicit drugs.

In their drug histories, the English dealers, compared with American, report more hashish as opposed to marijuana use, and have heavier late-teen and early-twenties hallucinogen use. Variations in other drugs, by age, exist but are inconsistent in direction and not frequent. There is at present a greater preference among the English for hallucinogens, in contrast to a greater preference for sedatives by Americans. Initiation into illicit use for the English dealer more often occurred via a same-age, same-sex friend and was more likely to occur in the 16 to 18 bracket. Coffee shops and other public places indoors and other less intimate settings were more often the scene of illicit initiation in London than in California.

With regard to dealing careers, upon meeting a dealer for the first time the English youth more often said he "approved" immediately of the dealer's trade—in contrast to the frightened or nervous California youth; and he was more often required to buy at cost than to receive as a gift his first illicit drug. The costs of drugs were, when money did change hands, considerably lower in England than in California. Amphetamines and hashish in London—as opposed to marijuana, sedatives, and hallucinogens in California—were the drugs first used. Substances sold in England were more often amphetamines, as opposed to early hallucinogen sale by California dealers. English dealers' first sales were concluded under the same circumstances as those of their first illicit use, especially in coffee shops and the like.

These first sales were mostly when they were 16 to 18 years old, whereas in the American sample the age of first selling ranges over more years, both before 16 and especially after 18. Linked to the older age at the time of the first sale is the older age for the Californians' first customers. Earlier commercialization of English dealing is suggested, not only by the prevalence of early purchase over sharing but by an earlier reliance on dealers (as opposed to friends and relatives) as initial sources for supply. English dealers probably were identified, (took on the role of the dealer) at an earlier age, as users in possession of salable quantities of drugs, since English dealers report that initial sales came about when others approached them; in contrast, the Americans generally had to go out to drum up business. Compatible with the earlier approval of the dealing role, English dealers more than American describe their response to becoming a dealer as one of indifference. Consistent with this less "flappable" self-portrayal, English dealers more often deny any concern over violating the law at the time of initial dealing-supplying and also more often deny any sense of guilt.

English dealers indicate a quicker start on their business careers, more initiating strictly commercial transactions. Early on, customers were not drawn from friends. Dealing with strangers had early consequences for the English dealers; for more of them report that in their early stages they were arrested, found out by parents or authorities, or cheated or robbed by their customers or business associates. These difficulties evidently have not deterred them, for more among the English sample are active dealers than among the California sample. The California sample contains more "sometimes" or casual dealers and terminated ones. The English sample contains more dealers who are considering quitting, and among these more who fear arrest and jail. English dealers also report more dissatisfaction with the dealer life, more pressure to quit from others, and a considerably greater fear of getting hurt—either by irrational customers or by gangsters cutting in on the business.

Reflecting on changes in dealing since they have been in the business, English dealers more than California ones comment on the growth of addiction and movement to hard drugs, on undesirable personality changes in dealers (egotism and avarice in particular), and on social changes such as a shift from earlier values and a growing inability for themselves to earn a living outside of trafficking in drugs. Economic considerations appear stronger in the English sample, for they emphasize that they can make more money dealing than in other work. Americans less often see dealing as the only way to earn money.

English dealers more than Americans include, among difficulties in leaving the life, obligations and fears associated with leaving an organization; that is, a fear of reprisal from organized criminals with whom they are in business. Americans, on the other hand, more often mention their need to remain dealing in order to maintain a supply of needed drugs for themselves. Should he stay in dealing and suffer as a result, the English dealer is less concerned than the American with hurting his family; he is, on the other hand, more concerned with the impact of misfortune arising from his dealing as it would hurt his girlfriend or wife. This may imply a greater peer-group value orientation among the English sample.

Reviewing developments in their careers, English more than California dealers comment on changes in their stock-in-trade, especially a shift from initial amphetamines and stimulants to hallucinogens and opiates and cocaine. Volume and profit differences are greater too for the English when the two total samples are compared. However, in dollar value the English dealers (even though more commercial from the start) made considerably less than American ones at the beginning of their dealing careers; even at the time of interview—when they have been in the trade a modal three to five years and report much increased profit—their profits are, on the average, only equal to American profits (in the $100- to $500-per-month range). English more than American dealers also report greater reliance over time on chemists as manufacturing sources and on other dealers for supplies. Their customers also have changed more during their dealing careers; strangers, casual acquaintances, and the "straight" becoming increasingly important as the English clientele. The diversity of the California sample again shows its effects in a wider distribution of customer ages in contrast to the English clientele; the Californians report both the youngest and the oldest customers. English customers are more often male and less often students than are Americans; those who do serve students in England are more likely to concentrate on university groups than are our California dealers, who serve lower educational levels. Compatible with the predominantly white characteristics of the English group, their customers are also more likely white. Habitual and regular users make up a greater portion of the English than American clientele.

In characterizing successful dealers, the English, unlike Americans, emphasize their "cool," inscrutable, careful nature and otherwise unflappable qualities—as opposed to the honest and trustworthy features prized by Californians. The English dealers also emphasize the prestige and admiration, the "ego trip" aspects of being a dealer. And English dealers are more likely to demean women as dealers, considering them paranoid and fearful, in contrast to more "sociological" judgments rendered by Americans in their attempts to explain the lesser frequency of dealing by women.

As for drugs considered incompatible with dealing, the English more often mention hallucinogens; Californians, amphetamines. The English specify amphetamines as a class of drugs which dealers can safely use and still conduct business, in contrast to Americans' opposite views. When asked about the general effects of drugs, the London dealers emphasize euphoria and awareness (produced mainly by cannabis and the hallucinogens) and "activity" (produced by amphetamines); the California dealers, in contrast, emphasize depression as a major effect of drugs. The bad effects of opiates are singled out more by the English dealers. Speaking of bad effects, the English emphasize the internal psychological side; Americans are attentive to external ones—in this case, arrest and imprisonment as consequences of use. On the other hand, Americans more than the English sample are in favor of a "stoned society."

Examining the activities of the two groups, we find that the English dealers report more street dealing, wholesaling, and marketing work; the Americans report more farming and manufacturing and, in general, more organizational complexity, specialization, and working agreements. English dealers more often report problems in securing supplies. The English dealers prefer to sell in London and to be in London. They prefer to buy in Central Asia (Nepal, Afghanistan, Pakistan, India) and in Africa, whereas Americans obtain their supplies in Mexico, the Near East, and the Far East. English drug deals are on a smaller scale than American ones, with the dramatic exception of hashish; and their lifelong profits are clustered in the low $1,000-to-$5,000 bracket. The modal English hashish deal reported by those trafficking in it is in the two-kilo to ten-kilo range.

Comparing their drug police, the English more often than Americans think of theirs as stupid and simpleminded in contrast to the egalitarian "they're like everyone else" American view. Local narcotics police are more derided for incompetence and the national "drug squad" more praised for skill than are their American counterparts. On the other hand, English more often than American dealers describe the ordinary police officer as "doing his job"; and the latter more often emphasize the self-righteous position of the American officer. As for direct experience with the police, more of the English dealers have suffered a drug arrest, but fewer have served time for drug offenses than have Americans. (There is no difference in the rate of nondrug offenses, which about half of both samples have experienced.) The California dealers more than the London ones admit to carrying a weapon (although 12 per cent of the London dealers do carry a gun). The English dealers less often file income tax returns and much more frequently break laws "for pleasure." The English believe, more than Americans do, that they are known to the police. Somewhat less often than Americans they describe themselves as professional criminals.

Evaluating the scene, today's versus yesterday's, the English dealers stress the greater present economic opportunities and the presence of gangsters and organized crime. Americans emphasize the greater involvement of youth, the greater variety of drugs, and the increase in gun toting.

In personal expectations and preferences, the English lean to the fine arts and the Americans to professions and business in the choice of straight jobs; the Americans lean to business and vocational courses in school and the English to social sciences. In national politics the English sample is more uninvolved or nihilistic, often denying the acceptability of any candidate (for Prime Minister).

As for background and status, the English more often come from Protestant families, report poorer present health and more worries over alcoholism, did not enjoy elementary or high school, felt disliked by teachers, were truant, have few friends, enjoy fast cars, do not have stable heterosexual relations, dislike the idea of settling down, and are impulsive spenders. The Americans owe larger amounts of money, although more of the English are in debt. The Americans require a much larger income to maintain their living standard. The English would be the more permissive as parents, more often allowing their children cannabis, speed, and hallucinogens (but, like Americans, the majority would not want their children to be dealers).

In self-description the Americans more often are keyed to the Protestant ethic; the English to the romantic one: unsure, searching, and roving. In contrast, the Americans more often are antagonistic to drug laws, calling for their abolition; the London sample—arguing for the retention of drug laws—emphasize medical-psychiatric disposition of users identified as having drug problems. The English, however, more often contend that present laws are unfairly enforced—not, as Americans say, because of their harshness but because the laws *are* egalitarian and do *not* provide for different handling for different people. Perhaps their more general support for drug laws as such accounts for the greater stated willingness of London dealers to pitch in and help control drug use themselves, particularly addicting substances. Asked what they wanted us to recommend, the English dealers more than Americans emphasize education.

In the rating section (keeping in mind that no reliability training for raters was conducted) the English dealers are rated, in contrast to the California sample, as more casual, long haired, clean, and well cared for, slowed in their responses, confused, and unreliable. Americans are more often seen as angry.

Comment and Summary

A sample of ninty-six English dealers was identified by Release workers, an English legal-aid and social-assistance group operated in

London by concerned young people. The London dealers are, in most ways, like the California sample of 480 dealers with which they are compared. Teen-age use and dealing, multiple-drug use with emphasis on hallucinogens, histories of drug and nondrug arrests, the development of business styles, and the immersion of dealing in the larger social context of drugs and with other delinquency—including the growth for some of violence—are observed in both samples.

Both groups believe that drugs are good things for people, and that what they do—as dealers—is morally right. Both English and American samples get psychological as well as social and economic gratifications from dealing. Dealing is part of a life in which drug use is central but where both dealing and use are social activities. Money is not the only aim in trafficking. English and American dealers are a "special" population—not only because they are dealers and delinquents but also because of their history of school, work, and family problems. Most are not—as far as our limited data allow us to estimate—madmen, drug slaves, or otherwise mythical creatures.

The average English dealers seen here do, on the other hand, differ from our average young American dealers in becoming more quickly commercial, less sociable, and experiencing faster and, we suspect, more jolting movement from middle-class straight family life to a criminal underworld. The differences observed between London and California dealers may be refined if we link them to our earlier analysis of American dealer subgroups and then draw some parallels. For example, the average English dealer in this sample is clearly like the American psychedelic dealers, serious or "sometime" in his preference for drugs and his stock-in-trade. He is not like the American lower-class opiate-using loser or experienced criminal who is deeply involved in addiction, and despair. He is like the American big-time dealer (cool and hip) in his commercialization and reduced drug sociability except that he is not the big-money success that the American big dealer is, and does not have the immunity from the law, or the comparative freedom from fear or danger, which the American's immersion in middle-class psychedelic dealing provides.

The average London dealer has some characteristics which strike us as peculiarly "un-American"; that is, as conforming to at least a stereotype of the British and their styles of doing business. We shall list these now—putting in parentheses the differences which suggest the characterization. We cannot be sure at this point whether our list reflects only our own stereotypes, whether it does tell us only something about the English sample, or whether it might be generalized to other English dealers. We simply offer our speculations for critical testing by others. The following English features strike us as generally (culturally) different from Californians:

controlled emotion (cooler, more disinterested)

male dominance (fewer women dealers, customers, more personal demeaning of female business competence)

more stable, less pathogenic families

delayed heterosexuality (more same-sex initiation, use, sales)

less opportunity for financial gain (drugs cost less, bring less profit even for serious dealers, although drug sales offer more earning potential than other available jobs)

difference in drug availability (hashish over marijuana)

less intimacy in social contact (more drug initiations and use in public places, less use in homes, more sales to strangers)

different business methods; specifically, less organization and less reliance on honesty and trust (an American small business ethic)

less evidence of a heroin-using, addicted, alcoholic, gun-toting slum-style user-dealer

more psychological "push" within the drug-using population for activity rather than tranquility, for "uppers" rather than "downers"—in contrast to the American theme (see Blum, 1971)

more personal romanticism and less commitment to the Protestant ethic (in self concepts, vocational interests, vocational goals)

greater attention to inner experience and internal or psychological determinants of behavior (inner-directed privatism) in contrast to American "extraversion" "other-directedness" (Riesman et al., 1953), and environmental-sociological explanations for one's own or others' conduct.

different preferences in international drug trafficking—sources in Asia or Africa as opposed to American buying in the Middle East and Mexico.

lesser English zeal for revolutionary or antiauthority ideology and social reform (more acceptance of cops, drug laws, and less approval of a stoned society than in their American counterparts).

more individual rebellion and greater individual movement away from straight institutions (breaking laws for fun, less peer involvement, coming from straighter families, more rejection of any candidates as offering political solutions, more removed from adult approval, more truancy) less egalitarian in viewpoint (wanting laws to be applied unequally), greater emphasis on inferiority in those disliked (such as drug police)

drug dealing as more often a genuine career path for loners than as an expression of one kind of (awkward) American sociability (fewer friends, less immersion of dealing in friendship context, more emphasis on private than on social facilitation in drug effects)

more support for the law as such; greater internalization of rule by law (more support for drug laws, approval of ordinary police, more fear of arrest and jail even though shorter sentences have been meted out)

less dealer involvement with the very young and, presumably, less prevalence of drug experimentation in lower grades; that is, drug use is concentrated among deviants or older youth, for example school leavers or university students (Wiener, 1970)—(fewer young customers; fewer students among customers; when students are customers, they are in university)

The foregoing are possibilities to be examined in a cross-cultural study of young English versus American drug dealers in relationship to their cultural milieu.

We call attention to the greater shift on the part of those English with origins in the middle- and upper-class straight families to the rough-tough drug underworld. Unlike the middle-class American who may experience but little that is new and shocking as a dealer, the London well born dealer, we infer, is more likely thrown into a new and uglier world. This circumstance leads us to ask if, for the British, this new class of profit-hungry, gangster involved, skilled, well educated, self controlled, prestigeful (both in family background and peer evaluation) youth may not pose something of a serious crime problem should their present drug dealing incomes—which are by American standards low—be seen by them as insufficient. Might these potentially competent offenders move out of the drug scene into other crime, for example robbery? We wonder if it may not be a signal of a major shift in English values and crime potentials, that 12 per cent of the London sample carry a gun. The trends suggested by the reports of gangsterism and violence do not bode well for keeping the English peace.

In this regard, we hark back to the complaint of the London underground press about the Americanization of dealing with its gangsterism and violence. The underground press was certainly sensitive to the experiences of the English dealers as here reported. Whether it is properly blamed on Americans is something historians can decide; what we suggest is, given the departure of these young Englishmen from the standards of their own family and society, that the roots of their rebellion and criminalization as well as their creative unusualness (referring to other aspects of the youth scene) are internal, not imports. That is to say, British family and social life must itself have the potentials for creating these phenomena even if the "model" is borrowed from Jesse James, Al Capone, Tim Leary, or (an export-reimported) Aldous Huxley. That these potentials for generating drug delinquency are less than those found in the United States is strongly suggested by comparing the prevalence of heroin use, violence, street delinquency, and the like.

Chapter 16

PHASES OF A GHETTO CAREER

This chapter describes some aspects of drug involvement as it is woven into a career line emerging out of the urban ghetto. The initial evidence for my account was gathered in the course of ethnographic field work as part of a larger study of youthful drug use in predominantly black ghettos of Oakland and the surrounding Bay Area.[1] In addition to numerous informal conversations, extensive participant observation, and life history interviews with key informants, a few central figures, those recognized by their peers as most knowledgeable about their world, were brought together in "panel sessions." Among several hundred participants seen, group interviews with key informants were held continuously over the past six years. As panel members gathered for group discussion and critically examined each other's experience, it was possible for me to separate individual experiences from those more collective in nature and to check the validity of my own observations. The following account suggests a few important lines of inquiry and does not represent an exhaustive study of drug dealing. It explicates a career line of a black

[1] The research techniques employed are described in more detail in Blumer, Sutter, Ahmed, and Smith (1967). Sutter (1969) presents a more comprehensive depiction of drug use worlds into which this analysis fits as one element. The more general ghetto context of social types and activities portrayed here is presented in Hannerz (1969) and Liebow (1967). See also Finestone (1960) and Milner and Milner (1972).

ghetto-raised youth who becomes (or fails to become) a hustler who may eventually deal in hard drugs.

Wanting to be the Baddest

Little tiny dudes, six to eleven years old, engage in the earliest form of drug involvement as they play near the ramshackle, scrawl-covered buildings of housing projects, near empty lots and playgrounds and around commercial establishments in the urban ghetto. Here they will confront a world of spontaneous play-groups and alliances. In seeking fun, partnership, and adventure, they swarm over the streets from nearby city blocks. The patterns of play activity are differentiated by the emergence of a distinctive set of especially bold and nervy little dudes, who begin to develop a reputation for being "bad." Having fun is often contingent on risk-taking behavior, and things like glue, paint thinner, gasoline or anything that can be manufactured on the spur of the moment become agents for distinguishing the bold and fearless from the timid and frightened. When drug use practices occur, they are usually woven into the embryonic posture of being bad:

> *We'd go on a Saturday and see who could sniff the most tubes of glue, man. This one dude, you know, he was about fourteen and we were about ten, and he was high, and we were all laughing in the park. We had our little bottle of whiskey with us, you know. Didn't even know what to do, dump the glue in a sock, and you know, roll it, and after you start sniffing, it's just something new and you flash. Throw the whiskey bottle away. I'm bad now! You go around with the other little cats.*

These particular bold little dudes are already prepared at this early age to engage in petty stealing, vandalism, and fighting. Physical assaults are woven into their daily routine as part of the spirit of play. Their high tolerance for aggression heightens a sensitivity to danger and awakens the need for self defense. To wander along the street alone, to ride a bicycle, or walk home after school can become an obstacle course. Lurking in the atmosphere is an ever present tension, a sense of fear which cramps the stomach with butterfly twitters. It becomes essential that a little dude meet violence by defending himself or engaging in fights to assert himself: "You got to be a rough little dude when you're coming up. You got to be to survive, man." The elevation of toughness to a supreme virtue is symbolized by bravery in the face of danger and the demeanor of a hard character.

This generalized sensitivity to danger does not mean that all children living under ghetto conditions are "belligerent little bastards." On the contrary, as particular play groups are differentiated from the main stream of children by their "nervy" and often public displays of aggression, they are in turn shunned and set apart by childhood associates. Despite a world with a high tolerance for violence and a threatening atmosphere, most children stay clear of rowdy little dudes and gradually form their own friendships and alliances: "There was this certain little group that were my age, but they was doing different things than I was doing. I was going to school and playing ball, pretty good little kid until I hit junior high, but they were running around fighting and sniffing glue and shit like that."

It is typical among the nervy little dudes to "act big" and to cultivate a reputation as "the baddest." Taking on the expressive patterns of fear-inspiring older dudes, lured by legendary tales of ferocious exploits, they strut about with a posture of arrogance and gradually set themselves apart from more conforming children, whom they regard as "punks."

> *You just want to be bad, man; it's in the air. . . . The little dudes around the block, they want to act older than they are, think it's all big and bad to beat up some kid on the street. . . . Fuck it, man! Everybody was a mess-up, all the kids in West Oakland. 'Cause when I was small, it was me and my cousin. We're the same age, and we were going to elementary school together, and all the thought on my mind was just rule the school man, rule the school. When I get in sixth grade I'm gonna rule the school, man, and that was my highest desire. I didn't care about nobody, and that's what I did. I ruled the school. I thought that was the greatest in the world. As far as we were concerned we were the baddest, and I thought that was boss* [*great*].

Drug involvement provides a mixture of fear, pleasure and confident hope in the face of new and unfamiliar sources of fun. Adventuring with aggression and techniques for altering consciousness and mood have an explosive potential which is deliberately sought out and cultivated among these little dudes. The potential danger of solvent inhalation, combined with the possibility of discovery and punishment, tends to heighten and intensify the intrigue associated with fun and being the baddest.

Associated with the quest for fun is an early awareness of "messing up"; for messing up can become a mark of distinction, and the attendant risk of "getting into trouble" is thrilling. Encounters with "adults," especially school authorities, increase steadily; these "children" are openly defiant, and their drug use practices are highly visible. Yet the little dudes rarely even imagine themselves as using real drugs, and there is no commitment to their use. Drug taking is fluid and unstructured, occurring on the spur of the moment during play. Through a process of exploration, different meanings are imputed to their tentative experimentation, altering mood states are discerned, and different sensations are grasped symbolically. This process of exploration is part of the initial phase in the developing experience with illegal drugs; while the cultivation of a bold and nervy character will lay the basis for becoming a cold dude.

As these bold little dudes pass through early adolescence, from around twelve to fifteen years old, they will form new partnerships and alliances. If they continue along the same course, directly expressing the spirit of masculine aggression, they will move into a genuinely "rowdy" stage, and being "bad" takes on new meaning. From the spirit of play in limited, spur of the moment situations, being bad develops into a central image and leads to a more serious and sustained belligerency in a wider range of situations. Progressive involvement with police also enters into the definition of being bad.[2]

"Low-riders" and "Fuck-ups"

Rowdy life, the "low-riding bag," is impulsive and unrestrained. Attempts are made to "terrorize" and elicit fear while in the presence of others. Boisterous and audacious conduct increases and criminal activity takes on a violent, even vicious character. It is well known that in some neighborhoods a rowdy group will simply convert the street corners and alleys into a restricted domain. Fighting is sought out; violence is courted in a deliberate attempt to create hazardous situations. A worthy character is a "bad" character, and to be bad at this time means to be rowdy, almost "crazy." The dudes who enter into the "low-riding bag" are often considered "crazy" in that they "don't give a shit about nothin' and nobody," even themselves: "You know, fuck it man! You want to fight, man, and you want to drink, and you want to fuck, and you want to steal, man. You gotta be bad, man, 'cause if you're not bad you ain't shit."

Over time these early-adolescent youths become the main representatives of physical prowess, eventually becoming known as the "badder crowd" in selected junior high schools, "hoods" and "thugs"

[2] Elements of these themes have been presented with sensitivity by Werthman and Piliavin (1967) and Feldman (1968).

in the eyes of upper- and middle-class high school youth; and "little gangsters" in the eyes of older dudes in the "fast life."

> *These are the types of dudes that when they are not even loaded* [*under the influence of a drug*], *they're vicious and sort of unruly, rowdy, you know. They carry it over when they are loaded. Go outside and yell in the street, pick on people that's passing by. You can be right there walking along with 'em, you know, and all of a sudden they'll say, "Let's go rip up that dude's suit," or "Let's go rip off that house right now, man," and they'll be in the house and pretty soon they're coming out with radios and tape recorders, you know. These are the cats who go out for terrorizing, just stone little gangsters. They take you off into another dimension somewhere.*

There is a readiness to consume a wide variety of intoxicant substances. Although liquor, mainly wine, is the favored and most often used drug, almost anything is likely to be seized. Sniffing volatile organic solvents is fairly common; the use of barbiturates (reds, yellows, blues, rainbows, christmas trees), other hypnotics, and amphetamine compounds takes on a patterned character; smoking marijuana, although less frequent than the use of other drugs, does enter into the repertoire of rowdy youth. There is also a growing competition between close associates, with frequent struggles to achieve the most exotic experience or to act in the most outrageous and bizarre manner after consuming whatever substance is known to alter consciousness and mood. The competitive character of drug use sets the stage for thrilling episodes which are later recounted in gossip sessions where romantic tales of prowess are exchanged and new reputations are built. "It's like you always got to be one step bigger than anybody else, you know. Like if everybody's drinking beer you goin' out and get some whiskey. So he's drinking wine and you go out and drop some pills. You always hassling just to show everybody what you can do."

Rowdy dudes seldom have the chance to use marijuana on a regular basis. Even though youngsters in junior high school often claim proudly that they "get loaded," that they're "wasted" or "ripped" on grass, and may even act out imagined roles, close examination reveals that marijuana use is episodic and relatively unsystematic. When on occasion marijuana becomes available, the pattern of use takes on the same characteristics as the use of alcohol and other intoxicating drugs. "Grass really sparks you, man. I mean I think the trip is out of sight. I can get loaded, man, but there's a dude that's sitting right there I don't like. I hate his mother-fucking guts, man; and if he says anything wrong, when I'm loaded, man, I can get up and hit him and think nothing about it."

The impending prospect of "getting busted" becomes an integral part of the world of rowdy dudes and enters into their conception of being bad at this stage. "Low-riders" begin to feel they are the targets of a massive conspiracy of school, police, probation, and even recreation authorities: "Everybody's down on me, man; they're messing with me; always on my case" expresses for many a proud realization that one is "bad" enough to be "wanted." The theme of "fucking up" expresses a mood of resignation to the fate of always "blowing it," always "getting busted" or ending up in jail. Being "wasted," the routine experience of inebriation on a wide variety of chemical agents, provides a convenient justification for having "fucked up" and also fits the attitude of careless bravado in the face of danger.

To be sure, the impulsive, violent and careless behavior occurring in groups of rowdy dudes has a marked impact on how they are treated by others, and in turn, how they define their sphere of life. Partnerships, cliques, and circles in the "low-riding set" definitely move in the direction of a segregated collective experience inside the ghetto community. Rowdy dudes form a distinctive world of social practice and belief and remain on the periphery of the illegal-drug market. Their dangerous and conspicuous behavior, coupled with their tendency toward violence, is a warning signal to experienced drug users and dealers. Reckless and irresponsible conduct is too great a hazard to those who deal drugs in the illicit marketplace and to most of the youth who consume drugs obtained through this market. Thus, before a dude who is in the "low-riding bag" can really get into the drug market, he has to mellow off. He must learn to "maintain his cool"; otherwise, he remains a "chump" who never listens, who never learns, who can't wake up to what's happening. He will be "iced" (kept at a safe distance and ignored) or downgraded by most of the dudes on the set:

> *The rowdy dude won't listen; he's too busy droppin' his low-ridin' hand; he won't look around and see what's happening. There's a lot of people that I wouldn't accept; they live in this world, and they don't know a damn thing about it, you know; they don't understand nothing; they don't know how to act around women; they don't know how to make money; they don't know what's the value of money; they don't know nothin' about nothin'. When I can detect this in a dude, you know, fuck him. I tell him after a while, "Say, ah, man, lookee here, you not*

righteous, you know. You ignorant, you know. You a damn fool. So just make it, man. I don't even want to talk to you!"

The rowdy dudes who fail to "lighten up" join the ranks of "fuck-ups," those who are recognized in later life as having been "raised by the state." They are taken out of circulation through death or incarceration and seem to "vanish" from the street scene by the time they reach their sixteenth birthdays. As "fuck-ups" they derive their primary identity from prison rituals and cliques where legends of great escapes are manufactured and elaborated in gossip sessions. During their prison experience they become what is known as "jailhouse slick," slick in the sense of learning all the hustling games from those who have failed. When they are released, they try to apply their jailhouse knowledge, usually "blow it," and return to the jailhouse. The "fuck-up," as a social type, does not seem to care whether he lives, dies, or remains in jail.[3]

Most dudes will "grow out" of the "low-riding bag" before joining the ranks of "chumps" and "fuck-ups." They either identify themselves with militant political activists, enter into a genuine spirit of sociability and party life, settle into fairly conventional school routines, or advance themselves in a variety of hustling games. Among those who continue their violent practices into later life, some will begin to develop a certain amount of discipline and self-control. They will "mellow off" or "lighten up," if for no other reason than to remain out of the jailhouse.

Mellowing Off

A more sociable pattern of life comes into being at a time when little dudes get interested in girls, develop a concern for their own appearance, and attempt to imitate the expressive styles of older cats on the set. By the time a rowdy dude moves into high school, an awareness of his exclusion from the mainstream of group life will usually force him to reflect on the consequences of his activity. Girls begin to "shine him on," ignore him, or rank him for not dressing right, not talking right and not acting right. Among the more thoughtful rowdy dudes there is an increasing concern that friends and acquaintances are getting killed, going to jail, or getting nowhere with their escapades of "terrorism"; while older cats are "getting high" and enjoying themselves. Thus, during the later part of junior high school, and especially upon

[3] See further Irwin's (1970) treatment of the "disorganized criminal's" world and "state-raised youth."

entrance into high school, there is a general movement toward cool sociability.

Passing from a "low-riding bag" into a cool round of life has a marked impact on drug-use practices. There is a dramatic shift to smoking marijuana as grass comes to symbolize a more refined and sophisticated style which is opposed to aggressive conduct. There is a concerted attempt to remain casual and composed, to cultivate poise and unruffled emotions. "See, people I know, after they got hip to weed, they just climbed out of that rowdy trip. They squared off completely, you know. Wanted to jump sharp, enjoy themselves and be mellow instead of getting all brutalized. That is definitely true. You don't hear much about gang fighting anymore even. People getting hip to weed."

The early outlines of a primitive system of drug distribution begin to emerge among the group of "cooler little dudes" around eleven or twelve years of age; however, the main source of marijuana is older relatives and friends in the neighborhood. Once in a while a youngster will have access to an ounce of marijuana which he distributes among his friends, but for the most part continuous access to marijuana symbolizes the *coming of age* in the ghetto. That is, a little dude "grows up" when he can "get loaded on weed" at will and participate in the round of life typical of older cats. If he is "fortunate" enough to have a "cool" older brother, he will be introduced to marijuana early in the game. Older dudes often "turn on" their younger brothers to prevent them from sniffing glue, drinking wine, or risking the chance of being arrested. The following comments by a seventeen-year-old dude illustrate the therapeutic value of marijuana in the "treatment" of glue sniffing and rowdy conduct:

> *I found out a lot about my little brother sniffing glue, and I used to whip on him thinking he'll hang it up man. You know, he got busted three times behind glue, and I couldn't reason with him at all, 'cause behind my back he would go sniffing glue with his younger partners who were all in that bag. So I says, if there's anything gonna make him grow up and see the light it's weed. If he gets loaded, he'll stop sniffing glue and be more cautious. Start the time machine going see, 'cause if you smoke grass you're bound to be with people that are older and more cool. So I started getting him loaded, and he's never sniffed glue since then, and he's never been busted again.*

Drug use practices among older dudes tend to filter down into the ranks of the emerging cool little dudes, and this diffusion process generates a give-and-take bartering system. Most of the time a youngster will simply "run across" a match box (⅕ ounce) of marijuana for no more than five dollars and often for nothing, simply as a favor. (This condition is of course contingent on the general supply of weed in the area.) He will learn how to clean the contents—removing seeds and twigs—and roll about fifteen "joints." Then he can pass around joints as an expression of friendship and trust, or he can sell the joints to his partners. In either case, the first experience of "turning on" his friends will really make him feel "boss" (superior). He must "have something going" for him; he must "really be into something," in the eyes of his partners.

A demand for marijuana and pills begins to increase, with a concomitant growth of the rudimentary give-and-take bartering system among the cooler crowds. Having continuous access to marijuana may alter the way a young dude begins to experience himself. He may like the way grass gives him confidence when he tries to rap to his number-one girl: "Hey, baby, what's goin' on? You wanna get high? You sure lookin' fine!" Here the little dude is starting to develop his conversation and grass is helping him along. Over time he may learn how to use grass to further advantage. Although everybody in his set seems to be getting high, not everybody can score his own grass. When he gets into high school, if he lives in certain Bay Area cities, he will have to have a "ride" (car) to really make it with his girls. He will also have to get his wardrobe together in mod fashion. This takes money, and money is scarce indeed. If he has made some pocket money by selling joints and then picks up the enterprising spirit of the hustling world, he will begin to "game a little harder." The attraction of developing a "hustle" combines with the existence of petty dealing opportunities to orient dudes in the direction of hustling:

> *When you playin' gangster, you hittin' on dudes, just kick ass wherever you be. But then you start playin', you know, you try to jump sharp. Don't be wearing them bell-bottom jeans and actin' crazy. The thing is where you want to be mellow. So I was startin' to get my game together. You try to mack* [*pimp*], *or you shoot pool, or you start dealin' a little weed or whatever. Everybody's got their little game and everybody's got their little front, and you're gonna get sharp.*

Getting Your Game Together

Before a dude can make big money, "top dust," he must learn how to "get his game together." He must do "whatever is right." Whatever is right depends on the situation at any instance in time.

You have to discover by yourself whatever is right for you. This may mean you have to "blow it" a few times and get back in the game. Drug dealing in the urban ghetto fits into the "whatever" dimension; it is right when the opportunity arises, and the individual is "ready."

It is the cool dude coming up on the set who is looking at the older cats, watching close, listening, knowing that he better hear if he wants to survive as a physical being with a self worthy of respect. He soon learns that dealings in the hustling life are nothing like the amiable transactions among previous friends. To remain in the "fast life" the dude must have audacity, ingenuity, knowledge, skill and "luck."

> *I was still fighting, you know, but I started to dig weed, you know, and I wanted to have my own. I didn't want to be getting it off somebody all the time. So I began hustling. This cat gives me one connection, and I think I had been smoking dope about two months, you know, and my mind was getting a little advanced, you know. I was starting to game. I just wasn't running with my old partners as much because I got in this bag with this dealer. I mean I was steady talking to him, and I was starting to get deals from him, you know, match boxes for two and three dollars. Well, one day I fell in, and I burned him. I did it on purpose, you know. I knew he was gonna find out about it, and I just took off two lids. So I come back the next day to see what the come down was gonna be, and he busts me. He says I burned him, and I told him, "Yeah, I burned you." And the dude dug me, you know. He say, "Well, that's all right." But I knew I had to watch him. . . . I was beginning to play now, you know, trying to be slick. I was trying to get myself together.*

Getting Slick

The game starts to get cold; competition is keen; and everything a dude has learned "coming up" will be put to the test.

> *You can't be a so-called hustler now and then find out your game ain't so tight, or your money ain't right, or you don't know nothin' about dealing. Let me school ya' before they fool ya'. A lot of dudes have this here phoney act, tryin' to be dynamic and soulful when they don't have all the moves to back their hand. How you gonna tell the teller and sell the seller? You can't sell the seller shit 'cause he's sellin' you! So after a while you read 'em, you know where they coming from. You know who to watch,*

> *what to say, when to say it, and how to play it. Let me tell ya', Jack. It's a cold game and you gotta be a cold dude. A poop-butt motherfucker in there dealin' gets pushed aside, fucked over, and stomped down.*
>
> *It's a cold game man. You got it down to where you don't care about anybody. You're trying to be slick, keeping your game tight, and that's all you care about. You're steady running, dealing some heavy shit, watching, doing a little bit of everything. You're that cold dude, and nobody's gonna mess with you. Whatever you say, they're gonna jump.*

If he can remain in the game, a dealer will meet people coming from different directions in the social order. Through his work he becomes increasingly aware of new opportunities for making money, meeting fine women, and gaining self respect, respect which is always contingent on his rising prestige and the maintenance of his position in the "fast life." Yet he discovers that to make money is not quite enough; he must also *show* that he is "qualified." This includes knowing how to "style." To be without sharp "threads" in the latest fashionable style, to be without classy jewelry and an expensive car means you're not ready yet. In addition, as most men know, in any game "you got to have a *Woman* or *Women* in your corner." So you use the "dust" made from dealing dope in order to "catch" yourself a girl, a bitch, a lady, or, if a dude is heavy enough, a full-blown *Woman.* If your game is really together, you might even get a Queen or Star in your corner, and then you are *there.*

When dope is within easy reach, and "you got your game up tight," you can deal in larger amounts of product, move away from street life, and begin to cultivate "class." The heroin market, including the kilo connections, the ounce men, the dealers in cut ounces, the street dealers in ten-dollar bags, the "hyps" who are "strung out," provides the opportunity for making "top dust," but the marketplace in cocaine is the place for the elite.[4] Cocaine is the "rich man's drug," and cocaine dealers move in the jet set of the underworld. As a member of the elite, the cocaine dealer likes "to get down," likes to "blow," digs "jamming" with "girl" (cocaine), and knows what he can do behind it: His conversation is strong, and his mind is sharp; his game is tight,

[4] For a fuller treatment of the heroin market in New York, see Preble and Casey (1969). See also Woodley (1971) for a description of the work day, etiquette, and perspective of a New York cocaine dealer.

and he can move all night. He has reached the goal of all dealers in the "fast life," that point where "all you do, man, is lay back and dress n' rest, dress n' rest, man."

The illegal drug economy may be viewed as a social and economic subsystem interpenetrating the larger capitalist economy. The spirit of enterprise infuses the hierarchy of distributors and dealers, while consumers invest in and sustain the marketplace activity. The spy system fostered by repressive drug control policies and the absence of regulations to ensure the manufacture of quality drugs tend to generate violence and chaos in the market. This makes for a "cold game" in which the players and dealers must stand alone in order to survive. The drug market, as it functions in the urban ghetto, provides opportunities for the otherwise unemployable, who are human surplus in the larger capitalist economy. Dealing drugs, for many, is the only way to earn a living and still remain a Man.

Comment and Summary

This chapter examined the way drug dealing forms part of a larger career line emerging out of the urban ghetto. Instead of concentrating on drug dealing per se, the changing context of drug practices among predominantly black ghetto-raised youth who may eventually deal in hard drugs is described. In the context of play activity among a distinctive set of bold and daring children, drug involvement becomes an integral part of "wanting to be the baddest." If these children pass into a genuinely "rowdy" phase of life during early adolescence, the celebration of prowess by overt displays of masculine aggression poses a threat to the mainstream of ghetto youth. There is considerable pressure to "mellow off," and drug involvement then is woven into a counterscheme which celebrates a more cultivated approach to life in the spirit of cool sociability. During later adolescence, the attraction of coming to possess a lucrative "hustle" combines with petty dealing practices to launch a number of youth into a "cold game" of drug dealing in the spirit of enterprise. For those who are "qualified" for the hustling world, the illegal drug economy provides an opportunity to make a living and still maintain the self-respect which characterizes manhood.

Chapter 17

THE SOCIAL STRUCTURE OF A HEROIN COPPING COMMUNITY

We have been studying heroin addicts in their natural setting in an effort to understand the factors contributing to the spread and maintenance of this disorder. In previous studies (Hughes, Crawford, and Barker, 1971; Hughes and Jaffe, 1971) we reported that (1) the majority of active street addicts in our urban area appeared to be organized for purposes of heroin distribution into neighborhood "copping communities," (2) an epidemiologic field team located at the local drug-distribution sites, called "copping areas," can obtain demographic and other epidemiologic data on the majority of copping community members, and (3) the field team can remove special samples from the copping community through experimental treatment projects.

During our visits to copping areas in various ethnic neighborhoods, we were impressed by the structural similarities of these drug-distribution networks and their high degree of social and geographical stability. The characteristic features of local distribution systems can be accounted for by two unique aspects of heroin addiction. First is the addict's need for a continuous drug supply to prevent onset of withdrawal symptoms. When he is sick and has money, he needs a place where he can go for symptom relief. Second, because these locations are frequently under police surveillance, the addict cannot walk

Reprinted from *The American Journal of Psychiatry*, volume 128, pages 551–558, 1971.

up to a dealer, pass him money, and walk away. Therefore, copping communities tend to develop a rather complex organization to protect their membership from constant police pressure. In this way they resemble delinquent gangs and other criminal organizations.

We describe here the role structure elaborated by the membership of one copping community studied for a period of one year. Data are presented showing the distribution of the membership in the various roles and the social and treatability characteristics of the occupants of these roles. Implications of the findings for prevention and control programs are also discussed.

Method

Methadone-maintained ex-addict field workers were assigned to four major copping areas on Chicago's South Side, where they were known and trusted. The choice of one particular copping area for intensive study was determined by the unusual competence of the field worker. By administering a survey card in the field, he obtained demographic and drug-use data on the majority of addicts frequenting this copping area. A weekly log was kept on the current addiction status of all copping community members for a twelve-month period. A "member" was defined as a heroin distributor or consumer who frequented the copping area for at least four weeks of the study period. The field worker's recordings were verified by professional staff through visits to the copping area and personal interviews.

Fifty-two members who were active during the months of April, May, and June, 1969, were offered a 50 per cent chance of immediate treatment if they participated in a questionnaire and home-visit study. The random assignment of participants to immediate treatment or to the four-month waiting list was made upon completion of the interviews. Thirty-four (65 per cent) cooperated with the project. A comparison of the effects of immediate treatment versus placement on the waiting list is reported elsewhere.

Each subject was rated on the Addict Psychosocial Functioning Scale (Schumann, Hughes, and Caffrey, 1971). This instrument evaluates addicts on eight subscales which assess severity of addiction, psychological and occupational functioning. Ratings were arrived at by consensus of a psychiatrist and two psychologists, one of whom conducted a clinical interview during the home visit. To provide a basis for ratings, the clinician who conducted the interview prepared a psychiatric history of each subject based upon questionnaire responses, interview material, and the field worker's report of how copping-community peers viewed the addict's social functioning.

Results

During the year of observation, 125 addicts and two non-heroin users were judged by field staff to be members of this copping community. Field staff determined that the majority could be assigned to one of the following primary roles: big dealer, street dealer, part-time dealer, bag follower, tout, hustler, and worker. Big dealers are defined as local wholesalers who supply street or part-time dealers, although they may deal directly to a few trusted customers. Street dealers sell heroin directly to consumers. Part-time dealers supplement their income by hustling or working, and move in and out of the dealer role for varying lengths of time. Touts carry out liaisons between dealers and consumers, sometimes steering customers to a particular dealer. They may also buy drugs for addicts who have no established connection with dealers. Bag followers attach themselves to dealers to support drug habits. The three in our study were attractive women who earned their drugs by enhancing a dealer's prestige or by carrying heroin on their persons because of the reluctance of police to search women on the street. Hustlers engage in various illegal activities other than drug distribution to support their habits; most commonly they are shoplifters. Workers maintain at least a part-time legitimate job, although most hustle as well.

This division of labor follows the functional requirements of drug distribution originally described by Preble and Casey (1969). However, our classification does not include roles in the distribution hierarchy above the neighborhood level. It also differs slightly from Preble's classification because of our desire to assign each individual to one primary role. The part-time dealer is the only label which we developed to meet this classification need. All other roles and definitions are based upon current use of these terms by heroin addicts in our community. Although some members were observed to carry out several distribution and consumer activities during the period of study, weekly recordings for a four-month period suggested a great deal of role stability over time.

The distribution of this copping community's membership according to functional roles is portrayed in Figure 1. One notes that a high proportion, 34 per cent, are primarily engaged in drug distribution. Only two members of this copping community are nonaddicted dealers —that is, motivated purely by economic gain. The figure also shows the distribution of females and police informers within the various roles.

Although 127 were considered to be active members of this copping community at some time during the twelve months, on the

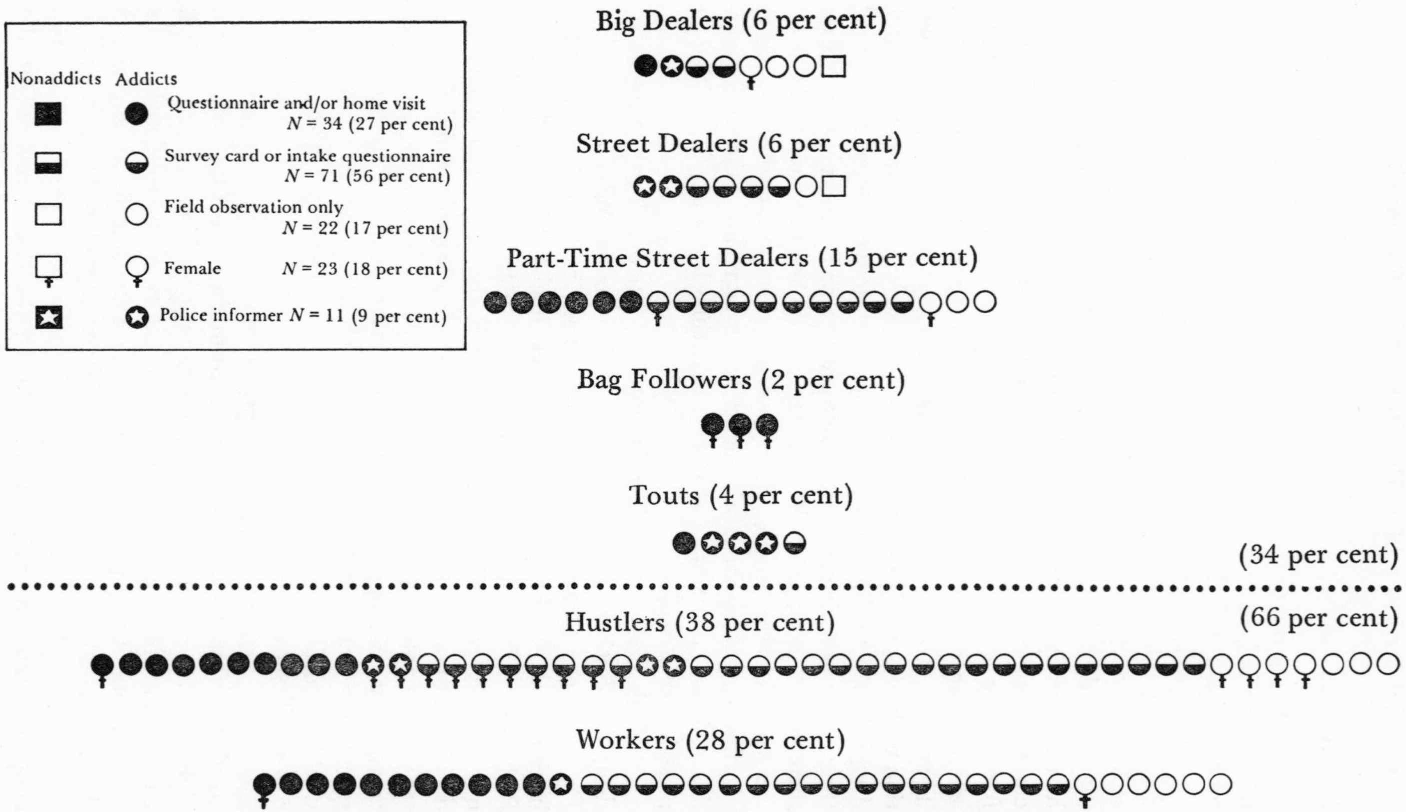

Figure 1. The distribution of copping-community members by functional role.

average only 56 per cent were reported to visit the area during any given week. New members entered because of relapse or movement from other copping areas when higher-quality heroin became available. Others stopped visiting because of being in jail, being treated, and for other reasons. For example, during the last week of August 1969, there was a total of seventy-seven active members: seven big dealers, three street dealers, eleven part-time dealers, one bag follower, five touts, thirty-one hustlers, and nineteen workers.

Demographic and Drug-Use Characteristics

Role occupants are compared on several demographic and drug-use characteristics in Table 2. Role in the distribution structure for men was not related to age or formal education. Women were most frequently hustlers and bag followers.

Role occupants did not differ as a function of age of first heroin use, although touts had been heroin users longer than others. This finding lends some support to the belief among addicts that chronic heroin use and repeated arrests cause some to lose their "nerve"—that is, to avoid dealing and hustling because of the higher risk of arrest. Instead they "hang out" in the copping area in low status roles, hoping to receive small amounts of drugs from their touting services. Bag followers had shorter addiction histories than other role occupants, which would be expected because the role requires that they be young and attractive.

TABLE 2

Distribution Roles Compared by Demographic and Drug-Use Characteristics

Mean for Each Subgroup (*n*)

Role	Age	Years duration of heroin use	Weekly cost of habit
Big Dealers	33.3 (4)	14.2 (4)	$1,000 (1)
Street Dealers	37.3 (6)	17.0 (6)	—
Part-time Dealers	37.1 (16)	18.2 (16)	$ 205 (5)
Bag Followers	23.0 (3)	2.7 (3)	$ 150 (2)
Touts	42.6 (5)	22.6 (5)	$ 100 (1)
Hustlers	36.2 (40)	15.4 (41)	$ 268 (7)
Workers	39.1 (30)	18.9 (30)	$ 111 (10)
Total	37.1 (104)	16.8 (105)	$ 208 (26)

Individuals in higher-level distribution roles reported more frequent heroin use and more expensive habits. However, the cost of their drugs might be considered an auxiliary expense of maintaining the distribution system and does not represent a personal expenditure. This framework for analyzing the economics of addiction, then, shows that it is erroneous to equate the huge habits of dealers with direct economic loss to the innocent public. Furthermore, workers, who reported less frequent use and less expensive habits, paid for their drugs largely through their own legitimate income. The true economic loss to the public would more appropriately be based upon the cost of the average daily habit of hustlers who bring into this illicit marketing system real dollars or goods obtained from illegal activities. It must be emphasized that the net dollar loss to the public occurs only once, no matter how many times money may change hands after it enters this system.

Standard of Living

The popular stereotype of the drug dealer pictures him living in luxury, with the street addict reduced to sleeping in abandoned buildings. To bring some clarification to this question, the intensive study subjects were ranked on several measures of living standard: (1) relative condition of housing, (2) general condition of neighborhood, and (3) monthly nondrug expenses such as rent, food, and clothing. Housing and neighborhood rankings were made on a standardized seven-point scale. A score of 1 signified unusual comfort and luxury; a score of 4, average accommodations; and a score of 7, extremely substandard conditions. A score of 8 was assigned to addicts who were "carrying the stick" (had no fixed place of residence).

Although the two big dealers did live better than other members of the sample, their housing and neighborhood ratings were only average (4.0). One big dealer lived in a lower-middle-class neighborhood in a neat but modestly furnished apartment. His working wife paid for food and rent and occasionally contributed to his legal fees on court cases. The other big dealer lived in hotel rooms, which he frequently changed because he kept drugs there. Some may be surprised by the relatively low standard of living of big dealers. However, it must be remembered that these individuals were defined as big dealers in this one copping community. Had we studied distribution roles above the neighborhood level or in other copping areas, we might have found the higher standards of living commonly associated with persons whom narcotics officers consider to be big dealers.

The three bag followers ranked just below big dealers on housing (4.7) and neighborhood condition (4.7). The eleven workers followed with ratings of 4.9 and 5.4, respectively. The six part-time dealers ranked next with a housing rating of 5.7 and a neighborhood rating of 5.5. The one street dealer visited received a rating of 6.0 on both housing and neighborhood. Hustling addicts ranked lowest on housing (6.9) and neighborhood condition (7.1), with five of the ten visited "carrying the stick."

Many of us assume that the addict pays rent, board, and family expenses just as we do (perhaps $200 to $400 per month) and that these living costs are borne by the public through theft and other illegal activities. This stereotype did not hold for the sample studied. Although three members of the intensive study sample were totally self-supporting, six "carried the stick," and the remaining twenty-five lived with others. When an addict lived with others, this almost always meant that his family or girlfriend paid the room and board, with the addict spending his entire income on drugs.

Psychosocial Functioning

Subjects who participated in the home-visit study were assigned scores of 0 to 100 on the following eight subscales: economic autonomy, severity of addiction, degree of subjective discomfort, employment fitness, degree of mental health, quality of interpersonal relationships, degree of criminality, and social attractiveness. A score of 0 on any subscale indicated severe malfunctioning; a score of 100 indicated perfect functioning in an area.

Compared with the rest of the sample, the two big dealers ranked high on economic autonomy, stability of interpersonal relations, and social attractiveness. They showed relatively little subjective discomfort and the lowest degree of mental disturbance. These findings are consistent with the requirements of the dealer role. Higher-level dealers must possess a certain degree of reliability and responsibility in order to maintain a stable distribution system, which is threatened by constant law-enforcement pressure and internal manipulation by addict members. This role also requires enough self-discipline to keep a cash reserve on hand and to use only a portion of one's heroin supply for one's own habit. Big dealers' high ratings on criminality and low ratings on employment fitness suggest that they would require extensive rehabilitation. Although the one street dealer in our sample exhibited a relatively high degree of mental disturbance, his other subscale scores, particularly employment fitness and criminality, were similar to those of big dealers.

The six part-time dealers in our sample tended to be addicts who had difficulty meeting the requirements of the dealer role. Frequently they were unable to "discipline" their habits or maintain a cash reserve in case they were "burned" (sold poor quality drugs). Some part-time dealers held jobs and dealt only enough drugs to support their own habits. They tended to score high on subjective discomfort, stability of interpersonal relationships, and social attractiveness. They tended to score low on economic autonomy.

Although the three bag followers did not have long addiction histories, they showed relatively high economic dependence and subjective discomfort. They were rated low on employment fitness, mental health, and stability of interpersonal relationships.

The ten hustlers tended to score low on all subscales except subjective discomfort. Although there was considerable variation among members, the subgroup as a whole scored low because the most severely disturbed persons appeared to be in this category. The relatively high degree of mental disturbance among hustlers suggests that this is a catch-all category with minimal role requirements. A severely disturbed individual who would have trouble meeting the requirements of a dealer role or the demands of steady employment could still hustle, even though unsuccessfully.

As a group, the nine workers were rated highest on employment fitness and lowest on criminality. They were also rated relatively high on mental health and social attractiveness, suggesting that they might be good treatment prospects.

Although the Addict Psychosocial Functioning Scale is still in its early stage of development, the findings presented here suggest that occupants of particular functional roles share certain characteristics that may be related to their choice of these roles as well as their ability to maintain them.

Treatability Characteristics

In an attempt to assess the treatability characteristics of role occupants, we compared the proportions entering treatment and the proportions remaining in treatment six months after their date of admission. Although the majority of subjects were assigned to methadone maintenance, some were assigned to other modalities such as therapeutic community and inpatient withdrawal. Therefore, our findings on treatment success must be viewed with caution.

Of the 125 addicted members of this copping community, fifty (40 per cent) entered treatment; and thirty (60 per cent of those entering) remained in treatment six months later (Table 3). As a group, workers were found to be the most favorable treatment prospects; that is, sixteen of the thirty-six entered treatment, and thirteen remained after six months. The relative success of workers can be partially ex-

TABLE 3

Distribution Roles Compared by Treatability Characteristics

Role (No.)	Admitted to treatment No. (%)	In treatment after six months No. (%)
Big Dealers (7)	3 (43)	1 (33)
Street Dealers (7)	1 (14)	0 (00)
Part-time Dealers (19)	9 (47)	6 (67)
Bag Followers (3)	3 (100)	1 (33)
Touts (5)	1 (20)	0 (00)
Hustlers (48)	17 (35)	9 (52)
Workers (36)	16 (44)	13 (81)
Total (125)	50 (40)	30 (60)

Note: Treatability data include all copping-community members known to enter treatment during the twenty-one-month period January 1969 to September 1970.

plained by their having already overcome one of the major hurdles to rehabilitation, obtaining legitimate employment. Not so readily explained is the finding that part-time dealers were most likely to enter treatment, with nine of the nineteen entering, and six remaining after six months.

The finding that big dealers, street dealers, bag followers and touts can be involved in treatment but tend to do poorly is consistent with our clinical experience. For example, we have observed a number of dealers who, after entering treatment, continued to sell drugs rather than seek legitimate employment. By continuing their illegal activities and by periodically returning to heroin use, they came under increasing pressure from clinical staff and eventually withdrew from the program.

Comment and Summary

We found that the drug-distribution community under study had elaborated a more highly differentiated system of roles than is usually considered—that is, a system involving only dealer and user. By studying drug use, personality, and treatability characteristics of the occupants of different roles, we were able to bring some empirical definition to this social system. Since drug-distribution role was not the basis for selection of the intensive study group, the sample sizes for most roles were too small to permit meaningful statistical comparisons. It must also be noted that the copping area studied was only one of perhaps twenty known to exist in the Chicago metropolitan area. The findings, then, should be viewed only as suggestive. Despite these limitations, the data suggest that the membership and dynamics of local heroin-distribution systems can be studied and perhaps altered by treatment programs.

Further field studies of the addict as a member of a definable distribution system should help to eliminate many of the myths surrounding the so-called addict subculture. For example, dealers in this neighborhood were not "pushing" heroin. The addicts, in fact, were in a seller's market—that is, they had to seek out the dealers. It may be that in such neighborhoods, where addiction is long standing, police surveillance and penetration prompt dealers to minimize the risk of arrest by selling only to trustworthy customers. One might expect an addict community experiencing less enforcement pressure to exhibit less structural differentiation, with dealers being more directly accessible to consumers. In such a setting one might see the "pushing" phenomenon and a buyer's market. It is interesting to note that Moore (1970) arrived at similar conclusions based upon purely theoretical considerations.

The distribution of police informers within this addict community is consistent with effective local enforcement penetration. For example, there is a concentration of informers in the tout role, which is perhaps the key communication position in the system. Although this aspect of our study is in an early stage, the ability to investigate police penetration into these systems may yield important clues to control. For example, the high degree of police penetration seen here may be partially responsible for the low incidence of new cases of addiction observed in this neighborhood (Hughes, Crawford, and Barker, 1971).

Despite the strategic location of informers, the system operates in a way that makes it difficult for local enforcement officials to arrest higher-level dealers. For example, during the period of study we noted that one big dealer in this copping area acquired four different felony charges for sale and possession of heroin. Shortly afterward he became suspected of being a police informer, lost his connections with the "main people" for drugs, and was forced to support his habit by hustling.

Although all heroin addicts share the same physical withdrawal symptoms, our findings indicate that addicts do not share the same psychological disturbance. By looking at the variation in psychopathology among addicts in their natural setting, our approach differs from studies carried out with the biased samples available in treatment or correctional settings. The approach used here permitted us to examine how differences in psychopathology might relate to the functional requirements of various distribution roles. It also incorporates the standards used by addict peers to judge one another in terms of social functioning. Although some professionals may consider all addicts to be sick, many members of the addict community are viewed by their peers as success models. Another result of our attempt to relate psychopathology to the social structure of this community was the location of the most disturbed members in the role with the lowest performance requirements.

The findings on treatability, if confirmed by future studies, may suggest improved treatment typologies and certain modifications in clinical practice. Our impression that major distribution roles were associated with lower motivation and higher dropout rates suggests that voluntary community programs might consider special approaches for involving and holding these groups. For example, one might obtain better results with big dealers by immediate hospitalization, thereby removing them from the temptation to continue dealing purely for profit. Alternatively, the demand for immediate behavioral change among big dealers might be postponed until they have worked through their initial difficulty in accepting the lower prestige of the patient role.

We are currently replicating our approach in different ethnic neighborhoods in order to assess local variations in role structure, membership distribution, and social and treatability characteristics of role occupants. Our search for an effective, medically oriented control strategy requires that we explore the usefulness of different operational models. For example, should local heroin-distribution networks be defined as disease-maintenance systems that might be eradicated through the use of public health field teams which involve the majority of active addicts in voluntary treatment and employ short-term quarantine for the small percentage who refuse treatment? Would it be useful to define these networks as illegal heroin maintenance systems which might be readily converted to neighborhood methadone-maintenance clinics? Or does their criminal role structure require that they be defined as deviant social systems best controlled by local law-enforcement pressure? In the absence of short-term quarantine laws, our intervention approach is limited to voluntary outreach projects. Nevertheless, we hope this intervention can be varied enough to permit experimental manipulation of the size, structure, and other characteristics of these drug-distribution networks, perhaps leading to their complete removal from some neighborhoods.

In summary, a field worker was assigned to a heroin distribution site or "copping area" in a Chicago Negro neighborhood for a period of one year. He identified and monitored 127 different dealers and consumers who were regular visitors to the site. Thirty-four of these addicts were involved in a home visit and outreach treatment project. These various sources of data permitted us to describe the role structure of this local heroin maintenance system, the distribution of members in various roles, and the social and treatability characteristics of role occupants. Our findings suggest that neighborhood heroin distribution systems are amenable to study and manipulation by treatment programs.

Chapter 18

DEALERS ON A CAMPUS

In fall 1968 we interviewed state university students who were being processed through health check-ups. These examinations are required for all who have dropped out for one quarter or more and for transfer students, freshmen, and newly registering graduate students. Three interviewing booths were assigned us in the health center, and during the three-day registration-examination period, 243 students out of 3,638 were seen. Sampling was unsystematic, for it was determined by time. Students A, B, and C waiting in line would be interviewed; during that twenty-minute interview period, forty students would pass to health stations beyond ours; when the interview was completed, the next students waiting in line for further stations would be seen. Thus we saw about every fifteenth student (if the line was slow and the interview fast, only thirty would pass). The effort to see as many as possible led to frantic work; four interviewers were on duty at all times, so that one could be resting while three worked.

The major sampling deficiency is the exclusion of the reregistering undergraduates and graduates, who were not required to be processed through the health center.

Seven per cent of the sample state that they have been or are drug dealers (a dealer defined as one selling illicit drugs repetitively and for profit). Two dealers are female, the balance male. All dealers have had experience as illicit-drug users. Two dealers describe themselves as regular dealers; others, as irregular or occasional dealers. Cannabis is the major sales item; hallucinogens rank second. Only a few have ever sold amphetamines (12 per cent) or opiates (6 per cent). This trade conforms to the "psychedelic" dealer pattern described for our variegated

California sample. Students describing illicit-drug experiences constitute 47 per cent of the sample. Nonusers comprise 53 per cent of the sample.

Since we have survey figures for a prior year on the prevalence of illicit use for that campus, we can compare our present (biased) sample with the earlier survey which had oversampled upperclassmen. In that 1966-1967 survey (N = 250) 33 per cent of the students reported illicit-drug experience. Either drug use has increased on campus or our returning (and more mobile or unstable in terms of student status) sample had higher use than other students. Perhaps both occurred.

From the sample we get an estimate of dealer prevalence in a (one or more times) illicit-user population of one dealer among every seven college users.

Families of Students

We wondered whether student dealers were nurtured in homes where parents had more benign views of illicit-drug use. We constructed an index based on the coding of replies to inquiries about parental attitudes toward drug use, classifying as "benign" those responses which indicate acceptance of at least some illicit use by the children (for instance, "Cannabis is okay even if heroin is not"); parental illicit-drug use; the absence of strong antidrug sentiments in the home; or "laissez-faire" descriptions, including acknowledgment by the student that he did not know what parental drug views were. We found that 50 per cent of the dealers' parents held "benign" views; 26 per cent of the parents of illicit users did so; but only 14 per cent of the nonusers' parents were benign about illicit-drug use.

All is not, however, benevolent acceptance. A larger number of student dealers (13 per cent)—compared with users (6 per cent) and nonusers (2 per cent)—say that their parents' attitudes toward illicit drugs have caused serious conflict between them and the parents. If a second constellation of family factors associated with dealing is one of conflict rather than acceptance, it follows that an important segment of dealers should describe themselves as generally in conflict with or not getting on well with their parents. This is the case. Twenty-six per cent of the dealers (compared with 7 per cent of the users and 1 per cent of the nonusers) say that they are alienated from their parents; and only 44 per cent of the dealers (compared with 59 per cent of the users and 74 per cent of the nonusers) characterize their family relationships as good.

This student view could have been affected by the marital status of parents. Yet among dealers 81 per cent report intact parental marriages; among users 79 per cent are intact; among nonusers 88 per cent are intact. Views could also be affected slightly by the native-immigrant status of parents. But 88 per cent of the parents of dealers (compared with 85 per cent of parents of users and 76 per cent of parents of nonusers) are both native-born United States citizens.

With regard to occupation, dealers' fathers are more often in white-collar jobs (57 per cent dealers, 46 per cent users, 44 per cent nonusers), less often in professional positions (12 per cent dealers, 20 per cent users, 12 per cent nonusers) and less often in blue-collar positions (31 per cent dealers, 29 per cent users, 40 per cent nonusers). Religious backgrounds suggest liberal or possibly conflicting parental faiths, but not agnosticism. We see that 19 per cent of the dealers' parents (compared to 5 per cent of parents of users and 4 per cent of parents of nonusers), are of mixed faiths; only 6 per cent of the dealers' parents (13 per cent of users' parents, 5 per cent of nonusers' parents) have no affiliation. Jews, Unitarians, and other (liberal?) smaller groups comprise 25 per cent of the dealers' families but only 18 per cent of users' and 8 per cent of nonusers'. It is the nonusing group whose parents stand out here as traditional; 40 per cent are Catholic (including Orthodox and Eastern) compared to 27 per cent of the dealers and users, and 43 per cent are Protestant, compared to 35 per cent of the dealers and users.

These findings do indicate that the families of drug-dealing students differ from those of nondealing illicit users and nonusers. The direction of differences suggest those found in our family study (Blum and associates, 1972) to discriminate high- and low-drug-risk families. Further, the families of dealers and nonusers may be conceived as extremes, with the families of illicit users, for the most part, occupying a middle position. Parents of nonusers are more often traditionally religious, working-class, and naturalized citizens who make their opposition to their children's drug use clear but do so in a relatively conflict-free context; for their children report generally good relationships with them and no conflicts created by drug use. Parents of dealers are at the opposite extreme, with two sub-syndromes proposed: (1) where the parents approve of or are indifferent to their children's drug use; (2) where the parents' opposition to drug use furthers the parent-child conflict already in existence in the family.

It also appears that parental conflict, as we infer it from divorce or mixed religious faiths, has a mild predisposing (or associative) role in the production of family constellations productive of drug dealing among offspring.

Students

If so, one would expect more psychiatric care for this group and, anticipating personal distress expressed in functional and psychosomatic complaints, more medical problems. That is the case. Among dealers 31 per cent report psychiatric visits as compared to 15 per cent among users and 9 per cent among nonusers. Medical problems are described by 19 per cent of the dealers, 4 per cent of the users, and 9 per cent of the nonusers. Surgical problems are described by 31 per cent, 13 per cent, and 10 per cent respectively. These differences cannot be attributed to social class, since more users than dealers are from professional (or professional plus white-collar) families, or to drug use as such, since nondealing users report fewer problems than using dealers.

Personal difficulties may also be inferred from the grade-point averages of the dealers, for they are lower than those of users or nonusers, more falling in the D to C group (6 per cent vs. 0 per cent vs. 1 per cent) and fewer in the B to A group (19 per cent vs. 36 per cent vs. 27 per cent). Note here that the highest (self-reported) grade points characterize users, so that drug use as such cannot be the determining variable in dealers' poorer academic performance. It may also be that the user group is "faking good." Left activists, who tend to be associated with drug use (see Lipset, 1971, citing L. C. Kerpelman), often report themselves in a more favorable light than their actual grade records warrant.

What about academic interests? Slightly more dealers major in literature (12 per cent vs. 8 per cent vs. 5 per cent), the arts (12 per cent vs. 4 per cent vs. 8 per cent), film-TV-radio-drama (7 per cent vs. 5 per cent vs. 3 per cent), life sciences (12 per cent vs. 4 per cent vs. 7 per cent), and physical sciences (7 per cent vs. 1 per cent vs. 1 per cent). Fewer dealers are found in engineering, education, languages, physical education, home economics, and mathematics. Perhaps artists and such are more willing to take on unusual social roles, of which dealing is but one. These academic interests also suggest curiosity, experimentation, and creativity as positive interests, as well as aversion to routine occupations.

Politics? In keeping with their other unusual stances, it is not a surprise that the student dealers more often describe themselves as New Left (26 per cent vs. 9 per cent vs. 6 per cent) or, appropriate for the "alienated," as apolitical (31 per cent vs. 22 per cent vs. 19 per cent). The Peace and Freedom party is the dealers' third bastion; 31 per cent support it, compared to 7 per cent of the users and 1 per cent of the nonusers. "Old-fashioned" Democrats and Republicans are more often found among the nondrug-using students—65 per cent of them affirming such traditional politics. Surprisingly, however, in view of their leftist leanings, dealers do not overwhelmingly favor student demonstrations (their campus had been the scene of some rather violent ones in the most recent past). They less often favor the activist demonstrators (strikes, sit-ins, bombings) than do users (18 per cent vs. 29 per cent) but do so more than nonusers (18 per cent vs. 10 per cent). Dealers are more often laissez-faire (13 per cent vs. 4 per cent vs. 6 per cent), reminding us of their apolitical stance—and of their parents' nonpositions on drugs.

Religion? No dealer describes himself as Protestant or Jewish and only 19 per cent call themselves Catholic, even though 63 per cent of their parents hold one of these affiliations. Twenty-seven per cent of the users claim these major affiliations—in contrast to 78 per cent of their parents. Sixty-two per cent of the nonusers claim these traditional affiliations, compared with 89 per cent of their parents. Only those dealers with Unitarian parents consider themselves also Unitarian. With that exception, our finding is that dealers and users have divorced themselves from the traditional religious roles and articles of faith which their parents held. This is compatible with findings from our earlier work (Blum and associates, 1969b).

We conclude that the student dealer on this campus, more often than users, feels himself apart from his family, is aware of greater mental and physical distress, takes a left-wing political stance which has a large admixture of apathy and admitted ambivalence, and does less well in college. Like the user, the dealer has rejected the religion of his parents. The dealer differs less from the nondealing user than he does from the nondrug user, who is in every respect more conventional.

Comment and Summary

Seven per cent of a sample of newly registering students undergoing health checks at a California college describe themselves as drug dealers, most dealing occasionally and most dealing in cannabis and/or hallucinogens. A total of 47 per cent (including dealers) describe illicit-drug experiences, a figure somewhat higher than earlier undergraduate survey data from that same school.

There is evidence that the families of dealers differ from families of nondealing illicit-drug users and nonusers. Parental approval of or indifference to illicit-drug use is greatest among dealers' families, as is conflict over drug use. In our sample conflict between the parents and the dealer child is also reported on other matters; and it is from these families that youths styling themselves as "alienated" most often derive.

Illicit users stand between dealers and nonusers on these matters.

Student dealers more often report psychiatric, medical, and surgical problems, a left-wing political stance which is colored with apathy and ambivalence, and poorer academic performance. Their problems and performance cannot be attributed to drug use as such (we have no data on intensity of drug use), since nondealing illicit users (by self-report) perform better than nonusers academically in this sample and, while reporting more family and personal disorders than nonusers, do not have them to the extent that dealers do.

We conclude that drug dealers identified on this campus suffer a greater burden of personal problems, many presumably family-related, than do nondealing illicit-drug users or nonusing students. We speculate that their willingness to engage in unusual and unlawful behavior may be linked not only to psychological distress but to inferred family approval of or disinterest in the values and behavior associated with illicit-drug use, thus providing a "nurturing" environment for their drug conduct. Their academic interests are compatible with curiosity, new role exploration, and aversion to conventional or boring routines.

We propose that the drug dealing of middle-class college youth has components—either within subgroups of dealers or individually within dealers themselves—which are derived from (a) involvement in illicit-drug use, (b) family conflict, (c) personal distress (psychopathology), (d) learning of approved novel or socially disapproved behavior within the family, (e) the development of conduct based on peer or personal interests in the absence of parental standards or guidance, and (f) personal curiosity, innovativeness, and dislike of routine or boring activities. We do not argue for these as a complete or thoroughly demonstrated set of contributing factors. We do suggest that they be kept in mind as one considers the personal origins of college drug dealing.

Chapter 19

DEALERS ON ANOTHER CAMPUS

We wanted to identify as many dealers as possible on a second college campus. We hoped to learn about dealing prevalence by kind of living unit. We also wanted to compare dealers with other students. To achieve these goals we set out on a two-year study of a major California university.

Our sampling procedure required interviews with at least two students (usually known to our interviewers) from every cohesive residence unit on campus—cohesive defined as a unit housing under ninety-five students, all of whom live together over time in daily contact with each other. By this definition, all fraternities, row houses (small university-run residences), on-campus cooperative and experimental living units, traditional university houses (such as women's residences), and each floor and wing of the dormitories are cohesive units. We also interviewed students in three kinds of residence units, or rather arrays of units, not considered cohesive: the university high-rise apartment houses, the (temporary) university trailer village, and the widely spread off-campus housing of students. At this university, trailers and apartments house from two to four single students per unit or married students. Off-campus housing ranges from solitary apartments to cooperatives and averages, we believe, two or three students per unit. We sampled every fourth trailer and apartment, interviewing two student residents in each. Off-campus sampling went through several stages. First, using the student directory, we identified all off-campus residents and selected systematically the first name on page 1, and second name on page 2, and so forth. We telephoned those selected and interviewed all of those who were at home and willing to see us. Telephoning leads, of course, to sampling bias, because some students are not-at-homes. In order to reach that most mobile sample who were never at home or moved faster than university records could keep up with them, we set up a special table on registration day. We offered (advertising via a sign) one dollar to all off-campus students who had moved three or more times during the last year.

Our sample of respondents consists of, among undergraduates, 165 of a total of 3,984 small-unit residents; 104 from among 590 trailer and apartment residents; and 203 of a total of 1,729 off-campus residents—including 36 highly mobile students responding to our registration-day appeal (22 undergraduates and 14 graduates). One hundred of 1,708 on-campus graduates were interviewed, as were 199 of 3,451 off-campus graduates. There were, in all, 771 residence interviews from among the total student body of 11,462.

Our assumption was that students in cohesive living units would be aware of drug use and drug dealing among their fellows and would speak frankly in discussions with our interviewers—mostly fellow students who were known to them and who were themselves drug-wise. Interviewers employed two schedules: one a living-unit description (how many students, car ownership therein, and so forth) and the other a drug-description inquiry (concerning the prevalence and frequency of illicit-drug use and dealing—among respondents and their fellow residents). We assumed also that those in trailers, apartments, and off-campus housing would not know of the activities of any but their immediate trailer, apartment, house, or commune mates. Their descriptions therefore were limited to their own units, and we sought to sample sufficiently among these units to provide a representative and reasonably accurate estimate.

Each respondent also was asked to introduce the interviewer to each drug dealer in the unit or, if the respondent was unwilling to make a personal introduction, to give an interview form to dealers. In such cases, the respondent sometimes administered the form himself, and it was subsequently collected from him.

We were introduced in this way to 111 dealers, 59 identified and referred from on-campus units and 52 from among the off-campus random sample. As we shall see, these 111 dealers represent only a portion of those estimated to be active on campus.

Difficulties in identifying and interviewing dealers were of several kinds. One was, as noted, that unit residents were sometimes reluctant to make introductions—not because they distrusted the interviewers but because, as they said, they were afraid that their dealer friends would not want to be identified to *any* outsider. Nevertheless, introductions were made.

As one school year came to a close, our studies were denounced by a member of Students for a Democratic Society (SDS) writing in the school paper. Although he didn't attribute malignant intent to the investigators, the article demanded that students refuse to participate in any work sponsored by the Department of Justice and the Bureau of Narcotics and Dangerous Drugs, because these were enemies of the people. There were also, on other occasions, vague threats to the project on the grounds that the investigators were "narcs" seeking to identify and arrest students. Our impression remained, however, that students cooperated in spite of all—hoping, as we did, that the findings would throw light on an important campus and general social issue.

A second problem hinged on definitions and self-concepts. We were seeking people who regularly sold drugs. Yet many students to whom we were referred denied that they were dealers, since they were very small operators engaged only in drug *transfers* and not in profitable big business. Our inquiries about net profits and gross receipts sometimes brought laughter; such business terminology seemed out of place to the students. To students, drug transfers are part of drug sociability. Most denied an interest in profit and insisted that there was little formalization of roles into source, dealer, customer, and the like. Their observations anticipate our findings. In any event, limitations on the number of dealers identified can partly be ascribed to the inappropriateness, in students' minds, of the terms "dealing" or "dealer" for the prevalent drug-transfer activities (see Goode, 1970; Carey, 1968).

A third set of problems in dealer case finding is associated with differential access to subgroups within a population. For example, dealers are most common in the group which we had the hardest time finding, the not-at-home, often-moving off-campus student. There were ten dealers among the thirty-six whom we did lure (by advertising) in that population. We cannot estimate the "real" size of that mobile population. Dealers appear next most frequently in the second-hardest-to-get-at population, the off-campus students in general.

Consider what might have occurred had we sampled every residence unit. Table 4 shows us the kind of population, its size, the number seen in it, the number of dealers referred and seen and, extrapolating, the number of dealers we might have expected to see if access to them were constant (at the same rate as our respondents introduced us). Table 4 suggests that total residence-unit (including off-campus) sampling could have led us to as many as 700 dealers. The table also shows

TABLE 4

Estimate of Accessible Dealers by Type or Residence

Graduates	Total size	Respondents sampled	Dealers seen	Estimate of accessible dealers number	Estimate of accessible dealers percentage
On-campus (including dorms and high-rise apts.)	1,708	100	2	2	0.2
Off-campus	3,451	199	17	290	8
Undergraduates					
On-campus (including dorms, fraternities, etc.)	3,984	165	41	41	1
On-campus (high-rise apts.)	126	30	4	16	13
On-campus (trailers)	464	74	12	75	16
Off-campus	1,729	203	35	280	16
Total	11,462	871	111	704	6%[a]

[a] Of total population of 11,462 surveyed.

that graduate students referred us to fewer dealers than undergraduates did, and that rates of referral to dealers are consistent (but not equal) for graduates and undergraduates. Lowest rates occur in the cohesive residence units; and the highest rates occur off campus (or in the trailer village).

The assumption made that a few students within any cohesive housing group would, in fact, be knowledgeable about the drug-using and drug-dealing conduct of their housemates leads to questions of accuracy of estimate, which will be touched upon again as we compare estimations derived in several ways. We did test reliability of this method: Taking two cohesive living units, we compared findings on it (a) by our method and (b) by a systematic within-house query by one of the residents. The results: When asked what percentage of the residents had had any illicit-drug experiences, respondents in one living unit gave an estimate of 60 per cent to our interviewer and 75 per cent to the in-house interviewer. Respondents in the other living unit estimated 33⅓ per cent (to our interviewer) and 65 per cent (to the house interviewer). Estimates of regular use were in greater agreement. Respondents in one house gave estimates of 25 per cent to our interviewer and 35 per cent to the in-house interviewer; estimates for the second house were 17 per cent vs. 20 per cent. Estimates on the number of persons who had ever sold showed a disagreement of 10 per cent for one house (10 per cent vs. 20 per cent) and 5 per cent for the other house (5 per cent vs. 10 per cent). The estimates of the number having sold regularly for profit were 10 per cent (to our interviewer) and 8 per cent (to the in-house interviewer)—a disagreement of 2 per cent for one living unit; and a disagreement of 3 per cent for the other unit (5 per cent vs. 8 per cent).

On the major items of interest to us, the reliability test in two houses suggests that an external interviewer using a few residents achieves substantially the same estimates as an internal informant (resident interviewer).

Student Descriptions of Use and Dealing

All descriptions and estimates in this section are based on respondents' characterizations of their own residence unit, whether a one floor wing (hall) of a dorm or a two-man off-campus apartment. For all units other than cohesive units, we have treated respondents' estimates as representative of the (unsampled) population from which they were drawn (for instance, the replies of thirty trailer residents are taken as fair estimates for all trailer residents) and have extrapolated—giving proper weights to the per cent of population resident in each strata—to arrive at total campus estimates for use and dealing.

First, with regard to illicit use, Table 5 shows estimates of one-time-or-more use and regular use (four times or more per week) for any illicit drug.

The data in Table 5 indicate that, consistent with our experience with dealer accessibility (Table 4), undergraduate respondents estimate more experience and more regular use of illicit substances than do graduates and that, consistently, on-campus use is estimated as somewhat less than off-campus use. The figures for any experience with drugs and regular use, extrapolated from residents' estimates, are compared in Table 6 with survey data from this same campus.

In the 1970–1971 survey, using respondents estimated that 70 per cent of the undergraduates had used illicit drugs; nonusers estimated 67 per cent.

TABLE 5

Illicit-Drug Use

(respondent estimates in percentages of total student population)

Undergraduate	Any past use	Regular and current use
On campus	70	37
Off campus	74	40
Total	71	45
Graduate		
On campus	36	7
Off campus	50	10
Total	45	9
Total for undergraduate and graduate	59	25

TABLE 6

Illicit-Drug Use on Campus

(historical trend)

Year	Sample	Some experience (percentage of sample)	Regular use (weekly or more) (percentage of sample)
1966–1967 [a]	300	21	14
1968 [b]	100	57	16
1969 [c]	201	69	16 (twice a week or more)
1970–1971 [d]	100	70	29 (8% at four times a week)

[a] Blum, 1969b
[b] Blum, 1969b
[c] Garfield, Boreing, and Smith, 1971
[d] Garfield, 1971

The residents' estimates for their living units, extrapolated to the student body, compare well with survey data for the same period for one-time-or-more illicit use (71 per cent vs. 70 per cent); but apparently either the residence members overestimated or the random sample underestimated percentages for regularity of use. Results from an earlier study of student drug use (Blum and associates, 1969b) show that users are the most accurate estimators of overall student drug experience.

Table 7 gives students' estimates of regular drug dealing, extrapolated to various living units and the student body as a whole.

TABLE 7

Estimates of Regular Drug Dealing by Type of Residence

Undergraduate	Percentage of students having regular dealing experience
On campus	
Dorms, fraternities, etc.	2
Trailers	13
Apartments	13
Total	4
Off campus	11
Undergraduate total	5
Graduate	
On campus	2
Off campus	7
Graduate total	5
Student Body Total	6

We see from Table 7 that cohesive living groups (dorms, fraternities, etc.) are estimated to have a lesser portion of their membership engaged in active dealing than are the smaller and more isolated on-campus dwellings; that undergraduates are estimated as dealing more than graduate students; and that, among both graduates and undergraduates, off-campus students are said to deal more than on-campus ones.

If we compare the estimates in Table 7 as one measure of dealer prevalence with our own experience in access to dealers (as shown in Table 4) we see that as far as rankings are concerned there is an exact correspondence: undergraduates high, graduates low, off-campus high, on-campus low, cohesive units low, isolated smaller on-campus units high. We also see correspondence between our estimate of accessible dealers as a proportion of total campus population and student estimates of regular dealer prevalence. Both yield an estimated 6 per cent of the student body as regular dealers. There is also good agreement in the two methods for dealing in each type of residence unit, there being no discrepancy greater than 5 per cent.

Turning now to the 1970–1971 random survey (Garfield, 1971) of undergraduates, we find that 14 per cent report having sold a drug at cost, but that only 6 per cent say they have sold for profit. The latter is the dealer definition used in this study inquiry. We see that

Table 4, Table 7, and the student survey are in remarkable agreement on the number of dealers on campus using that definition.

If we examine estimates of regular use of illicit drugs for the several types of undergraduate on-campus residences, we find that regular use for apartments and trailers is said to be over twice as great as for dormitories and other cohesive living units, 72 per cent as opposed to 32 per cent. Considering that regular users are much better customers than irregular or past experimenters only, we can understand the reportedly greater number of dealers serving the trailers and apartments than the dorms, fraternity houses, and women's row houses. The proportion of regular users who would then be dealers in the cohesive units is 6 per cent as compared to 18 per cent in the other units.

If we disregard the possibility of artifact due to errors in estimating, we may attribute this increased prevalence of dealers among regular users in trailers and apartments, compared to dorms and houses, to three additional features. One is that the estimate of any use of illicit drugs is greater for trailer-apartment dwellers (80 per cent to 69 per cent). In the former, then, there would be a larger population of irregular users. Second, cohesive units are just that—places where there is or can be daily residence contact; a dealer can supply one large unit more readily, and, if several dealers are residing in the same unit, customers may be assured that a source is near at hand. In contrast, trailers and apartments are physically separate; residents do not come in contact as easily and are less likely to know who has what supply on hand when; consequently, a regular user is more likely to become a dealer to assure supplies for himself and others in this more fragmented situation. Also, we believe, sheer distance may play a role. It is less convenient for a user to have to walk across a trailer village or to another high-rise building to get drugs than to be able to go to a supplier across the hall or walkway. In these circumstances there should proliferate more dealers, each serving fewer customers but thereby assuring his own as well as their convenience. In arguing for physical proximity and spatial separateness as partial determinants of the emergence of dealers from a population of users, one is reminded of the work by Festinger and his associates (1950), which showed that friendship patterns among college students are often based on the accident of who lives next to whom.

Dormitory, fraternity, and row-house residents were asked where their suppliers lived. The majority reported one or more of the following: (a) that their dealers lived near their rooms; (b) that they were supplied by dealers elsewhere in the building; and (c) that, counting all students who on one occasion or another supplied their unit, most lived outside the dorm. These replies show that proximity can be only one factor, for students move around within the building to traffic in and use drugs, and they rely on a variety of dealers from outside their residence as well. The distribution estimate that places the majority of all dealers serving a residence outside it implies that (a) to maintain a supply on campus a user must know a variety of sources; (b) the dealer role is both rare enough and specialized enough that only a minority in any campus using population become regular dealers, so that users must seek out a widely distributed group of persons; and (c) drug use itself is a phenomenon occurring outside of residence units, so that upon visits, while socializing, the user will enjoy supplies provided by his "hosts" in other quarters. A dealer, to sustain himself in that role, must have customers. Those dealers not in large self-contained living units (that is, those dealers in apartments, trailers, and off-campus residents) must serve students outside their dwelling in order to have a clientele. Their interests are served by developing a supplier relationship with people in other living units. One would expect that dealers living in self-contained large units with many residents who are heavy users would find less need to supply outside the unit. However, this would not be the case for dealers who, successful in supplying a heavy clientele, develop good off-campus sources for themselves and, finding the income a pleasure, then move a step upward to become a big dealer on campus.

In our sample two small coeducational living units proved to have the greatest on-campus regular use. These units also proved to have the greatest number of dealers per capita—a fact that does not emerge in Table 7 because these were exceptional living units, far from the norm of dormitories, fraternities, and women's row houses in general.

At the other extreme, one expects that units in which there is no drug use will not generate dealers; if any members of these units do deal, it will be outside the unit and among persons other than its residents. Both of these expectations are borne out by the data and by impressions. Within the two heavily using coed living groups, dealers are described as within-house oriented. That orientation is linked not only to customer availability but, according to respondents, to an in-group social orientation. At the other end, women's row houses sometimes report no use and no dealing. Those women dealers found were in coed units or, in one case, a girl who dealt in company with her boyfriend, who was a major supplier.

With regard to other features of dealers, respondents described most of the dealers in their unit as being their own age; 10 per cent were older, 0.5 per cent were younger. Dealers were also described as males in 99 per cent of the cases, and 87 per cent were students in the university. Ten per cent of the dealers serving the campus were nonstudents (Gentle Jim of Chapter Four was one of them); 2 per cent were students from other schools; and 0.5 per cent were faculty or staff. Most dealers were described as serving ten clients or less, with a modal profit of $26 to $50 per month. Seven per cent of the respondents said that dealers they knew averaged zero profit; 7 per cent said that their acquaintances averaged over $100 each month. Cannabis and hallucinogens were the major stock-in-trade. As for sources, one fifth said that the dealers they knew obtained their drugs locally or in nearby cities; 0.5 per cent said that they went over the border or out of state; most said that dealers on campus supplied each other.

With regard to the attitudes toward dealing in their living units, the majority (73 per cent) described them as live-and-let-live. Seventeen per cent reported approval by residents; 6 per cent indicated that the majority disapproved (disapproval of dealing occurred most often in women's units where there were no spontaneous users and no dealers); and 4 per cent said that their members occasionally pitched in to promote dealing (to help find dealers and sources).

Asked about drug problems, 10 per cent of the living units were described as having one or two persons with drinking problems; 1 per cent indicated that there were several members with alcohol difficulties. Illicit-drug problems were more common. One fifth of the living units reported one or two overusers; 4 per cent reported three to four overusers; 4 per cent reported five to six overusers; 72 per cent reported no drug "abuse." These estimates contradict the 1966–1968 findings on that same campus—namely, that alcohol-related difficulties were more numerous than illicit-drug problems. One assumes that with the advent of regular illicit use there are more people with drug problems.

Dealer Reports

Recall that we interviewed 111 dealers out of an estimated 700 whom we calculate would have been accessible had we been able to sample every residence unit on and off campus. The number of accessible dealers is the same as the overall number of dealers described by students as being in their residence unit. This encourages us to believe that we were able to find most dealers in those units we did sample. Alternatively, it means an unhappy coincidence of consistent student error in underestimating dealer activity in their living units and our inability to find many dealers in these residences through the search method we employed.

The dealers whom we interviewed proved to be upperclassmen

(75 per cent), males (95 per cent; 74 per cent of the students are males), white (95 per cent; compared with total white enrollment of 92 per cent), with grade-point averages of B (the average also reported by the 1970–1971 random sample of undergraduates, although male users are slightly lower than other students). Note that these are self-reports of grades. Lipset (1971), citing L. C. Kerpelman, comments that leftist-activists (a greater than average drug-using group) report their grades (and traits) as more favorable than they are in fact. We must leave the possibility open, then, that our dealers falsify and may have poorer grades than other students. This would be consistent with data from our study of junior and senior high and the dealer census in a different college (Chapters Eighteen, Twenty-Three, and Twenty-Four). Nearly all use alcohol; 99 per cent currently use illicit drugs. Most of those who use illicit drugs use cannabis at least weekly, and less than 10 per cent use either amphetamines or hallucinogens on a regular (monthly) basis. Five per cent report opiate or barbiturate use once a month. Many report that they did not begin illicit-drug use until they arrived in college, although the younger dealers report earlier initial use (that is, the class of 1974 started earlier than the class of 1971). We thus see a movement within two years from initial illicit use to regular dealing.

Most sell cannabis; about one fourth sell hallucinogens or speed occasionally. No more than one third sell more than once a week, and most report reduction in present over past sales. Most (80 per cent) buy cooperatively with other campus dealers, and most buy from one another. The campus dealers' first source is another undergraduate. Off-campus sources are mostly local, with some from neighboring cities. Student dealers' off-campus suppliers are slightly older—averaging age 23. Average profits are under $50 a month. Six per cent make over $100 (net) a month. We find that descriptions by residents of living units are in good agreement, on those items (sex, age, monthly income, drug sources) where comparison is possible, with what dealers themselves say.

Ten per cent of the dealers have been arrested on nondrug charges, 5 per cent for drug-related offenses. This compares with 10 per cent of nondrug arrests (all of those arrested were users) among a random sample of undergraduates, and 1 per cent drug arrests (plus 2 per cent alcohol-related offenses) reported in Garfield (1971). As for their careers, 25 per cent of the dealers were unsure about their plans. This compares with the 1970–1971 random sample results, where 22 per cent of the drug users but only 3 per cent of the nonusers were uncertain about their vocational futures. Two fifths of the dealers said they intended to continue selling drugs, at least during their college careers.

Dealers were asked to estimate the number of dealers on campus. Three fifths of those venturing an estimate said there were less than 200. Only 8 per cent said there were 500 or more. If we contrast this "expert" opinion with our experience estimate, resident student estimates, or survey findings, it is remarkably low. Why? Possibly the undergraduate dealers thought only of the undergraduate community in which they deal and live. If so, then their modal estimate (which we coded in a frequency classification of 100 to 200), say 150, would represent only 2.4 per cent of the undergraduate student body of 6,303. Possibly these campus dealers have but limited exposure to one another and therefore do underestimate, by a factor of ⅓, the number of dealers on campus. Possibly also, the off-campus interviewees often identify the same dealers, raising the number erroneously. This does not explain the high numbers in the trailers, but that population is much smaller and would not raise the total N so much.

The most probable explanation, we believe, is that suppliers have developed a more rigorous definition of a dealer; that is, they conceive of a dealer as someone who is heavily involved in regular profit making. In that case, our dealers are indeed correct in their low estimates; for the data show that most campus suppliers are dealing irregularly, confine themselves to a very narrow clientele, make very little money, and are pursuing noncriminal career goals. Our (nonquantified) sectors of the interview show users and dealers both emphasizing the social-communal aspects of drug use and drug sharing. The "professional" dealer, whose primary role is a dealer and who works hard to make money, is a rare bird, if he exists on campus at all. Indeed, only 3 per cent of our dealers report making over $250 a month. Given the otherwise excellent agreement among resident respondents, survey sample data, and the dealers, we believe that the student who looks like a dealer to those he supplies—and who is a dealer in the eyes of the law—nevertheless may not consider himself one. Similarly, when asked to identify others in that role, the student supplier has a definition which excludes most of those who qualify as dealers in the eyes of other students, our research group, and the law.

Personality Test Results

Would psychological tests demonstrate any differences in personality or values between dealers and users if one controlled for environmental factors? To find out, we selected three fraternity houses on campus and sought in each illicit users who were dealers. We compared them with a matched sample of illicit regular users who were not, and have not been, dealers. Since all of the regular users in the three houses had done some sharing or selling of drugs, we decided to define a "dealer" as someone selling for a profit at least once a week and grossing over $200 a year. "Nondealers" were those dealing for profit rarely or not at all.

We sought to match dealers and nondealing users on academic majors, careers choices, grade points, class standing, alcohol use, sexual activity, political predilections, and family income. Close matches were made on majors. There were six out of ten in each group in the social sciences, and three in each group in science-technology. The remaining were a matching failure. Close matches were also made on career plans. Four dealers and five users had not chosen a career, and law had been selected by three in each group. Class standing also correlated positively. The grade point average of dealers was slightly lower than that of users (2.9 vs. 3.3). Alcohol use was essentially the same as was frequency of sexual intercourse. Political matching was less close; among dealers were five radicals, three liberals, and two conservatives; among users were one radical, five liberals, one "none," and three conservatives. Family income was also a poorer match, for dealers' parents averaged $15,000 annually and users' parents about $23,000. As a check on our selection criteria, we recorded income from illicit-drug sales; dealers averaged gross receipts in the prior year of $2,180 (one had made $15,000) whereas users averaged $77.50.

To this sample we administered four psychological tests, each of which had discriminated on that same campus between users and nonusers in our earlier study. These were the California Psychological Inventory, the Strong Vocational Interest Blank, the Allport-Vernon Study of Values, and the Myers-Briggs Type Indicator.

On the fifty subscales tested for significance of differences (using student T-scores), none proved significant at $P = <.05$ (although by chance one expects several to have done so). Furthermore, there was only one "trend" which exceeded $P = <.20$.

The sample is small, but the magnitude of differences on the various psychological tests scales is so low that—given the requirements for residence and personal matching—only immensely expanded sampling might conceivably have yielded significant differences. Such an expansion probably would have foundered on matching failures and the confounding of social homogeneity as one was forced to move beyond high-illicit-use fraternity houses into other types of residences. In any event, we didn't have the money to afford the exercise.

Just as we have found that dealers are not different people from regular users in any absolute way, for we find all dealers to be illicit users and all regular illicit users in these three residences to have dealt at one time or another, we now propose that dealers and regular users—once matched for background, activities, and residence—are not different people either in terms of personality traits, vocational interests, personal values, or the Myers-Briggs Jungian typology of sensitivities. If this is the case, then drug dealing as opposed to regular illicit-drug using within carefully defined situations and drawing from an homogeneous population is not a matter of personality as measured by the tests we used.

Comment and Summary

Drug experimentation is common on campus. Regular illicit-drug use characterizes from one third to one half of the students; at least one third have violated laws pertaining to dealing by having supplied (free) drugs to others; and a portion of students—we estimate about 6 per cent—have become consistent suppliers to their fellow users. These suppliers come from the heavier drug-using sectors and are characterized by having greater drug use than the average drug user on campus as we measure the latter by means of surveys. These dealers are less involved in intensive on-campus living, for they are more often found living off campus or, if on campus, in the smaller and more isolated atmosphere of apartments or trailers. Dealing is almost exclusively masculine and is an upper-classman's trade. Our data and our impressions indicate that being a campus dealer is not a permanent occupation, although we suspect the underlying drug involvement is fairly constant. The campus dealer is not otherwise criminal. In comparison with the variegated dealers in preceding chapters he is nondelinquent and almost arrest-free. Most campus dealers aim toward legitimate vocations. Nevertheless, among both dealers and users, vocational plans are less clear than among nonusers; and the few nondrug delinquencies that do occur are more likely to be among users-dealers than nonusing students.

Information gathered in this phase of our inquiry was limited primarily to dealing prevalence. Since, however, dealing is one correlate of intensive use (Goode, 1970), it is possible to supplement the comparison of dealers with other students by extrapolating from other information on drug use gathered on this same campus (Blum, 1969). This information compared intensive with less intensive drug users. It revealed a continuum of features with nonusers placed at one extreme and intensive users at the other. For example, intensive users were older, from wealthier families, were in disagreement with their parents, held left wing political convictions, were irreligious, personally dissatisfied, distrustful of authority, pessimistic, disappointed, had more dropout experience, and had parents who themselves used illicit drugs and had considerable experience with approved drugs. Clinical descriptions drawn from tests and observations in that study also fit the clinical impressions gained from dealer observations during this inquiry. Boredom, romanticism, empty parental relations, mourning over poverty of interpersonal emotions, free spiritness, a blighted Dionysian intensity, peer dependency, an absence of purpose, and risk-taking are traits which we suspect more often characterize dealers compared with their nondealing peers who do not use drugs.

Psychological tests were given to regular dealers in three high-illicit-use fraternity houses on one campus. These dealers were compared to regular illicit users in the same houses who were matched on grades, majors, career plans, political stance, use of alcohol, frequency of sexual intercourse, and (poorly so) parental income. The definition of "dealer" was someone selling once a week or more with annual gross receipts of $200 or over. There were no dealers who were not regular illicit users and no regular users who had not, at one time, dealt. Results show that no personality trait, personal value, vocational interest or (Jungian) character sensitivity distinguished between users and dealers in this similar population. We conclude that once the major variables which account for selection into the groups for which we controlled (residence, majors, career choice, etc.) are excluded, personality characteristics are not in evidence as determinants of who will or will not become a drug dealer in environments where regular illicit drug use is the rule.

Chapter 20

AMERICAN COLLEGIAN ABROAD

Approximately three hundred colleges and universities in the United States sponsor or approve overseas study programs. Every year over 25,000 American college students study abroad, some on campuses maintained by their American institution, others under approved programs within European universities. In addition to these resident students, there are the travelers. In 1969, for example, one and a half million passports were issued to Americans for European travel. Since passports are good for five years and since there are over four million current passports, we can hazard that in 1970 there were *at least* 50,000 additional young Americans in Europe as tourists. Since some portion of these resident and touring students will be drug users before they leave American shores, since a few may be expected to begin drug use abroad as part of their experimenting with a variety of new experiences, since some will be dealers bringing to Europe a know-how in drug distribution, and since some will find in Europe either new drugs or new markets, we undertook two studies and one tour with an eye to learning more about drug dealing and the American student abroad.

Overseas Campus A

There were eighty-one undergraduates in residence on this European campus, located in the heart of a fine city. Seventy-nine of them (thirty-nine men and forty women) agreed to participate in our inquiry. Their modal age was 20, most were juniors, humanities constituted the preponderant major, politically most classed themselves as liberal, and almost half had gone to private prep schools. Their overall grade-point average was 3.2 (B). While on campus in the United States, prior to going to Europe, the majority reported irregular wine consumption, irregular marijuana smoking and hashish use, and no experience with hallucinogens. In total experience, 87 per cent had used alcohol, 76 per cent marijuana, 56 per cent hashish, 23 per cent mescaline, 8 per cent LSD, and 22 per cent other drugs (including opiates and special substances).

While the students were overseas, for a six-month period, wine consumption and hashish use increased in regularity; marijuana and hallucinogen use declined. The shifts in wine, marijuana and hashish consumption are all significant at the $p = <.001$ level. When we compare total illicit-drug use in the United States and overseas, disregarding the kind of drug, we find no significant change. Sixty of seventy-nine students were users at home; sixty-one were users overseas. When we talked to these same students after they came home from Europe, we found a slight increase in drug use (not statistically significant). Sixty-five are in the ranks of the illicit users. Our conclusion so far is that the prevalence of illicit-drug experience does not change with European campus residence, nor does wine experience as such.

The use of some substances increases considerably in regularity, while others decline in regularity. Availability and convenience are the key variables; marijuana and hallucinogens were available in the United States but not in Europe; hashish was available in Europe but less so in the United States. Wine was available in both but to a lesser extent in the United States, where wine is not as easily available to underage 20 year olds.

The seventy-nine students were divided into seven subgroups: nonusers (no experience with any illicit drug), $N = 14$; ex-users (used in United States but not overseas), $N = 3$; new users (used in Europe for the first time), $N = 7$; users (both in United States and Europe), $N = 36$; ex-dealers (in United States but not in Europe), $N = 7$; new dealers (for the first time in Europe), $N = 5$; and dealers (in United States and in Europe), $N = 5$. We see from this that prevalence rates may have been the same but that different people may be involved; that is, some start and some stop use when they go to Europe, and some start and some stop dealing. There are more chronic users, both in the United States and in Europe, than chronic dealers. We presume that for these collegians use rather than dealing is the more central and stable feature of their lives.

We compared the seven subgroups on their majors, politics, prep school background, and on the regularity of their drug use, both in the United States and overseas. Although inspection indicated trend differences, because the subgroup Ns are small, statistical significance is not obtained. Recombining subgroups into illicit users who have never been dealers in contrast with nonusers, we find the nonusers significantly ($P = <.05$) more often to have attended prep school and to be politically to the right. Those who have stopped using drugs by the time of their European residence are also more conservative, a trend, $P = <.10$. New users were compared to all others on an interview item asking them to rate the risk of being caught using drugs. There was a trend $P = <.10$, for new users to rate the risk as relatively large compared to the risk others felt. One surmises from the trend that the lack of risk felt by experienced users is a function of safe experience in use. It is also possible that the late starters (new users) are more apprehensive or conforming people. (See Blum and associates, 1969b, for the characteristics of abstainers and their slow but positive response to drug-use opportunities in college.)

Ex-dealers did not differ from the remainder of the sample. Although there was a tendency for them to have been more frequent marijuana users only (not dealers or nonusers), the ex-dealers tended toward conservatism. Chronic dealers differed from the remainder of the sample in that they had been, $P = <.01$, the most regular users of marijuana in the United States and also the most regular users of hashish while in Europe. As for new dealers, they also tended to be greater marijuana users in the United States and hashish users in Europe than the rest of the sample. All dealers, as a group, differed significantly, $P = <.01$, from all nondealing users, as a group, in these same two areas. Our conclusion regarding dealers is, as Goode (1970) has shown, that drug dealing is a function of the regularity of illicit-drug use; that is, the greater the drug involvement, the more likelihood of dealing. We also note that there are a total of ten people who at least occasionally supply others with drugs in a total using population of fifty-eight persons.

Overseas Campus B

Overseas campus B is isolated in the country in contrast to campus A, and is, in consequence, more of a self-contained community. At the time of the study there were eighty students (fifty male and thirty female), five faculty members, and three administrators, one of whom was a graduate student. All students and faculty were in their twenties and thirties, as was the young administrator; the two directors were over 40. All students but only those faculty identified as involved with drugs were interviewed; in addition, those identified as dealers were observed and periodically reinterviewed for the six months of their European stay. Many of the students had a history of marijuana or hashish use. While in Europe nearly half (thirty-six) reported regular hashish use (three times or more per week). Two of the five faculty were also regular users, as was the younger administrator. Although each student was told upon his arrival that his being found to use, possess, or deal in illicit drugs would lead to his expulsion, it soon became clear that this rule, like the few other regulations on campus, was a public policy statement not intended for enforcement. The involvement of faculty and administrators in use affirmed the informal acceptance of discrete use in contrast to formal policy.

Our interest in this investigation was not, as in campus A, in the prevalence of use or changes in drug use, but in the dealers—how they traded and what their roles were. On campus B, there were four student dealers supplying, for profit, the thirty-nine users (themselves included). There was also one faculty and one administrator dealer.

Student Dealers. Student dealers are specialized—two trading in hashish, one mescaline, and one marijuana and hashish. Sam, the mescaline dealer, is a white, 19-year-old fraternity member with a B+ average. He tried his first illicit drug at age 17 and made his first sale at 18. He uses hashish and mescaline about once a week. Bob, the dealer in marijuana and hashish, is 21 years old, white, a senior, and a fraternity member. He has a B grade average and plans to attend law school. He uses marijuana once a week and hashish about once a month. He tried an illicit drug for the first time when he was 18, and made his first sale when he was 20. Mary is a 19-year-old white girl, a member of the Women's Liberation Front, and the heaviest drug user among the dealers. Both her consumption of illicit drugs and her grades climbed during her stay overseas. She uses marijuana or hashish daily and LSD, methamphetamine, or mescaline on occasion. In her own words:

> *I was not a heavy dope smoker because I didn't like to inhale anything—cigarettes, dirty air, anything. This is the first quarter I've done a lot of dope constantly. This is also the first quarter I've done a great deal of my work, consciously gotten out and done things, traveled and enjoyed myself and thought a lot.*

Dick, the last of the quartet, is a 21-year-old male senior with a little better than a B grade average. He first took an illicit drug at age 18 but did not make a sale until he was 21. He uses hashish and marijuana often and mescaline on occasion.

Bob, the student who sells marijuana, obtained his first supply from the United States—parcels which were sent from a false name and address in the United States to a false name at the overseas campus. There, unclaimed parcels were given to one of the administrators for forwarding or retention until they were claimed. He held them until the dealer called for them, both wanting to be sure that the parcels hadn't been checked by customs. Bob had no fear of being caught, since he felt protected by the false-address scheme and "laws against entrapment."

Bob says that he came to sell by chance. A pusher approached him in the center of the country's capital, asking if he was interested in buying large quantities of hashish. Bob, on what he says was a spur of the moment, said "yes."

Mary, the major hashish supplier on the campus, obtained her entire supply locally. She also met her supplier "by chance." After she was introduced by a mutual friend to this local dealer, discussion arose about dealing and she decided it was worthwhile to become a dealer. At first the hashish was delivered to the campus by her supplier, who received his payment upon delivery. Arrangements were made by phone. With time, the method of delivery changed. This is how Mary says it works:

> *You get a call at 6:30, catch a train to the city at 8:00, wait in the station for half an hour past the predetermined hour and finally two faces come out of nowhere. You split with them, drive off to the pad of the higher-up guy, walk in, sit down, talk around, listen to good music, talk, exchange raps and dope stories, discuss the American situation, and maybe smoke some dope. Then the talk gets to the immediate situation. You discover it'll cost* [*about $24*] *more than the last buy but it's OK 'cause you've got the money. Then you check out the stuff for weight, size, texture, smell, color, etc., talk more on general dope—other markets, etc., then split. You never know the cat by more than a first name and you never could find his home again personally if you had to. The two guys drive you home, you sit and talk, say goodbye—that's it.*

Mary also purchased supplies for the fourth dealer, Dick. His sales were, however, quite small.

Three of these dealers had their own independent sources. Sam, the mescaline dealer, initially brought his supply of drugs from the

United States, carrying his capsules with his toilet articles and clearing customs without question.

All four dealers sold drugs on their home campus in the United States before coming to Europe. Sam, the mescaline seller, reports that in Europe his sales dropped from three sales to one a week. His gross monthly receipts fell from $75 a month to about $33 a month, and his European profits were only $10 to $15 per month. Bob, the marijuana peddler, was a minor dealer on the home campus and remained so on the overseas campus—his was a $5 monthly net profit. Mary, as the major supplier of hashish to the overseas campus, enjoyed a net profit which increased from $5 per month on the home campus to $40 per month in Europe. Her gross receipts rose from $40 per month to nearly $100 per month. Dick's hashish gross receipts fell from $30 per month to $20 per month, but his profits went up from pittance to pittance, a dollar per month to $5 per month. The increase in net profits of the hashish dealers was due to a virtual monopoly on hashish sales which they had on campus.

None of the four sold outside the campus. They felt safe from arrest, dealing in the isolated university community.

All four dealers gave the same two reasons for their dealing: one social and altruistic, the other financial; they wanted to provide an easily available supply of illicit drugs for their friends, and they wanted to make some sort of profit. One, for example, said that he sold marijuana "partly to be able to finance my own purchases of drugs, somewhat for personal profit, and partly so that others in the group can have access to drugs." The mescaline dealer, Sam, expressed similar sentiments. The hashish dealers, both of whom enjoyed rising profits in Europe, seemed more interested in money. Mary, who did most of the business, said, "I sell so that I can make enough money to go on my three-week break." Dick, the other hashish dealer, used his (meager) profits to buy his own "dope." Although only two of the dealers, Sam the mescaline peddler and Bob the marijuana peddler, came to Europe with plans to sell drugs, all of them plan to continue their operations for an indefinite time. They do not believe that their dealing has interfered with their plans for conventional careers. Sam expects to marry and be a writer, Bob plans to enter law school, and Mary plans to pursue a career in broadcasting. Dick's plans are uncertain.

None has had any trouble with the law, either in the United States or in Europe. Bob and Sam do not plan to cross international borders again carrying illicit drugs, nor do the other two plan to risk taking drugs across international frontiers. They have learned that students were "suspect" by customs, and they don't want to take the risk of being caught.

Mary told us that she felt safe on the home campus because "nobody bothers about it [illicit drugs] and because it [the criminal law] is so absurd." Overseas she felt "a little more" secure on campus than off. Dick said that drug dealing is equally dangerous anywhere. Bob felt safe because he sold only to friends and because he considered the campus a sheltered area. Sam agreed that a dealer on a university campus in the United States or in Europe is safer than elsewhere.

Faculty Dealers. A young faculty member and the young administrator also distributed illicit drugs. Both sold only hashish, and both sold it only on rare occasions. Each contended that his only customers were friends whose own supply had run out. The young administrator said, "I've had some to spare, a friend hasn't had any, and I agreed to share." The young faculty member asserted that he supplied "because [I am] a decent guy." Both would say only that their profits were negligible.

The faculty member is young, white, and European. He was introduced to marijuana by some of his students when he was 22 and at the time of the interview used marijuana and hashish often (at least four times per week). He first sold hashish at age 24.

The young administrator is a 23-year-old white male on a leave of absence from a United States graduate school. He first used marijuana when he was twenty, and he had become a heavy user (at least four times per week) of both marijuana and hashish. He made his first sale when he was twenty-one. His sales were less at the European campus than they were at the home campus.

The faculty member was supplied by students, and the administrator obtained his drugs from friends on and off campus. The latter, a native of the country, had better contacts "outside." The faculty member told us he was safe dealing on the campus. The administrator does not plan to continue dealing whereas the faculty member said that he will continue to sell.

Unlike the four student dealers, these two dealers have carried and planned to continue carrying cannabis across international borders. Neither has had any difficulties with customs.

Dealers Compared with Others. There is little to distinguish the outward demeanor and dress of the drug dealers from that of the other members of the campus community. Their appearance ranges from the clean-cut, conservative dress to the more "hip"-looking styles. In their plans, views, and interests, we could not distinguish dealers from others on campus.

Attractions of Dealing. Some were attracted by the excitement and "romantic" intrigue associated with dealing. The young faculty member was, he said, influenced by the excitement of dealing and by the fact that it brought him friends and acceptance among the using students. Mary was intrigued by the undercover aspects of drug peddling. She liked her "double life" ("a Miss Jane Bond"). The others emphasized that they liked the extra money (which was so little for these well-off students that we must be skeptical of that claim). There was a real advantage in terms of their own drug use: by finding sources and buying drugs to sell, they assured themselves a cheap, readily available supply. Since dealing took little time, was fun, and involved, as far as they could see, no risks, why not?

An Eyewitness Account

One summer a knowledgeable fellow, our Traveler, recently graduated with a bachelor's degree and in addition familiar with our dealer studies, accompanied some of his dealing acquaintances as they made their rounds in Europe, North Africa, and the Near East. One of these was a millionaire by virtue of having, at one time, made and resold an immense wholesale purchase of LSD illicitly made in the laboratories of a large chemical-pharmaceutical concern. The others were mostly small-time dealers, supplying drugs for themselves and friends and getting traveling money. Some made $100 to $200 per month but not for many months. All dealt in hash, and about a third sold "mescaline." During this trek our Traveler made notes for our project, recording nothing that would be incriminating if the notes were seized but, as a tourist's diary, sufficing to remind him upon return home of those matters we now remark upon.

First, with regard to dealing prevalence, Traveler met an estimated 150 to 200 other young Americans while on his tour. He talked to about thirty of these, long-haired and of casual appearance, about their own or others' drug use and dealing. Among those who were visibly hippie, Traveler states that he found almost none who were not dealing in illicit drugs. Another external indicator of dealing had been, in earlier years, the sale of *Herald Tribunes* on street corners in Paris, London, Amsterdam, Copenhagen, and Nice; newspaper selling had served as a front for moving about and meeting customers. During 1970 Traveler's expert companions commented on the reduction of American newspaper vendors; they attributed the reduction to increased enforcement everywhere or, at least, a feeling of increased surveillance by local and national police in Europe.

Traveler believes that there is sufficient intercommunication among touring American youth who are also users and dealers that a body of knowledge and lore builds up about the "best" and "worst" places to buy and sell. (This is supported by the agreement among types of dealers in our Bay Area study as to where to go abroad to buy.) In the summer of 1970 Amsterdam was rated first in this small timers' guide to where to traffic in Europe. Amsterdam is described as a drug users haven because of small penalties against users and dealers, the expectation that enforcement will be minimal given the existence of legal "sanctuaries" (social clubs) for use within the city, and the expectation that Dutch law will shortly legalize cannabis. As a commercial center for trafficking, it has the advantage of being central. This allows dealers going and coming from other European nations to meet easily there. During his two-day stay, Traveler witnessed the transfer of 20 kilos of cocaine in Dam Square and heard of an equal additional quantity that was available.

The dealers place Paris as the city of second rank for drug commerce. Traveler's acquaintances there said that they imported via Marseilles; but usually the arrangements for drug transactions, including storage and transportation, were conducted in Paris, the business capital. In Paris both French and American youth are active in drug dealing. At the small-scale level, the deals are often made in particular cafes. All drugs are available there, as is also the case in Amsterdam; but Traveler believes that opiates constitute a greater portion of the French than the Dutch trade for the young American dealer. Any young American with some experience and interest can do business in Paris; some have done very well. Indeed, as an extension of the invasion of European markets by American enterprise, Traveler states that young Americans are likely to do as well or better in the drug business in Paris than Frenchmen. He believes that because of their having more capital, more stateside experience in dealing, more connections (because of the wide social networks in the United States involved in dealing and because Americans abroad move about and make friends easily), American youth are likely to control more drugs and more "territory" and to have greater access to sources and dealers than French dealers do. Indeed, some of the Europeans that Traveler met complained of American imperialism in the drug trade. This Continental complaint echoes exactly the one quoted in the Prologue from the English underground press.

Traveler had occasion, through his companions (in crime), to get acquainted with several big dealers. Their traffic routes are described as converging on European capitals (especially Paris and London) from opiate and hashish sources in the Near East or North Africa (Central Asian drugs being transhipped also arrive from the Near East). One feature surprising to Traveler was that some of his acquaintances spoke of importation to Europe via "less suspect" rerouting shipments with Near Eastern origins through Eastern Europe (Czechoslovakia, Yugoslavia, sometimes Hungary or Poland) to the West. In addition, dealers draw upon warehoused supplies of opiates, amphetamines, and barbiturates, which had been manufactured legally in past years but were now held in very large quantities by wholesealers to the illicit trade. When one country allows a substance illicit in another to be imported and exported legally—or without police interference even if technically illegal—that country, of course, becomes a center for smuggling operations. Traveler comments that his companions and their colleagues use Italy for amphetamines and Germany for methedrine in this way. Amsterdam's role has already been noted. Lebanese, but not non-Lebanese citizens, are able to work in Lebanon selling hashish and opiates. Foreign dealers in Lebanon have, he says, more difficulty securing the informal underground equivalent of "work permits" from local police—or criminals—than do natives.

Traveler's higher-echelon friends described smuggling into the United States as a very special business problem. They indicated that they prefer to employ as couriers regular travelers and regular routes, particularly seamen and airlines personnel and the offices and facilities of major respectable importing concerns. New Orleans and Baltimore are, for Traveler's acquaintances, the major ports for import. From these cities, drugs (narcotics especially) are then sent to East Coast cities. Traveler's acquaintances said that the methedrine market is in transition. Until very recently, German production and exports dominated the market, with Bay Area producers second, but now other manufacturers are competing. In consequence, the profits (they said that theirs had been about 800 per cent on meth purchased either in Germany or San Francisco and sold in New York City) will be reduced as greater supplies become available. Traveler's wealthiest companion, the LSD magnate, described his source as English and stated that most of his deliveries were through the mail, five-gram lots (sufficient for twenty thousand 250-microgram administrations) being usual.

As with other cross-cultural business affairs, Traveler indicates that his companions found easier working relationships in countries where the culture is akin to the American one. In some places, however, the local population of drug merchants has accommodated sufficiently to Western ways so that young American dealers can profit even in "strange" environments. All of Western Europe, with the exception of Spain, is classified by Traveler's friends as a place congenial for Americans for dealing, since Americans can understand and do business with local traffickers there. Turkey and Morocco are stranger places, but there the marketplace is so established that a serious dealer can learn readily and expect to do business satisfactorily. Lebanon, on the other hand, is not only not Western; it has, reportedly, protective policies for local citizens plus serious enough enforcement endeavors that the young American, however drug-wise, may be ill-advised to work independent of established native backers and partners. The same may be true for larger Asian producing countries.

Traveler's companions and their colleagues did express themselves clearly on their preferences. They prefer to live and deal on the Continent (France, Holland, England, etc.) rather than to locate in the Near East or North Africa, where they secure their supplies. Thus, for cannabis and opiates, they are traveling buyers and importers rather than exporters from producing countries. Amphetamines and hallucinogens, on the other hand, are manufactured on the Continent. Life in Paris for the young American dealer does not mean what it may evoke to the reader—romance and lots of fun. Traveler describes the lives of the people he knows there as tedious and sometimes sterile. They are, viewed through the eyes of a "busy" American, inactive. They get up around noon, have a cheap lunch, drink coffee and beer, and talk. Some are flamboyant and splurge at the fine restaurants, but most dealers have considerable entertainment expenses in their bar bills for dozens of clients plus assorted hanger-on acquaintances. Most that Traveler knows are in an alcoholic haze most of the time, for alcohol is the drug which they say is appropriate to social and business dealings; besides, it is not safe to "use" other drugs publicly in Paris. Further, some of his acquaintances (like some of ours in the Bay Area study) fear that hashish or the opiates interfer with their business acumen; others are ex-addicts who have gone through withdrawal from heroin and now avoid that drug.

Traveller's low-level friends and their colleagues are not involved with syndicates. Some of them are involved in minor ways in opiate and cocaine import-export and traffic without sensing any "stronghold" from other organizations including larger syndicates. For their heroin-cocaine activities, which may net them no more than $2,000 to $3,000 per year, no elaborate international network is required. These Americans ordinarily will be aware of local (native) crime groups who are, like themselves, involved in local dealing; and if the American wishes to expand contacts, sources, or distribution, he may elect to involve himself with local criminals for the purposes of importation to and distribution within European countries. Should the American wish to become a heavy dealer in opiate or cocaine—and sometimes hashish—he is likely to tie in with organized groups which may have other criminal interests as well. Traveler knows a few such dealers and believes that to make it big smuggling "hard" narcotics into the United States one must participate in some kind of enduring organization. Such involvement does not mean permanent ties with the Mafia per se, although it can mean working with Corsicans, Frenchmen, and Sicilians.

As far as the purity of what they sell is concerned, Traveler says that, as elsewhere, a middle-class dealer who cares for his reputation will want to maintain it by handling high-quality products. Others, more calculating, cut quality on occasional batches, reasoning that if most are good, their reputations and clientele will remain whereas an occasionally tampered batch can readily be explained away. Because drugs are readily available at reasonable prices to importers and wholesalers, the pressure to adulterate is not great except for those for whom short-term increased profit margins are of prime importance.

When Traveler compares Bay Area dealers he knows—and he knows several hundred—with his European acquaintances, he finds that in both groups the serious ones embark with intention to profit. For both groups dealing is, like most businesses, difficult, and profit is not assured; this is particularly so for the dealer whose interests are in sociability and pleasure and not to a twelve-hour-a-day grind. Dealing has its drawbacks for those who abhor commitments to bureaucratic organizations, whether straight or crime syndicates. Like other businesses, dealing depends upon shippers and clients, but in the drug world these may be erratic people. Consequently, many hours are spent waiting rather than working. To these problems are added the precautions which the threat of arrest imposes both at home and abroad. As for differences, the middle-class American abroad differs from his Bay Area counterpart in that, in the Bay Area, drug dealing is interesting and is immersed, for the psychedelic-cannabis set, in a community where there is much support and acceptance. By contrast, in Europe—even with the advent of the transcultural hippie—dealing is not so much fun. It is not an "in" thing to do. It is not a free and easy part of an adolescent-and-early-twenties ethos, where the majority use and where many adults—including family and teachers—do not strenuously disapprove. The American dealer who lives abroad is not in a scene which is the center of sympathetic attention and whose members are encouraged to consider themselves the wave of the future. Whatever the local underground may say of itself, Traveler believes that Europe is less generous in its acclaim for youthful experimentation or revolution; in consequence, the dealer is confined to a narrower group of friends, many of them expatriates like himself. Therefore, unless he is getting very rich—which is rare—Traveler predicts that he will get bored and come home, or be busted and remain for a long cold season in European prison. Those there, says Traveler, know this and consider their foreign venture temporary; "get ahead and get out," they say, because, for most of them, the good life requires something more than money.

Comment and Summary

It is obvious from the three sets of reports, two campuses and one grand tour, that there is no evidence that the American collegian behaves any differently in Europe than in America with regard to his willingness to use drugs illicitly or to engage in illicit dealing. Prevalence rates for experience and dealing remain constant, although some individuals drop in and others drop out of the dealing scene. For all in our sample, being a resident dealer abroad is a transient experience; the collegians return home to use and deal in the United States; the expatriate nonstudent (or former one) "gets his bread and gets out."

There is evidence that the drugs most used are those most readily available and those consistent with prevailing local life styles. The grand-tour report also emphasizes convenience: trading in countries where smuggling and transactions are easiest, and living in countries more akin to the cultural styles to which the American dealer is accustomed.

With regard to the impact of the laws, one observes that the American abroad continues his illicit use and dealing as at home even though he is aware that local penalties may be more consistent and stiffer than in the United States. Those on campuses appear to enjoy sanctuaries in Europe which are of the same order as those in the United States. The expatriate dealer enjoys no sanctuary; and, as the grand-tour report suggests, the dealer trades off higher risks in Europe in return for the greater ease of dealing defined by cheapness and variability of available supplies.

Chapter 21

HOLY ROCK BIBLE COLLEGE

At the gate of Holy Rock Bible College, located in California's beautiful wooded hills, a sign proclaims, "The end of the world is nearer than you think! Hallelujah! Praise the Lord!" The religious character of the college is pervasive. In order to be admitted, a student not only must meet academic standards but "a definite experience of Christian conversion is also essential." A large portion of each student's program consists of religious studies, and many major in such areas as "Bible-theology, Ministerial, Missions, and Pre-seminary." The student is required to attend chapel and prayer sessions several times each day and church services on Sunday. All students must engage in "student ministry activities" such as "Street Evangelism" and "Visitation Evangelism." Grades are assigned for these activities.

The college's strict discipline is exemplified by this statement from the *Student Handbook:* "The following are not permitted: Participation or involvement in gatherings where dancing, social or otherwise, is exercised. Possession and/or use of any forms of alchoholic beverages, tobacco, marijuana, and other drugs. Attendance at public theatres."

Five hundred and forty-two students, 280 men and 262 women, attend Holy Rock—107 living off campus, 360 in dormitories, and 75 in other types of college-provided housing. Our sample of 102—61 men and 41 women—was drawn from the dormitory residents. All dormitory residents present during the period when the interviewer was on campus were approached and asked to cooperate. There were no refusals. The age range of our sample was from 18 to 22.

One of us moved into the dormitory at Holy Rock for one weekend, after having paid three visits and becoming acquainted. During that stay, we interviewed the 102 sample members.

Twenty students described themselves as exdealers. Ten indicated that they had used illicit drugs (most regularly) but had not sold them regularly and for profit. The remainder—70 per cent of our sample—denied any experimentation or use with any illicit psychoactive substance. At the time of the interview no student was either selling or using any illicit drug. Our evangelical group, then, contains within it a 30 per cent sector who are "reformed" users, 20 per cent of whom are exdealers. Their reformation, in our opinion, contains two elements: one, a very dramatic shift in values and in conduct in the direction of Christian salvation (as they see it); the other, a continuation of conduct which, at an inner level, is an expression of what went on before. In this, the drug dealers more than the nondealing users stand out as examplars. The nonusers, more conventional folk, are undirectional.

We report here only the major findings, based on trends observed within the sample (not subjected to statistical testing). We find that the exdealers are more often freshmen but older, indicating that they are starting Bible college later than their fellow students, be the latter either exusers or the nonusers. They are also more likely to be taking evangelical-theological studies. In contrast, exdealers have no interest in the social sciences but one fifth of the nondealing exusers and the nonusers are majoring in social sciences.

Exdealers and exusers more often have come from urban environments; the nonusers, from rural ones. Poverty characterizes the parents of the exdealers less than the others.

Politically the exdealers are both least conservative and most apolitical. Only among the nonusers are no political radicals to be found. The exuser group is least involved in student organizations, and they report the fewest number of friends, although essentially all the students are sociable and have some friends.

Arrest histories reveal a far greater frequency of arrest for both drug and nondrug violations among dealers than among exusers or nonusers—and little difference between the latter two groups. Even so, half of the exdealers report that they have never been arrested. Given the fact that most of the dealer sample were juveniles during their dealing life, it is no surprise that juvenile offenses such as running away and curfew violations are included. Drug histories show strong differences. The exdealer group began smoking and drinking at an earlier age (two fifths before age 10) than the other two groups, and a small number of these exdealers have continued to use both cigarettes and alcohol; in contrast to the group of exdealers, none of the nonusers report any current use of tobacco or alcohol. Ninety-five per cent of the exdealers had used marijuana; 85 per cent had used heroin; half had used cocaine; and the majority had used sedatives, hallucinogens, and amphetamines. In the exuser group the variety of illicit experience had been far less, and only marijuana had been used by the majority. Most of the dealers had peddled marijuana; a small minority had also sold heroin; and most had sold other substances.

All of the students in the sample deny any current use of illicit drugs, although some exdealers admit marijuana use as recent as within six months of the interview. The reasons offered for stopping that use—which, for dealers, was both extensive and intensive—are of interest. We asked first, however, about their stopping smoking. Most of the exusers and two fifths of the exdealers were religiously motivated to quit.

> *God told me to stop. I found I no longer had a need for tobacco.*
>
> *My body is the Temple of the Holy Spirit. Jesus lives inside my heart and I wouldn't want Him to suffocate.*
>
> *Smoking isn't necessary, for I've found satisfaction in a high ideal.*
>
> *Jesus Christ proved to me that smoking was wrong.*

Exdealers as well as exusers also report that they quit smoking because of health hazards or because, for various reasons, they no longer enjoyed the experience. Cessation of drinking was even more often a matter of religious conviction.

> *Liquor gave Satan a perfect chance to play games with my head, therefore influencing my life into sin and destruction.*
>
> *Before I found the true and living God, I needed these escapes to provide happiness. But now that I have a personal relationship with the Creator of this Universe, I am satisfied with His love.*
>
> *I found the ultimate high with Jesus.*

As with alcohol, the majority of dealers and users state that they quit the use of illicit drugs for religious reasons.

> *I found a better high in Jesus. Jesus can't even be compared to drugs. Jesus is reality. I'd have to come down to light up a joint.*
>
> *Grass was a substitute for real joy and peace that can only be found through Jesus Christ and at best it is a poor substitute. Grass is temporary and illusionary, but Jesus is real and satisfies the inner longings of my heart.*
>
> *Heroin was destroying my mind mentally and my body physically, and God cured me of that habit.*

Of the thirty exusers and dealers in this sample, only six give other reasons for quitting than those arising from religion and conversion. "Not liking it," "fear of jail," and a belief in the harmful effects of marijuana are mentioned. The importance of religious experience to the exusers (all dealers had been users) as a group, in contrast to the nonuser Holy Rock students, is demonstrated in another way. More of the dealer and user group intend to be ministers than do other students; we have already noted the predominance of religious studies among the dealers especially.

These students reveal a remarkable Christian fatalism concerning their career plans. Many of them say that they cannot plan or predict a career ten years in advance, for that depends on "the will of the Lord." These career doubts are interwoven in conversation with the expectation of the Second Coming:

> *I hope to be in heaven ten years from now.*
>
> *I expect to be with Jesus Christ for all eternity ten years from now. I really believe that.*

Half of the exdealers, one third of the exusers, and only 17 per cent of the nonusers speak in what we coded as fatalistic terms; that is, their career depends on Jesus's intentions for them. Further, the dealers and users are certain that the Second Coming will be within ten years—which is the date we used when we talked to the students about their careers and what they expected to be doing then.

What do these Pentecostal students have to say about legalizing marijuana? They are against it. All nonusers and nondealing exusers feel that way; two exdealers want it legalized. Indeed, half the sample want stricter laws, punishments for marijuana. Many of the exdealers and the nondealing users (but only 18 per cent of the nonusers) give religious reasons for their opposition to legalization: "I honestly was all for legalizing grass until I found Christ. Since that time I've realized that all drugs are Satan's counterfeit of Christ." Among the nonusers, beliefs that marijuana leads to hard drugs, or that it is physically or psychologically harmful, more often account for their stance.

Comment and Summary

If dealing is, as we believe that it is for many, a transitional state, where do they go when they quit? Some went, we saw, to communes, of which Consciousness III (Chapter Fourteen) was an example, there to live an agrarian-mystical life (but usually not for long). At Holy Rock we find a similar phenomenon, except that whereas Consciousness III attracted a better-educated middle-class group, Holy Rock seems more to attract the children of blue-collar and lower-echelon white-collar strata. At Holy Rock we do see their next step on the path of changing life, which is, after drug peddling, conversion to the living Christ and the denunciation of Satan's tools and counterfeit coin, illicit drugs, and the drug life.

Yet Holy Rock is not the end of a career for young people; it is a beginning, one which like drug dealing itself seems uncertain. Consider the fatalism of half of the exdealers, who have happily surrendered to Christ's will and in doing so avow that they cannot be sure what the next decade holds—even though they are involved in theological studies and plan on evangelical ministerial futures. Comparing this joyful embrace of ambiguity as well as of Christ by dealers (and exuser nondealers) more than by the nonuser students, one asks whether these are not people committed to being uncommitted (see Keniston, 1960).

If the embrace of uncertainty, of a "now" orientation, and of a plunging surrender to Dionysian experience—be it drug intoxication or the mystical revelations of Jesus here and now—is the case, then the two experiences, drug dealing and Holy Rock, have more in common than might at first be thought. We shall address the obvious differences too, but for the moment consider some further similarities, the more readily to understand the appeals of the two experiences and of the movement from chemical to spiritual vocation.

Both experiences are simultaneously private and social. In both settings the associates are likely to view themselves as the elect. In both, a special language, ritual, and morality set the members off from nonmembers. Experiences are emotional rather than rational. Orientation is not toward community or social action, nor on money making or doing good, but on a state of feeling or being. As Maslow (1964) puts it, these are "peak experiences." Consider the parallel drawn by an ex-user himself: "Drugs used to make me happy and make me high; they became my reason to live. But now I've found a better high in Jesus." Compare also the two following statements:

> *A great power was present; I felt that this might be what the prophet had imagined was God. It continued for almost an hour and then I lapsed into unconsciousness.*
>
> *I felt a great force was with me. It was the Lord.*

The first statement comes from an LSD user on another campus studied; the second, from a student at Holy Rock who had never used drugs.

If one wishes to take a less positive view than William James (1902) did of the mysticism to be evoked within man, one might emphasize instead that drugs and the "Call" do offer a way out of a sometimes unpleasant real world. Compare the words of one student in the campus survey (Chapter One): "When I'm stoned I don't have to worry about Vietnam or grades or my parents. I'm in a special world and problems aren't there" with the words of a Holy Rock student: "A long as I'm with Jesus nothing bad can happen to me so I don't have to worry about anything. Accepting Him as my personal Lord and Savior solved all my problems."

Both the student at Holy Rock and the dealer on the street are in a central position in relation to their peer group. In the evangelical scene he is the minister of Jesus, one of the chosen few whose sight is considered clear and whose words are prophetic. In the drug scene he is the "righteous" peddler, ministering drugs to the community. Both are advocates and priests around whom a group revolves. Presumably this centrality is more important to the dealer become evangelist than to his peers who became neither.

That the sacred role—whether as Leary's holy dealer or at Holy Rock—is personally rewarding in prestige and power is not to be overlooked. Insofar as both roles—dealer and evangelical minister—allow for the expression of unusual personal qualities—akin to what Radin (1957) said of shamans—then the individual achieves through "ministering" a social resolution for what are likely to be powerful irrational forces. In either instance the individual seeks a unique competence serving the (presumably less strong) irrational forces within his congregation. Yet we must emphasize the seeking or proclaiming of such competence rather than its achievement, for the Holy Rock student has quit dealing before he was old enough to succeed (on the basis of data on successful dealers), and here at Holy Rock he has only announced his calling and has yet to achieve it. If his uncertainty about the future is prognostic, we deem it likely that at least some will never achieve a real ministry. If that is so, we are in both instances looking not just at uncommitted people but at unpersevering ones as well, that is, at failures.

If that is true, then perhaps proselytizing can better be understood, for dealers and evangelists are missionaries out to convert others to the faith. In *Utopiates* (Blum, 1964a) we considered proselytism at some length. Suffice it here to say, as we said in Chapter Ten, that for one who needs reassurance from others about a role or an ideology which he himself has embraced with doubt, proselytizing can be an outcome. Missionary zeal can also express a singular cast of mind, the focus on one way of life above all others, a fanatical bent or a *True Believer* (Hoffer, 1951). In any event his own importance increases as the size of his congregation grows, while the act of persuasion itself is a form of triumph. As the dealer moves to evangelist and takes his clientele with him, he doubly triumphs and in doing so may twice enjoy proofs from others of his own power and the righteousness of his way.

Let us take two cases—Tim and Sammy. Tim, age 19, is a sophomore at Holy Rock. He has never used an illicit drug and does not drink or smoke. He has wanted to be a minister since age 15. "Jesus is the center of my life." When Tim came to Holy Rock, "Jesus fulfilled my desire to belong to something or some group." Now "Jesus is rapture." It is his duty to save souls and being the Lord's servant is the most valuable, the most commendable way that one can use the life the Lord has given. Tim works hard and perseveres, not just for the Lord, not just for the souls to be saved, but also because he is *of* the religious community. His own conduct reflects on his church and his friends and family. We expect Tim to succeed in the future as he has in the past.

Sammy is a 23-year-old freshman at Holy Rock. He gives this drug history.

> *I started using when I was 11, first wine and smoking marijuana, then I started sniffing glue. I started shooting stuff for three years and when I was 15 I started selling marijuana. My brothers used drugs, my sisters used drugs, two of my brothers were heroin addicts, one of my sisters was too, and two of my sisters were prostitutes.*

I got involved in drugs because I was lonely and unhappy. I was a child that was filled with hate. I had it in for everybody. I found happiness in drugs, so I used them. I found happiness in drinking, so I drank. When using or drinking I didn't have to worry about my problems. I carried on like this till I was 20. I used heroin for about five years and I was strung out on it off and on. I was in and out of jails; I used instead of committing suicide.

I wanted to identify with the other kids; I wanted to become part of a group, to be like the other guys. So I started carrying a knife and used more drugs. I cut a few people and I got cut a few times. Drugs became my life. I lied a lot, stole a lot, cheated a lot, and I used my friends to get money to buy drugs. That's all I cared about. I started out using a $5 spoon all the way up to $100 a-day habit.

When I was dealing I was making close to $700 to $800 a week. I was dealing heroin, opium, acid, mescaline, methedrine, reds—just about every known and some unknown drugs. I worked for a few people for three years just dealing, and I traveled to a few states and I transported from Mexico and from Panama into the U.S. When I was in New York for a while the most money I ever had in my pocket was maybe $15,000 to $16,000. This made me feel important. I started pimping too. I wanted to be a really cool guy, so I started pimping girls and got them to using heroin. They'd come and they'd beg and they'd cry and beg me and ask for a fix. And they'd go out of their way to do anything, just to get a fix. . . . I had to show my friends that I was tough. I had to be tough to be a dealer. I found that dealing wasn't just an everyday thing; it's a round that you get into that you just don't break away from quite easy. It's either your life or their life. You don't care about other people's lives; you don't care whether they live or die. You just care about the money.

I couldn't live up to the standards of dealing. I found myself in a mental hospital. After I got out I said, "Well, I'm going to kick my habit now," but every time I said that I was going to kick my habit, I found myself dealing again, always acid or something else. It would lead down from one joint to a couple of tablets of acid, a few reds, then always back to heroin. It would always go back to the same thing. It seemed like that stuff just possessed my body so much that I couldn't pull away from it.

I quit for a few months one time, and a friend of mine came up and he offered me a joint, and he said, "I know where we can get some heroin, but we have to rip it off." We went down to steal the heroin from the people; we stole it all right; we stole a couple of ounces and the guys caught up with us and they threw me out of a two-story window and just about broke my back. I found that I was running from a lot of people because I had ripped them off. I started ripping people off instead of dealing. I'd rip someone off, then I'd sell what I got, and then I'd rip someone else off again and sell that.

I got busted about two years ago. I got busted for transporting, for forgery, for burglary, attempted manslaughter, and had about five or six counts against me. I'd been picked up before, but no one ever proved anything; but it seemed like this time I was going to prison. But instead they sent me to a mental hospital. I stayed there about six or seven months. While I was in the mental hospital, I was dealing heroin to patients, and I was using heroin myself. I was using about $85 to $90 a day worth of heroin. I sneaked in the heroin through my friends. I got busted in there, in the hospital, and I knew that this time there wasn't any way out. But a funny thing happened. God just seemed to step into my life at that time. There was a guy, an exheroin addict, telling me about the Lord. He started witnessing to me about God. He told me about the love of God. I didn't want to believe him. It took this guy six months to tell me about the love of God. I went to church before. I had thought about God, but God wasn't anything to me in my life. I was just atheist and rebellious. I didn't care about no God. I didn't care whether God lived or died.

I got out of the hospital; I found that I was up here at the Bible college. A friend had brought me up to the Bible college, but I still went through all kinds of different hassles. I was really sick, physically and mentally. My mind was still messed up pretty bad. Up at this Bible college I seen all these religious fanatics running around, preaching the word of God to everybody, preaching this big game. To me it was just a big game. Well, I found that day I was lonelier than ever. My friend he helped me to get an apartment, and he'd bring me up to the Bible college. I was still using—I needed heroin to keep me going, and I kept using heroin and kept using it. After two weeks of coming up here listening to these religious fanatics, one day I was up in my room, and a strange thing happened to me. I don't know how to explain it—

> *how to put it into words, but it was a voice that just called me. It was something I never heard before. It was a voice that spoke to me clearly. It was a voice that assured me of something new and something good. This voice started talking to me. It led me away. It told me, "Come out of the filth that you're in, come into the righteousness of me." It just kept repeating over and over. It was really freaking me out, so I decided to go for a walk. I went for a walk in a secluded part of the Bible college here and I broke down for the first time in my life, really, really broke down, and cried. I broke down. I saw myself for what I was. I was high that day on heroin, but God touched my life that day. He cured me of my habit of heroin right there. He cured me of my habit of smoking. He gave me a purpose. He gave me something to live for, gave me a life. I found myself. I had had the vision where I just seen everything. I was cured.*

By our lights, Tim has known where he has been going for a long time and, in getting there, has kept his perspective on himself and his relations to others. He is, nevertheless, by urbane standards, a religious fanatic. Sammy's has been a much more disturbed career. Coming from one of those pathogenic families (see Chapter Eleven), he has seen the worst of street life and could not survive in it. He did not become a successful dealer but became instead a rip-off artist, at risk of his life. His adolescence was a series of experiments and failures, each bringing something worse in its wake. His use of a variety of drugs could hardly have improved his judgment or ability to cope, whatever they may have done for his temporary relief or by way of giving him some sorry purpose in life. He became psychotic and, while in a mental hospital ward, he was told about "the love of God" by an exheroin addict. Still later—again in the presence of an accepting and religious friend—he began his association with Holy Rock, peripheral at first but gradually becoming more intense until, as we know him now, he is a student and ministerial candidate.

One may view the call of God, as Sammy tells us of it, in several ways, depending on one's own perspective. Clinically, one could argue that Sammy remained psychotic and was still hallucinating, but that what he believed was God was at least a friendly hallucination, one which was restorative in that it was a symptom of an effort to make his disintegrated self whole again. It advised him of a way for his guilt to be assuaged and his inadequacies to be countered. Sammy remains mentally ill but is in remission. That Godly voice came, appropriately, at a time when Sammy's resources—his friend, the proselytizers at Holy

Rock, his own awareness that he was miserable and wanted to change his slow maturation out of adolescent confusion—enabled him to resolve his misery in a way that he and society would both agree represents a considerable advance.

At another level one may wonder whether Sammy has not found in his Holy Rock friends the kind of approval and acceptance for which he has so long been looking? Here at last there is status—not for the striving addict, dealer, pimp, and rip-off artist, but for one who was once all of these. Sammy as Prodigal can rest on his laurels, an elder statesman of delinquency, so to speak. Before Holy Rock's approbation is secure, however, Sammy must be an initiate; and that requires, as the printed admission statement affirms, that God as well as the registrar concur in his admission. For Sammy, who has long used hallucinatory drugs and whose ego is none too firm, the demand to script the voices which speak to him should not have been too difficult a requirement. This does not imply any conscious faking or less than full conversion; it simply notes that Sammy is the kind of person who could fulfill the requirements of the missionaries just as they, in offering him a less painful life, fulfilled his.

Both of these interpretations are consonant with what Sammy has told us of his life. They may be a bit too pat as after-the-fact accounts tend to be; we have no reason to believe that we could have predicted Sammy's conversion prior to the event any more than we could predict now, without a base in follow-up studies, what he will be doing ten years hence—assuming, not as he does, that the Day of Judgment be not then at hand. Based on data in the variegated dealer sample, one does anticipate that most teen-age dealers will not continue as such and one can discriminate now between those who become more criminal and those who become less. Yet given Sammy's proclivities for death-dealing activities, we would probably at first glance have considered him a case destined to go down the tubes. We are, in fact, still worried about him, not because of his conversion but for fear it may not last.

But we have not come to grips with what is for Sammy and Holy Rock the most profound issue. It *is* awesome that he did change, moving from a derelict addict and dealer to Christian virtue. He says he changed because God came to him. Were that the case, then all of our interpretations would but specify preliminary conditions for readiness to hear that Word.

Sammy's account is a valuable one because it tells us so much about what can happen to dealers. It is a limited account because it tells us only about Sammy and only that about him which was on his mind when we talked to him. It does not tell us about others at Holy Rock who had also been in the dealing life. We suspect that many of them are youths with a conscience, a conscience that had been filled with guilt as well as derogatory opinions about the self.

People deal with guilt in many ways. One can deny it, at some emotional cost, while at the same time punishing oneself as Sammy did. (He once even threatened to kill himself.) Some turn it inward and become depressed. Some go into psychotherapy or respond well to the combination of punishment, penitence, and sometimes even treatment which juvenile correctional facilities offer. Some simply change and reorder their lives. Some repent and seek forgiveness. The latter solution is most likely to have religious implications, for repentance is of sin as well as of misbehavior or good times lost. The forgiveness one seeks can be God's as well as man's. Some of the exdealers at Holy Rock are repentant.

The repentant sinner is a favored guest at the Pentecostal. He is living proof of Satan's work, but his presence is proof of Jesus' love and the power of His word. The repentant sinner—popular publicly these days, too, in the person of the exaddict haranguing high school audiences against drug use—can be a dramatic figure whose personal testimony reassures the audience that the straight and narrow path they have followed is the right one after all. Perhaps as Roche (1958) has suggested for the criminal trial, one needs these displays from time to time to reenergize the suppressors in us all which lead us not into temptation.

The dealer as repentant sinner is the Prodigal himself who comes to Holy Rock acknowledging, "Father, I have sinned against heaven and in thy sight." Although that college may offer up no fatted calf, it does offer appreciation now, as well as the Kingdom of Heaven shortly. Holy Rock is, we believe, particularly proud of the Prodigals in its midst. So blessed is the prodigal that one wonders if the exdealer's testimony does not itself become elaborated and ritualized.

Sammy's tale is chock full of sin as well as retrospective contrition. It also has those psychosocial insights which conform to a latter-day theory of drug use and delinquency as arising from loneliness, despair, unhappiness, and hostility. Probably Sammy came to these understandings on his own, but one cannot rule out his having learned them as part of his training at Holy Rock. If genuine, his perspective as well as his change is profound. If less than that, Sammy is still at work conforming to the special role of acceptable deviant which others have cast for him.

Let us quickly summarize, then. A study was undertaken of

dealing and dealers at a Bay Area Bible college. A sample of 102 dormitory residents out of a total population of 542 students was interviewed. There were no students using or dealing drugs, and most were not smoking or drinking either. Nineteen per cent, however, had been drug dealers, and another 10 per cent had been illicit users without having sold drugs regularly for profit. Most of the dealers had histories of marijuana, heroin, hallucinogen, and amphetamine use, and half had used cocaine. The nondealing exusers had used marijuana but, as a group, had been much less widely and intensively involved in illicit drugs.

Among the nearly one third of the Bible college students who were reformed, the major reasons given for their giving up drugs—illicit and licit—was religious conversion. This was least often the case with tobacco. The importance of the religious experience is also demonstrated by the fact that more exdealers and users were taking Bible studies (the college offers other majors) and more planned to be ministers than their peers without illicit-drug histories. Christian fatalism was marked among the former group, for most had put their careers in the hands of the Lord. As a group they are opposed to legalizing marijuana, and indeed half want punitive sanctions increased. Among exusers and dealers, opposition to use is also religiously grounded, but this is not the case among students without illicit-drug histories.

Chapter 22

COLLEGE FACULTY

When we set out to study dealing on campus, we thought it well to include faculty in our sample. Our intention was to gain information on possible illicit drug distribution practices and the correlates of such conduct. We also wanted to identify some of the factors that accounted for *not* dealing in circumstances where dealing was easy—where illicit drugs were present, police surveillance was difficult, and buyers were near at hand. The intentions which guided the examination of faculty also were present as we looked at other groups of respectable adults: pharmacists, physicians, detail men, and narcotics officers.

One would expect some professors to be dealers. Consider that in an early study of exotic drug use from 1962 to 1964 (Blum, 1964), one group of LSD users—which we called the informal professional sample —included a number of academics. Another group, the informal black-market sample, included graduate students who were turning on or being turned on by faculty; and some of the younger of these students were teaching assistants or part-time teachers in nearby undergraduate institutions—simultaneously students and faculty. In our current situation, given the fact that faculty once were graduate students, some very recently, why wouldn't they continue their "recreational" styles? They are surrounded by students who use; they do have legal sanctuary (see Blum and associates, in press); and in their work they are dedicated to considering the novel favorably.

At the level of scholarship and social policy formulation, one also finds academics in the forefront of the fight to liberalize drug laws, as for example to legalize marijuana (Kaplan, 1970; Grinspoon, 1971), or to abandon the criminal law as a means for influencing that conduct termed "vice" (Packer, 1969). We believe that this public debate which pits some academicians against law enforcement spokesmen reflects a pervasive difference between academicians and law enforcement personnel over how human behavior is best influenced and what conduct deserves criminal sanctions. In an earlier investigation (Blum and Wahl, 1964) we learned that academicians and narcotics police did indeed look at drug users differently. Given these demonstrations of liberalism in the academic community, one might well expect a university to be a protective, even a nurturing environment which encourages faculty to deal in drugs.

First Estimate

Despite the seeming likelihood of such faculty actions, in our study of dealers on campus student and dealer informants agreed that only 0.5 per cent of all drug sources were faculty and staff. On that campus there are about 1,029 faculty and 5,848 staff; so, by any proportionate split, there could not be many professors involved. In the course of research, which has looked at various forms of drug use on that campus for almost ten years, we have heard of only one faculty member (not a graduate assistant) dealing illicitly. (The LSD proponents had been proselytizing at a time when that was still legal.) We did find proportionately more faculty dealing on one small overseas campus (see Chapter Twenty), but that is a very different situation—small, informal, and foreign.

Second Estimate

The foregoing were preliminary facts. We also checked with the police in nearby Comfort (Blum and associates, in press) and in the county sheriff's narcotics unit and learned that they had no professors on their suspect list as dealers. That list is simply an accumulation of reports to police intelligence at various levels of documentation. As another step, we considered our friends and acquaintances. Among the four of us, we know well (intimately enough to know about informal social behavior including drug use) perhaps one hundred faculty on campus. On that list of intimates we could identify no dealers, although several had been early LSD missionaries or had, as graduate students, probably dealt. We could identify other peccadillos —adultery, some income tax evasion—a chap who consistently cheated calling line shots in tennis, even someone who long ago had been a cat burglar, but no current drug dealing.

As an added step one of us interviewed intensively eight junior faculty (of a total of nine) of a department with a large number of students. Those interviews were supplemented by conversations with senior faculty and a review of all those social occasions on which, since there had been illicit-drug use, faculty dealing could have emerged. Two facts were evident. All those junior faculty members have used marijuana and still do occasionally but do not now use any other illicit psychoactive drug. They began as students and continue now, but with reduced frequency and involvement. The other fact is that none of these junior faculty now deal or would now consider dealing, be that defined either as regular profit-making or even such technical violations of the law as selling at cost or consistently giving or sharing one's supply with others.

As a final step we conducted a formal survey. We sent letters to every associate professor on campus, inviting participation in thoughtful discussion of faculty codes and conventions which would extend to drug matters. Of the 118 contacted, only thirty-five were willing to talk with the graduate student doing this portion of the work. This rate of cooperation is lower than that of physicians (Chapter Twenty-Five) in returning anonymous, mailed questionnaires—and physicians are notorious for noncooperation in surveys. We surmise from this several things. One is that a graduate student has very little clout in securing faculty cooperation. Second, we infer real resistance to talking about faculty codes to strangers, perhaps especially to strange graduate students. Third, we confess that it was a poor interview—much too long and rambling. Fourth, faculty can be remarkably resistant to cooperating in research, for in our family study (Blum and associates, 1972) we also had turn-downs from colleagues whom we had known for years but who surprised us by their antipathy to social science investigation. We would, at this point, tangentially note that in the family study, noncooperation is associated with other psychosocial features (see also Shippee and Blum, 1958).

From the thirty-five faculty members we did see we learned a great deal that was relevant to our inquiry. Foremost we found that none of the sample dealt drugs, and we also learned something about why they did not.

To come to an understanding of faculty behavior, we examine the professorial role, that is, the relationship of the academician to his institution, his colleagues, his students, and to predicated self-images. Our consideration is based upon an analysis of interviews and observational data among the 144 individuals who constituted our sample, either as intimate acquaintances or formally cooperating subjects. We sat as a group at regular intervals to review what we were hearing and seeing; we sought to identify the themes—faculty characteristics which appeared to account for nondealing—which emerged in the interview and observation material. When we agreed that a theme was present, we pursued it further in the next round of interviews and observations. The result of this approach is not a quantified set of data, but rather a set of explanatory concepts.

Faculty Conduct

We have noted that most of the junior faculty we know do smoke marijuana from time to time; those who are more regular users seem also to fall into other nonconforming patterns of dress and (non-Marxist) radical politics. Most have an "I can take it or leave it" attitude.

> *When I'm offered grass by friends or at parties I smoke . . . otherwise not. I rarely take the trouble actively to seek out a dealer . . . although I may share—and pay for my share—if someone else provides the impetus. Marijuana is more likely to be provided by faculty (but not in* my *department) or by graduate students—these are people at least one step removed from anyone I call a dealer.*

> *I've never seen evidence of grass at any parties given by faculty members, nor have I been offered it by any of my departmental colleagues in any social setting. One, two occasions I've been offered a joint at parties which graduate students gave where a small number of relatively hip—almost all junior—faculty were invited.*

> *The use of marijuana by faculty in the presence of their graduate students is not frequent but does occur. It occurs at the initiative of the student, not the professor. A couple of the junior faculty I know have smoked in the presence of undergraduates, but again it was the student rather than the professor who offered the grass and both times it was in the home of the student.*

> *Marijuana doesn't play an important role in most faculty's lives or consciousness. There is little reluctance to use it or to admit use, but there is obvious reluctance to offer it to one another or to students. The supply channel between faculty and students is a one-way street from students to faculty. Comparing junior faculty to graduate students, I'd say that the faculty use less now than when they were students and they use it less now than their*

own students do. Whether this is diminished opportunity—socially because of reluctance rather than any drug availability—a less active partying or social life, or due to conflict between the old student way and "adult professional" roles, I can't say. Perhaps it's attitude change toward drugs, but my hunch is that this is least important.

In our sample was one young professor who got caught "gardening"; that is, he was growing marijuana in his back yard. Arrested and indicted, he faced what he thought to be the certain fate of an extended leave of absence in the local pokey. He was wrong. His department head and the university administration intervened; a personal petition was made to the judge on his behalf, with a law school professor preparing the special plea. These interventions were successful and his case received little publicity on or off campus. The matter has not been brought up by anyone, and there have been no serious repercussions in his career for this man who confesses himself "sadder but wiser."

The use of other drugs is rare. Some have used hallucinogens: LSD, mescaline, and peyote. This group includes the older professors, associated with the earlier romanticism of LSD, as well as junior faculty who had their experience as students. There was, in our sample, one faculty member whose LSD use came to public attention through an accident in which his 4-year-old son drank a tiny vial of the stuff stored in the refrigerator. The child recovered and the father was not charged by the police. There was no department or university censure. The incident passed and, as far as we can determine, left no official bruises. Some of his colleagues do, however, consider him a dangerous fool, a judgment which may leave unofficial bruises for a long time.

Comparing their behavior as graduate students with their present actions, we do see a shift in attitudes. Those junior faculty who took LSD would not now take it even if it were offered. Younger faculty are more likely to have used a variety of drugs and to know from their own experience—or that of their peers—more of the drug scene than are older professors. One, for example, who knew those involved in the early LSD days (those referred to in the *Utopiates* sample), said he never knew what they were doing at that time even though he was acquainted with them: "I used to wonder why they lay out on the grass not moving or staring vacantly into space. I thought at the time they were bombed [drunk] and had no idea they were on LSD." There is active disinterest as well:

I've no idea where drugs come from. I suppose there are some on campus but it doesn't interest me. No, I can't tell you anything about dealing or for that matter using either.

I don't think we have any drug problem. If students use them, it's out of curiosity. They're young, after all, and it's a form of childish experimentation.

Only one among the professors interviewed expressed envy or a kind of self-criticism for failure to be "in touch" with what he imagined the drug scene to be: "I don't know why the hell I'm teaching Sumerian. Drugs are where the students are." There is also the escapist view: "Only problem students would use drugs. They're an escape from reality."

Faculty Views

There is strong opposition to the current legal stance on marijuana use. Few faculty believe that young people should be busted for smoking dope, although most grant that the serious dealer deserves prosecution. The dealer is blamed not for his marijuana trading but for trafficking in other drugs as well; there is, we infer, general opposition to the use of other substances. Most, but not all, want marijuana legalized and can think of no alternatives better than that. There is awareness that some marijuana users do have trouble handling its effects, so qualifying proposals such as the licensing of users (after establishing their psychological health) are made. Few propose that marijuana serves much positive function except as a pleasant social pastime to be enjoyed in moderation. Although claims for insights, consciousness expansion, or spiritual achievement are rare, one faculty member feels its use is helpful in radicalizing students, pitting them on an issue they understand against the oppressive establishment. Another feels that it does "awaken individuals to the possibility of alternative ways of thinking, feeling, experiencing, and knowing."

Upon probing, one concludes that most faculty are not well informed on the properties of psychoactive drugs and are not acquainted with the complexity of issues at stake. The defense of drug users and drug use—which is strong among junior faculty—arises from their general libertarian posture and not from any faith in the value of drugs. Their ignorance of drug effects is likely to be projected on to students. Faculty seem convinced that for other than cannabis the students wrongfully assume safety and positive effects. They emphasize that students may not be aware of "dangers"—which faculty are hard pressed to define or document on the basis of their own scientific knowledge. Yet faculty feel they are better informed. They would agree that theirs is a more conservative stance than that of the "typical" student.

Even if the (mostly junior) faculty do use marijuana, their attitudes toward other drugs, about students' drug-information levels, and toward dealers are much like those of the public in general (Gallup and Davies, 1970); perhaps faculty give greater emphasis to nonpunitive handling (except for dealers) and more generally favor marijuana legalization. We conclude—and this is our thesis—that, despite significant changes in student life style and general university conflict, faculty lives, especially in the highly competitive prestige university, have remained largely conventional. Conventional is used in a dual sense here, meaning not only adherence to society's standards of morality but also a peculiar adaptation to the setting of a university. This adaptation is illustrated in the concept of the "working personality."

The Working Personality

The concept (Chinoy, 1955; Walker and Guest, 1952; Hughes, 1958; Wolensky, 1956) describes a distinctive set of opinions and conduct which characterizes a given occupational group. A professor has a working personality. The major stated job components which contribute to it are writing, research, and teaching. The three unstated elements are not rocking the boat (being discrete and cooperative), being politically savvy (aware of how power is distributed and attained), and accepting the major articles of faith of the university community. Both stated and unstated requirements can contribute to anxiety and define acceptable and unacceptable behavior. Among the stated job components, the teaching role, which brings the professor in contact with the student, offers the most opportunity for those social exchanges and friendships which could contribute to the sharing of psychoactive drugs (whether alcohol or marijuana) and to dealing. Certainly teachers do develop social ties with students, yet friendships and informal behavior are constrained by the professorial role itself, for professional, institutional, and adult peer and hierarchical commitments take precedence over the norms of students in setting standards for how teachers are to behave. The weight of these is immense because they are internalized as well as externally constant. Students' invitations to the professor to join in their life styles or students' challenges to those who express antiauthoritarian or antiintellectual values to prove personal worth by showing "relevance," "radicalism," or "restructured priorities" fill but a small portion of the academician's life space. The political challenges, which one would expect to be most connected with drug proselytism and therefore to possible drug dealing, come from a minority of students. So the professor is protected not only by the admonitions of the establishment and his internal commitment to it, but by the standards of many students who do not seek to radicalize their faculty. The professor, like other humans, will remain attentive to the hand that feeds him.

The professor who is confronted by strong pressures from students to join them, whether in radical politics or in that drug involvement which precipitates dealing, ordinarily adopts one of two postures. He either seeks to reaffirm the establishment values he holds dear—thus appearing more distant and unyielding than ever to the young Turks; or he makes some informal adjustments, social steps which aim to prove he is not rigid or unsympathetic. He adopts long hair, sandals, and sport shirts and accepts proferred marijuana cigarettes, but he does *not* change his formal conduct with his colleagues unless he is compelled to prove to students he isn't really a professor at all.

A few faculty for whom the system is totally unsatisfying may actually, or for manipulative purposes, identify with a revolutionary student constituency. Some act out their disappointment or disillusionment with the power structure which has not rewarded them as they believe they should be rewarded. Others seek to turn the students into their own political arm through which they can gain power to demand institutional changes which they themselves seek. Some egg students on to live these fantasies which they themselves are afraid to translate into action. At the opposite extreme, some faculty oppress those students who challenge the status quo either out of emotion and conviction or because they deem their support for such oppression an avenue to achieve personal power believing that the university hierarchy harbors an oppressive view behind its mollifying public statements.

Only one of these types might conceivably be tempted to trade in drugs, and that is the disillusioned fellow who identifies with a youthful revolt against his own establishment. Even in such a case the youths with whom he identifies must be heavily involved in use and admire dealers without simultaneous ambivalence or derogation. Strict Marxist students will not be among them, for theirs is an antidrug stance both on moral and political grounds.

The faculty member has already achieved his status—however ambitious he may be for more—through conventional routes and has committed himself for many years of study and hard work to an academic career. Such routes, self-discipline and commitment, are the antithesis of the careers and motives which we have observed in dealers at any level. This is a fundamental point. Long before the faculty member accepts his appointment he has been part of a way of life for which drug dealing could not be central. As a student he may have played (Huizinga, 1955) with such conduct, but it could only be amusing transitional behavior discarded on the way to something more important.

To be a dealer can be for an adolescent one way of integrating desires, pleasures, and capabilities—as well as resolving problems. Being a dealer is rarely something an adult comes to without having had early and intensive involvement in drugs. The only example we have seen of an adult coming to dealing, *de novo,* is the professional criminal who makes a rational business decision to enter a thriving market. Not only is the usual adolescent drug-using background not productive of professors, but the adult circumstances for a *de novo* choice are simply not present in academe. There is neither criminal know-how, criminal values, nor marketing opportunities which make dealing more attractive than maintaining oneself as a professor. We grant it could happen; we simply state that it is very unlikely. Tim Leary is not the ordinary man.

Antimercantilism

Another theme we found revolved about earning money. Speaking about the American academic, Von Mises (1956) said: "As conditions are under capitalism, a man is forced to choose between virtue and poverty on the one hand and vice and riches on the other. He, himself, thank God, chose the former alternative and rejected the latter." Von Mises is poking fun, for the poverty-stricken but virtuous professor is a myth. Virtue may indeed lead to a life of poverty, but training and expertise do not a saint make. In fact, it has been suggested that long, systematic graduate training militates against idealism (Becker and Geer, 1958). Even so, that virtue which faculty embrace and which is expressed in the myth of poverty does require denunciation of greed. One may trace this attitude to St. Paul, himself a priestly scholar, who proclaimed that the love of money is the root of evil. The implication is that those who do not seek money are less evil. Traditionally teachers, for whom the classics have until recently been a source of standards, have expressed contempt for the mercantile class whose pursuit of money is paramount. The scholarly virtue as publically set forth resides in the pursuit of truth, not cash.

It is not that professors hate money. Far from it. It is simply that it must not be sought aggressively or publicly; being a merchant is bad form, it is a loss of virtue. Our colleagues during interviews strongly denied that money-making was important to them or occupied much of their time. Some said they would feel guilty about making money; others said they'd be ashamed to be entrepreneurs. Some confessed that it might just be a matter of ability—the only thing they knew how to do was what they were doing now. A philosophy professor was the only one who admitted he wished for more creature comfort. He specified new golf balls. Since he is making around twenty thousand dollars a year, we are confident he can achieve this dream without having to become a drug dealer.

To be a merchant is to be less than a scholar; mercantilism is below his dignity. Scholars sell, but ordinarily they don't sell *things*. They sell their time, their books, their ideas, and their services. They prefer income in the form of salary to riskier money earned in the hustling combat of commerce. Antimercantilism is fundamental in accounting for the immunity of the professor against drug dealing; no merchant he, no competitor in real commodities bargaining, he cannot commit himself to commerce in drugs without the loss of virtue.

Self-Respect

More than public virtue, drug dealing bears on self-respect. The faculty agree that dealers ought to be prosecuted, are criminal, and are unworthy. How could a self-respecting man, grown in the nurturant surround of an ethical system which worked, where one could be honest and still prosper, exchange his pleasure in himself for a self-image that would only give pain? As Becker (1958) points out:

> *In fact, the normal development of people in our society (and probably in any society) can be seen as a series of progressively increasing commitments to conventional norms and institutions. The "normal" person, when he discovers a deviant impulse in himself, is able to check that impulse by thinking of the manifold consequences acting on it would produce for him. He has staked too much on continuing to be normal to allow himself to be swayed by unconventional impulses.*

We believe that faculty reject the criminal role of the dealer because it is incompatible with their self-respect.

In Loco Parentis

The organization of the university embraces a peculiar authority system—*in loco parentis*. That concept is based upon temporary displacement of authority from parents to trusted elders who act as guardians. Parents, having placed their "trust" in the university for the safekeeping of children, expect faculty to be their surrogates or to act as family-employed tutors, baby sitters, or guards, depending on the parents' wishes. Even though within the university there is ambivalence and debate over this role, expectations for acting *in loco parentis* are strong and account for one flank of the sanctions upholding conventional behavior. One can see how the professor, expecting himself or being imposed upon to act as a parent, assumes conduct forms which might otherwise be rejected. It is in this regard, for example, that the incest taboo may become more than a peripheral issue in teacher-student relations. One does not go to bed with one's "adopted" daughter. Here too one can see that as a universal parent for his flock even the "swinging" professor may be loathe to take on the "corrupting" role of the drug dealer. Further, it is already sufficiently risky to corrupt youth with ideals which one does strongly believe in and which are the core of the professional self—Socrates standing as the symbolic hero for all teachers, or Scopes in this century. The incompatibility of being the parent surrogate and the prophet of a new ethic outlaws the low-gain, high-risk, disharmonious enterprise of being a drug dealer.

The Mark of Cain

People fear that when they deviate from standards which they themselves hold or which others hold for them they may be caught. Put differently, a la Goffman (1963), they fear stigmatization, and unless they are accomplished deceivers of the sort that informers, spies, and dealers are, the ordinary man believes that truth will out. Stories of witches tell us that they have strange birthmarks; Count Dracula's beady eyes revealed his true character too. If a child is told masturbation will make black hairs grow out of the back of his hand (and some are told that), he is likely to pay close attention to those hands. So it is that the professor who considers straying from the straight and narrow will be deterred by fears that the mark of Cain will appear to reveal his actions to his colleagues. This confidence that deception will be found out when one has strayed underlies the considerable success of the lie detector. In a university, the belief in the mark of Cain symbolizes the intensive scrutiny which the academic community constantly gives its members. Were a professor to deal drugs, it would be discovered by his collegues as self-fulfilling prophecy, if nothing else, for the tongues of the hounds of academe wag incessantly.

Conventional Misconduct

Human frailties are allowed a professor; for example, he may maintain a mistress, although he would do well to be sure that she is not also sleeping with students in his department and regaling them with stories of her older lover. We have seen that happen and know that, while no administrative or career damages need be incurred, gossip spreads, and an image is created which is incompatible with the conventional one the professor usually prefers. Having a mistress may be an envied enterprise among professors sitting in judgment as males. But being a drug dealer is neither envied nor accepted and so is not part of acceptable or conventional misconduct.

One kind of drug use is. That is drinking. We speak not of the nigh-on universal social drinker but of being drunk.

> *Drinking is the dissipation of choice. It's the only form of conspicuous consumption which is condoned and I could even say you can make a positive reputation by inbibing prodigious amounts of alcohol. Such people are colorful—about as colorful as you dare get. Of course there are the nuts and kooks who drink so much that it ruins their judgment and professional competence. Then it's not colorful, just the end of the road.*

It is neither conventional nor unconventional to engage in heterosexual frivolity off campus and with people not members of the university. To move one's affairs onto campus is either to engage in conventional misbehavior (eyebrows raised, but otherwise passable) or to begin to take chances.

> *I wouldn't date a girl who lives in a dorm; those girls get together and talk; they even lend each other vaginal jelly or birth control pills if it comes to that. It's too public.*
>
> *When I used to teach at a small college—that's where I met my wife—my colleagues asked me who it was that they'd seen me walking across campus with. When I told them she was my fiancee, they all relaxed and congratulated me.*
>
> *I consider sex with students bad. I don't mean it's bad sex, but I mean it's a poor idea.*
>
> *I think you can move a little if you know what I mean, but within limits, within limits if you understand. Some chaps I know will restrict themselves to faculty wives, others will screw graduate students but not in their own department; a swinger will screw the [graduate] girls in his own department, but generally speaking, undergraduates are out of bounds.*
>
> *Oh yes, I know of a few cases with undergraduates, junior*

bachelor type faculty mostly; but even if they end up getting married, some people consider it in bad taste.

I used to go to bed with students—I was a bachelor then—but my rule was always to wait until they'd completed any course they were taking with me. I didn't think it was fair otherwise and, frankly, I didn't want to be under that kind of obligation when it came to giving them a grade.

It's not what you do with the students, but how carefully. Every time I think of screwing one, I say to myself, "How will that one read in the newspaper?"

I have a friend who is, I guess you'd say, athletic. He'll fuck them on the floor of the lab, the desk in his office, after office hours, between classes, you know; he's ambitious about it. But still, never on the quad and not on the chapel altar either. I don't think he's religious; he just wouldn't like all that attention.

Frankly I've never heard of it. I mean, I suppose it could happen in some very unusual circumstances, but no, I don't think so, not intercourse between faculty and a student—not here.

Whereas earlier in this century heterosexual promiscuity, defined then as intercourse with other than wives, led to some of the greatest men being fired from their universities (psychology, mathematics, philosophy, economics—all had their stellar scandals), these days one can't be sure what would happen. That is the case for homosexual conduct too. The way to keep anything from happening is to remain discreet. For example, a homosexual male was under consideration for tenure. The department head was told that he had "tendencies." The head replied that that was "exactly the kind of information I don't want to know about." As one professor put it, "Whatever you do, do it in such a way that the administration is not put into the position where they must admit there has been an act of indiscretion." Or another: "The most serious crime is getting caught. It makes very little difference about what." By implication we see that not only is the indiscretion intolerable, so is its observation and reporting. One assistant dean told the incoming freshmen: "We don't want to know who is using pot or where it's being done on campus."

Uncertainty

The demand for discretion, including audience as well as actors, makes it difficult to know what the limits are. "The problem of judgment is that there seldom are explicit criteria upon which judgments can be made. The whole thing is subjective unless stated regulations have clearly been broken. Otherwise it's negotiable."

We found considerable diversity of views as to whether there *was* a faculty code governing ethics, politics, and the like. "I'm absolutely certain you couldn't define such a code. Within reason what one does is up to the individual"; or: "Of course there's a code. Here it's based on excellence"; or: "I don't know if there's really a code or not. No one talks about it, but there are things you do and don't do. The telling question really is, what gets you fired?" Another faculty member seemed to sum up the situation very nicely.

> *Codes and conventions here are a sleeping giant. If you wake it up with something monstrous, it acts, but mostly to insure that peace and tranquility are restored. There's a rule of thumb: don't bother with moral deviates as long as they're discrete, but fire—or don't give tenure to—the political ones. The political ones by definition refuse to be discrete. Consider the case of B . . . He had to splash himself all over, wanted to destroy the university itself—very embarrasing. Still to dismiss him is embarrassing too —a very awkward situation.*

Their Brothers' Keepers

As we mentioned earlier, we found that young faculty are more likely than are older ones to smoke mariajuana. Perhaps they are also more likely to mix socially with students and to be tempted to share or deal drugs as part of being sociable. Yet these same young faculty are those for whom the upward struggle for promotion, for tenure, and for professional reputations is most pressing. The standards used in promoting and in giving tenure are, within the university, unclear. All that is known is that most do not get tenure. On the basis of our interviews we also suggest that most do want it. In a situation where ambition is strong, standards are unclear, and anxiety is high, we propose that those already committed to self-control and the long professional road are apt to be exceptionally careful, to conform to what they fear may be required as well as to known requirements. In this, as in their research or writing, young faculty members' eyes are on the jury before the crime is committed. The jury consists of everyone: students, peers, and department heads. All have watchful eyes and ready tongues and are their brothers' keepers.This form of social control, reminiscent of that in a small cohesive town, mitigates against drug dealing.

Blackmail

A man need not be a coward to be careful. Anyone with an ounce of foresight will think twice before putting his fate—lock, stock, and tenure—in the hands of someone who is not in intimate trust. Students and faculty ordinarily do not share such trust. To the contrary, the relationship is a formal one, partly based on the exercise of power which rests in the hands of the professor. Were that professor to engage in illicit behavior which could come to the attention of a student, the teacher would reverse the power balance. Since drug dealing is a social activity which does come to the attention of a large number of people, and since in the university those people are mostly students, the drug dealing professor would be placing a weapon in the hands of unknown as well as known others. Given the motivation for a redress in the balance of power which arises necessarily as a function of student ambition and vulnerability, it is assumed by professors that some students would use knowledge of professorial drug dealing to extort good grades, favors, recommendations, and the like. Fear of blackmail is a fundamental reason for faculty adherence to the straight and narrow in their activities involving students.

Pecking Order

The university is hierarchically based. The caste system is well demarcated, from undergraduates through assistants to professorial ranks and higher. It is within the undergraduate ranks that drug dealers are spawned. Dealers there may have a chevron more than the other privates—though even that is uncertain—but only in the barracks crowd, not in full view on parade. For a professor to take on a role which at best serves to give informal status to the lowly is reverse achievement. If anything characteristizes faculty at a major university, it is *not* the desire to be demoted. Ambition is nigh a universal. Realizing the strength of this drive for status is crucial in comprehending why faculty do not deal.

Anyone who would deal would have to shift his reference group, caring more for students than for his faculty brothers. Some who have done research on college teachers and teaching (Sanford, 1967; Katz, 1968; Stevens, 1967; Bush, 1958; and Conte and Mason, 1970) point out that professors concern themselves little with the sentiments of the undergraduate. For example, Tolstoy (1967) holds that "education is the tendency toward moral despotism raised to a principle," and Goodman (1962) contends that spite rather than affection characterizes the professorial views of undergraduates. If so, why would the teacher seek the equivalent status and approval of those in whom he has no interest and who may be demeaned as lesser creatures? And to pursue that pointless approbation by means such as dealing which are patently mischievous? Hardly!

The Serpent Forefended

There are further reasons to avoid involvement. If at a more psychodynamic level teaching is, as one of our sample insisted, an "erotic business" in which teachers really are sexually attracted to lovely young creatures—male or female—yet dare not love them (the history of education having long since insisted that pedagogy not be pederasty), perhaps one can in defense only turn away from them. From love to indifference is a cruel step, but it does ensure that one avoids the temptations which arise out of intimate social contact. To be close enough to be a drug dealer is close enough to enflame other passions—as our dealers' accounts of sexual access make quite clear. Should such intimacies—sex *and* dealing—take place, the professorial house of respectability might well tumble down and with it one's institutional security and self-regard.

Security and Risk

From time to time we have touched on the theme of security. Faculty ambition is not only for the fruitful life of the mind and the rewards, uncertain as they be, that an antiintellectual (Hofstadter, 1964) society offers, but also for those typically human concerns, certainty and a position. The desire for security expresses itself in preoccupation with tenure. Most of our respondents considered tenure both a good and a bad thing, but no other topic so occupied the conversations when faculty considered our questions regarding conventions and the unconventional. If security is the object of desire and tenure its attainment, then one does not venture to risk. One of us has been studying gamblers (Martinez and LaFranchi, 1969). The contrast is great between the risk-taking, crises-responsive, self-destructive, magically minded compulsive—and passive—gambler (Bolen and Boyd, 1968) and the ordinary professor. The drug dealer may not gamble with cash, but a gambler with life he is, and in this risk-taking he differs from the professor as a type.

Primacy of Intellect

Our respondents exalt the primacy of intellect, the respect for ideas, and the excitement of the search for knowledge. This orientation may imply a retreat from practical matters. The ivory tower does imply a style of life. It is far from the hurly-burly and one wants it that way, for too much activity and worry mob the creative mind. Drug dealing may be, for youth, an uncommitted life but it is anything but contemplative and worry-free. For all the dealers' romantic talk of "cool" and "easy," being irresponsible, what they do does not free them to think. The professor prefers the latter to the former and in so doing has another reason not to peddle dope.

Our colleagues emphasized the positive when they spoke of the intellect. There was a sense of mission, zeal for reason, their being torchbearers for the lamp of knowledge. Indeed, one of the bookplates of the university shows seated Minerva, lighted lamp beside her, bestowing her gifts to a kneeling supplicant. These days that posture is being challenged, but the general image remains. One does not wish to dim wisdom's lamp. The younger faculty who were marijuana smokers, discussing why they did not use more powerful drugs, said they did not wish to dull the illumined mind. That mind is not only the tool of their trade but as a Platonic ideal represents their role and strivings. Older colleagues who use only alcohol trust that drug not to interfere, but they do not trust other substances. For those who admire a lucid mind and who would be known as clear thinkers, it is truly inconsistent to become involved in drug use, to be "stoned out of one's mind." We have learned from observations on dealers that involvement is the *sine qua non* for becoming a dealer, for dealing arises from such immersion. In contrast, faculty who do use drugs use them sparingly and are in control. They are less involved than when they were students. Even then they were playing, just as their students are playing today. In the past some faculty had become deeply involved with LSD, but even then the dream was of greater insight, creativity, and understanding through the use of hallucinogens (Harmon and others, 1966; Stafford and Golightly, 1967). Thus their ostensible aims were compatible with their intellectual mission; whether they were, in fact, also lured by other gratifications is another matter. In any event their experience has shattered the LSD dream, and those who were involved and whom we saw recently now claim to be abstainers. For them and for most faculty who have never gone the hallucinogenic route, faith in the primacy of intellect—be that itself myth or reality—makes it impossible to use or, as dealers do, to advocate and expedite the use of substances which are, or are believed to be, anathema to the intellectual's tenets of faith.

Comment and Summary

We have, in incomplete ways, examined the role of faculty as drug dealers. Our estimates are that few university faculty members deal in drugs. At first glance one may consider them a group at high risk of such behavior—given the past experience of many as drug-using graduate students, their presence in a youthful environment where use and dealing are accepted, their sanctuary from arrest should they choose to use/deal discreetly, and their liberal values which characterize middle-class users/dealers. Because they do not deal nevertheless, we thought it well to consider what prevented them. On the basis of what our colleagues told us, our own observations, our own experience, and a bulk of theory and conjecture, we have discussed "immunizing" features. They are many but may be summarized as a commitment to conventional goals, considerable reward or hope of reward for avoiding mischief, plus considerable risk arising from engaging in unaccepted as opposed to simply unconventional misbehavior. There is, further, faith in the primacy of intellect and a belief that intellect can only be subverted, not enhanced by the intensive involvement either in a drug or in a criminal life, one or the other of which is a prerequisite for serious—as opposed to playful—drug peddling. For those interested in the prevention of dealing, one may consider the faculty member as a developmental model. We call attention to the fact that prevention or deterrence, using this model, does not rest on legal sanctions, although these may be peripheral considerations. Rather it depends upon an early and consistent dedication to convention and immersion in a watchful community where conduct is controlled not by what is either said or threatened but by anticipation of and identification with the standards of an academic collective.

Chapter 23

DEALERS IN HIGH SCHOOL

Over the last several years one of the county school systems (San Mateo) in the Bay Area has conducted a county-wide survey of illicit-drug use among its high school students. This survey has shown a high rate of drug use among young people of high school age and also indicated that an extremely rapid increase in the proportions of students using drugs occurred between 1968 and 1969. At the senior high school level, tobacco, LSD, and amphetamine usage was generally less in 1970; the rate for marijuana use increased but to a lesser extent than that which occurred between 1968 and 1969. In general, girls have lower rates of usage than boys, although this difference is diminishing. Also, seniors have higher rates than freshmen, but it appears that younger and younger people are being initiated into drug use.

Goldstein (1971) observes that findings on high school use from various locales are highly consistent. His Pittsburgh investigation found that initiation to illicit-drug use was by a same-sex friend in a social situation with others present. On psychological tests he found users more than nonusers to be poised, nonconforming, critical, impulsive, self-centered, having a reduced sense of well-being, insecure, pessimistic about their future careers, disorganized under stress, rebellious, flexible, and with aesthetic and social values rather than economic, political, or religious values.

The evidence for the widespread prevalence of experimentation with illicit drugs and for the frequency of regular illicit use, particularly of marijuana, suggests that drug dealing should occur where young people of high school age are in contact. We have seen from our studies of the variegated dealer sample that such contacts—leading to the initiation into illicit use, its continuation, and for some the development of dealing interests—are reported primarily at parties in homes but also in public gathering places such as coffee shops, in parks or on the streets, in institutions, in cars, or even on school buses. Less often mentioned as places for drug use are schools as such. (Ten per cent of our junior high sample reported drug use at school.) But dealing does occur on the campus, and high schools are a good place to learn more about teenage dealers.

We selected for study a high school in San Mateo County, where the principal and other administrators, while not participating in any way in the study, did allow our researcher free rein on the campus. Our method was simple. We had with us for a research internship an Antioch College student who had graduated the previous year from that high school. During the autumn of 1969 he adopted the role of the high school graduate returning to the old campus. Unlike most of that breed, who spend brief but glorious moments strutting about in their college colors, our intern spent several hours each day for three months chatting, watching, and, in confidence, interviewing. He did not serve under any "official cover"—that is, he was not introduced as bearing an administration stamp of approval (although unofficially he had that) but rather appeared as an old graduate, now interested in drugs because of his college exposure thereto, who was taking in the scene. He bragged a little, listened and admired a lot, and in the end had uncovered what he felt to be most, if not all, the illicit dealers of drugs on that campus.

The school has 1,900 students. Most are middle class. Approximately 20 per cent of the students are Negroes. On that campus 129 dealers were identified (four of these were actually eighth graders from another school who came to sell). A dealer was defined as anyone distributing illicit drugs. Sales ranged from five times or less per month to two hundred times per month.

What are the high school dealers in our sample like? Half are 15 or 16 years old; one third are 17 or 18. All classes (years) are represented; but (in order) seniors lead juniors, who match sophomores, who lead freshmen in numbers. Four fifths of the dealers are male and 92 per cent are white. Two thirds report a grade average of C, whereas in the school as a whole only 35 per cent receive a C average (40 per cent receive B or better average, and 25 per cent are below a C). More Bs than Ds are represented, but not a single A-average student is a dealer. Arts and crafts are the foremost subject interests reported, followed by social science and English, including literature. Less than one fifth are interested primarily in the hard sciences or mathematics. For the student body as a whole, attendance at courses other than those minimally required for graduation indicates these preferences: English, 40 per cent; mathematics and hard sciences, 45 per cent; art, 15 per cent. (Social science, being a four-year required course, could not be accurately represented.) Among outside interests, the passive one of listening to music ranks first, sports are second, motorcycling and cars rank third. Less often mentioned are "being with people," being with girls, using drugs, or being outdoors.

A drug-history inquiry indicates that three quarters drink alcohol at least occasionally and that all have used illicit drugs. It must be kept in mind that in all drug-use replies, students report what they thought they used. As Blum and associates (in press) show, they are often misled. For most (86 per cent) marijuana was the first illicit drug, and the modal age for initial use was 13 to 14. Two dealers began marijuana use before age 11; one fourth, at ages 11 or 12. For most (75 per cent), present marijuana use is regular, four times or more per week. About half report use of LSD, the majority once a month or less. Speed is used by a minority and then rarely. Barbiturate use is reported by two fifths, with use about once a week most often cited. Two fifths also report infrequent mescaline use. Opiates have been used by 17 per cent, with use either once a week or daily. As for drugs used in the past but not now regularly used, we find over one third saying that they have tried opium and another 11 per cent reporting past heroin experimentation. Asked when they first supplied drugs illicitly, most of the sample began at age 13 or 14. Seven per cent say that they began at ages 11 or 12; one says that he started as a child of 10.

We asked about the lifetime incidence of illicit distribution (how many times in all they had sold or given away drugs). The modal incidence is also the top end of the scale, 200 occasions or more. At the other end, one fourth supply drugs ten times or less. Marijuana leads in sales five to one over LSD and eight to one over barbiturates, the two runner-up drugs.

We are uncertain about present (at time of interview) sales activity. It appears from their replies that one fourth have already "retired" in the sense that they no longer are dealing. Of those still at it, infrequent rather than frequent sales are the rule. One fourth report sales once a week; and 7 per cent of the dealer sample are active dealers, selling daily. Marijuana and hallucinogens are most frequently sold followed by barbiturates and amphetamine (either speed or bennies).

In terms of a market, these dealers state that they sell off campus as well as on; indeed, only 10 per cent restrict themselves to their fellow students. Yet on-campus sales are more frequent. About one fourth report eleven or more sales the past month off campus; three fifths report that number of on-campus sales. Average net profits vary considerably, from zero to over $200. (Bragging may occur here, be reminded.) Among those still dealing actively, 9 per cent say that they make more than $100, and 35 per cent say that they make less than $5 (including no profit at all). Gross receipts are, of course, higher, with only 10 per cent reporting a gross under $5 and 38 per cent reporting a gross of $100 or more. Sales do not appear limited to a particular class or sex, although males predominate, as do white and middle- or upper-class customers. Most customers appear to be friends or acquaintances. There are barriers to sales; race is one, for some white dealers do not sell to black students; most commonly the barrier is that dealers do not sell to strangers. Off campus, most customers appear to be students, including those in elementary school; and most are from nearby towns.

The majority describe shifts in their selling over time, with most saying that at the time of interview they sold less than they did in the past; and some no longer sold at all. Many stopped or slowed down for summer vacations—presumably they and/or their customers were away. Very few "manufacture" in the sense that they roll cigarettes or encapsulate chemicals, but farming is another matter. Over three fourths state that they have planted and/or harvested cannabis locally. Most buy from other dealers; most do so cooperatively, so that together their pooled resources purchase cheaper or more convenient units—for example, kilos or bricks of pot. Most use several sources to assure supplies; when a shortage occurs, the majority keep what they have on hand for their own use rather than selling it to others. Pleasure before business is the rule. Sources are other dealers on the campus, as well as students from other high schools and, to a lesser extent, college students and "street" dealers in San Francisco itself. A few are supplied by their sibling dealers. Suppliers are older than these dealers; the median source age is about 20; most white and local. A minority claim knowledge of the Mafia, and 9 per cent claim that they themselves know someone in the Mafia.

We asked dealers to estimate the number of student dealers on the campus (current as well as exdealers). The majority estimate 5 per cent or less. The 125 (plus four eighth-grade visitors) whom we identified as dealers represent approximately 7 per cent of the students. We think theirs is a fairly accurate estimation.

Discussing arrest, the majority say that they do not feel safe from arrest simply because they are dealing on or near their high school campus; most claim close calls, and one fourth say that they have already been arrested for a narcotics offense. Two fifths say that they have been arrested for other than narcotics offenses. Nearly all say that they have friends who have been arrested for narcotics offenses.

Asked to consider their future, the great majority expect to be out of dealing soon; only 12 per cent of the sample (N = 16; 0.8 per cent of the total student body) expect to deal for the rest of their lives. Why do they expect to quit—or why have they quit already? "Too risky" is the most and only common reply, one fifth offering that explanation. Almost all expect to go on to straight jobs; a few expect to go on to college. Would it change their present lives much to give up dealing and using? Most say no.

We asked for their recommendations to parents, citizens, teachers, and the United States government regarding sales and use of drugs. The recommendations are, in order: legalize marijuana and hashish (presumably for teenagers), 58 per cent; maintain present penalties on all drugs except cannabis, 29 per cent; bring drug laws into concordance with statutes governing use and sale of alcohol and tobacco, 12 per cent; legalize all drugs, 11 per cent.

Comment and Summary

A sample of 125 high school dealers (and four eighth-grade visitors to the campus) was obtained over three months' observation and interviewing on campus by a recent grad. This represents 7 per cent of the school's student body and approximates, we believe, the active and recently active dealer population. Dealers have a history of early drug use and, compared with the students at large, have lower grades, a greater interest in "soft" or "liberal" subjects, and lower career aspirations. They also experience nondrug arrests. Most are not serious dealers; most do not make much money, and most expect to quit within a year or two. Even for this more delinquent—and, we suspect, less able, underachieving, and passive—population, dealing seems a short-term activity. We cannot accurately assess the impact of past or the threat of future arrest on the group.

The genesis of the high school dealer is clearly linked to his own drug use, which seems to be of an earlier, heavier, and more multiple sort than that of his peers. That implies his exceptional interest in drug experiences and involvement in drug-using groups. This drug use can also be transient, at least for some, if we take as evidence their past experimentation with drugs—heroin and other opiates, for instance—

which are no longer reported used. Whether or not their optimism is in order is another question; but what seems clear to us is that seen through their eyes neither their drug use nor their drug dealing interferes with "normal" life as a student or with their conventional goals; for neither what they are doing now nor what they plan to do depends either on taking or giving up dealing and drugs.

As for the kind of people these dealers are, other than statistically deviant in terms of what they are doing now and conventional in their plans, we can hazard guesses based on comparisons with their fellow students. For one thing they are heavy on arts, crafts, social sciences, and English—the "soft" or "liberal" subjects which also characterize the earlier college drug users (Blum and associates, 1969b). One infers that they tend to be passive and aesthetic—given their music-listening preferences—which is also compatible with findings from older users. Their low grade averages suggest either a lack of academic interest or abilities, an inference which is in line with the fact that only a few (less than one fifth) speak of going on to college—even though the school they attend sends 32 per cent of its graduates to two-year colleges and 32 per cent to four-year colleges. They are in addition a delinquent lot and presumably a more maladjusted one, given the prevalence of other-than-narcotics arrests in two fifths of the sample. Whether they lack for funds or simply want more money we cannot say, but some certainly are moved to make a buck, dishonestly if need be. Some few at least are—we venture to propose—braggarts, for we take their "Mafia" claims as that, although at age 16 there may be nothing special about such outlandish claims. About one fourth, according to interviewer rating, are "hippie" types in dress and hair styles. What this means in terms of personality can only be guessed; if the findings of McGlothlin, Cohen, and McGlothlin (1967) on older students interested in LSD are applicable, one would expect greater inner-intuitive sensing, hypnotic susceptibility, psychopathic (delinquent) trends, and the like. Blacker, Jones, Stone, and Pfefferbaum (1968) have emphasized the passivity and self-defeating character structure of hallucinogen users in their teen years; these findings too would be consistent with the little we have observed, as would Goldstein's (1971) observations. We call attention to the similarities between this group and both our college and junior high school dealers (Chapters Nineteen and Twenty-Four).

One wonders about the impact of arrest on this group. Obviously they have not been sent to jail for long, or they would not have been on campus and appropriately age placed by school year as they were. Yet a goodly minority have been arrested; nearly all have friends who suffered drug busts. It may be this has helped shape their decisions to give up dealing before they are really into it. The risk factor is mentioned as a reason for quitting; but by only 9 per cent. Perhaps, then, the absence of long incarceration has actually been in the best interests of everyone in these cases, for it allows those so disposed—even when they have continued occasional dealing—to move toward their conventional goals of a nondelinquent life. The positive pull of work, risk avoidance, and their current respectable student roles are best attributed to positive socialization and appeals inherent in normal living. Yet we speculate that the experience and/or threat of arrest likely has been a stick which has helped some, at least, to keep their eye on the straight-life carrot. We consider the implications of our data for policies directed toward teenage dealers in Blum and associates (in press).

Chapter 24

DEALERS IN JUNIOR HIGH SCHOOL

In 1971 we attempted to identify drug dealers in a junior high school in one suburban community. For our study, 346 students out of the school population of 1,317 in the seventh, eighth, and ninth grades were selected at random (random numbers table and the school enrollment lists). As required by regulations, the parents of the students selected were sent a stamped return postcard on which they were asked to certify their permission or refusal for their children to participate in the anonymous drug inquiry. Approval from 287 families (83 per cent) was obtained. These students were invited to one of two special assembly areas, where they were given a questionnaire. Six members of our research staff supervised the questionnaire administration. Of the 287 students, 274 appeared for the assembly and completed the inquiry form; the rest were absent that day. We do not know what bias is introduced by the nonparticipation of 21 per cent of the students designated in the original sample. We shall assume that the sample participating are reasonably representative of junior high school students in a sophisticated Bay Area community, and that students' replies reflect reasonably well their conduct and views.

Dealers were defined as those students affirming, in response to questions, that they have sold or are now selling drugs at cost or for profit. This definition is less stringent than the one applied to all other dealer samples, for it requires neither sale for profit nor repetitive supplying. The definition does conform with the technical provisions of the criminal law, which specify supplying or intent to supply as (dealing) acts subject to greater penalty than mere possession. Our purpose in liberalizing the definition in this sample was to identify in this 12- to 16-year-old age group those who had begun supplying others but might not have embarked yet on profitable selling. Recall that data from the variegated dealer sample indicate that for youngsters who become dealers there is a transitional period after illicit use, where supplying—via sharing or gifts or profitless sale—may take place prior to the first sale.

Drug Experience

Alcohol and tobacco purchase, supplying, and use (outside the home) are illicit for all of these junior high youngsters. Nevertheless, a majority had used alcohol three or more times in the twelve months preceding questionnaire administration. There is an unsteady increase in prevalence by age for wine, beer, and hard liquor but not for cigarettes. A minority are cigarette smokers. However, the eighth-grade girls in this sample report the highest prevalence for smoking (49 per cent), wine (66 per cent), and beer (70 per cent) use and equal the ninth-grade boys in hard-liquor use as well (45 per cent). Seventh- and ninth-grade boys report greater experience with each of these drugs than do the girls. Paradoxically, seventh- and eighth-grade boys are most often likely to report little or no use of alcohol or tobacco.

Experience with drugs which are both disapproved and illicit (that is, with narcotic and dangerous drugs as defined by law) is less common than experience with alcohol and/or tobacco. No experience with marijuana, for example, is reported by 77 per cent of seventh graders, 63 per cent of eighth graders, and 66 per cent of ninth graders, with only minor sex differences. Reported cannabis use (marijuana, hashish, or both) three times or more in the last twelve months is 10 per cent for seventh graders, 20 per cent for eighth graders, and 17 per cent for ninth graders. Children admitting present use most often characterize their use as occasional or regular in the seventh and eighth grades, whereas ninth-grade boys say that they use cannabis often. Peak regular use is among eighth-grade girls (21 per cent).

Inquiry as to (one or more time) LSD or other hallucinogen use during the past year also yields an eighth-grade peak prevalence. Only 2 per cent of seventh-grade boys or girls, 22 per cent of eighth-grade girls and 23 per cent of the boys, and 12 per cent of the ninth-grade girls and 11 per cent of the boys report hallucinogen use. Five per cent of seventh-grade girls, 11 per cent of the boys; 26 per cent of the eighth-grade girls, 22 per cent of the boys; and 7 per cent of the ninth-grade girls and 11 per cent of the boys report illicit barbiturate or tranquilizer use, exclusive of medical prescriptions.

As for stimulants (amphetamines and/or cocaine), 2 per cent of the seventh-grade pupils report one-time-or-more illicit experience, either with amphetamines or cocaine, in the last year—as do 7 per cent of the eighth- and ninth-grade youngsters. Opiates (exclusive of approved medical use) are reported by 2 per cent of the seventh-grade girls, none of the boys; by 1 per cent of the eighth-grade girls and 7 per cent of the boys; and by none of the ninth-grade girls but by 6 per cent of the boys.

Because we did not have earlier data on junior high drug use, we proceeded to inquire more about it so as better to understand dealing. We find that most illicit-drug use is done with one or more close friends, that party use ranks second, and that solitary use is least common (described by about 5 per cent). Locales for drug use vary, with the home more common for seventh graders and home and young people's "hang-outs" about equal for other students. An average of 8 per cent say that they use illicit drugs on the school grounds.

Where do they get their drugs? Inquiries reveal that same-age friends are the most common source of illicit drugs, with older friends second, and "professional" (nonstudent) dealers rare. Only about 10 per cent of those currently using illicit drugs report obtaining them from sources who are "professionals" as opposed to friends or relatives. We take it that the sources of supply, then, are mostly the student suppliers identified in the next section.

Dealing

Past supplying of drugs in the legal-technical sense (that is, sharing, giving, giving at cost, or selling for profit) is reported, overall, by 23 per cent. It is most common among our eighth graders (30 per cent) and among ninth-grade boys (27 per cent) and least common among the seventh graders (16 per cent). Sharing and giving is the most common form of supplying; giving at cost ranks second; and selling for profit is least prevalent. Profit sales are age and class related; 1 per cent in the seventh grade, 2 per cent in the eighth grade, and 4 per cent in the ninth grade are so engaged.

Fewer students now supply actively than have done so in the past: about 8 per cent of seventh graders, 20 per cent of eighth graders, and 16 per cent of ninth graders describe themselves as current suppliers to others. In the eighth grade, sharing and giving predominate over profit making, as does giving at cost. However, among both seventh and ninth graders now active in supplying, selling for profit is as frequent as selling at cost. Perhaps this means that the more involved suppliers—whom we presume to be current suppliers—have already found that it is as easy to sell for profit as for no profit. Sources for these suppliers tend to be friends of their own age, with either relatives (siblings) or older friends ranked second.

Dealers, Users, and Nonusers

All dealers report the use of illicit drugs; nevertheless, for our analysis here, we separate user-dealers from those users who deny supplying drugs to others. The dealers, those selling at cost or for profit, constitute 7 per cent of our sample; nondealing current users constitute 28 per cent; and students denying any experience with illicit drugs constitute 65 per cent of these junior high pupils. Dealers in the sample are older (median age 14) than users (13) and nonusers (13).

There are only slight differences in family characteristics. With regard to ordinal position, more dealers are youngest siblings than are users and nonusers (42 per cent vs. 35 per cent vs. 33 per cent). The marital status of parents is not different; intact marriages characterize the families of about 80 per cent of all students. The educational level of the father is slightly higher for dealers, 84 per cent having completed college, as compared to 75 per cent among users and 74 per cent among nonusers. The same holds for mothers' education; 64 per cent of dealers' mothers hold college degrees (vs. 56 per cent of the mothers of users and 61 per cent of nonusers).

Dealers do differ in other respects. With regard to grades, 21 per cent of the dealers characterize themselves as in the top 25 per cent of their class, as opposed to 47 per cent of users and 50 per cent of nonusers. (Possibly our random sample oversampled students with better grades among users and nonusers, or the grade reporting is inaccurate—reflecting modesty or low self-esteem among dealers.) Similarly, more dealers deny knowledge of their class standing (32 per cent vs. 14 per cent of users and 16 per cent of nonusers). Ambivalence toward or dislike of school is more prevalent among dealers, 90 per cent declaring that school is always or sometimes a bore or waste of time, compared to 66 per cent of users and 41 per cent of nonusers expressing that negative opinion of school.

Organized peer activities, in the form of outside-of-school or school-sponsored clubs, are less common for dealers; 16 per cent report outside youth-group interests, as compared to 21 per cent of the users and 24 per cent of the nonusers. Eleven per cent of the dealers are in school-sponsored activities, as opposed to 29 per cent of users and 32 per cent of nonusers. Conversely, artistic interests do characterize the dealers more than others; 89 per cent claim interests and/or participation in arts-crafts-music, as opposed to 56 per cent of the users and 62 per cent of the nonusers. As for future educational-vocational plans, the dealers more often reject higher education. Eleven per cent say that they do not intend to go to college; 63 per cent say that they do; the rest are uncertain. In contrast, only 4 per cent of the users reject college and 76 per cent plan to attend college; among nonusers, there are no outright rejections and 92 per cent with plans for college. Dealers do not differ from the other groups in their sports involvement (which is high for all), participation in church groups (low for all), or in having friends (most have good friends).

There is a striking difference in the evaluation of parental roles and conduct as deduced from students' statements about the adequacy of drug information given to them by their parents. Thirty-two per cent of the dealers, compared to 19 per cent of the users and 9 per cent of the nonusers, state that their parents were ignorant or otherwise uninformed about drugs. Only 26 per cent of the dealers believe that their parents gave them correct information, compared to 45 per cent of users and 63 per cent of nonusers.

Comment and Summary

A random sample of 346 of 1,317 junior high school students was selected, of whom 274 completed a questionnaire in a supervised school assembly. The majority of students had used alcohol and a minority had used tobacco on three or more occasions in the twelve months prior to inquiry. Experience with other illicit drugs is less common. Among these, marijuana is the most common, with nearly one third reporting at least one experience and one fourth of the eighth graders reporting current occasional use and one fifth (girls) describing regular current use. Hallucinogen use is less frequent—although, again, nearly one fourth of the eighth graders had at least one-time use the prior year. Stimulant use—either amphetamines or cocaine—also occurs, but a maximum 7 per cent of any class report it. Opiate use is also rare, with a maximum 7 per cent (eighth-grade boys). Junior high school drug use is, for the most part, social and takes place at home or in "hangouts." Eight per cent report illicit-drug use in school. Most receive their drugs from same-age friends. Only 10 per cent of those using indicate that they are supplied by "professionals" (older persons who are not part of their immediate friendship or family group).

Supplying drugs to others is acknowledged by about one fourth of the students. The most common form is to share or give drugs away. Only 7 per cent sell at cost or for profit. We calculate that one out of four current users in junior high deals at least occasionally. Profit sales increase with class level. Sources for dealers are, as with other users (and all dealers are users), same-age friends, siblings, or older friends.

When dealers are contrasted with users and nonusers, family differences are slight; dealers do have better-educated parents. On the other hand, dealers do not do as well in school, derogate school more, reject college plans, and are not as involved in organized youth activities in school or out. Much more than others, dealers claim that their parents have deceived them about or are themselves ignorant of drug matters. We infer from this both derogation of parents and parent-child conflict. The dealers more than other students express interests in arts, crafts, and music, and they show signs of opting out of the conventional system—and of avoiding their parents' footsteps—by less often planning to go to college. But the poor grades, derogatory school view, and lack of college plans cannot be attributed to underprivileged status, for not only is the school middle-class, but the parents of the dealers more than those of other students have college educations. (Eighty-four per cent of their fathers have college degrees).

Constraints upon the inquiry—which had to be school- and parent-approved in a district sensitive to any outside studies that are not curriculum oriented—prevented our asking direct questions about personal problems or family relations. We believe that the data support an inference of poorer school and family adjustment among dealers than among their peers. The data do not suggest poor peer adjustment as such, given the reports of friends, but show that conventional peer activities in other realms are less popular than with other students. Dealers' expressed interest in artistic pursuits does suggest a possibly greater desire on their part to be expressive, creative, and—as we see from their behavior—unconventional. These developments are also compatible with data from our earlier studies (Blum and associates, 1969b), which suggest that children of better-educated parents take the lead in exploring unconventional paths and in expressing dissatisfaction with traditional institutions: the family, school, custom, and the law itself.

Chapter 25

PHYSICIANS

The physician plays a critically important role in drug distribution. Through his hands yearly pass more than two hundred million prescriptions for psychoactive drugs (Lennard, Epstein, Bernstein, and Ransom, 1971). Along with the pharmacist, who dispenses over-the-counter drugs directly and prescriptions on order, the physician is the gatekeeper for all but folk remedies, alcohol, tobacco, and illicit substances (although he may dispense drugs in such a way as to become an illicit channel). The physician is a teacher to his patients (Balint, 1957); he teaches them methods of caring for their illnesses, preventive habits, and accepted forms of drug use. It is likely that in this latter role he shapes people's views about what is safe and unsafe, approved and disapproved, so that they, in turn, as parents or relatives, pass along that counsel.

Physicians engage in a wide range of behaviors with regard to the use and prescription of psychoactive drugs. This chapter explores, by means of hypothesis testing, factors which account for varying rates of drug dissemination and for behavior which encompasses using, recommending, and prescribing drugs, as well as maintaining drug-dependent patients and controlling drugs in the physician's own office. At the extreme end of the spectrum of drug dissemination, one finds a few physicians who, in the eyes of the law, "abuse" powerful psychoactive substances in the way they distribute them to others and by personal consumption. The latter group run some risk of coming to the attention of their own professional associations and law enforcement agencies. We open this chapter with cases drawn from government files.

Illustrative Cases

There are multiple areas in which physicians have been involved in abuse of controlled dangerous substances. The following cases depict some typical abuses by professionals of various types of drugs.

During the 1960s considerable publicity was devoted to what came to be known as "fat doctors." These practitioners used many types of drugs to accomplish weight reduction "painlessly," without dieting or exercise. Wholesale weight-reduction programs were inaugurated, employing thyroactive drugs, cardiac glycosides, amphetamines, diuretics, vitamins, hormones, and laxatives.

One physician conducting such an obesity practice was treating a teen-aged boy with a thyroid preparation, digitalis, amphetamines, diuretics, and other drugs. The combination of these drugs was considered responsible for producing a lowered blood potassium level, which causes an increase in the irritability of the heart muscle. This increased irritability resulted in a particular type of irregular heart rhythm and muscular paralysis. The patient died despite efforts to improve the potassium level, electrical cardiac stimulation, and cardiac massage. The conclusion of the complex medical investigation was that the boy's death was a result of the combined effects of weight-control medications causing myocardial (heart muscle) irritability, cardiac arrhythmias, and critically reduced serum potassium levels.

A similar case involved a thirty-eight-year-old housewife and mother who was taking pills dispensed by her physician for weight reduction. This patient was shown to have been on doses of thyroactive substances which were much higher than those prescribed for any known medical indication in order to accomplish weight reduction. After driving her daughter to school one morning the woman died at the steering wheel of her car, and death, again, was attributed to her weight reduction regime.

An interesting feature of the weight reduction programs conducted during this era is the fact that enormous quantities of thyroid-type drugs were being used and digitalis-like medications were being administered to people who did not have a valid medical indication for these drugs. One drug company was producing a product containing a thyroactive drug which was available in one-grain pills. Most practitioners assumed that the one-grain dosage form was equivalent to one grain of thyroid extract. After sufficient study, it was determined that one grain of this substance was actually equivalent to more than nine grains of thyroid extract, and patients receiving three or four of these pills a day were receiving the equivalent of thirty to forty grains of thyroid extract daily. It is generally accepted that even in an individual who has had his thyroid surgically removed, replacement therapy usually does not require the use of more than five grains a day.

Obviously people on such therapeutic regimes could be expected to become thyrotoxic and clinically suffer from hyperthyroidism. This condition, in addition to the toxic effects of the digitalis preparation in patients who have no medical indication for them, could be expected to produce a serious or perhaps fatal outcome.

Physicians were shipped these drugs directly by the manufacturer and were taught their use; they were also told how to conduct an obesity-type practice and were given office management instructions. This type of practice was examined by Congress and subsequently by the medical profession. During the past few years there has been an apparent diminution in the number of practitioners who deal solely in the treatment of weight reduction utilizing this dangerous technique.

The application of methadone, a synthetic narcotic, in the treatment and rehabilitation of heroin addicts has also been abused considerably. This technique involves supplying large doses of oral methadone to selected patients on a daily basis as a part of an overall rehabilitative effort utilizing a range of therapeutic services and monitoring procedures. A number of physicians who have treated heroin addicts with methadone omitted vital control procedures and precautions necessary to prevent some rather disastrous effects. Some of these physicians obviously had a profit motive; others had apparently convinced themselves that they were helping the addicts.

One such doctor was prescribing methadone, along with other narcotic drugs, tranquilizers, and barbiturates. Drugs from his program were being sold illicitly on the street. No other types of therapy were being provided, and no monitoring procedures were being used to ensure that patients were actually benefiting from the program. Patients employed as janitors were stealing prescriptions from the doctor's office. Forged prescriptions were later discovered by investigations of drugstore records. One individual was shown to have purchased more than eight hundred Dilaudid tablets (a potent synthetic narcotic) in one month. These tablets had a value of about $10 each at that time on the illicit market. Undercover agents found their way into this program and, without any medical exam, were given prescriptions for large quantities of narcotics. Obviously, such loose practices have been responsible for drug dependency in previously nonaddicted individuals and for the deaths of young drug users resulting from overdosage.

This particular physician was confronted with evidence showing that he was responsible for an intolerable situation in his community.

After provision was made for the care of his patients elsewhere, the doctor agreed to stop this type of practice and no prosecution was deemed necessary.

Another example of a loosely controlled methadone program is the case of a young physician in a large northern city who prescribed and dispensed methadone without any semblance of a doctor-patient relationship. This physician had more than two hundred addict patients, each of whom was seen from one to three times a week. The fee for the initial visit was $20 and subsequent visits cost the patient $10 each; if the methadone was dispensed by the physician, an additional charge was made. Often no physical examination was made; the doctor only placed a strip of litmus paper in the mouth of the patient in order to assess the pH. Urine samples were collected without supervision upon the pretext that thin-layer chromotography would determine the abuse of other substances, but apparently the urine specimens were not actually tested.

This physician was believed to have been an addict himself; he had been ordering tremendous quantities of a drug containing barbiturates from a mail-order drug dealer. A covert investigation was initiated by both local and federal enforcement officials during which undercover agents visited the physician and, without examination, were given prescriptions for methadone; in some instances, methadone was dispensed in amounts of fifty to more than three hundred 10-milligram tablets. Prescriptions were issued at each of sixty-eight visits made by agents; during some visits, the agents were not even seen by the physician but were given prescriptions by his office nurse.

This doctor claimed to be conducting a methadone maintenance program, but he was unregistered with the federal government as a distributor of controlled substances. Additionally, he had taken no security precautions to prevent theft of drugs or prescriptions. An audit of the doctor's records disclosed that the physician, over a period of time, had purchased 714,000 10-milligram tablets of which 709,000 went to the methadone maintenance program. Neither the physician nor the program could account for the 5,000-tablet shortage. Under pressure from local and federal authorities, the doctor discontinued these practices and left the area, again eliminating the necessity for prosecution.

A more sophisticated case of methadone abuse concerned a board-eligible psychiatrist who had given up his private practice to devote full time to operating a treatment center for narcotic-dependent individuals. The center had thirteen full- or part-time physicians and several sociologists on its staff.

The psychiatrist asked the Food and Drug Administration

(FDA) for an Investigational New Drug Application. The protocol he submitted outlined what appeared to be an excellent treatment facility. Based on the scientific merit of his application the FDA approved a Notice of Claimed Exemption for an Investigational New Drug, which provided authority to conduct his methadone maintenance program. The program began on a small scale but soon mushroomed into a large facility with approximately three thousand patients. There were no apparent selection criteria. The fee for the initial visit was $20, and each subsequent visit ranged from $5 to $20. Methadone tablets, as well as other medications, were dispensed and were included in the fee. The treatment center was alleged to have been grossing more than $150,000 a month.

After receiving several complaints from concerned citizens and an inquiry from a Congressman regarding methadone abuse arising from this treatment center, the Bureau of Narcotics and Dangerous Drugs began an investigation. An undercover agent claiming to be addicted to Demerol was admitted to the clinic and was interviewed by two members of the professional staff. They advised him that Demerol was a barbiturate and that barbiturate addiction should not be treated with methadone, which is an addictive narcotic drug. After a short consultation, a cursory physical examination was given to the agent. A urine sample was collected, but without awaiting the results of the urine test, a seven-day supply of methadone was dispensed to the agent.

Over a period of thirty days the agent made seven visits to the treatment center, and on each visit he was given a week's supply of methadone. A urine sample was collected each time, and in spite of the fact that no drugs (including methadone) showed up in the urine, the agent was never questioned. On one occasion an agent was able to purchase methadone after admitting that he was not an addict and that he had only injected heroin three times.

Bureau agents audited the center's records on the amount of methadone received and dispensed. The audit revealed a gross discrepancy in the amount of methadone dispensed. After the Bureau provided the FDA with the results of its investigation, the FDA terminated the Notice of Claimed Exemption for this program. This action in effect made the program illegitimate under both Food and Drug Administration and Bureau of Narcotics and Dangerous Drugs statutes. Provision was made for patients in this program to be cared for at other treatment centers in the immediate area.

Another important aspect of drug abuse involves the drug-dependent professional. In a rather typical case a physician came to the attention of the Federal Bureau of Narcotics as the result of inquiries made by a state bureau of narcotics in 1940. During the course of the investigation, this doctor admitted that he had been addicted to narcotics for at least a year and that he had administered to himself nearly all the morphine he had purchased on his government order forms. His federal narcotic registration expired in June 1940, and he promised not to request registration renewal for a period of six months; in addition, he agreed to undergo therapy at the U.S. Public Health Service Hospital in Lexington, Kentucky. He was treated and discharged after one month in the hospital.

In November 1943 the doctor was arrested in a midwestern city after a fire in his hotel room. He was discovered with 15 cc's of morphine solution, 80 cc's of morphine-atropine solution, a hypodermic syringe and needle, as well as several unidentified drugs which were probably barbiturates, in both tablet and capsule form. He was then returned to the hospital in Lexington for an extended period of time.

The state board of medical examiners revoked his license to practice medicine in October 1946. However, in March 1947 he petitioned the board for restoration of his license and a favorable judgment was rendered. In October 1953, both the doctor and his brother were charged with falsifying narcotics records. The brother forged the doctor's signatures on prescriptions. Ultimately, the doctor was acquitted, but his brother received a two-year suspended sentence. The physician surrendered his narcotics tax stamp in November 1955 and agreed not to attempt reregistration under the Federal Narcotics Law until July 1956.

In May 1956, this physician was indicted on fourteen counts for violations of the Federal Narcotics Law. He was arraigned and released on $5,000 bond. Subsequently, in June 1956, he was again arrested after unknowingly delivering twelve Dilaudid tablets to federal narcotics agents, paid for with marked money which was later found in his possession. He was ultimately sentenced in federal court in 1957 to five years' imprisonment.

His license to practice medicine was again revoked by the board of medical examiners late in 1957. In 1958, he pleaded guilty to six counts of the 1956 indictment and was sentenced to three years' imprisonment, to run concurrently with the five-year sentence previously imposed.

Factors Associated with Dissemination Rates

There have been a number of studies of physicians in relationship to such matters as prescribing, behavior toward patients, and their own illicit use. Coleman, Menzel, and Katz (1959) examined physician acceptance of new drugs and the spread of prescription practices. They found that propensities toward earlier prescribing of new compound drugs were related to information exposure, past experience, and medical-social activity. Prescriptions for new drugs were first written by those who had partners, attended meetings, had already used similar drugs, and had considerable contact with other physicians. Prescription habits, as such, have been found (Lee, Draper, and Weatherall, 1965) to vary among physicians by locale, to be correlated in that prescriptions for various classes of drugs are consistently high or low (Joyce, Last, and Weatherall, 1968), and to vary depending upon the speciality of the M.D. (Cooperstock and Sims, 1971); for example, psychiatrists least often gave hypnotic-sedatives and stimulants but most often prescribed tranquilizers and antidepressants. Prescription rates vary with the training period of the physician, with those graduating after 1950 favoring tranquilizers over barbiturates. Older physicians in one study (Cooperstock and Sims, 1971) wrote larger prescriptions (longer duration of use) than younger ones, a finding consistent with that of Hayman and Ditman (1966), who found that younger psychiatrists and surgeons prescribed for lesser periods of time.

Balint, Hunt, Joyce, Marinker, and Woodcock (1970) examined repeat-prescription practices and found that both patient and physician characteristics influence the prevalence of repeat prescriptions. The researchers concluded that the repeat prescription is itself symptomatic of a kind of relationship between doctor and patient—namely, one in which the patient's complaint has psychological origins; the patient keeps at a distance from the doctor; and the doctor does not directly handle the tension he feels in the relationship but alleviates it by acceding to the patient's demand for repeat medication. Physicians who accept negative aspects in a relationship give fewer such prescriptions. That prescribing provides advantages for the physician is suggested by Lennard, Epstein, Bernstein, and Ransom (1971), who note that it can provide him with a sense of accomplishment and impart a feeling of mastery in the relationship.

That physicians may use drugs to control patients who are otherwise demanding ("crocks") has been suggested in a study (Blum, 1958) which found on wards in a poor-quality high-malpractice hospital a higher rate of sedative prescription—and greater nursing freedom to "quiet" patients—than in better hospitals. Prescription rates have also been found to vary (Appleton, 1965) among residents depending upon the nervousness and inexperience of the physician. Mendel (1967) also reported that experience and training affected prescription rates. Student physicians who were early instructed to refrain from prescribing prescribed much less after the training period.

As with the Balint, Hunt, Joyce, Marinker, and Woodcock (1970) work, prescriptions have been found to vary consistently depending upon the patient's nonmedical characteristics alone. Levine (1969), for instance, has reported that females receive most psychoactive prescriptions; and Shepherd, Cooper, Brown, and Kalton (1966) found that women more than men are treated for psychiatric problems with psychoactive agents. Patient age is also a variable, affecting prescription practices, for as females turn 16, their risk of being prescribed psychoactive agents increases markedly. Cooperstock (1970) also found a higher rate of psychoactives given to females.

Physicians' own drug use also has been the object of inquiry. Vaillant, Brighton, and McArthur (1970) in a twenty-year follow-up found that a group of students who became physicians used more stimulants, sedatives, and tranquilizers but no more alcohol and tobacco than a control group did. Many of the physicians' drugs were self-prescribed. Heavy use of drugs, alcohol, and tobacco tended to occur simultaneously; the heavy users were found to be those who had been least psychologically sound in college. Among those physicians using drugs heavily, one third of their serious illness, measured by time in hospital, was associated with self-medication or alcohol overuse. Vaillant, Brighton, and McArthur (1970), studying physician self-prescriptions, concluded that these physicians deny to themselves any risk of drug-related illness or disability, and have a sense of invulnerability to untoward drug effects and sometimes a certain self-indulgence (our word, not the investigators')—that is, at the end of the day the doctor feels he "deserves" something too after "giving" things all day to others.

Other components in physician self-prescription, particularly that linked to narcotics addiction, have been described by Duffy and Litin (1967), Modlin and Montes (1964), and Pearson and Strecker (1960). These components include problems of childhood, marriage, and work adjustment; the availability of drugs; the physician's magical belief in his own invulnerability to addiction; and unrealistic aspirations, resulting frustrations, real overwork, and subsequent distress. Generally, the onset of narcotics dependency is in the late thirties or early forties and is preceded or accompanied by alcohol problems. Psychologically, physician addicts resemble other narcotics users (Hill, Haertzen, and Yamahiro, 1968).

In reviewing this literature, as well as our experience with physician subjects in other research (Blum, 1960), we can distinguish a group of factors which ought to bear on physicians' own drug use and their prescribing in regular ways. Our study here tests for expected relationships between and among these variables.

Method

We constructed, pretested, and revised a questionnaire which included several (untested) scales intended to measure a physician's position on matters of opinion and attitude. The questionnaire also included a previously developed and refined scale (Blum, 1957), the Doctor Opinion Questionnaire (DOQ), which measures physicians' views of patients along a continuum previously found to be related to the probability of generating malpractice-prone relationships.

Aside from the fact that our scales other than the DOQ have not been tested for reliability or subject to item analysis, scaling, and so on, our inquiry suffers several other limitations. One is that we lack a guarantee of an independent measure of prescription practices. We gave detailed instructions to cooperating physicians on how to record prescriptions for the week prior to questionnaire completion and offered to pay their assistants for compilation; but only 7 per cent of the physicians sent in bills, and we cannot say, since the forms were mailed in anonymously, whether others followed our instructions on measuring prescriptions.

We suffer, too, from a shortage of cooperating physicians. We had sought the help of two medical societies in conducting this study but were rejected on the grounds that the results might embarrass the membership. We distributed three hundred forms through informally cooperating physicians located in one drug-help clinic, one university health center, one state mental hospital, one large community hospital, one large clinic, and a number of small private-practice groups. In addition, individuals in private practice with whom we had contact were invited to participate. Forms were returned by one hundred physicians: seven general surgeons, twenty-four internists, eleven general practitioners, eleven pediatricians, thirty psychiatrists, and seventeen other specialists. Because our sample contained a disproportionate number of psychiatrists and because other work has shown that their prescribing practices—and their outlooks—are different, we have analyzed our data in two groups: psychiatrists, $N = 30$, and all other physicians, $N = 70$. We do not know what bias differentiates our sample from nonresponding physicians; we suspect that the physicians in our sample have a greater interest in research and in the effects of drugs and less suspicion of or sensitivity to "outside" looks at medical practice. Because of the limitations, this should be considered a first-stage inquiry.

We assume that our cooperating doctors differ from Bay Area physicians as a whole and are not representative of them.

Sample Characteristics

On the basis of their replies, our cooperating sample can be described generally as healthy (few with past or present disabilities), not feeling stressed (about 15 per cent were ranked high on stress), but actively taking medications (only one fifth were ranked low on self-medication). Regarding psychoactive drug use, one third have prescribed sedatives for themselves; one fourth have prescribed tranquilizers; one fourth have prescribed analgesics; one fifth have prescribed stimulants; and 7 per cent have prescribed muscle relaxants in the preceding twelve months. Psychiatrists, more than other physicians, use more tranquilizers (37 per cent vs. 21 per cent). No differences in rate of use greater than 4 per cent occurred between the two groups for the other drugs. In the preceding five years, 16 per cent of the sample have prescribed opiates for themselves; nonpsychiatric physicians acknowledge such use at a rate three times greater than psychiatrists.

Work loads range from four to three hundred patients seen during the five days prior to form completion. About half of the psychiatrists saw twenty-five or fewer patients in that time; the majority of the nonpsychiatric physicians saw between fifty and one hundred patients. Among psychiatrists, the majority (54 per cent) wrote prescriptions during that time for fewer than 25 per cent of their patients; among nonpsychiatric physicians the majority (74 per cent) gave prescriptions to half or more of the patients seen. Sixty per cent of our sample maintain some dependent patients on drugs.

Measuring control of office drugs, we learned that in about one third of the offices all staff do have access to drugs and that, for 86 per cent of the sample, no records are kept of (nonopiate) drug supplies. About 15 per cent say that drugs in their offices have turned up missing.

As for their own recreational drug use, about two thirds are not heavy drinkers (three drinks or less—wine or alcohol—over the past weekend) or nondrinkers. About one fifth smoke tobacco (27 per cent of the psychiatrists; 14 per cent of the others); and more than one fourth have tried marijuana (63 per cent of the psychiatrists; 13 per cent of the nonpsychiatric physicians). Ten per cent of the total sample report LSD use, again with psychiatrists dramatically in the lead, 30 per cent to 1.4 per cent for the nonpsychiatric physicians.

Physicians as Drug Disseminators

There were four separate counts employed to measure a physician as a drug disseminator: (a) prescribing volume, the total number of prescriptions written over the five full days preceding form completion; (b) average prescription rate or score, measured as the total volume divided by the number of patients seen during those five days; (c) over-the-counter (OTC) volume, a report of the total number of over-the-counter substances recommended to patients during the five-day reporting period; (d) over-the-counter (OTC) rate, the average number of OTC preparations recommended per patient seen. A test of the relationship among these components shows, for psychiatrists, that (a) correlates $r = .51$ with (b), $r = .11$ with (c), $r = .02$ with (d); (b) correlates $r = .19$ with (c) and $r = .09$ with (d); and (c) correlates $r = .06$ with (d). A test of the relationship among these components for other physicians shows that (a) correlates $r = .63$ with (b), $r = .60$ with (c), and $r = .27$ with (d); (b) correlates $r = .29$ with (c) and $r = .28$ with (d); and (c) correlates $r = .96$ with (d).

Our expectation was that high disseminators by each measure would have more confidence in drugs than low scorers would; would receive lower DOQ scores, indicative of discomfort and psychological distance in the doctor-patient relationship; would report more personal illness; and would themselves use more pharmaceutical preparations.

Trust in Drugs. This is an attitude dimension which contains two components: (a) confidence in the therapeutic efficacy of drugs and (b) beliefs as to the malevolence, inefficacy, or benevolence of drugs (the general utility and impact of pharmaceuticals). We tested our expectation that prescription measures would be correlated with dissemination (measures (a) and (b)) and with trust in drugs (measures (a) and (b)) for psychiatrists and separately for other physicians. Among the eight tests, all correlations were in the expected direction; in four $r = <.20$, and in two $r = <.30$. None was significant at the .05 level. The two strongest correlations linked beliefs about the nature of pharmaceuticals to prescription volume ($r = .32$) and to average prescription rates ($r = .34$) among psychiatrists. Among eight correlations of OTC (over-the-counter) volume and average rates with drug confidence and beliefs, all were in the expected direction, with none significant at the .05 level, however.

On the basis of these findings, there is a trend for prescription rates to be mildly associated with physicians' trust in drugs. The relationship between trust in drugs and physicians' recommendations of over-the-counter substances remains unestablished.

Reasonableness in Doctor-Patient Relationship. The twenty-item DOQ was used to test our expectation that greater drug dissemination would characterize the less "reasonable" (more uncomfortable, less information-giving) physicians. Correlating DOQ scores (the lower the more reasonable) with prescription volume and average rate per patient, we find five in the expected direction and three not. Among psychiatrists, $r = .35$ ($p = <.08$) for DOQ and average prescription rates per patient.

Physicians' Health. We expected that the health of the physician, measured by reported disabilities past or present, would be related to drug dissemination—specifically, that physicians with greater ill health would (presuming their own greater experience with medication and what might be termed a self-based sickness orientation) propose more for others. Correlating health with prescription measures and over-the-counter recommendations, we find five of eight in the expected direction, two significant at the .05 level. The strongest relationship is demonstrated between being a less healthy psychiatrist and OTC volume, $r = .50$ ($P = <.04$), as well as OTC per patient average rates, $r = .44$ ($P = <.03$). Among psychiatrists, poorer health and average per patient prescription rate correlate $r = .24$ ($P = <.21$).

Self-Prescriptions and Patient Prescriptions. We expected, in line with the preceding hypothesis, that current medication use would be linked to drug dissemination. There were several component measures of medication including (a) how many prescription drugs the physician was currently taking, (b) how many OTC preparations he was taking, and (c) how many times he had self-prescribed in the preceding twelve months. A subsidiary set of measures (c′ 1 . . . . . . 6) recorded the frequency of self-prescription for specific psychoactive drugs: stimulants, tranquilizers, analgesics, and muscle relaxants for twelve months preceding; and controlled medication (narcotics such as Percodan, Demerol, morphine) for the five years preceding form completion.

When dissemination variables (a) through (d) are correlated with own-medication measures (a) through (c), among the twenty-four tests (twelve for each physician group) only about half (fourteen) are in the expected direction of greater dissemination and greater own use. For psychiatrists, three are above the .45 level; two of these, $P = <.001$. Psychiatrists who self-prescribe also are high prescribers, $r = .38$ ($p = <.05$); and psychiatrists who use OTC substances are likely to recommend large numbers (volume) of OTC preparations to others, $r = .87$ ($P = <.001$) and to have high average per patient OTC recommending rates, r = .67, (P = <.001). The volume of OTC preparations recommended also correlates positively, r = .45 (P = <.07) with self-prescription. Among psychiatrists, high current self-medication (self-prescription in particular) does correlate with being a high drug disseminator.

In examining specific psychoactive medications (c′ 1 . . . . . 6) used in relationship to being a drug disseminator, we report only those where r = <.30. We find that psychiatrists who prescribe high volumes use more sedatives, r = .31 (P = <.16) and more stimulants, r = .39 (P = <.07) and those with high average patient prescription rates use more stimulants, r = .32 (P = <.11). Among other physicians those with high prescribing volume are higher on stimulant use, r = .33 (P = <.01). Since stimulant use is the prevailing specific medication, we wonder if there is a "high activity" need underlying both; that is, a felt need to be stimulated and a propensity to appear active with patients by writing them prescriptions.

Physicians' Medication Practices

We also predicted that physicians high on drug taking would be in ill health (have more past and present disabilities than those who are low on drug taking), would feel that physicians receive poorer medical care than other patients, would be high users of social and illicit drugs, and would feel themselves under stress.

Health. When correlations are run between health and physicians' use of medications, eight of nine are in the expected positive direction. The strongest relationship is between psychiatrists' ill health and their own use of OTC preparation, r = .40 (P = <.03). Among nonpsychiatric physicians, the strongest relationship is between illness and the total prescription drugs now in use, r = .29 (P = <.02).

Medical Care for Physicians. In two questions we sought the opinion of physicians about the quality of care that physicians receive; a score was given to the position on the scale ordered for replies. Correlations were run between the foregoing measure of esteem for physicians' medical care and their drug-taking—own-medication measures (a), (b), and (c). Among the six tests, three were in the expected direction; three were not. None was greater than r = .22 and none was significant at the .05 level.

Use of Social and Illicit Drugs. We expected a relationship between the use of pharmaceutical preparations and the rate of use of "social" drugs (alcohol, tobacco) and of illicit ones. Alcohol users were ranked into high, medium, or low, based on the distribution of replies on amounts and regularity of use. Tobacco use was classified as present or absent. Illicit use was classified as present or absent for marijuana and for LSD.

A total of twenty-four correlations yielded positive relationships, among which two were greater than $r = .22$, none significant at $P = <.05$ level. The strongest association was in a direction opposite to that anticipated: high self-prescribing psychiatrists are not tobacco smokers, $r = -.45$ ($P = <.01$).

With regard to specific psychoactives used, psychiatrists who use analgesics tend not to smoke, $r = -.36$ ($P = <.05$), but those who use muscle relaxants do, $r = .44$ ($P = <.01$).

Stress. Felt stress was measured by the position on a scale (rarely, sometimes, often) of a physician responding to ten queries—including, for example, his feeling overworked, suffering marital unhappiness, worrying about his children, experiencing financial difficulties. A sum score was obtained, and physicians were ranked into three groups based on those reporting. Felt stress was correlated with the three self-medication variables (a) through (c) for both physician groups. Five out of six were in the expected positive direction, of which three were significant at the $P = <.01$ level. Stronger relationships occurred in the nonpsychiatric physician group than among psychiatrists. We find that the physician who feels that he is under a high degree of stress self-prescribes more, $r = .52$ ($P = <.001$), and is taking more substances prescribed by others, $r = .49$, ($P = <.001$).

Examining correlations of .30 and over for specific psychoactives used in relationship to felt stress, we find that nonpsychiatric physicians who are high self-prescribers of stimulants tend to be under high stress, $r = .33$ ($P = <.006$). Psychiatrists with high self-prescription of sedatives are under high stress, $r = .31$ ($P = <.09$) as are those who self-prescribe controlled substances (narcotics), $r = .34$ ($P = <.10$).

Other Relationships

Space does not allow us to discuss our findings with regard to other expected relationships, as, for example, when we examined the correlates of unreasonableness, of physician health, of views about psychoactive substance use, and of their practices and philosophies with regard to control over drugs. But compared to the findings just reported our crystal ball proved cloudy. We noted a close correspondence between beliefs about the need to control drugs and the physician's own reported non self-prescription of narcotics, $r = -.89$ ($P = <.001$).

In addition to testing hypotheses, we took advantage of computer capabilities to run a series of "shotgun" tests of relationships among other variables which we conceived to be important but where neither theory nor hunch guided us to predict directions for outcome. Using a series of opinion measures and our scales, we ordered physicians' replies and, letting the computer hum, emerged with only 409 where $r = .30$ among 3,500 tests. A number of these sets of findings proved interesting to us, but we can discuss only a few here, all of these based on relationships where $r = .30$. (The reader interested in the details, including correlation coefficients—not as demonstrations of fact but as the basis for hypotheses that he may wish to pursue—is referred to our full report: Report to the Bureau of Narcotics and Dangerous Drugs, Contract J-68-13, July 1971.)

Drug-Confidence Score. Psychiatrists with high confidence in the therapeutic use of drugs tend to be unwilling to use medications; to believe that pharmaceuticals are basically malevolent; and to require that psychoactive drugs, including euphoria-producing ones, not be used outside of medical practice. They tend to maintain strict control over access to drugs in their offices and do not maintain dependent patients on drugs. They are, however, willing to help patients with their questions about drugs. Physicians (other than psychiatrists) who have a high degree of confidence in the therapeutic use of drugs tend not to control the drugs strictly in their office and not to exert that control formally.

The most interesting feature here is the relationship between therapeutic confidence and a belief in the malevolence of drugs and also the belief that psychoactives should be under strict medical control. This, coupled with their emphasis on control, strongly suggests that these physicians believe in the *power* of drugs, a power that must be controlled.

Nature of Pharmaceuticals. Psychiatrists who feel that drugs are basically benevolent in nature tend to use stimulants but not muscle relaxants. They tend to have a low degree of confidence in the therapeutic use of drugs but approve the use of psychoactive substances recreationally. They tend to prescribe in large volume and at a high per patient rate. They are not strict in controlling access to drugs in their offices. They tend to have an informal approach toward their patients. Physicians (other than psychiatrists) who feel that drugs are benevolent in nature tend to be unaware of losses of drugs from their offices.

We propose that the psychiatrist who trusts in the benevolence of drugs but not their therapeutic efficacy—and who initiates their use through prescription, approves their use recreationally, and does not control his own office stocks—is at opposite poles philosophically from the psychiatrist who has confidence in the therapeutic benefits of pharmaceutical agents. The latter believes that psychoactive drugs heal but have dangerous powers, and he insists on control. The former believes that drugs do not heal, apparently are not dangerous, and may readily be used in and out of medical practice. The particular view that a physician holds ought to make a considerable difference in what he teaches his patients by prescription, by example, and through conversation. A physician who holds the benevolent-drug view would teach a casual approach compatible with high patient use and, as in our high-risk families in the family study (Blum and associates, 1972), possibly an optimistic willingness to explore illicit drugs as well. A physician with the opposite view would, we presume, teach the dangers of drugs and insist on controlling their use—a position compatible in child rearing with the conduct of low-risk families in the family study.

Side-Effect Cognizance. Psychiatrists who are not very concerned with drugs' side effects are more likely than others to have tried LSD. They tend not to strictly control the access to drugs in their offices. They are confident that patients can be counted on to use drugs wisely. Physicians (other than psychiatrists) who tend to dismiss the dangers of drugs' side effects are alert to drug needs in their patients and supply them with maintenance doses of habituating drugs. These doctors do not themselves use tobacco.

Confidence in Patients' Use of Drugs. Psychiatrists who have a high degree of confidence in the care with which patients use drugs tend to be unconcerned with drugs' side effects, tend to let the closeness of their relationship to patients influence their decision to respond to patients' requests for (medically questionable) drugs, and tend not to be helpful with patients' questions concerning psychoactive substances.

Physicians (other than psychiatrists) with a high level of confidence in the care with which patients use medications tend to have suffered more ill health themselves than physicians doubting the patients' responsibility in the use of pharmaceuticals.

Number of Patients Seen. Psychiatrists with large patient loads tend to be willing to take medication and to use sedatives and stimulants. They generally approve of the use of psychoactive drugs for pleasure and do not disapprove of social drug use. They write many prescriptions and have an informal approach to their patients. They tend to be aware of drug dependence among their patients and to emphasize control via the criminal law in regard to illicit drugs.

Physicans (other than psychiatrists) with large patient loads tend to write a large number of prescriptions, advise the purchase of over-the-counter drugs, and prescribe at a high average rate per patient.

Control over Office Drugs. Psychiatrists who exert strict control over the drugs in their offices more often than those with careless security use tranquilizers and muscle relaxants. They report themselves under a high level of stress, appear alert to drug dependence among their patients, are strict when asked for psychoactive drugs by young patients. Their response to requests for psychoactive drugs is affected by their personal relationship with the patient. These psychiatrists are more likely than others to use tobacco.

These physicians have a high degree of confidence in the therapeutic use of drugs, consider the dangers of drugs' side effects, feel that pharmaceuticals are basically malevolent, and disapprove of use of psychoactive drugs outside medical practice. They do not write many prescriptions and they give prescriptions to a small percentage of their patients. Their DOQ scores suggest greater hostility toward their patients. They are less likely than those less careful about drug security to have tried LSD.

Physicians (other than psychiatrists) who strictly control the drugs in their offices treat all requests from patients for psychoactive drugs equally, that is, they are not influenced by their personal relationships with the requesters. They are not "law-and-order" minded in regard to the control of illicit drugs, and handle situations involving the use of drugs by members of their staff in an impersonal fashion.

Response to Drug Requests. Psychiatrists who respond to requests from patients for psychoactive drugs in a formal manner (that is, do not accede readily) tend not to suffer from ill health, not to use over-the-counter drugs, not to self-prescribe, and not to use sedatives or stimulants. In contrast to more acquiescent doctors, they feel that pharmaceuticals are basically malevolent in nature, and that the use of psychoactive substances should be limited to medical practice. They do not write many prescriptions in toto and do not advise people to buy over-the-counter drugs. They strictly control access to the drugs in their offices but are unaware of losses. They do not supply many patients with maintenance doses and do not grant requests from young patients for psychoactive drugs. They respond equally strictly to these requests regardless of the young patients' life styles.

Physicians (other than psychiatrists) who respond to requests for psychoactive drugs in a formal manner have a low level of confidence in the quality of medical care received by physicians, are unwilling to help a patient with questions regarding drugs, do not smoke, and are less likely than others to try LSD.

We call attention to the response of psychiatrists to patients' requests for psychoactive drugs, since it appears to be a key feature of the drug-controlling physician; that is, the low disseminator who is not likely to contribute to any increase in the use of mind-altering agents by his patients. This type of physician holds that drugs are malevolent (dangerous in nature's scheme); he is reluctant to use them himself (and, being healthy, does not need to use them) and is reluctant to prescribe or recommend OTC substances. He refuses to maintain dependent patients on drugs and is not swayed by superficial appearances (for example, a student vs. a hippie) in deciding whether to prescribe a psychoactive drug requested by the patient.

Maintenance of Drug-Dependent Patients. Psychiatrists who supply dependent patients with maintenance doses suffer from ill health, use over-the-counter drugs, and self-prescribe. They use stimulants but not analgesics. They do not have confidence in the therapeutic use of drugs and do not approve of marijuana. They advise the purchase of over-the-counter drugs in volume and at a high per patient rate. They tend to approach requests for psychoactive drugs in an informal manner (to accede more readily) and to be aware of dependence among their patients, but are not willing to be helpful with their patients' questions about drugs. They tend more to alcohol use themselves but to have a basically negative opinion about drugs.

Physicians (other than psychiatrists) who supply maintenance doses to dependent patients tend not to be concerned with drugs' side effects. They are realistic in their view of the doctor-patient relationship.

Psychiatrists and Other Doctors

Both in the hypotheses testing section and in the shotgun readings, one thing is consistent above all. Psychiatrists differ from other physicians on almost every variable. Our psychiatric sample shows greater diversity and, within that diversity, greater cohesiveness among subgroups, which allows more correlations to emerge. It may be that the differences between them and other physicians are due to psychiatrists' being more willing to express extreme positions and to be internally consistent in what they say and do.

Comment and Summary

The areas where expected relationships emerge in some strength or consistency are between trust in drugs (measured both as confidence in effects and beliefs about the nature of pharmaceuticals) and dissemination practices (both in giving prescriptions to patients and in recommending over-the-counter substances to them). Thus, physicians who are the high disseminators are also those who believe that drugs are efficacious and that nature, in her role as pharmaceutical chemist, is benevolent. Some doctors are not particularly trustful of drugs; for example, one fourth of the psychiatrists and 13 per cent of nonpsychiatric physicians consider pharmaceuticals as more dangerous than useful.

A second set of relationships has to do with physicians' own drug use and their health. Physicians who have had more past or present disabilities also use more prescriptions and OTC preparations and do more self-prescribing. Use of medications also is strongly linked to felt stress (work, marital, financial) in the physician's life. This finding that felt stress contributes to self-medicating behavior suggests that drug use—including nonpsychoactive compounds—is a response to life problems. Since a physician's own drug use is linked in some ways to the rate at which he prescribes or recommends drugs, one can posit that stress—or factors underlying stress—is an intervening variable which ought, in the future, to predict which physicians will be high disseminators.

A third set of relationships, weaker, bears on control of drug access in the physician's office and his own social-recreational drug use. Those who control in one place control in another—not consistently and in all ways but at least in enough ways to make sense. It is the same person who is running an office and going home to drink at night, and it appears that his approach to both has some consistency in it. The control variable is strongest, however, *in* the office; for it is the high-control physician who most rejects using opiates from his own narcotics cabinet.

A fourth set of relationships are built around the dimension of trust in drugs. At one extreme is the psychiatrist who has confidence in the therapeutic efficacy of pharmaceuticals; his confidence is linked to his conviction that drugs are essentially malevolent, powerful, and consequently must be controlled both in the office and in social use. At the other extreme is the physician who trusts in the benevolence of drugs. That belief is linked to disparagement of the power in these substances, for such a physician considers drugs to be therapeutically worthless, is not concerned with the unsupervised social use of pleasure-giving substances, and is willing to prescribe drugs at a high rate. This dimension of trust linked to a conception of power and the subsequent need and responsibility for control is fundamental.

We now set forth some ideas about physician types. These are to be taken as tentative but worthy, we think, of further exploration.

The antidrug psychiatrist feels that the nature of pharmaceuticals is basically malevolent and that the use of any psychoactive substance should be strictly limited to medical practice. He writes few prescriptions and gives them only to a small percentage of his patients. In his opinion, the side effects of drugs can be dangerous and should always be kept in mind. The access to any drugs which are kept in his office is strictly controlled. He is uncomfortable or distant toward his patients and responds to their requests in a formal, perhaps even unfriendly manner. He does have a high degree of confidence in the therapeutic use of medication. Perhaps he prefers to use drugs therapeutically than to become personally involved with his patients. Conservative in many ways, he is also less likely to have tried LSD than are his colleagues.

The over-the-counter advocate, a psychiatrist, strongly recommends OTC preparations. He uses them himself to alleviate his own discomfort, some of which is associated with ill health. Informal, responsive, and empathic with the difficulties of his patients, he is alert to their drug problems and sympathetically supplies maintenance doses to those who are dependent. A conventional person, he disapproves of marijuana. He is reluctant to encourage that which is out of bounds, is uncomfortable in discussions about illicit conduct and responds with a "law-and-order" attitude on such nonmedical matters.

The high-prescribing psychiatrist writes prescriptions at a heavy rate, feeling confident that pharmaceuticals are safe and believing that psychoactive drugs are an important modality in the treatment of emotional and mental disorders. With his staff he is relaxed, perhaps overly so, since access to the drugs in his office is not strictly controlled. Nevertheless, he keeps (as most of his colleagues do not) strict records and is alert to the possibility that drugs might be stolen. A reasonable man in the doctor-patient relationship, he is informal and relaxed about patient requests for psychoactive drugs. He is aware of those among his patients who are dependent on drugs, and he is willing to become personally involved with and helpful toward those of his patients with drug interests or problems. He is, nevertheless, conventional, even touchy, about the social use of drugs; for he accepts the need for enforcement controls over the social use of drugs.

The high-prescribing physician writes many prescriptions and advises his patients to get over-the-counter preparations. He carries a large patient load, so that his drug disseminating is a quick way to take care of his patients. He is probably not "psychologically" oriented, and one wonders about the adequacy of his relationship to patients or even the quality of care he renders.

The stressed physician (not a psychiatrist) feels discomfort in his life—arising, he believes, from overwork, marital difficulties, financial problems, dissatisfaction with career, and difficulties with his children. These are pressures he finds hard to handle. He responds with a high grade of use of prescription medications and doses himself whenever he feels unhappy, overwhelmed, or unloved. He is particularly likely to use stimulants, probably for their mood-lifting effect.

The formal physician is somewhat unbending, perhaps lacking inner confidence; he distrusts his colleagues and the quality of medical care he himself can receive. He finds it difficult to talk to patients and gives short shrift to their questions. A self-controlled person, he avoids drugs himself, especially their social or illicit use.

The zero correlation man is missed in our typologies, which emphasize visible correlations. They overlook the "invisible" men among whom there are no detected regularities between and among drug attitudes, opinions, use and dissemination. What are these physicians like? We have no idea.

In summary, one hundred physicians cooperated in an inquiry directed to discerning relationships between a hypothesized set of dimensions of attitude and conduct bearing on their distribution of drugs to their patients and on other drug-related behaviors. Psychiatrists proved to be different from nonpsychiatric physicians in their replies, and more relationships were obtained among them than among other physicians. The limitations on our work require us to be cautious in accepting our findings.

Relationships have been obtained for drug dissemination by physicians and their confidence in drugs, between their own use of drugs and their health histories and their felt stress, and between the degree of office control (security) of drugs and the physicians' own use and beliefs about drugs. There is a group of physicians who believe drugs are efficacious and dangerous and act accordingly, using them sparingly, controlling them, and disapproving of nonmedical use. In contrast, there are more casual physicians who disseminate heavily, care not about unsupervised use, but doubt both dangers and efficacy. Patient load is related to high dissemination of drugs; concern over drug side effects is linked to a variety of other cautions. A physician's response to his patients—whether in their requests for drugs or information—is also linked to the degree of drug disseminating as well as to the physician's own drug experimentation and his willingness to maintain dependent patients on drugs.

Chapter 26

PHARMACISTS

Among the licensed groups which buy and sell psychoactive drugs, pharmacists are unique in that their primary function is the distribution of drugs directly to the public. As legitimate drug dealers, they provide important services in support of the nation's health and comfort. The typical family in this country requires eighteen to twenty prescriptions per year, which are filled by more than 100,000 pharmacists currently in practice in this country.

The pharmacist has a concern with illegitimate traffic for several reasons. In the first place, his pharmacy is subject to thefts from illicit users or dealers. Second, the pharmacist is the object of manipulation by users and dealers, who submit counterfeit or forged prescriptions, try to shoplift, or simply wheedle or seek to bribe in order to obtain psychoactive drugs for nonmedical use. Third, the pharmacist, as a knowledgeable person in the chain of distribution, may learn something of the mechanism of drug diversion itself (diversion defined as the mechanism by which drugs produced by legitimate manufacturers are somehow channeled to illicit markets). The chain of legitimate distribution involves the manufacture; all transporters (truck, railway, postal employees, and other handling personnel); all warehousemen, sometimes detail men who transport samples; packagers and wholesalers; and, ultimately, the pharmacist or dispensing physician. Diversion may occur at any point in the chain, including the pharmacy itself.

To learn about the problems and pressures faced by pharmacists, we searched the literature and could find only isolated accounts of individual pharmacists who had engaged in illicit practices. For this reason, we undertook to interview a sample of pharmacists in San Francisco, with an eye to learning from them something of the problems and perspectives of these legitimate drug dealers and to learn too, if we could, something about diversion.

Method

We took every fifth name from the *Directory* (California State Board of Pharmacy, 1969) for the County of San Francisco. Of the total number selected in this fashion (256), fifty-five were contacted, and thirty-seven (66 per cent) agreed to an interview. Initial contact with the pharmacist was by the interviewer's walking in during slack periods of the business day without previous contact and asking for the pharmacist on duty. The interviewer attempted to interview him on the spot by saying: "I would like to have several minutes of your time to talk to you about drug problems." The study was then briefly explained, and the questions were presented as stated on the questionnaire. If the pharmacist appeared hesitant, the interviewer mentioned that any questions the pharmacist did not wish to answer would be omitted. If the pharmacist did not wish to talk at that time, other arrangements were suggested. When several pharmacists were on duty in the same store, we selected the acting manager. A letter of introduction was often used and assurance of complete confidentiality was given. A thirty-one-item interview was designed to illicit attitudes and opinions of the pharmacists about a variety of subjects, including illicit activities by pharmacists and the pressures that are put on them to distribute drugs in either unapproved or questionable circumstances.

Results

The majority of our pharmacists had received four or more years of pharmacy training, were sole or part owners of the store in which they worked, were members of several pharmaceutical associations, and worked in stores employing three or more nonpharmacist employees. In these respects the persons interviewed are like other pharmacists in California (Day and Clare, 1968). The distribution of clientele by class, age, or ethnic characteristics linked to pharmacy location was (in order) middle class (46 per cent), working class (12 per cent), multiclass and ethnic group (9 per cent). The remaining percentage was composed of persons on pension and welfare, black, Spanish-American, and Oriental. Both by the kind of clientele served and by location, the drug stores in the sample cover a cross section of San Francisco's population.

Prescriptions filled per month range widely, from a few hundred to over 2,500, with two thirds of the stores filling between 500 and 2,000. Prescription sales represent between 16 per cent and over

70 per cent of the total dollar sales of the pharmacy, with 41 to 50 per cent as the modal point. The majority of pharmacists consider their activities to be more or at least as much professional as business oriented and, in fact, prefer the professional role to the business role. Most indicate that they are content with their choice of career.

When asked about drug abuse, pharmacists agree that prescription more than over-the-counter (OTC) drugs are the ones abused. Most (71 per cent) have faced problems from customers (or physicians) linked to what they regarded as the abuse of drugs. In such cases—for instance, when patients are overreceiving prescription substances—the pharmacist usually calls the doctor to discuss his concern with the number of repeat prescriptions or the size of the order. For OTC drugs, pharmacists remove from view or easy reach those items of stock which they suspect of being purchased for abuse potential. In some cases the OTC drug has been discontinued. Among OTC drugs, cough syrups, inhalants, minor tranquilizers, sleeping preparations, antihistamines, and asthma-control agents are, in that order, believed to be purchased by their customers for their psychoactive effects rather than for the stated purpose of the medication. Two per cent of the pharmacists suggest that laxatives can also be used in that fashion. Only 9 per cent believe that no OTC drugs are being abused.

Other steps taken by pharmacists to control customer use which was suspect include calls to the police when patently fraudulent prescriptions have been presented or when shoplifting of drugs of abuse has occurred (one fourth reporting such action) or talking directly to a customer, voicing their concern for the patient's repeat purchase of one or another substance.

Pharmacists were asked whether Americans in general tend to rely too heavily on psychoactive substances, even when used legitimately. Four fifths of the pharmacists interviewed hold that people do indeed use more psychoactives than they should and that alternative, nonchemical means for handling emotions, moods, sleep cycles, and so forth, should be utilized.

As for the frequency with which OTC preparations are abused, most pharmacists (79 per cent) state that such purchases (or shoplifting) come to their attention no more than four times a year. Twelve per cent report about one incident a month; 6 per cent, two to five incidents a month; and 3 per cent (one pharmacist), six to ten incidents per month. Whether these low percentages are due to the lack of information by the pharmacists or are indicative of low abuse of OTC products is not known. Available data support the view that very few people use the pharmacist as a source of advice on drug actions, benefit, and side effects (Jang, Knapp, and Knapp, 1970).

With regard to loss of controlled drugs and narcotics, as well as OTC substances, through theft, *every* drugstore had experienced burglary or robbery during the preceding twelve months. For the majority there had been only one or two such events, but some stores had frequently been the victim of robbery or burglary. We asked the pharmacists how often customers came in seeking narcotic or dangerous drugs, either without any prescription or with inadequate authorization. The majority say that such incidents occur at least several times a month; one fifth say that they occur at least once a day.

In discussing diversion of drug products, two thirds feel that diversion occurs on a widespread scale or is a serious problem within selected parts of the country. Only 14 per cent contend that diversion is an uncommon phenomenon. Regarding the role of pharmacists themselves in illicit traffic (diversion), one fourth of the sample said they know of pharmacists who have been guilty of such offenses.

We cannot estimate accurately the percentage of pharmacists actually engaged in illicit distribution; for, if anything was clear, it was the self-protective behavior of pharmacists in the study. Unlike our sample of illicit dealers—who are open in discussing their illicit behavior simply because it *is* their life and they accept it—the respectable professional must conceal any illicit conduct in order to maintain his self and social respect. One finds justifications—excuses, rationalizations, and so forth among respectable offenders, embezzlers, for example (Cressey, 1953)—but we do not encounter such defenses among regular criminal drug dealers when the interviewing relationship is well established. In any event, none of our pharmacists admit to illicit diversion. We did get identification of two drug stores as ones possibly engaged in illicit traffic. We checked these against police records (including informants' reports) and sent an experienced agent to one store to observe and try to make a buy. (We could never find the other store open.) No positive information or conduct emerged to justify the allegations made. A review of police information indicates that an average of one to two pharmacists per year are arrested in the City for illicit dispensing (and related practices). Informant reports identify twelve individual pharmacists, out of a total population of about 584, as ones engaged in illicit practices. If informant reports plus police arrest reports are within the range of accuracy, the prevalence of illicit diversion among pharmacists would be at a rate of about 2 to 3 per cent ($N = 14$). It is possible that some of the pharmacists who refused to cooperate fall in this category; for—of two groups of pharmacists who claimed to be "too busy" to be seen—the first were, in fact, high-volume successful men, but the others were found, upon observation of their stores, to be inactive and operating without assistants. Whether they were simply embarrassed over their status, noncooperative in general, or more at risk of illicit practice would be worthy of investigation.

Exploration of the diversion problem focused on other personnel who could or, to the pharmacists' knowledge, had been involved. We rank these in order of the pharmacists' views of the frequency of their complicity in diversion: (1) jobbers-wholesalers-warehousemen, (2) nonprofessional hospital and pharmacy employees, (3) detail men, (4) physicians, (5) janitors, (6) nurses, (7) pharmacists, (8) police officers including narcotics agents, (9) veterinarians, (10) clinical researchers, and (11) pharmacy interns.

Regarding the narcotics and dangerous-drug-control laws, about one third of our pharmacists feel that present laws are adequate and necessary, whereas the same proportion hold them to be too restrictive or unenforceable. Some consider present laws too lenient or otherwise filled with loopholes, and some complain that laws should be, but are not now being, enforced.

We presented the pharmacists with hypothetical situations and asked them what they would do. In one, a known addict presents a proper and legal prescription for narcotics. What would the pharmacist do? One third say that they would refuse to fill it; one third would check with the doctor; one fourth would fill it. In the next case, Mrs. Smith, a regular client, requests a refill for a drug which requires her physician's approval for refill. The doctor cannot be reached by the pharmacist, and the customer insists. How many pharmacists would acquiesce to her demand if it was for a chronic medication which she had received many times before? Answer: 41 per cent. What if it was an amphetamine preparation which the customer had received many times before? Answer: 15 per cent. And if it was a barbiturate with many prior prescriptions? Answer: 15 per cent. But what if it was an amphetamine or barbiturate which she had received only once before? Answer: 3 per cent would give it to her. What if it was a life-sustaining drug (digitalis, nitroglycerin, etc.)? Answer: 50 per cent. If it was a narcotic and the patient was in pain? Answer: 11 per cent. And if it was a narcotic and the pharmacists could not ascertain whether the patient was in pain? Answer: 6 per cent would give it to her. What would the pharmacists who would not fill the order without authorization do instead? Answer: For chronic medication (unspecified), barbiturates received often before, and life-sustaining drugs they would give a few doses to the patient; for the other drugs, they would ordinarily wait for authorization.

In a third hypothetical situation, an unknown customer, claiming to be an epileptic, presents herself at night; she also claims to be from out of town and says she has forgotten her Dilantin capsules. She asks for enough to tide her over until she sees a doctor. The story as it is presented to our respondents gives a hypothetical reply from a pharmacist, who says he cannot sell her the capsules without a prescription but does give her three capsules with the recommendation that she see a doctor; he offers to recommend one if she so desires. Our pharmacists were asked whether they agreed with the handling of the situation in this way; four fifths of them did. Those agreeing were then asked whether they would agree with the same handling if she had asked for phenobarbitol (30 mg.). Again, half agreed with the dispensing practice.

Comment and Summary

The pharmacist as businessman and paramedical professional is often in a bind, caught between the demands of the client, who is a customer for many items besides drugs, and the demands of the law that governs drug dispensing.[1] Professionalism is a source of pride and preferred to the businessman image or activity; consequently, one suspects that, both during and after training, the pharmacist as a striving professional more than as a merchant internalizes the rules and concepts governing safe and lawful prescription. As *his* rules, they are an anchor for him in dealing with the questionable requests of customers. In this light, one can understand the complete acceptance of the concept of control through law which characterizes this sample. It is this identification with control and with laws which, we posit, also colors the pharmacists' beliefs as to who is responsible for drug diversion, for pharmacists attributed criminal diversion primarily to nonprofessional people.

These judgments about where diversion occurs and who is responsible for it may be correct. Whether correct or not, we propose that the hierarchy of knaves as presented represents something else as well, and that is a conception of the world. It is a conception which presumes an order of things, a unity, in which there is a right and there is a wrong and that which is right is simultaneously an article of faith, a set of shared values, an internalized conscience, and a way of behavior. That conception implies that the medical-pharmaceutical-legal codes which govern the use and distribution of drugs and constitute proper

[1] For a discussion of trends in the practice of the pharmacist and macro- and micro-aspects of his multiple roles, see Knapp and Knapp (1968).

authority are an adequate body of wisdom in service of the protection of laymen, and do provide a satisfactory set of business relationships. We posit that the current body of drug laws and regulations as these affect dispensing and distribution arise from belief, are supported by faith, are precepts practiced because the values are internalized, and are enforced on others when others fail to subscribe to the well-intentioned health and business morality of the professional establishment and its minions. In this event, one would expect knowingly illicit diversion to be practiced by those who lack this professional image and faith, who are less socialized to the norms of the profession via schooling, who are less beholden to the middle class from which this professional ethic arises, have less to gain from adherence to the ethic, enjoy less prestige in adhering to norms, suffer less peer pressure because they are not members of professional associations and are, in any event, poorer or less satisfied with their lot and income. Who would these be? Any lower-level employee, any sharp businessman who is fighting his way up, any pharmacist or other professional who is himself an outcast in his group. These are the people the pharmacists describe as engaged in illicit diversion and we would think that any future research would do well to test that sensible expectation.

It is also likely—and comes as no remarkable observation—that the general values of the middle class, of which we see the professional as a "culture carrier," eschew crime per se, or at least those visible, immoral, and indelicate delinquencies which illicit-drug dealing implies. These same moral and status constraints may not be so salient when it comes to "sharp" business practices, income tax evasion, and white-collar crime as such.

Whoever does the diverting of drugs, it is likely that the pharmacist, as one of the principal channels for drug dissemination, will share in the responsibility for correcting over use. If law-enforcement techniques were ever to be successful against the street dealers, it would be the pharmacist who would quickly feel pressure to meet the demand created by diminished supplies available from illicit dealers.

As pharmacists look around them to see who it is they know doing diversion—either unlawful distribution to others or use for themselves—it is noteworthy that they rank the physician as foremost diverter among the professionals. Even more noteworthy: they rank their own pharmacy interns as least delinquent—perhaps because the intern embodies the ideals of the student professional, the golden seminarian, untarnished by either actual opportunity or the ugly pressures of the real world of business. Can it be that the physician's foremost rank is more than a mirror of what is often alluded to, the physician's actual vulnerability to opiate addiction (Modlin and Montes, 1964)? Might it also be a status ranking, showing the heart's secret desire, the pharmacist nobler than the doctor in a society where the doctor is, in the public eye, graced with higher status than the pharmacist? Might it also be that a trace of vengeance lurks in the appraisal? It was not unknown during the study—or outside it—to learn that there was no love lost between the commanding (prescribing) physician and the obedient (dispensing) pharmacist when the relationship is posed—as physicians have been known to do—in that light. Perhaps the pharmacist, wounded in past status encounters with the physician, mindeth not to call attention to the latter's venal side. These are speculations, but not impossible ones.

The pharmacist's own strong professional commitments do not fully protect him from the immediate situation when a customer wants something which the law says he cannot give. So it is that a goodly portion (two fifths) of our pharmacists complain that current laws are too restrictive or otherwise unenforceable. Credence is added to what they say as we examine their response to hypothetical situations—situations which would, we assume, lead to underreporting rather than overreporting of such minor unlawfulness as the unauthorized dispensing of prescription drugs implies. Some candidly admit that they would give unauthorized amphetamines, barbiturates, or narcotics to a known customer with a prior prescription. The situation here is one which is interpersonal and where prior medical sanction exists. The pharmacist, as a professional, does make judgments independent of the written rules when he ascertains that his judgment, not the rules, is a more just (or more businesslike?) arbiter of the patient's needs. Many of our pharmacists would also dispense, without being paid, barbiturates to an unknown customer without evidence of prior medical sanction. Again, the demand they face is personal, the need portrayed by the patient is real, the service they render is humane and in the way rendered brings the dispenser neither gain nor can it bring harm (not two capsules of barbiturate in any event) to the patient. Again, the real situation (well, the hypothetically real one) is balanced against the rules. For half the pharmacists, independent judgment and the benign assumption of honest need on the part of the patient wins out. In a very minor way, the natural law—one's moral obligations as one sets them oneself—is here elevated over the written one, just as in large and perhaps grotesque ways the illicit-drug peddler does the same. We must conclude that any human being with access to drugs and felt obligations to others may dispense psychoactive substances in technically unlawful ways. The consequences of this fact of life should be disquieting only to those who have adopted a philosophy of perfection in the accountability of all controlled drugs in our society.

The other problems that the pharmacists describe represent tension arising from the conflict of being a controlling professional and the business demand to please the customer. On the part of the pharmacy student, the conflict between business and professional and scientific roles is intense, especially so since the scientists and educators who populate the schools of pharmacy do not hold the practice of pharmacy in high esteem. Control of the profession rests to a large degree with the practitioners and pressures on pharmacists, for high volume is likely to remain as the most direct route to success. Future trends, such as the introduction of more dispensing points for easier and faster procurement of drugs—a drive-in vending machine pharmacy?—will increase the problems associated with restricted access to dangerous drugs.

Pharmacists commonly are asked to provide dangerous or narcotic drugs for which no sanction can be given. Furthermore, their stores are burglarized and their shelves pilfered. They are faced with the problem of dealing with doctors and dentists who sometimes treat prescription pads as if they were scratch paper. It is small wonder that "pharmacists . . . generally underestimate what the public expects of them" (Knapp, Knapp, and Edwards, 1969).

Yet, extending beyond these stark signs of drug-dependent persons seeking supplies by any means is the larger problem of the overuse of psychoactive substances by the public. These pharmacists, who make the better part of their living from the sale of prescriptions alone, have come to believe, presumably from their knowledge and observation, that Americans in general rely too much upon those chemicals which the drugstore sells. The pharmacists' dilemma should be seen in this light.

In summary, a number of San Francisco pharmacists were interviewed. Most have experienced problems with clients abusing drugs; prescription substances more than over-the-counter ones are implicated. All are faced with pressures from customers to secure drugs illegally; all have experienced thefts, shoplifting, and the like, as one expression of a larger problem—a too-extensive reliance by the public on psychoactive materials. They consider diversion of drugs from legitimate sources to illicit trade to be serious and commonplace; most attribute to nonprofessionals in the distribution chain the responsibility for that theft and deceit which is diversion's mechanism. Pharmacists themselves appear deeply committed to a professional ethic and support the existing structure of legal controls over drugs. They are, however, faced with day-to-day situations which require the exercise of judgment, and in those circumstances many admit to the use of professional judgment which may run counter to the letter of the law. They do not admit to any acts which can be construed as unprofessional or illicit traffic as such, although some do know of pharmacists who have themselves been guilty of diversion for profit. On the basis of their estimates, such conduct is rare. An independent police arrest and informant report estimate of the prevalence of illicit diversion among pharmacists yields a rate of 2 to 3 per cent.

Chapter 27

PHARMACEUTICAL SALESMEN

Pharmaceutical houses do not advertise their products, prescription drugs, directly to the consumer patient; rather, their efforts are directed at the physician, for he is the gatekeeper who controls what the patient will take. Although the drug industry relies on conventional advertising, to the tune of three-quarter billion dollars a year (Garai, 1966), its prime device is through the drug company's representative, the detail man. It is the task of the detail man to see physicians; to give information about his company's existing products, their application and advantages; to create anticipatory interest in new products under development by the company; to offer general educational materials about pharmaceutical products and the industry; to jog the physician along on the first step of learning to use a company product; and to give him samples of drugs manufactured by his firm for trial use with patients.

The sales value of the detail man must be considerable, for the average cost of each of his visits to one physician is almost $8 compared with the cost per reader of about one penny for typical magazine advertisements (U.S. Department of Health, Education, and Welfare, 1968). That sales value has no doubt been demonstrated in practice measured by revenues; it has also been documented in scholarly literature. Coleman, Katz, and Menzel (1966) report that 57 per cent of the physicians in their sample indicated that the detail man was their initial source of information about the new drugs covered in that study. Fassold and Gowdy (1968) found that 46 per cent of their medical sample considered detail men to be the "most informative and/or most acceptable type of drug advertising," and Hagood and Owen (1967) report that 85 per cent of the physicians in their study gave detail men "a strong vote of confidence." Given his influential role not only as salesman but as a promoter of new drugs, one must consider the detail man not only an important link in the chain of drug distribution but a teacher of work-a-day pharmacology as well.

Since detail men do occupy important roles in the drug-distribution chain, carrying and giving samples as well as advising prescription behavior, we decided to include them in our study. Our goal was to identify, through them, points in the distribution chain where illicit diversion—a form of "white-collar crime" in drug dealing—might occur. We had hoped to gather two samples: one from ethical pharmaceutical houses (which adhere to codes of conduct in advertising and distribution) and the other from "pill mills" or "bathtub suppliers" (which do not adhere to such codes). Unfortunately, we were able to locate only ethical detail men; we found the "pill mill" detail men elusive, and with our limited resources (to be exact, nonexistent resources, since this was a voluntary and unfinanced endeavor) we were unable to locate many or secure the cooperation of any.

Twenty detail men working in the Bay Area and representing most of the ethical houses constituted our sample. We inquired first about their personal drug use. Most of them claim to be conservative in the use of psychoactive drugs; for example, only 10 per cent have recently used prescription sedatives. About half admit that they keep for their own use samples of psychoactive samples given to them for distribution to physicians. The majority say that this is a common practice among detail men. This unsanctioned (nonprescription) use for oneself occurs more often than more frankly illicit distribution, for only 15 per cent indicate that they would distribute—or have distributed—samples in their possession to others. All claim that they would do so only if in their judgment the recipient had a health reason (sleeplessness, fatigue, etc.) justifying their action. On the other hand, the majority of our sample state that some detail men do sell samples to make extra money. As for their own use of illicit drugs, one fifth of this group (median age 37) acknowledge that they themselves have used marijuana.

Asked to consider sources of drug diversion known to them, the majority contend that some physicians and detail men are engaged in such diversion. Three of the twenty say that they themselves have been approached and invited to participate in illicit sales; the majority hold that it is unlikely that detail men would themselves be asked to play a major role in diversion. The average estimate is that 5 per cent of the detail men and 5 per cent of the physicians known to them are engaged in such traffic.

The following diversion methods are listed: (1) A physician requests—and then sells—large supplies of samples from as many detail men, representing different companies, as possible. (2) Drugs are diverted during shipping. Theft from trucks is particularly common. Mail theft also occurs. One fifth of the sample have themselves suffered such losses of consigned psychoactive drugs. (3) Pill-mill (generic) houses intentionally engage in sales to consumers whose credentials are dubious but not checked. (4) Wholesalers divert drugs outright, selling them to illicit dealers and covering up through fraudulent accounting. One device is to arrange "theft" of supplies. (5) Certain companies or wholesalers ship directly to Mexico, without concern that the recipient is probably unqualified (not a pharmacist or physician), and intends the drugs for the illicit United States market. (6) Sales are made to legitimate Mexican recipients, who in turn divert (penalties there for such traffic in nonnarcotic compounds are light) to illicit dealers. (7) Counterfeit drugs are marketed. For example, capsules used for barbiturates are filled with inactive substances (sugar, talcum powder, etc.) and sold by wholesalers to illicit traffickers, who peddle them as genuine. (8) In the laboratories of legitimate enterprises (pharmaceutical houses, pharmacies, chemical labs) chemists independently produce—or steal—drugs, which are illicitly marketed. (This procedure was called to our attention by someone not in our original sample.) (9) As aforementioned, detail men themselves sell samples or, in liaison with traffickers, procure substances for illicit sale.

All of the detail men are in agreement that psychoactive drugs should be controlled. The majority feel that controls should be made more stringent on amphetamines and sedatives. The majority hold that present controls are adequate for the distribution of narcotics through legitimate channels. Only one detail man argues for decreasing narcotic-control measures (for reducing the paper work, required by current laws, e.g. triplicate prescriptions etc.). On the other hand half of the sample are in favor of legalizing marijuana; three feel that LSD should be available on prescription.

Comment and Summary

These detail men are strongly control-oriented with regard to opiates, sedatives, and amphetamines and in their own conduct indicate conservative use of these substances. Nevertheless, half do "divert" to themselves, which is technically illicit; a few may divert to others illicitly, although for benign rather than monetary reasons. Most are in agreement that their detail-men colleagues and their physician customers do sometimes engage in frankly illicit traffic; but no more than 5 per cent of either group are considered likely to be criminal.

In contrast to their drug conservatism, their obvious wish to present themselves as honest (which we believe they are), and their strong control orientation toward many substances, one fourth of this very "straight" sample have used marijuana and one half recommend its legalization. We take these men as an informed and practical-minded group. We must surmise that theirs is not a libertarian but a pragmatic argument for drastic reduction in present marijuana controls.

Chapter 28

NARCOTICS OFFICERS

Consider this to be the introduction to the study that might have been. It had been our intention—based on a desire to provide perspective on enforcement and drug dealing and also to gather information which would aid in the selection, training, and management of narcotics officers—to compare samples of officers known for honesty and competence with those with less happy performance records. We failed on three counts. We learned of only one agency which had conducted any self-study of honesty and dishonesty among its agents. That unit was unable to release its data publicly, even though it had taken administrative action internally or, when indicated, had prosecuted wayward officers. Consequently, that one department could not serve as our work base. The second failure was in obtaining funds to conduct the same study in a second department where we had a special situation: widespread corruption described to us by several informants, who were disgusted with their dishonest colleagues within the department, and a new chief who was about to clean house. Our third failure was in persuading narcotics officers in the metropolitan area in which we did work to be frank with us about problems of illegal conduct among their fellow officers. Unlike drug dealers, who accept their criminal lives, narcotics officers, like pharmacists and physicians, want to keep their reputations in the straight world and so do not, as illicit dealers do, speak easily to investigators about the seamier side of their own lives—if there is one.

Background

We did expect to find narcotics officers who were acting illicitly; for, in the course of our work with dealers, we had both direct and hearsay evidence of such activities. For example, 5 per cent of the big-money dealers said that they paid off the police as part of their working arrangements. Recall too that these admissions came less readily than others; for at the beginning of our conversations with dealers, only those who were dealing with foreign police admitted to bribing officers. This in itself suggests, first, that corruption among officers varies by place according to the local standards for honesty and procedures for selecting and supervising officers and, second, that illicit enterprises which involve officers in collusion with dealers are only reluctantly discussed even by dealers; for the dealers stand to lose not just their connections or "shade trees" but can be subject to reprisals if word ever gets back.

During our work we also received reports—some of them direct admissions—in underdeveloped drug-producing or transhipping countries about narcotics or other law-enforcement officers' involvement in illicit traffic. Practices described include accepting bribes, facilitating smuggling, acting as sales agents, acting as investors (in a kind of commodities market), and acting as bodyguards and, at the extreme, as robbers, comanagers for large operations, or assassins. We did not hear direct admissions of such activities as we worked within the United States; however, the one very large department which conducted a "self-study" reported bribe taking, robbing dealers of money and drugs, giving drugs away in return for information, and selling seized drugs to wholesalers. It also found officers arresting competitors in order to protect a dealer operating under the officer's "umbrella", or providing information to a protected dealer by warning him of impending raids, seizures, or other threatening police activity. Also, in working police departments, we did hear from officers that some of their colleagues were engaged in lesser peccadillos such as keeping back a portion of drugs (mostly marijuana) seized to give away to their own user friends or for their own use (see Blum and associates, in press). That some narcotics officers have tried illicit drugs is no surprise; if young they are part of the same youthful population where the majority are likely to experiment with marijuana. Indeed, in 1962-1964, in a study of the beliefs of narcotics officers (Blum and associates, 1964), such admissions were made. That a few should continue to use must also be expected, given a combination of youth, access to drugs, and perhaps an image of oneself as a swinger.

Serious corruption within narcotics squads is, we think, almost inevitable. In spite of the increasing availability of selection and management techniques designed to improve police personnel, many departments are primitive. Furthermore, narcotics-law-enforcement bureaus operate in the larger context of corrupt departments in corrupt cities. Given the presence of predisposed personnel, the absence of good supervision, and an atmosphere of corruption, how can one expect that the temptations which arise in the course of vice investigations—where there rarely are complainants and where work is undercover and conducive to conspiracies—will be universally resisted? One would expect the contrary.

We are limited in our examples to published information, although some additional data which we cannot publish have been made available to us. Consider the testimony of the chief counsel of the State Commission of Investigation in New York (*New York Times*, April 6, 1971), who held that "shocking examples of corruption" in part account for the fact that the New York City police department, at least in the recent past, has "no appreciable effect on the flow of drugs" and that its heroin-control effort is "a monumental waste of manpower and money." Corruption described includes "extortion, bribery, giving contradictory evidence in court to effect the release of narcotics suspects, improper association with people involved in drugs, and the direct involvement of police officers in the sale of narcotics." The chief counsel, Joseph Fisch, also criticized police practices, particularly the quota system, which penalizes detectives for low arrest rates and thus forces them to ignore complicated higher-level dealing in favor of busts of street addicts. Poor training and supervision in the detective division were also charged. This report is consistent with confidential studies made over the last decade in Eastern cities by other groups. For example, one confidential report indicated that one fourth of the narcotics enforcement personnel were suspected of serious involvement in illicit conduct concerning drug dealers.

Corruption within narcotics-law-enforcement agencies can better be understood if one keeps in mind the pressures for arrest in an investigational arena where most work is clandestine and where, in consequence, police come to rely on informants who usually are themselves illicit-drug users and dealers. The relationship with an informant is a delicate matter (Blum, 1972), a matter of give-and-take. As Skolnick (1966) well demonstrated, it is also a matter of investigators' developing their own codes of conduct, which can be independent of constitutional requirements, and the administrative edicts of their own department. Insofar as officers within vice units do become autonomous and begin making their own rules, they then become, we suspect, more disposed to violations of the criminal law as they work in tandem with informant offenders.

Corruption within narcotics bureaus must also be seen as a

special case—perhaps one of the most likely cases, given the working environment, of police corruption. Reiss (1971) has done the most comprehensive work in this area. Using as a measure the observations of investigators riding with 597 patrolmen eight hours a day over six weeks, Reiss found that the proportion of policemen committing crimes in the company of the nonpolice observer was, in Chicago, 30 per cent; in Boston, almost 27 per cent; and in Washington, D.C., nearly 21 per cent. The crimes included theft from already burglarized establishments, assaults on citizens, accepting bribes, and shaking down deviants or offenders (extortion). If, in these cities, patrolmen are open enough about their criminality to expose themselves to outsiders in so short a time, should we expect a real rate of offenses for vice investigators to be any less?

It would be unfair to leave it at this. There is no evidence that felonies committed by on-duty officers are as high as 20 per cent in other cities, where a different milieu exists. And where felony rates among officers are high, should one not expect that to reflect the attitudes and habits of the citizenry at large? Students of the "dark number" (that is, crimes committed as opposed to reported) have long noted that most citizens do themselves admit to having committed felonies (Wallerstein and Wyle, 1947). The rate and kind, of course, differ with backgrounds, personalities, opportunities, and risks. Should we realistically expect it to be different among police officers?

Corruption

During the course of one year we sought to identify the kinds of corruption among narcotics officers which arose as part of their work in the drug scene. We also hoped to estimate prevalence of such conduct and to identify factors conducive to it.

In that year we interviewed (exclusive of the work reported in Blum and associates, in press) eighty-two individuals selected for their likely knowledge of narcotics officer conduct. We also drew informally upon acquaintances in local police and dealer circles. The formal sample included officers of one large city and a state agency; a group of convicted dealers, with whom group discussions in prison were set up; and a few select informants who were working for narcotics agencies and whom we "turned around" to inform for us on the activities of their employers. Because we ran into a stone wall with most officers and among some convicts, we must treat reports with some measure of caution. Curiously, convicted dealers were less damning than informants and those few officers who talked, even if in parables.

Contact with Dealers and Informants. If we consider the dealer under police suspicion or arrest as the most likely source of temptation, one wants to know at what rate temptation, in the form of personal experience with offenders who have something to offer an officer in return for services rendered, might arise. A two-man narcotics detective team in the major city of our inquiry will handle 75 to 100 arrested suspects a month. At any one moment they are likely to be in contact with 300 dealers, suspects not arrested or those already arrested and in jail or on bail. The average team is likely to have from three to five informant contacts per day (usually by telephone or in a secure meeting place) and, during one month, will be in touch with 100 working informants who are valuable enough to continue. At higher levels of investigation, the contact load is reduced but is intensified and may mean frequent meetings with only five or ten informants working on a few major cases. Opportunities are, we conclude, considerable, should suspect, informant, and narcotics agent be of a mind.

Paying Informants. Informants work, in part, for love and pride. They also work to avoid their own prosecution (Blum, 1972; Skolnick, 1966). But beyond these, they work for money. An average two-man team will pay up to twenty informants $10 or $20 during one month. If the bust is a big one, informant fees go up to $100 in the Bay Area. This means that officers will be handling perhaps $400 in cash—which, in many departments, is "unvouchered" (that is, requires no informant-signed receipt), since an informant is understandably loathe to sign what could be his execution warrant. It is in this pay-off area, we were told (by informants themselves and a few officers), that chiseling begins. The simplest device is for the officer to collect $20 for a pay-off and to pay only $10 or, if receipts are required, to insist that the informant sign for $20 in order to receive $10. An escalation of this chiseling turns the officer into a dealer; for, instead of paying out any funds, he will pay off a user informant "in kind," giving him seized drugs and keeping all of the cash for himself. There was agreement that only a small fraction of agents do this.

Buys. Cash also changes hands when officers make buys as part of the evidence gathering in a case or as part of working their way up the ladder from small-time to bigger dealers, proving themselves as customers as they go. An average two-man metropolitan team will spend $500 to $600 a month on twenty to thirty buys. In higher-echelon traffic, buys are fewer but more money is involved, sometimes in the tens of thousands of dollars. When three to five buys have been made, sufficient to prove a man is a dealer, the bust occurs. It is at this time—either in the field, in headquarters, or after jailing—that the officer leans on the suspect to turn him into an informant.

We have been told of chiseling with "buy" money, but we have no admissions to that among our sample of officers. What takes place is this: The officer keeps the "buy" money for himself and pays off the informer in barter with other drugs or stolen goods or, as in any expense-account chiseling, simply by spending less than he records.

Bribe Offers. We tried to estimate the number of bribes per month offered to or requested by officers. Among the group of thirty convicted dealers, only one spoke of a serious bribe request, one in which his arresting officer visited him in jail and said the state would "lose interest in his case" for $3,500. Another spoke of a bribe attempt on his part which had been rejected by the officer, who said in a fatherly way, "Look, son, you appear to be in trouble already. Don't make it worse by trying to bribe us." Among narcotics officers, one estimated the rate of bribe offers at not more than three out of one thousand arrests. Another officer recalled only one serious attempt, this one "brokered" through a fellow officer on behalf of a rich dealer. These "serious" bribe offers are contrasted with those that are discounted as "rituals," for at time of arrest most street-level dealers are said to say in effect, "Oh man, take all my bread, take all my stuff, just let me go."

There was agreement that among chronic addicts and serious dealers in the class especially vulnerable to arrest (that is, among the criminal dealer group), word does spread as to individual officers' predilections. The agent, for instance, who estimated 3/1,000 bribe offers over arrest said his demeanor discouraged more. "I look straight and I have always been a mean, cold, fair son-of-a-bitch . . . who lets them know that when I get them, they've been got!"

One dealer in the convict sample considered it a bribe on the part of arresting officers to offer to turn him loose and to pay him in return for his becoming an informant. If one uses that criterion, that of the police bribing by giving money and freedom, then of course all narcotics officers are so engaged. Since such offers are often successful, recently busted dealers who soon return to the street must explain their "luck" to their suspicious colleagues. Under such circumstances the dealer-turned-snitch is likely to lie by saying something to the effect, "I laid five G's on them and the fuckin' pigs took it." Officers attribute the rumors of their cupidity to such origins.

Officers themselves contended that buy-offs had been, in fact, common in the old days but that—with higher personnel qualifications, higher salaries, and more modern police management—things have changed. As one said, "Hell, nobody is going to risk $14,000 a year for less than $100,000, and nobody has that kind of money for a buy-off."

As for the informant reports, these too yield a low rate. Our most competent and trustworthy one counted cases he had witnessed and came up with 5/2,000 buy-offs. One of them, for example, involved a $9,000 payment to three officers, of which the informant received only $200. He was so angry that he said he went to another police agency to complain.

Drug Sales. Only one case of drug dealing in the marketplace by a narcotics officer was reported to us from among our eighty-two discusssants. The report was by an informant who told of making a marijuana buy and being surprised later to learn that the man he'd fingered had been identified as an officer.

Unconstitutional Acts. Skolnick (1966) has identified failures of narcotics agents to observe the law, particularly search-and-seizure rights. Our officers agree that they enforce the "intent" of the law rather than its wording. That is, they will engage in harassment and other unconstitutional acts in order to interdict dealing. For example, an officer learns that a dealer has received a shipment. His informant is not "reliable" in the eyes of the magistrate, so that a warrant cannot be obtained. They know further that arrest without a warrant will not hold up in court. "So we just rip the dealer off, kick in his door, grab his stuff, leave him enough to support his habit, and flush the junk down the toilet"; or again, "We take a guy's stuff from him when we've got him dirty and we know the case won't hold up in court. We take him on because we know he is dealing, but we don't have reasonable cause. We know that but we don't tell *him* that"; or again, "We take the stuff and tell him we're going to book it against him, but that we won't put him in if he'll cooperate. We turn a few informants this way but not many." Seven of the thirty imprisoned dealers also said they had suffered this form of "justice without trial."

Not all rip-offs of dealers by men wearing badges are done by the police. A stolen or false police badge can be used by a robber as well. One such event came to our attention. A burglar had stolen an officer's gun and star from his home. He used both in ripping off a dealer to whom he announced himself as a narcotics agent. The dealer, completely cleaned out, couldn't believe the thief was really a cop and took a drastic step, one almost unheard of in the case of a dealer rip-off: He called the police. The thief was picked up within a few minutes in the same neighborhood and booked for armed robbery, possession of narcotic drugs, possession of stolen property, and impersonating a police officer. The latter charge was dropped because arresting officers and the prosecutor felt uncomfortable about the bad company that nobler charge was keeping.

Theft. The seizure of illicit drugs, even if they are destroyed, is theft. Theft of other goods occurs. Both officers and informants agreed to this. Convicted dealers were less likely to know about it because once they returned to their homes after arrest they could hardly know whom to blame for the disappearance of their valuables. Officers are said to be most likely to steal hand guns, binoculars, tape recorders, portable television sets, shoulder weapons, and expensive tools. If cash is on hand, it is easily stolen.

One informant said that he had sold a pistol legally and with bill of sale to a man who later was a suspect in a guns-for-drugs deal. The informant helped set his customer up for sale of stolen property, for which he was arrested. The suspect had no drugs but did have the weapon. Two days later the informant was offered the gun by one of the officers, who was grateful for the informant's help in their recovery of merchandise worth $30,000. The informant appreciated the offer but pointed out that the gun legally belonged to the suspect.

The story leads one to wonder if officers involved in investigation and arrest may not develop a proprietary feeling about the goods of the offender. They have chased their quarry and taken him and his. Is not what he had—since he was criminal and his goods ill-gotten—now by rights theirs? If such thinking does occur, then one can see how readily the property and cash of a dealer might disappear during police search at the time of arrest.

Although there was agreement that theft of a dealer's residence is the most prevalent form of "corruption," one which most officers have probably been guilty of, the incidence of such theft is not high. It is our belief that most narcotics officers are not in business as thieves and, consequently, will not consistently burglarize the premises of an arrested dealer.

Contributing Factors. Among those who told us of illicit acts we inquired as to contributing factors. These were believed to be personality, departmental status, departmental affiliation, and circumstances. Offending officers were said more likely to be people with (neurotic) problems, who were apt to be living beyond their means—boozers, swingers, and the like. It was also claimed that young uniformed policemen, not yet advanced but eager to make their way, might thoughtlessly try to make a name for themselves by using drugs seized in arrests to buy information leading to a big bust when, in the ordinary course of things, they would not have access to adequate buy money. A similar course of events was described for several men who were unpromoted and frustrated in middle age and appeared willing to take risks to achieve departmental recognition through arrests based on unwise moves. Departmental affiliations appear to bear on police criminality because, in a comparison of two agencies, five men in one agency were identified as offenders, whereas none in a second agency was so identified. This may be an accident of case finding; but if it is not, it supports the role of milieu as a factor determining how police behave. As for circumstances, it was agreed that in the Bay Area, where departments insist on honesty, the dishonest man has to act privately or in league with his investigating partner. We assume that the less public a bust, the more likely are private dishonest arrangements to be undertaken without risk.

An Informant Reports. One of the informants whom we turned around is an ex-burglar who has worked for the last six years as an informant, mostly in the narcotics area. He had been a professional burglar, making a tax-free $100,000 a year but, upon marrying and having children, was persuaded to give up the life. As a professional informant, he maintains a borderline role—lawful but in criminal company; and by working 80 to 90 hours a week, he makes about $800 per month (taxable). At present he meets with the police often, averages twenty to fifty buys a month from lids to 25 kilos of marijuana and probably a few ounces of heroin. He has never used illicit drugs and refuses them when they are offered to him, as they are, by narcotics officers—either in lieu of pay or as a medium of exchange when working the drug scene. He observes that in addition to his own experience he has been present when other informants have been given drugs in return for dealing.

He describes other criminality which he has witnessed: bribe taking, theft of money from dealers or from their premises, and the theft of valuables. He states that it is common for officers to keep back a portion of drugs seized, for use not only in buying information but as gifts to addict or user acquaintances whom they like. These may be considered investments in future information. Some officers do use drugs, marijuana especially, and sometimes amphetamines, self-prescribed from illicit stock. He has, in one instance, found an officer to be dealing in drugs. On other occasions he has been the victim of chiseling, by signing vouchers for monies not received. During the course of the study he was working a case where a female dealer was "popped" (arrested). "They took all her drugs and money; then they told her to get out of town for a couple of days, they weren't going to book her. They told her all they wanted was a free piece of tail, her stash, her money, and that was it, except they didn't want to see her around for a while. She obliged."

"I've also been paid off to stay away from certain people and certain places. When this happens, they told me that some 'benefactors' were involved."

The informant opines, "The narc in a big department has gone through a long struggle to get there [investigator rank]. He has had to fight his way through a lot of competition and having arrived he feels some benefits are due him. You cannot but expect that a high percentage can't resist knocking down a little on the side when they get the chance."

This informant, who likes and is good at his work and who likes his officer coworkers as well, is not unduly critical of the officers' knocking down. Indeed, he observes that such men enjoy his company because with him—a professional criminal—they can relax, which they can't do with their incorruptible colleagues. His belief that many narcs are crooked on occasion should probably be viewed in part as an expression of a bias to see others as not more worthy than himself. Elsewhere (Blum, 1972) we have shown a significant association between being oneself corrupt and attributing corruption to others. The accuracy of such assessments versus the naive and trusting ones remains to be determined. One wonders if the trait of Machiavellianism (Christie and Geis, 1970) is associated with the dimmer view of mankind.

Comment and Summary

Some forms of criminality in which narcotics officers engage have been identified. Difficulties in research in this area are noted, and the uncertain nature of our findings is emphasized. The criminality of narcotics officers should be considered within the perspective of the milieu of their city and department in general. In the Bay Area there is rough agreement among our three major classes of informants—narcotics officers, snitches, and convicted dealers—that the most common violations are of civil rights rather than the criminal law. Second in frequency appears to be theft of objects from the premises of dealers upon arrest. At least a strong minority of officers are likely to have engaged in both sets of violations. Chiseling on expense accounts (mostly informant pay-offs) also occurs. Much less frequently, one estimates, there is trading narcotics to informants in return for information. Because of the rarity of reports coming to our attention during one year of endeavor, we presume that such matters as theft of drugs for resale, involvement in drug traffic, or taking bribes are very infrequent occurrences. For the latter our only data lead to a rate of not more than five bribes taken for every two thousand user-dealer arrests.

Whatever the local rates, there is good evidence that criminality among the police is a serious problem in other jurisdictions. That, combined with the admitted frequency of civil rights violations, leads to the conclusion that in order for the narcotics-law-enforcement personnel to abide by the high standards of honesty and regard for civil liberties which a modern city expects, there must be continued emphasis on improvements in the selection, training, and management of police personnel. Given the realities of corruption and self-interest in certain cities, it would be foolish to hope for major changes only as a result of steps taken solely within departments. Furthermore, given the continued difficulties of enforcement of vice laws where temptations outweigh complaints and where, necessarily, the officers are exposed to two standards of morality (users versus the straights) and must adjust, at least partially, to each in order to work effectively, one ought not to hope for the full suppression of police criminality which arises in connection with their work on the dealing scene.

We cannot provide prevalence rates, but we can offer generalizations which we think make sense. One is that not all the people dealing drugs or involved in crime in association with dealing are the "bad guys" (self-identified drug dealers). Some of those committing felonies are "good guys" (that is, cops who are also robbers). Second, of the crimes which narcotics officers commit in association with their role, dealing as such is rare. The opportunities are greater and the risks are less if they engage in bribe taking, theft, extortion, protection, and the like. Third, the prevalence of offenses depends on factors that affect other police criminality: individual background, personality, adequacy of supervision, the degree to which corruption is accepted by others in the department and is part of the political-business life of the city in which the police work, and situational factors such as opportunity and the sophistication of the dealers. Fourth, the majority of local narcotics officers have at one time or another committed felonies in connection with their work. These appear to be less frequent, however, than those acts which violate the constitutional rights of the offenders on whom they are targeted. For the Bay Area we would guess that the incidence of robbery, burglary, graft, and the like, is low—occurring in not more than one in a hundred arrests and perhaps at the rate of only several per thousand. In other regions documented rates are much higher; we conclude that there are differences in police criminality by department.

EPILOGUE

Those illicit dealers and that illicit traffic in psychoactive drugs which have received our attention have proven to be both simple and complex. Simple in the sense that for dealers dealing comes naturally. It arises from their immersion in the drug life and is a consequence of it. Such immersion represents personal values, interests, and methods for coping which are transmuted into the special activities and self-images which constitute being a dealer. Insofar as drug dealing is like other things that young people do when they are experimenting, learning what pleases them, finding what costs as well as benefits accrue to any vocational role, then becoming a dealer is but one of many possible developmental activities.

But it *is* different, and complex, for dealing is a delinquent pattern, as evidenced by both law and behavior—proclamations of righteousness on the part of psychedelic dealers to the contrary. Dealing is a particular form of delinquency which is woven into and becomes expressive of the values and circumstances of particular sets of backgrounds and of immediate environmental situations. For the middle-class "sometimes" dealer it reflects, in an extreme way, self-centered but gregarious "freedom," the roots of which we saw in our study of high-drug-risk middle-class families (Blum and associates, 1972). For a lower-class black like Cobra, it is the way a sharp fellow, cool and tough, can make money and achieve status and even "live better than a pimp." For the middle- or even upper-class fellow, that "cool-man-hip-on-a-big-dealing-trip," very real money-making interests and business competence are interwoven with other time-honored American traditions: free enterprise, personalized business relationships, being your own boss, eschewing government regulations and taxation, plus a little bit of the fearless frontiersman. Mixed in are newer strains of social philosophy—the sociable, magical, mystical, pleasurable, free-and-easy establishment-disdaining, and mock radical values common in the youthful drug scene. For a man like Lobo peddling is different still: a functional "solution" to his multiple addictions; a way of avoiding starvation for one without skill, training, or opportunity; a continuing excitement for an old rake who never wanted to go straight; a vestigial spiritual and intellectual expression for his (other) Yacqui medicine-man self; and it allows him to be a prideful leader, still able to kill and face being killed in the Pancho Villa bandito tradition.

The foregoing are but illustrations, reminders that dealers are different and that dealing brings different gains and losses to those involved. With the variation in persons and circumstances which affect who deals, how he deals, and what happens to him, one cannot but conclude that the one label *dealer* embraces many persons, capabilities, commitments, and outcomes. We saw that clearly within one small copping community where roles were clearly distinguished, with life styles, capabilities, and treatment results almost perfectly predictable from the community role (that is, the level and kind of heroin activity).

Dramatic outcome differences will also be seen, qualitatively and quantitatively, when one compares different places where people have gone when drug pushing is over (Blum and associates, in press). Consciousness III was almost totally abstinent. Its residents combined a New England hardiness and individualism in tilling the soil with a casual disinterest in drugs and coupled that with a pervasive nondrug mythology and magic which, depending on the stance of the viewer, could be interpreted as profound mysticism, pervasive religious sentiment, playful (if not childish) irrationality, narcissistic self-exaltation, or psychotic process. Holy Rock was also abstinent and religious but hardly disinterested in drugs. To the contrary, exdealers there, its Prodigal Sons, were as fiery antagonists to drugs as they had been enthusiasts for them.

Dealers, deterred dealers, and postdealers in institutional settings—public schools and colleges, correctional facilities, and communes—are still transitional. Where they are going we cannot be sure; on the basis of demonstrated capabilities, rearrest statistics, degree of dealing criminal involvement, and career data for groups—as opposed to the rhetoric or uncertainty of individuals—we can make guesses. Our guess is that all or almost all of the ordinary college kids will pass beyond dealing to more conventional careers, although we do predict a higher likelihood of unconventionality in later life for them than for those who are not dealers. The commune groups we looked at have passed beyond illicit drugs, Haight-Ashbury or Fillmore style, and have the inner resources to consolidate that experience, but because they are unusual people pursuing an unusual life, one expects that there will be no well greased track (or rut) for them to follow. We predict, therefore, greater variability than in the already-conventional college youth, and since some commune members are, we suspect, quite mad, we also presume proportionately more social failure. Holy Rock is an Old Testament prophet's joy, but, for latter-day prognosticators who try to stick to social science, it is unfirm ground. How many of the dealer converts will stay converted, given their short-term faith that the Day of Judgment can only be ten years hence, we cannot say. It is no great shakes to anticipate that arrested drug offenders will have futures predicated on the same recidivism predictors that work (rather inefficiently) to predict outcomes for other violators. Who would not expect the teenage middle-class juvenile with a good family and only drug arrests to be a better risk for straightening out than the slum raised 30-year-old without marital ties or straight job history who is putting in his time at San Quentin running a heroin ring? Unfortunately, a study like ours, which catches people only where they are and has only on hearsay where they have been but does not follow them where they are going, can do no better than guess at outcomes.

We have, so far, stressed complexity—that is, that not all dealers are alike, that dealing does vary by place and circumstance, and that different risks and gains are involved. Now let us note some constancies. There is, foremost, common illegality and a tendency among young dealers to have committed nondrug offenses as well. There is also a common history—first teenage involvement in illicit use and then in illicit sharing or giving. There also occurs, necessarily in career development, some early learning about sources, prices, customers, and the like. More successful dealers learn much more. There are too cross-cultural and cross-class similarities, attested to not just by the indistinguishable hippiedom among Western European and North American youths (with some Asian kids now joining in) when they are seen congregated in Amsterdam, Katmandu, or Tangiers, but also by the humming testimony of our computer showing that young London and California dealers are more alike than different. In our data one sees no major differences in dealing that are functions of race or ethnicity. Language and styles vary perhaps, but they reflect what we hold to be, on the basis of our family research (Blum and associates, 1972), mostly within-family factors which vary in turn with socioeconomic class and with pathogenic parental constellations of the sort that Robins (1966) describes. There is also a peculiar constant—that curiously steady 7 per cent dealing among all students in the junior highs, senior highs, and nonevangelical colleges and universities we surveyed. That percentage leads us to the rough estimate that about one fifth of the regular users of illicit drugs engage in repeated sales for profit sufficient to qualify them for the dealer role. But, based on our histories and on the findings of others, we know that most regular users have violated the laws, technically at least, pertaining to supplying.

The constant which links dealing to use not only is affirmed among our young dealers but extends, qualitatively, to that respectable sample of physicians among whom those who were themselves greater drug users disseminated drugs more both by prescription and by recommending purchase of over-the-counter remedies. We also found in that sample some relationships between own use, confidence in drugs, approval for nonmedical use, and, willingness to maintain drug-dependent patients on drugs. Also, in our family studies we found that parents who used more drugs (alcohol, prescription substances, illicit substances) had children who more often used illicitly and at high risk, and it is from this latter sample that drug dealers are drawn. We conclude that the phenomenon of illicit drug dealing is intimately linked to matters other than delinquency, in particular to the practices of people (dealers, doctors, parents) in taking and giving legal as well as illegal psychoactive substances. These practices are in turn demonstrably associated with sets of values which include not just confidence in drugs and philosophies as to who should be allowed to use drugs under what circumstances but, as the family work showed, beliefs associated with permissiveness, freedom, self-realization, and the like.

We were not sure when we set out how much overlap there would be between our family research (Blum and associates, 1972) and our dealer research; we now believe that the findings of the family study essentially prescribe the conditions for the dealing career. Conversely, looking backward, the dealers' own descriptions of their families allowed us to identify family constellations observed elsewhere as well as one very important family constellation uncovered in the dealer study but not observed in the family work—that of the disorganized, poor pathogenic (or sociopathogenic) family with a high rate of parental criminality and drug dependency. In the family study we could not achieve the cooperation of these families.

In the dealer study we did not attend primarily to the "immunizing" features which account for why some people who are users do not "progress" to regular drug sales for profits. Our family findings give us excellent predictive capabilities for drug risk but not for dealing as such. Earlier student work—ours and others—also provides adequate and consonant capabilities for estimating the characteristics of illicit users as opposed to nonusers. The information we have which helps predict who among users will be a dealer is limited, especially since it is of the retrospective or here-and-now sort. The student data (junior high, senior high, and college) do indicate that dealers are more uncertain about their careers, perform less well in school, may be more ill, are more alienated from family politics and religion as well as from their parents, and use more drugs more intensively than do their peers who use illicitly but do not deal regularly for profit. These findings repeat almost exactly earlier descriptions of differences between collegiate users and nonusers. And when we compared intensive users versus less intensive ones the same variables (those above plus consistent others) operated according to the rule "the more, the more likely" (for example, the more alienation the more likely intensive use).

Whether there are differences between dealing users and nondealing users in terms of personality characteristics, as conventionally defined as test or self-description traits, remains an open question. Our data from one college where we had a broad sample discriminated by dealing habits alone suggest that the dealer is psychologically different from nondealing regular users, for example, will more often report himself ill and see a psychiatrist. But when we selected a very narrow (and small) sample within two already homogeneous populations and then matched dealers and nondealing users as closely as possible prior to testing, no personality differences emerged. One has the impression that it is not only difficult but possibly foolish to seek to separate internal features of a young person (trait scores on a test) from his external features (family religion, politics) if the mix of background, experience, group memberships, and identifications, values, interests, and personality characteristics may well be clusters or syndromes which together predict the likelihood of dealing or not dealing. As one narrows the differences among people on these sets of factors which together do discriminate dealing and nondealing, one expects less variation in behavior. Or, conversely, when one finds people who are very much alike in their drug use and choice of drug peers, then the small distinction between those dealing now and those not dealing now ought not to carry with it expectations of major differences in either adjustment traits or biosocial correlates.

Goode's (1970) work on marijuana users offers powerful evidence that the degree of drug involvement, itself predictable on the basis of family and personal characteristics, is in turn the major discriminant between having used and not sold, and having used and sold. That intensity-of-involvement variable among youthful users is defined by features such as age of onset, number of using friends, length of use, variety and regularity in drugs used, drug dependency, presence or absence of anchors in conventional life styles, attitudes toward drugs and their use, peer support, and, we suspect, personality functions. Most of these same features have been shown (with a somewhat different definition of involvement) to distinguish peyote users from nonusers in the quite different environment of the Navajo (see Aberle, 1966); thus strengthening the argument that in diverse settings involvement in unusual drug-using groups is likely to depend on a variety of linked social developmental experiences. In our dealer study itself, where the definition of involvement is the degree of seriousness and professionalization, work complexity, time in the dealing life, acquaintance with other serious dealers, engagement in interstate and international trafficking, and so forth, we find that involvement predicts profits and violence. But not exactly the same predictors are involved for profits and for violence. For the latter we must be cognizant of various kinds of involvement: for example, involvement with an essentially criminal lower class interested in heroin versus involvement with a middle-class group interested in marijuana and hallucinogens.

In our work here we briefly examined situations where people were exposed to what others might consider the temptation of dealing. We did that to comprehend how it was that dealing did not occur as well as to make estimates of prevalence. Our data were weak in each of those instances, either about the extent of dealing—as with narcotics officers—or as to "hardness" regarding factors retarding dealing—as with our observations of faculty. We are reasonably confident that our impressions are correct, but the reader with preferences for hard data will have little reason to accept our faith. Among pharmacists commitment was to wholly conventional strivings, values, and life styles, and our inference was that only marginal pharmacists would be tempted to illicit diversion. Among physicians dissemination (not diversion) was linked to particular views and habits; our statistically supported inference was that stress was an important mediating variable associated with use and dissemination. Among professors conventions are ill defined but risks, values, and commitments are clear enough—all of which account for an almost zero dealing rate, although some do, nevertheless, use illicitly. That contradiction makes professors, like physicians, like detail men, good people to look at for features which restrain dealing or, put differently, make drug dealing quite unappealing because so many more important and approved activities are incompatible with a role which is beneath their maturity and dignity. The stress mediator in physicians and the marginal commitment to the profession among pharmacists, which make for increased possibilities of risk-taking conduct vis-à-vis drugs, are parallelled among professors by, we suggest, severe career dissatisfaction, a peripheral place in the establishment or resistance to convention arising out of radical values, personal psychological distress, or identification with youthful (delinquent) ways rather than adult (conventional) ones.

During this study we met no fabled dealers—Corsicans, Sicilians, Turks, Laotions, or such like—of the sort held responsible for major international traffic and journalistically described as the men behind the scenes—big dealers but not users. We met some older dealers who were no longer using much and some who denied current interest in drugs, but in general we must characterize our dealers—in every setting and at every level from the losers to those making a million dollars a year—as users first and dealers second (sequentially) and as users to the core as far as their affiliations with the drug scene are concerned. Like abstinent alcoholics some were beyond using but they were of as well as in the scene. Even the older criminals whom we met, like Cobra, who had moved into the market for the money, had prior social ties to users and dealers and were heavily involved in drugs for personal purposes, if only for short periods of time. Our experience makes us reasonably confident that the personal life of an American drug trafficker, especially those young people who constitute most of the using and dealing population, is heavily invested in the drug scene. The question might come to mind, do those master-mind traffickers exist, those criminals who sit in high places, whose interest is above it all, strictly commercial, and who eschew drugs for themselves entirely? Like students who have gone to the zoo to see the llamas but do not have time for elephants, we can say only that we have heard of elephants but have never looked for one or had the chance to see him. We hope that when the time comes we will learn more about them than we did about the Mafia, for recall that we did meet dealers who claimed Mafia ties if not identity. But we looked at them and found it hard to believe. Can it be the same with elephants, that we would not recognize one if we saw one? Or is it conceivable that there are no elephants, only camels pretending? We really do not know. We suspect that there will be readers who do.

Two large matters—elephants or no—do require our attention. One has earlier been noted; it is that drug dealing begins as a developmental process which is visible in adolescence and which for some, on the basis of family data, would be visible at conception. Thus, whatever one's preoccupation with dealing as an adult phenomenon, its roots are early and profound. In consequence, concern with dealing cannot, it appears to us, be divorced from general issues pertaining to family planning, mental health preventive measures, early case findings for delinquency, and the like. Even if our data are not representative for those nonusing adult traffickers who may exist in the United States, they do bespeak the prevalence of widespread drug dealing among youth and the origins of that conduct prior to the first illicit sale. To address dealing as a social problem (or a legal one) requires that we keep these origins and the development process in mind.

The second major matter has to do with the present societal response to dealing—the criminal law and police intervention. In Blum and associates (in press) we—all of us who have been involved in the total study—consider some facts pertaining to intervention as derived from studies of police, drug traffic, and prisons. But the data derived from the work reported here make it clear that arrest does occur and does matter. As dealers stay in the life the risks increase, and these color the psyches as well as social relations of dealers. Recall the concern with being "paranoid," the expressions of fear and suspicion, and the growth of precautions, distrust, and the like among those dealers either long in the game or most vulnerable to arrest. Recall too the evidence, as we interpret it, that fear of arrest may be responsible for the reduction of dealing among some and that the fact of arrest did appear, when arrested and nonarrested dealers were compared, to play some role in the decision to retire, if not from all delinquency at least from dealing. The data are not so clear as to allow one to correctly estimate the consequences of arrest, but they do affirm that arrest is by no means insignificant emotionally and socially. Whether the influence is positive or adverse depends on the person in question and the values of the viewer. The impact of arrest as well as the risks for arrest vary with the characteristics of the dealer. For example, among those making big money, arrests were common but appeared to have little role in deterring business. As before, the principle for evaluation of dealing careers and consequences is the need to be specific—who, what, where, and how. Since drug dealers are not alike, the impact of their experiences on their development is different too.

The major questions about dealing for many people may not be those to which we have primarily addressed ourselves so far. We have sought information about profiles and careers of dealers, prevalence of dealing, contrasts between dealers and users, environments and commitments which mitigate against dealing, and identification of differences among dealers linked to one or another phenomenon of interest—violence, getting rich, being arrested, and the like. We have not addressed ourselves to the issue of societal response.

Except for looking at arrest as a component in lives—that is, as described by or inferred from dealers—we do not know how the criminal law works in action. What are the policies of narcotics squads and how do these fit in with their results? What dealers do the police seek and whom do they find? And what happens when a young dealer is convicted and sent to juvenile hall? Does his dealing stop? What about the adult offender sent to prison? Does he enter a sanitized environment or is there drug traffic behind the walls as well? And, speaking of traffic, what are some of its components as viewed not from the standpoint of dealers but as dealing, an activity which involves commerce, money, and organization? Not all identified dealers go to jail or prison; some of the youthful ones in particular may be referred to medical psychological facilities instead. What happens to them in one of these? Does medical intervention make a difference? All of these are important inquiries which, along with the evidence presented here, have bearing on what we think may be the major question in the minds of many: What ought to be done?

As part of our effort to comprehend drug dealers and dealing we undertook to get additional information which does bear on the question of policy, what ought to be done. We did conduct studies of police departments, vice squads, dealing in prisons and in juvenile halls, treatment in a psychiatric ward for young drug users and dealers, international drug traffic patterns, and what dealers sell (that is, the issue of illicit drug purity). The results of those inquiries are presented in Blum and associates (in press). Because the presentation of facts alone may guide policy but may not either identify the issues or lead to viable solutions, it is necessary to go beyond studies to analyze issues as well as data and to integrate these into recommendations which take cognizance of the political, social, and moral framework in which the major forms of intervention take place. Such integrative positions coupled with recommendations affecting the criminal law, government action, interventions with individuals (psychiatric, correctional, drug abuse programs), education, the pharmaceutical industry, and international drug legislation and programs are also to be found in Blum and associates (in press).

BIBLIOGRAPHY

ABERLE, D. *The Peyote Religion Among the Navaho*. Chicago: Aldine, 1966.

ADVISORY COMMITTEE ON DRUG DEPENDENCE. "Cannabis: A Report." London, 1968. (Commonly known as the "Wootten Report.")

ADVISORY COMMITTEE ON DRUG DEPENDENCE. "Powers of Arrest and Search in Relation to Drug Offenders." London: HMSO, 1970.

ALBEE, E. *Who's Afraid of Virginia Woolf?* New York: Atheneum, 1962.

APPLETON, W. S. "Snow Phenomenon." *Psychiatry*, 1965, *28*, 88–93.

ASHCROFT, G. *Military Logistic Systems in NATO: The Goal of Integration. Part II: Military Aspects*. Adelphia Papers, #68. London: The Institute for Strategic Studies, June, 1970.

BADEN, M. M. "Medical Aspects of Drug Abuse." *New York Medicine*, 1968, *24* (9), 466.

BALINT, M. *The Doctor, His Patient and the Illness*. New York: International Universities, 1957.

BALINT, M., HUNT, J., JOYCE, C. R., MARINKER, M., and WOODCOCK, J. *Treatment or Diagnosis: A Study of Repeat Prescriptions in General Practice*. Philadelphia: Lippincott, 1970.

BALL, J. C. "The Reliability and Validity of Interview Data Obtained from 59 Narcotic Drug Addicts." *American Journal of Sociology*, 1966–1967, *72*, 650–654.

BALL, J. C. and CHAMBERS, C. D. *The Epidemiology of Opiate Addiction in the United States*. Springfield, Ill.: Thomas, 1970.

BANFIELD, E. C. *The Unheavenly City*. Boston: Little, Brown, 1970.

BARRETT, E. "Police Practice and the Law—From Arrest to Release or Charge." *California Law Review*, 1962, *50*, 11–55.

BARRON, S. P., LOWINGER, P., and EBNER, E. "A Clinical Examination of

Chronic LSD Use in the Community." *Comprehensive Psychiatry*, 1970, *11* (1), 69–79.

BATES, W. M. "Occupational Characteristics of Negro Addicts." *International Journal of the Addictions*, 1968, *3* (2), 345–350.

BEAN, P. "Social Aspects of Drug Abuse: A Criminological Study of a Group of London Drug Offenders." *Journal of Criminal Law, Criminology and Police Science*, 1971, *62* (1).

BECKER, H. *Outsiders: Studies in the Sociology of Deviance*. New York: Free Press, 1963.

BECKER, H., and GEER, B. "The Fate of Idealism in Medical School." *American Sociological Review*, 1958, *23*, 50–56.

BENTEL, D. J., and SMITH, D. E. "The Year of the Middle Class Junkie." *California's Health*, 1971, *28* (10), 1–5.

BERG, I. A., and BASS, B. M. (Eds.) *Conformity and Deviation*. New York: Harper and Row, 1961.

BERKOWITZ, L. *Aggression: A Social Psychological Analysis*. New York: McGraw-Hill, 1962.

BEWLEY, T. "Recent Changes in the Pattern of Drug Abuse in the United Kingdom." *Bulletin on Narcotics*, 1966, *18*, 1–13.

BLACKER, K. H., JONES, R. T., STONE, G. C., and PFEFFERBAUM, D. "Chronic Users of LSD: The Acidheads." *American Journal of Psychiatry*, 1968, *125* (3), 341–351.

BLOOMFIELD, L. P., and LEISS, A. C. *Arms Control and Local Conflict*. Vol. I: *Summary*. Cambridge, Mass.: Massachusetts Institute of Technology, Arms Control Project, February, 1970.

BLUM, E. M., and BLUM, R. H. *Alcoholism: Modern Psychological Approaches to Treatment*. San Francisco: Jossey-Bass, 1967.

BLUM, R. H. *The Psychology of Malpractice Suits*. A Report of a Study prepared for the Medical Review and Advisory Board of the California Medical Association. March 1957.

BLUM, R. H. *Hospitals and Patient Dissatisfaction*. San Francisco: California Medical Association, 1958a.

BLUM, R. H. *The Psychology of Malpractice Suits*. San Francisco: California Medical Association, 1958b.

BLUM, R. H. *The Management of the Doctor-Patient Relationship*. New York: McGraw-Hill, 1960.

BLUM, R. H. "The Jailer's Revolt: Iron Doors Give Way to Open Doors." *This World, San Francisco Chronicle*, February 3, 1963, pp. 16–19.

BLUM, R. H. (Ed.) *Police Selection*. Springfield, Ill.: Thomas, 1964.

BLUM, R. H. "The Polygraph Examination in Law Enforcement Personnel Selection." *Police*, 1967a, *12* (2), 60–75.

BLUM, R. H. *Task Force Report: Narcotics and Drug Abuse.* The President's Commission on Law Enforcement and the Administration of Justice. Washington, D. C.: U. S. Government Printing Office, 1967b.

BLUM, R. H. "Drugs and Violence." In *Crimes of Violence*, Vol. 13. A Staff Report to the National Commission on the Causes and Prevention of Violence. Washington, D. C.: U. S. Government Printing Office, 1969.

BLUM, R. H. "To Wear a Nostradamus Hat." *Journal of Social Issues*, 1971, 27 (3).

BLUM, R. H. *Deceivers and Deceived: Observations on Confidence Men and Their Victims, Informants and Their Quarry, Political and Industrial Spies and Ordinary Citizens.* Springfield, Ill.: Thomas, 1972.

BLUM, R. H., and Associates. *Utopiates: The Use and Users of LSD-25.* New York: Atherton, 1964.

BLUM, R. H., and Associates. *Society and Drugs: Social and Cultural Observations.* San Francisco: Jossey-Bass, 1969a.

BLUM, R. H., and Associates. *Students and Drugs: College and High School Observations.* San Francisco: Jossey-Bass, 1969b.

BLUM, R. H., and Associates. *Horatio Alger's Children: Family Factors in the Origin and Prevention of Drug Risk.* San Francisco: Jossey-Bass, 1972.

BLUM, R. H., and Associates. *Drug Dealing: Intervention and Policy Alternatives.* San Francisco: Jossey-Bass, in press.

BLUM, R. H., and BLUM, E. *Health and Healing in Rural Greece.* Stanford: Stanford University Press, 1965.

BLUM, R., and DOWNING, J. J. "Staff Response to Innovation in a Mental Health Service." *American Journal of Public Health*, 1964, *54*, 1230–1240.

BLUM, R. H., and OSTERLOH, W. "Keeping Policemen on the Job: Some Recommendations Arising from a Study of Men and Morale." *Police*, 1966, *10* (5), 28–32.

BLUM, R. H., and OSTERLOH, W. "The Polygraph Examination as a Means for Detecting Truth and Falsehood in Stories Presented by Police Informers." *Journal of Criminal Law, Criminology and Police Science*, 1968, *59* (1), 133–137.

BLUM, R. H., and WAHL, J. "Police Views on Drug Use." In R. H. Blum and associates, *Utopiates: The Use and Users of LSD-25.* New York: Atherton, 1964.

BLUMER, H., SUTTER, A., AHMED, S., and SMITH, R. "The World of Youthful Drug Use." *Add Center Project, Final Report.* Berkeley: School of Criminology, University of California, 1967.

BOLEN, D. W., and BOYD, W. H. "Gambling and the Gamblers." *Archives of General Psychiatry*, 1968, *18*, 617–630.

BROTMAN, R., and FREEDMAN, A. *A Community Mental Health Approach to Drug Addiction.* U. S. Department of Health, Education and Welfare. Washington, D. C.: U. S. Government Printing Office, 1970.

BROWN, W. P. B. *The Police and Corruption.* Washington, D. C.: The President's Commission on Law Enforcement and the Administration of Justice, 1967.

BUENO, D. V. "The Problem of Drug Addiction in Mexico." In R. T. Harris, W. M. McIsaac, and C. R. Schuster (Eds.), *Drug Dependence.* Austin: University of Texas Press, 1970.

BURCHARD, W. "Role Conflicts of Military Chaplains." *American Sociological Review,* 1954, *19*, 528–535.

BUSH, R. N. "The Human Relations Factor: I, Principles of Successful Teacher-Pupil Relationships." *Phi Delta Kappan,* 1958, *39*, 271–273.

CAHALAN, D. *Problem Drinkers: A National Survey.* San Francisco: Jossey-Bass, 1970.

CALEF, V., GRYLER, R., HILLES, L., HOFER, R., KEMPNER, P., PITTEL, S. M., and WALLERSTEIN, R. S. "Impairments of Ego Functions in Psychedelic Drug Users." Paper presented at the Conference on Drug Use and Drug Subculture. Asilomar Conference Grounds, Pacific Grove, California, February 1970.

CAREY, J. T. *The College Drug Scene.* Englewood Cliffs, N. J.: Prentice-Hall, 1968.

CARLSON, R. and BRISSON, L. "Mayor of San Francisco tied in with Mafia: web that links San Francisco's Mayor Alioto and the Mafia." *Look Magazine*, September 23, 1969.

CASTANEDA, C. *The Teachings of Don Juan.* New York: Ballantine, 1968.

CHAMBERS, C. D., MOFFETT, A. D., JONES, J. P. "Demographic Factors Associated with Negro Opiate Addiction." *International Journal of the Addictions,* 1968, *3*, (2), 329–343.

CHEEK, F. E., and others. "Deceptions in the Illicit Market." *Science,* 1970, *167*, 1276.

CHEIN, L., GERARD, D. L., LEE, R. S., and ROSENFELD, E. *The Road to H: Narcotics, Delinquency and Social Policy.* New York: Basic Books, 1964.

CHERUBIN, C. E. "Investigations of Tetanus in Narcotic Addicts in New

York City." *International Journal of the Addictions*, 1967, 2 (2), 253–258.

CHINOY, E. *Automobile Workers and the American Dream*. Garden City, N.Y.: Doubleday, 1955.

CHRISTIE, R., and GEIS, F. *Studies in Machiavellianism*. New York: Academic Press, 1970.

CLARK, E. "Three Students in Five Have Tried Drugs." (London) *The Observer*, May 2, 1971.

CLOWARD, R. A., and OHLIN, L. E. *Delinquency and Opportunity*. New York: Free Press, 1960.

COHEN, A. K. *Deviance and Control*. Englewood Cliffs, N. J.: Prentice-Hall, 1966.

COHEN, M., and KLEIN, D. F. "Drug Abuse in a Young Psychiatric Population." *American Journal of Orthopsychiatry*, 1970, *40*, 448–455.

COLEMAN, J. O. X., KATZ, E., and MENZEL, H. *Medical Innovation: A Diffusion Study*, Indianapolis: Bobbs-Merrill, 1966.

COLEMAN, J., MENZEL, H., and KATZ, E. "Social Processes in Physicians' Adoption of a New Drug." *Journal of Chronic Diseases* (St. Louis), 1959, *9* (1), 1–19.

COLON, JOSÉ. "Marijuana." Advisory Task Force on Drugs Report of the White House Conference on Youth, 1971.

CONTE, A. E., and MASON, E. R. *Drug Abuse: A Challenge for Education*. Trenton, N.J.: Urban Schools Development Council, 1970.

COOPERSTOCK, R. *Sex Differences in the Use of Mood-Modifying Drugs: An Explanatory Model*. Toronto: Addiction Research Foundation, 1970.

COOPERSTOCK, R., and SIMS, M. "Mood-Modifying Drugs Prescribed in a Canadian City: Hidden Problem." *American Journal of Public Health*, 1971, *61* (5), 1007–1016.

COUMBIS, R. J., ALBANO, E. H., and LYONS, M. "Drug Detection in Urines of Commercial Blood Bank Donors." *Journal American Medical Association*, 1970, *214* (3), 596.

CRESSEY, D. R. *Other People's Money*. New York: Free Press, 1953.

CRESSEY, D. R. "Theft of the Nation: The Structure and Operations of Organized Crime in America." *New York Review of Books*, 1969, *13* (5), 11. Also published by Harper and Row, 1969.

CRUTCHER, J. A. "Lead Intoxication and Alcoholism: A Diagnostic Dilemma." *Journal of Medical Association of Georgia*, 1967, *56*, 1–4.

DANIELS, D. N., GILULA, M., and OCHBERG, F. (Eds.) *Violence and the Struggle for Existence*. Boston: Little, Brown, 1970.

DAY, R. L., and CLARE, M. "The Associations, Pharmacists and Continuing Education Activities of California: A Report from the University of California School of Pharmacy." San Francisco, September 1968.

DE ALARCON, R. "The Spread of Heroin Abuse in a Community." *Bulletin of Narcotics*, 1969, *21* (3), 17–22.

DE ALARCON, R., and RATHOD, N. H. "Prevalence and Early Detection of Heroin Abuse." *British Medical Journal*, 1968, *2* (5604), 549–553.

DE FLEUR, L. B., BALL, J. C., and SNARR, R. W. "The Long-Term Social Correlates of Opiate Addiction." *Social Problems*, 1969, *17* (2), 225–234.

DENSEN-GERBER, J., MURPHY, J. P., and RECORD, W. J. "The Changing Face of Addiction: An Adolescent Confrontation." Paper presented at the International Institute on the Prevention and Treatment of Drug Dependence, Lausanne, Switzerland, June 9, 1970.

"Diseases Related to Narcotics Addiction Cause More Deaths among New Yorkers Fifteen to Thirty-Five Years Old than Murder, Suicide, Accidents, or Natural Causes." *New York Times*, August 15, 1958.

DISHOTSKY, N. I., LAUGHMAN, W. D., MOGAR, R. E., and LIPSCOMB, W. "LSD Use and Genetic Damage: A Critical Review." Paper dated October 1, 1970, Research Department, Mendocino State Hospital, Mendocino, California.

DOERINGER, P. B. "Ghetto Labor Markets—Problems and Programs." Harvard Institute of Economic Research, discussion paper 33, June 1968, p. 9.

DOORENBOX, N. J., FETTERMAN, P. S., QUIMBY, M. W., and TURNER, C. E. "Cultivation, Extraction and Analysis of Cannabis Sativa L." Paper presented at the New York Academy of Science, Conference on Marijuana, New York City, May 1971.

DOUGLAS, M. *Dealing: Or the Berkeley-to-Boston Forty Brick Lost Bag Blues*. New York: Knopf, 1971.

DUFFY, J. C., and LITIN, E. M. *The Emotional Health of Physicians*. Springfield, Ill.: Thomas, 1967.

DUSTER, T. *The Legislation of Morality: Laws, Drugs and Moral Judgments*. New York: Free Press, 1970.

EISENBERG, W. V., and TILLSON, A. H. "Identification of Counterfeit Drugs, Particularly Barbiturates and Amphetamines, by Microscopic, Chemical and Instrumental Techniques." *Journal of Forensic Sciences*, 1966, *11* (4), 529.

ERIKSON, E. H. *Childhood and Society*. New York: Norton, 1950.

ERIKSON, E. H. *Identity: Youth and Crisis*. New York: Norton, 1968.

EVANS, W. O., and KLINE, N. S. *The Psychopharmacology of the Normal Human.* Springfield, Ill.: Thomas, 1969.

FASSOLD, R. W., and GOWDY, C. W. "A Survey of Physicians' Reactions of Drug Promotion." *Canadian Medical Association Journal,* 1968, *98,* 701.

FELDMAN, H. "Ideological Supports to Becoming and Remaining a Heroin Addict." *Journal of Health and Social Behavior,* 1968, *9,* 131–139.

FESTINGER, L., SCHACTER, S., and BACK, L. *Social Pressures in Informal Groups: A Study of Human Factors in Housing.* Stanford: Stanford University Press, 1950.

FINESTONE, H. "Cats, Kicks and Color." In M. R. Stein and M. White (Eds.), *Identity and Anxiety.* New York: Free Press, 1960.

"First Annual Pot Report Turns Up Nothing New; Penalty Changes Asked." *Drug and Drug Abuse Education Newsletter.* Washington, D. C., January 1971.

FROEDE, R. C., and STAHL, C. J. "Fatal Narcotism in Military Personnel." Paper presented at the Twenty-Third Annual Meeting of the American Academy of Forensic Sciences, Phoenix, Arizona, February 1971.

FROSCH, W., ROBBINS, E., and STERN, M. "Untoward Reactions to LSD Resulting in Hospitalization." *New England Journal of Medicine,* 1965, *273,* 1235.

FULTON, C. "An Analytical Study of Confiscated Samples of Narcotic Drugs." *International Microfilm Journal of Legal Medicine,* 1965, *1* (1), Card 2–G1. Also in *NAPAN Newsletter,* 1964, *2* (2).

GALLUP, G. H., JR., and DAVIES, J. O., III. "Gallup Poll." *Washington Post,* May 26, 1969; April 10, 1970.

GARAI, P. Quoted in S. Malitz, "Psychopharmacology: A Cultural Approach." In Symposium: Non-Narcotic Drug Dependency and Addiction. *Proceedings of the New York County District Branch, American Psychiatric Association,* March 10, 1966, p. 10.

GARFIELD, E., BOREING, M., and SMITH, J. P. "Marijuana Use on a Campus: Spring 1969." *International Journal of the Addictions,* 1971, *6* (3), 487–491.

GARFIELD, M., and GARFIELD, E. "A Longitudinal Study of Drugs on Campus." Unpublished paper, Institute for Public Policy Analysis, Stanford University, 1971.

GAY, G. "Changing Drug Patterns in the Haight-Ashbury Subculture." *Journal of Psychedelic Drugs,* 1971, *4,* 3.

GOFFMAN, E. "On the Characteristics of Total Institutions: Staff-Inmate Relations." In D. Cressey (Ed.), *The Prison: Studies in Institutional Organization and Change*. New York: Holt, Rinehart and Winston, 1961.

GOFFMAN, E. *Stigma: Notes on the Management Spoiled Identity*. Englewood Cliffs, N. J.: Prentice-Hall, 1963.

GOFFMAN, E. "Where the Action Is." In *Interaction Ritual*. Chicago: Aldine, 1967.

GOLDING, W. G. *Lord of the Flies*. New York: Putnam, 1954.

GOLDSTEIN, J. W. "Getting High in High School: The Meaning of Adolescent Drug Use." Paper presented to the American Educational Research Association, New York, February 1971. (Report No. 71–3, Department of Psychology, Carnegie-Mellon University, Pittsburgh, Penn.)

GOODE, E. *The Marijuana Smokers*, New York: Basic Books, 1970.

GOODMAN, P. *Compulsory Mis-education and the Community of Scholars*. New York: Random House, 1962.

GRINSPOON, L. "Marihuana." *Scientific American*, 1969, *221* (6), 17–25.

GRINSPOON, L. *Marihuana Reconsidered*. Cambridge: Harvard University Press, 1971.

GRUPP, S. E. "Prior Criminal Record and Adult Marijuana Arrest Dispositions." *Journal of Criminal Law, Criminology and Police Science*, 1971, *62* (1), 74–79.

HAGOOD, W., and OWEN, J. "The Image of the Drug Industry as Seen by Town and Gown." *Virginia Medical Monthly*, 1967, *94*, 110–114.

HAMPSHIRE CONSTABULARY. "The Police Aspect of Drug Abuse in Hampshire." *Community Health*, 1969, *1* (3), 140.

HANNERZ, U. *Soulside: Inquiries into Ghetto Culture and Community*. New York: Columbia University Press, 1969.

HARMON, W. W., and others. "Psychedelic Agents in Creative Problem-Solving: A Pilot Study." *Psychological Reports*, Monograph Supplement 2–V19, 1966.

HARRIS, R. T., MC ISAAC, W. M., and SCHUSTER, C. R. *The Problem of Drug Addiction in Mexico*. Austin: University of Texas Press, 1970.

HAWKS, D. V. "The Dimensions of Drug Dependence in the United Kingdom." *International Journal of the Addictions*, 1971, *6* (1), 135–166.

HAYMAN, M., and DITMAN, R. "Influence of Age and Orientation of Psychiatrists on Their Use of Drugs." *Comprehensive Psychiatry*, 1966, 7, 152–165.

HELPERN, M. "Crime in America—Heroin Importation, Distribution, Packaging and Paraphernalia." *Hearings before the House Select*

Committee on Crime, June 27, 1970. Washington, D. C.: Government Printing Office, 1970.

HILL, H. E., HAERTZEN, C. A., and YAMAHIRO, R. S. "The Addict Physician: A Minnesota Multiphasic Personality Inventory Study of the Interaction of Personality Characteristics and Availability of Narcotics." *Research Publication of the Association for Research on Nervous and Mental Diseases*, 1968, *46*, 321–332.

HOFFER, E. *A True Believer*. New York: Harper and Row, 1951.

HOFSTADTER, R. *Anti-intellectualism in American Life*. New York: Knopf, 1964.

HOME OFFICE (United Kingdom). "UK Statistics of Drug Addiction and Criminal Offences Involving Drugs." London, 1970.

HUIZINGA, J. *Homo Ludens: The Play Element in Culture*. Boston: Beacon Press, 1955.

HUGHES, E. *Men and Their Work*. New York: Free Press, 1958.

HUGHES, P. H., CRAWFORD, G. A., and BARKER, N. W. "Developing an Epidemiologic Field Team for Drug Dependence." *Archives of General Psychiatry*, 1971, *24*, 389–394.

HUGHES, P. H., and JAFFE, J. H. "The Heroin Copping Area: A Location for Epidemiologic Study and Intervention Activity." *Archives of General Psychiatry*, 1971, *24*, 394–401.

INTERDEPARTMENTAL COMMITTEE, Her Majesty's Stationery Office. "Drug Addiction." Second Report. London, 1965. (Commonly known as "Second Brain Report.")

IRWIN, J. *The Felon*. Englewood Cliffs, N. J.: Prentice-Hall, 1970.

JAMES, I. P. "The Changing Pattern of Narcotic Addiction in Britain, 1959–1969." *International Journal of the Addictions*, 1971, *6* (1), 119–134.

JAMES, W. *The Varieties of Religious Experience*. New York: Random House, 1902.

JANG, R., KNAPP, D., and KNAPP, D. A. "Reactions of the Public to the Pharmacist as a Drug Adviser." Paper presented to the Academy of the General Practice of Pharmacy, Washington, D. C., April 1970.

JOHNSON, N. "Turning on the Vice President." *Federal Communications Commission News*, September 17, 1970.

JOYCE, C. R. B., LAST, J. M., and WEATHERALL, M. "Personal Factors as a Cause of Differences in Prescribing by General Practitioners." *British Journal of Preventative and Social Medicine*, 1968, *22* (1), 170–177.

KALANT, O. J. *The Amphetamines*. Springfield, Ill.: Thomas, 1966.

KAPLAN, J. *Marijuana: The New Prohibition.* New York: World Pub.; 1970.

KATZ, J. *No Time for Youth: Growth and Constraint in College Students.* San Francisco: Jossey-Bass, 1968.

KATZ, J., LOZOFF, M., BOCHNER, A., and HUNKELER, E. *Effects of Coed Housing on Male-Female Relationships.* In press.

KENDALL, R. S., and PITTEL, S. "Three Portraits of the Young Drug User; Comparison MMPI Group Profiles." Paper presented at meeting of Western Psychological Association, Los Angeles, April 1970.

KENISTON, K. *The Uncommitted.* New York: Dell, 1960.

KNAPP, D. A., and KNAPP, D. "An Appraisal of the Contemporary Practice of Pharmacy." *American Journal of Pharmaceutical Education,* 1968, *32,* 747–758.

KNAPP, D. E., KNAPP, D. A., and EDWARDS, J. O. "The Pharmacist as Perceived by Physicians, Patrons and other pharmacists." *Journal of American Pharmaceutical Association,* 1969, *NS9* (2), 80–82 and 84.

KNAPP COMMISSION. "Report." *Criminal Justice Newsletter,* New York City, 1971, 2 (14), 109.

KOVACH, B. "Communes—the Road to Utopia." New York Times Service as reported in the *San Francisco Chronicle,* January 4, 1971, p. 6.

KRIPPNER, S., and FERSH, D. "Paranormal Experience among Members of American Contra-Cultural Groups." *Journal of Psychedelic Drugs,* 1971, *3,* 109–114.

LEARY, T. "On Dope." *Quicksilver Times,* December 8–18, 1969.

LEE, J. A. H., DRAPER, P. A., and WEATHERALL, M. "Primary Medical care: Prescribing in Three English Towns." *Milbank Memorial Fund Quarterly,* 1965, *43,* 285.

LENNARD, H. L., EPSTEIN, L. J., BERNSTEIN, H., and RANSOM, D. C. *Mystification and Drug Misuse.* San Francisco: Jossey-Bass, 1971.

LERNER, M., and MILLS, A. "Some Modern Aspects of Heroin Analysis." *UN Bulletin on Narcotics,* 1963, *15* (1), 37–42.

LEVINE, J. "The Nature and Extent of Psychotropic Drug Usage in the United States." Statement before the Subcommittee on Monopoly of the Select Committee on Small Business. U. S. Senate: 9, 1969.

LIEBOW, E. *Tally's Corner: A Study of Negro Streetcorner Men.* Boston: Little, Brown, 1967.

LINDESMITH, A. R. *The Addict and the Law.* Bloomington: Indiana University Press, 1965.

LIPSET, S. M. "Youth and Politics." In R. K. Merton and R. Nisbet (Eds.), *Contemporary Social Problems* (3rd ed.). New York: Harcourt, Brace, Jovanovich, 1971.

LYTHGOE, H. C. "Character of Illicit Liquor on the Massachusetts Market." *New England Journal of Medicine*, 1928, *198*, 228–230.

MAC SWEENEY, D., and PARR, D. "Drug Pushers in the United Kingdom." *Nature*, 1970, *228*, 422–424.

MAFIA SERIES OF ARTICLES. *Life Magazine:* January 31, February 14, February 28, May 2, May 30, October 24, November 21, 1969; April 10, May 29, June 12, 1970.

MANHEIMER, D. I. "Marihuana Use among Adults in Two San Francisco Bay Area Locales." In S. M. Pittel (Ed.), *Drug Use and Drug Subcultures*. Washington, D. C.: U. S. Government Printing Office, 1971.

MANHEIMER, D. I., MELLINGER, G. D., and BALTER, M. B. "Marijuana Use among Urban Adults," *Science*, 1969, *166*, 1544–1545.

MARSHMAN, J. A., and GIBBINS, R. J. "The Credibility Gap in the Illicit Drug Market." *Addiction*, 1969, *16*, 4.

MARSHMAN, J. A., and GIBBINS, R. J. "A Note on the Composition of Illicit Drugs." *Ontario Medical Review*, 1970, *37* (9).

MARTINEZ, T., and LA FRANCHI, R. "Why People Play Poker." *Transaction*, 1969 (Summer), 20–25.

MASLOW, A. H. *Motivation and Personality*. New York: Harper and Row, 1954.

MASLOW, A. H. *Religions, Values and Peak Experiences*. Columbus: Ohio University Press, 1964.

MATZA, D. *Delinquency and Drift*. New York: Wiley, 1964.

MAY, R. *The Meaning of Anxiety*. New York: Ronald, 1950.

MCGLOTHLIN, W. H. "Effects in Man of Short- and Long-Term Use of Cannabis: Research Aspects." Working paper prepared for the World Health Organization for a Conference in Geneva, December 1970.

MCGLOTHLIN, W. H., COHEN, S., and MCGLOTHLIN, M. "Long Lasting Effects of LSD on Normals." *Archives of General Psychiatry*, 1967, *17* (5), 521–532.

MENDEL, W. "Tranquilizer Prescribing as a Function of the Experience and Ability of the Therapist." *American Journal of Psychiatry*, 1967, *124* (1), 16–22.

MERTON, R. K. *Social Theory and Social Structure*. New York: Free Press, 1957.

MILES, W. C. "Present Status of Alcoholism." *8th Medical Surgeon*, 1935, *97*, 177–180.

MILLS, J. "I Have Nothing to Do with Justice." *Life Magazine*, 1971, *70* (9), 56.

MILNER, C., and MILNER, R. *Black Players*. Boston: Little, Brown, 1972, in press.

MODLIN, H. C., and MONTES, A. "Narcotics Addiction in Physicians." *American Journal of Psychiatry*, 1964, *131*, 358–365.

MOORE, M. *Policy Concerning Drug Abuse in New York State*. Vol. 3: *Economics of Heroin Distribution*. New York: Hudson Institute, 1970.

MORRIS, J. N. *Uses of Epidemiology*. Edinburgh and London: E. & S. Livingstone, 1957.

MORTON, A., MUELLER, J., OHLGREN, J., PEARSON, R., and WEISEL, S. "Marijuana Laws: An Empirical Study of Enforcement and Administration in Los Angeles County." *U.C.L.A. Law Review*, 1968, *15*, 1501–1585.

MURRAY, H. A. *Thematic Apperception Test*. Cambridge: Harvard University Press, 1943.

MYRDAL, G. *An American Dilemma, The Negro Problem and Modern Democracy*. New York: Harper and Row, 1944.

NATIONAL COMMISSION ON THE CAUSES AND PREVENTION OF VIOLENCE. *To Establish Justice, To Insure Domestic Tranquility*. Final Report, 1969. Washington, D. C.: U. S. Government Printing Office, 1970.

NATIONAL INSTITUTE OF MENTAL HEALTH. *Alcohol and Alcoholism*. Washington, D. C.: U. S. Government Printing Office, 1969.

PACKER, H. *The Limits of the Criminal Sanction*. Stanford: Stanford University Press, 1969.

PEARSON, M. M., and STRECKER, E. A. "Physicians as Psychiatric Patients: Private Practice Experience." *American Journal of Psychiatry*, 1960, *116*, 915–919.

PEPPER, C. "Crime in America: Heroin Importation, Distribution, Packaging and Paraphernalia." In *Hearings before the House Select Committee on Crime*. June 25, 1970, p. 3; October 5–6, 1970, p. 189. U. S. Government Printing Office, 1970.

PHARMACEUTICAL INDUSTRY OPERATIONS. *Annual Survey Report, 1968–1969*. Washington, D. C.: Pharm. Manu. Assoc., 1969.

PITTEL, S. M., CALEF, V., GRYLER, R. B., HILLES, L., HOFER, R., and KEMPNER, P. "Developmental Factors in Adolescent Drug Use: A Study of Psychedelic Drug Users." *Journal of the American Academy of Child Psychiatry*, 1972, in press.

PREBLE, E., and CASEY, J. J., JR., "Taking Care of Business—The Heroin

User's Life on the Street." *International Journal of the Addictions,* 1969, *4* (1), 1–24.

RADIN, P. *Primitive Religion.* New York: Dover, 1957.

REDL, F. "The Psychology of Gang Formation and the Treatment of Juvenile Delinquents," *Psychoanalytic Study of the Child,* 1945, *1,* 367ff.

REICH, C. A. *The Greening of America.* New York: Random House, 1970.

REISS, A. J., JR. *The Police and the Public.* New Haven, Conn.: Yale University Press, 1971.

RIESMAN, D., GLAZER, N., and DENNEY, R. *The Lonely Crowd.* Garden City, N. Y.: Doubleday, 1953.

RINKEL, M. *Specific and Non-Specific Factors in Psychopharmacology.* New York: Philosophical Library, 1963.

ROBINS, L. N. *Deviant Children Grown Up.* Baltimore: Williams and Wilkins, 1966.

ROBINS, L. N., and MURPHY, G. E. "Drug Use in a Normal Population of Young Negro Men," *American Journal of Public Health,* 1967, *57* (9), 1580–1596.

ROCHE, P. Q. *The Criminal Mind: A Study of Communication between Criminal Law and Psychiatry.* New York: Farrar, Straus and Giroux, 1958.

SAN MATEO COUNTY SCHOOL STUDY. "Five Mind-Altering Drugs: The Use of Alcoholic Beverages, Amphetamines, LSD, Marijuana and Tobacco, Reported by High School and Junior High School Students, San Mateo County, California, 1968, 1969, 1970." Department of Public Health and Welfare, The Research and Statistics Section, San Mateo, California.

SANFORD, N. *Where Colleges Fail.* San Francisco: Jossey-Bass, 1967.

SANFORD, N., and COMSTOCK, C. *Sanctions for Evil.* San Francisco: Jossey-Bass, 1971.

SCHACTER, S. *The Psychology of Affiliation.* Stanford: Stanford University Press, 1962.

SCHELER, M. *Ressentiment.* New York: Macmillan, 1961.

SCHOFIELD, M. *The Strange Case of Pot.* London: Pelican, 1971.

SCHULTZ, L. G. "Why the Negro Carries Weapons." *Journal of Criminal Law, Criminology and Police Science,* 1962, *53* (4), 476–483.

SCHUMANN, S., HUGHES, P. H., and CAFFREY, E. "Addict Psychosocial Functioning Scale." Unpublished manuscript, Department of Psychiatry, University of Chicago, 1971.

SCHUR, E. M. *Crimes without Victims—Deviant Behavior and Public*

Policy; Abortion, Homosexuality, Drug Addiction. Englewood Cliffs, N. J.: Prentice-Hall, 1965.

SHELDON, W. H. *Varieties of Delinquent Youth: An Introduction to Constitutional Psychiatry.* New York: Harper and Row, 1949.

SHEPHERD, M., COOPER, B., BROWN, A. C., and KALTON, G. *Psychiatric Illness in General Practice.* London: Oxford University Press, 1966.

SHEPPARD, C. W., and GAY, G. R. "The Changing Face of Heroin Addiction in the Haight-Ashbury." *International Journal of the Addictions,* 1971, *6,* 4.

SHIPPEE-BLUM, E. "The Uncooperative Patient: The Development of a Test to Predict Uncooperativeness in Medical Treatment." In J. Block, E. Shippee-Blum, and J. Vitale (Eds.), *Supplemental Studies on Malpractice.* San Francsico: California Medical Association, 1958.

SKOLNICK, J. *Justice Without Trial.* New York: Wiley, 1966.

SMITH, D. E., and LUCE, J. *Love Needs Care: A History of San Francisco's Haight-Ashbury Free Medical Clinic.* Boston: Little, Brown, 1971.

SMITH, J. P. Addendum to "Final Report," Bureau of Narcotics and Dangerous Drugs Contract J-68-13, 1971.

SMITH, R. *The Marketplace of Speed: Violence and Compulsive Methedrine Abuse.* Unpublished manuscript, 1971.

STAFFORD, P. G., and GOLIGHTLY, B. H. *LSD: The Problem-Solving Psychedelic.* New York: Universal Pub., 1967.

STATE OF CALIFORNIA, DEPARTMENT OF JUSTICE, DIVISION OF LAW ENFORCEMENT, BUREAU OF CRIMINAL STATISTICS. "Drug Arrests and Disposition in California, Reference Tables, 1969."

STEIN, K. B., SARBIN, T. R., and KULIK, J. A. "Further Validation of Antisocial Personality Types." *Journal of Consulting and Clinical Psychology,* 1971, *36,* 177–182.

STEVENS, J. M. *The Process of Schooling.* New York: Holt, Rinehart and Winston, 1967.

STORER, J. Testimony, "Organized Crime and Illicit Traffic in Narcotics." *Hearings before the House Permanent Subcommittee on Investigations, July 30, 1964.* Washington, D. C.: U. S. Government Printing Office, 1964, p. 742.

SUTHERLAND, E. H. *The Professional Thief.* Chicago: University of Chicago Press, 1937.

SUTTER, A. G. "Worlds of Drug Use on the Street Scene." In D. R. Cressey and D. A. Ward (Eds.), *Delinquency, Crime and Social Process.* New York: Harper and Row, 1969, pp. 802–829.

SYLVESTER, E., and OREMLAND, J. Personal communication, 1969.

TALBOTT, J. H. "Tetanus in Addicts." *Journal of the American Medical Association*, 1968, *205* (8), 584–585.

THAYER, G. *The War Business*. New York: Avon, 1969.

TOLSTOY, L. *Tolstoy on Education*. Trans. by L. Wiener. Chicago: University of Chicago Press, 1967.

UNGERLEIDER, J. T., FISHER, D., FULLER, M., and CALDWELL, A. "The Bad Trip—The Etiology of the Adverse LSD Reaction. *American Journal of Psychiatry*, 1968, *124* (11), 1483–1490.

U. S. DEPARTMENT OF HEALTH, EDUCATION, AND WELFARE. *The Drug Makers and the Drug Distributors*. Task Force on Prescription Drugs. Washington, D. C.: U. S. Government Printing Office, 1968.

U. S. DEPARTMENT OF HEALTH, EDUCATION, AND WELFARE. "The Natural and Synthetic Materials." In *Report to the Congress from the Secretary; Marihuana and Health*. Section III. March 1971, pp. 13–19.

U. S. SENATE. "Organized Crime and Illicit Traffic in Narcotics." *Hearings before the Permanent Subcommittee on Investigations of the Committee on Government Operations, 88th Congress*. Part 3, 1963, 1964; Part 4, 1964; Part 5, 1964.

VAILLANT, G., BRIGHTON, J., and MC ARTHUR, C. "Physicians' Use of Mood-Altering Drugs." *New England Journal of Medicine*, 1970, *282*, 365–370.

VON FRANZ, M. L. *Puer Alternus*. Middlesex, England: Spring Publications, 1970.

VON MISES, L. *The Anti-Capitalistic Mentality*. Princeton, N. J.: Van Nostrand, 1956.

WALKER, C., and GUEST, H. *The Man on the Assembly Line*. Cambridge: Harvard University Press, 1952.

WALLER, C. W. "The Chemistry of Marihuana." Paper presented to American Pharmaceutical Association, Chicago, April 14, 1971.

WALLERSTEIN, J. S., and WYLE, C. J. "Our Law-Abiding Law Breakers." *Probation*, 1947, *25*, 107–112.

WEEKS, C. C. "Hooch poisoning." *British Medical Journal*, 1942, *1*, 596.

WELLISCH, D. K., GAY, G. R., and MCENTEE, R. "The Easy Rider Syndrome: A Pattern of Hetero- and Homo-Sexual Relationships in a Heroin Addict Population." *Family Process*, 1970, *9* (4), 425–430.

WERTHMAN, C. "The Function of Social Definitions in the Development of Delinquent Careers." In The President's Commission on Law Enforcement and Administration of Justice, *Task Force Report:*

Juvenile Delinquency and Youth Crime. Washington, D. C.: U. S. Government Printing Office, 1967, pp. 155–170.

WERTHMAN, C., and PILIAVIN, I. "Gang Members and the Police." In D. J. Bordua (Ed.), *The Police: Six Sociological Essays.* New York: Wiley, 1967.

WHITE HOUSE CONFERENCE ON YOUTH. Final Report of the Intern Task Force on Drugs for the White House Conference on Youth, 1971.

WIENER, R. S. P. *Drugs and School Children.* New York: Humanities Press, 1970.

WILSON, J. Q. *Varieties of Police Behavior: The Management of Law and Order in Eight Communities.* Cambridge: Harvard University Press, 1968.

WINICK, C. "Maturing Out of Narcotic Addiction." *Bulletin on Narcotics,* 1962, *14,* 1.

WITKIN, H. A., DYK, R. B., FATERSON, H. F., GOODENOUGH, D. R., and KARP, S. A. *Psychological Differentiation.* New York: Wiley, 1962.

WOLENSKY, H. *Intellectuals in Labor Unions: Organizational Pressures on Professional Roles.* New York: Free Press, 1956.

WOLFE, T. *The Electric Kool-Aid Acid Test.* New York: Farrar, Straus & Giroux, 1968.

WOLFGANG, M., and FERRACUTI, F. *The Subculture of Violence.* London: Tavistock, 1967.

WOODLEY, R. "An Introduction to Flash." *Esquire,* 1971, *75,* 79–83.

YOUNG, J. *The Drugtakers.* London: MacGibbon & Kee, 1971.

ZABLOCKI, B. D. "The Social Structure of Drug Based Communes." Paper presented at the Conference on Drug Use and Drug Subcultures sponsored by the Center for Studies of Narcotics and Drug Abuse of NIMH and the Department of Psychiatry Haight-Ashbury Research Project of Mt. Zion Hospital, San Francisco, California, at Asilomar, California, February 1970.

ZIMRING, F. E. "Perspectives on Deterrence." NIMH Center for Studies of Crimes and Delinquency, Washington, D. C., 1971.

INDEX